LANGUAGE POWER

Second Edition

Dorothy U. Seyler
Northern Virginia Community College

Carol J. Boltz

Random House  New York

Second Edition
987654321
 All inquiries should be addressed to Random House, Inc., 201 East 50th Street, New York, N.Y. 10022. Published in the United States by Random House, Inc., and simultaneously in Canada by Random House of Canada Limited, Toronto.

Library of Congress Cataloging in Publication Data
Main entry under title:

Language power.

Bibliography: p.
1. English language—Rhetoric. I. Seyler, Dorothy U. II. Boltz, Carol J., 1943–
PE1408.L3186 1985 808'.042 85-2130

ISBN 0-394-34139-2
Manufactured in the United States of America

Acknowledgments

"The Power of Words." From A WORD-A-DAY VOCABULARY BUILDER, by Bergen Evans. Copyright © 1963 by Bergen Evans. Reprinted by permission of Random House, Inc.

"The Human Use of Language" by Lawrence L. Langer. Copyright 1977 by Editorial Projects in Education, Inc. Reprinted by permission of The Chronicle of Higher Education.

"Words to Live Without" by Colman McCarthy. *The Washington Post,* February 6, 1972. © 1972, the Washington Post Company. Reprinted with permission.

"Good Usage, Bad Usage, and Usage." Article by Morris Bishop. © 1980 by Houghton Mifflin Company. Reprinted by permission from *The American Heritage Dictionary of the English Language,* pp. xxi–xxiv.

"Contexts." From LANGUAGE IN THOUGHT AND ACTION, Fourth Edition by S. I. Hayakawa, copyright © 1978 by Harcourt Brace Jovanovich, Inc. Reprinted by permission of the publisher.

Reprinted by permission of the Harvard Business Review. "Clear Writing Means Clear Thinking Means . . ." by Marvin H. Swift (January–February 1973). Copyright © 1973 by the President and Fellows of Harvard College; all rights reserved.

"Clutter." From ON WRITING WELL, Second Edition, by William K. Zinsser. Published by Harper & Row Publishers, Inc. Copyright © 1980 by William K. Zinsser. Reprinted by permission of the author.

"The Word" from FULLY EMPOWERED, by Pablo Neruda. Translations copyright © 1967, 1969, 1970, 1975 by Alastair Reid. Translated from PLENOS PODERES, copyright © 1962 by Editorial Losada, S.A., Buenos Aires. Reprinted by permission of Farrar, Straus and Giroux, Inc.

"The Watcher at the Gate" by Gail Godwin. Copyright © 1977 by The New York Times Company. Reprinted by permission.

"Silences." Excerpted from the book SILENCES by Tillie Olsen. Copyright © 1965, 1972, 1978 by Tillie Olsen. Reprinted by permission of Delacorte Press/Seymour Lawrence.

"Why I Write" by Joan Didion. Reprinted by permission of Wallace & Sheil Agency, Inc. Copyright © 1976 by Joan Didion. First appeared in *The New York Times Book Review.*

"The Exact Location of the Soul." From MORTAL LESSONS, by Richard Selzer. Copyright © 1974, 1975, 1976 by Richard Selzer. Reprinted by permission of Simon & Schuster, Inc.

"On Being Female, Black, and Free" by Margaret Walker, from THE WRITER ON HER WORK, edited by Janet Sternburg, is reprinted by permission of W. W. Norton & Company, Inc. Copyright © 1980 by Janet Sternburg.

"The Naked and the Nude" by Robert Graves. Published by Doubleday & Company. Reprinted by permission of the author.

"Silent Questions," excerpted from the book CRAZY TALK, STUPID TALK by Neil Postman. Copyright © 1976 by Neil Postman. Reprinted by permission of Delacorte Press.

"Watching Out for Loaded Words," by Frank Trippett. Copyright 1982 Time Inc. All rights reserved. Reprinted by permission from TIME.

"Metaphors: Live, Dead, and Silly." From ON WRITING, Roger Sale. Copyright © 1970 by Roger Sale. Reprinted by permission of Random House, Inc.

"Metaphor and Social Belief" by Weller Embler. Reprinted from ETC., Vol. 8, No. 2, by permission of the International Society for General Semantics.

"The Gettysburg Address" by Gilbert Highet, from A CLERK OF OXENFORD: ESSAYS ON LITERATURE AND LIFE. Reprinted by permission of Curtis Brown, Ltd. Copyright © 1954 by Gilbert Highet, © renewed 1981 by Helen MacInnes Highet.

John C. Merrill, "How TIME Stereotyped Three U.S. Presidents," *Journalism Quarterly,* Autumn 1965. Reprinted from *Journalism Quarterly* with the permission of the publisher.

Bradley Miller, "Cutesy," *The Washington Post,* March 23, 1980. Copyright © 1980 by Bradley Miller.

Paul Stevens, "Weasel Words: God's Little Helpers." From I CAN SELL YOU ANYTHING by Carl P. Wrighter. Copyright © 1972 by Ballantine Books, Inc. Reprinted by permission of Ballantine Books, a Division of Random House, Inc.

"Advertising's Fifteen Basic Appeals" by Jib Fowles. Reprinted from ETC., Vol. 39, No. 3, by permission of the International Society for General Semantics.

"It's Natural! It's Organic! Or Is It?" Copyright 1980 by Consumer's Union of United States, Inc., Mount Vernon, NY 10550. Reprinted by permission from CONSUMER REPORTS, June 1980.

Neil Postman, "The Parable of the Ring Around the Collar: and other irreverent observations on the religious nature of commercials." Reprinted with permission from PANORAMA Magazine. Copyright © 1980 by Triangle Communications Inc., New York, New York.

"The Rhetoric of Cow and the Rhetoric of Bull" by D. G. Kehl and Donald Heidt. Paper delivered at the Convention on College Composition and Communication in March, 1984. Reprinted by permission.

Leigh Montville, "Made In Heaven," *The Boston Globe,* May 15, 1983. Reprinted courtesy of *The Boston Globe.*

Excerpt from Freshman Registration issue of the Harvard Lampoon, Fall 1973. Published by Harvard University. Reprinted by permission.

James J. Kilpatrick, "The Highfalutin and the Mighty." Reprinted by permission from NATION'S BUSINESS, July 1974. Copyright 1974 by NATION'S BUSINESS, Chamber of Commerce of the United States.

"The Language of Bureaucracy" by Henry A. Barnes, from *Language in America.* Published by Western Publishing Co. Reprinted by permission.

Diane Johnson, "Doctor Talk." Reprinted by permission of THE NEW REPUBLIC, © 1979 The New Republic, Inc.

"Lawyers and Their Language Loopholes" by Ronald Goldfarb, from *The Washington Post.* Copyright by Ronald Goldfarb. Reprinted by permission.

"Psychobabble." Reprinted by permission of Cyra McFadden. Copyright 1978 by Cyra McFadden.

"Journalese as a Second Tongue" by John Leo. Copyright 1984 Time Inc. All rights reserved. Reprinted by permission from TIME.

Tom Shales, "Videospeak," *The Washington Post Magazine,* January 23, 1983. Reprinted by permission.

"The Language of Prejudice" by Stephen Steinberg, from *Today's Education.* Reprinted by permission.

Robin Lakoff, "You Are What You Say," MS., July 1974. Reprinted by permission of the author.

"The Desexing of English" by Sol Steinmetz. Copyright © 1982 by The New York Times Company. Reprinted by permission.

"Give Up Six Words and Change Your Life" by Marian and George Burtt, from *Glamour.* Reprinted by permission.

"Talking New York" by Deborah Tannen. © 1981 by Deborah Tannen. Reprinted from New York Magazine by special permission of Rhoda Weyr Agency.

"Tune That Name" by Justin Kaplan. Reprinted by permission of THE NEW REPUBLIC, © 1984, The New Republic, Inc.

"The Language of Clothes." From THE LANGUAGE OF CLOTHES, by Alison Lurie. Copyright © 1981 by Alison Lurie. Reprinted by permission of Random House, Inc.

"next to of course god america i" is reprinted from IS 5, poems by E. E. Cummings, by permission of Liveright Publishing Corporation. Copyright 1926 by Horace Liveright. Copyright renewed 1953 by E. E. Cummings.

"Politics and the English Language." From SHOOTING AN ELEPHANT AND OTHER ESSAYS by George Orwell, copyright 1946, 1974 by Sonia Orwell. Reprinted by permission of Harcourt, Brace Jovanovich, Inc.

"The Language of War" by Haig Bosmajian, from *The Language of Oppression.* Reprinted by permission of the publisher.

Ellen Goodman, "The Words Race," *The Washington Post,* November 27, 1982. © 1982, The Boston Globe Newspaper Company/Washington Post Writers Group. Reprinted with permission.

"I Have a Dream." Reprinted by permission of Joan Daves. Copyright © 1963 by Martin Luther King, Jr.

"White English: The Politics of Language" by June Jordan from *Black World,* August 1973. Copyright © 1980: June Jordan.

Barney Frank, "Is This a Dagger Which I See Before Me?" *The Washington Post,* July 27, 1983. Reprinted by permission.

Stephen Gillers, "Behind the War Metaphor," THE NATION, March 27, 1982. Copyright 1982 by THE NATION Magazine, The Nation Associates, Inc. Reprinted by permission.

"Democracy" by E. B. White. From THE WILD FLAG (Houghton Mifflin Company). © 1943, 1971 E. B. White. Originally in The New Yorker.

Fred Bruning, "Why People Distrust the Press," MACLEANS, January 16, 1984. Reprinted by permission.

"Journalism and the Larger Truth" by Roger Rosenblatt. Copyright 1984 Time Inc. All rights reserved. Reprinted by permission from TIME.

"Our All-Too-Timid Press" by Tom Wicker. Copyright © Tom Wicker, 1975, 1977, 1978. Reprinted by permission of Viking Penguin Inc.

"An Ethical Dilemma: Responsibility for 'Self-Generating' News" by J. K. Hvistendahl, from *Grassroots Editor.* Reprinted by permission.

"Of Privacy and the Press" by Arthur Schlesinger, Jr., from *The Wall Street Journal,* October 24, 1978, p. 24.

Meg Greenfield, "Must Reality Be Off the Record?" NEWSWEEK, April 16, 1984. Copyright 1984 by Newsweek, Inc. All rights reserved. Reprinted by permission.

Peter Funt, "Television News: Seeing Isn't Believing," THE SATURDAY REVIEW, November 1980. © 1980 SATURDAY REVIEW Magazine. Reprinted by permission.

Preface

Being asked to prepare a second edition is much like being asked back to a friend's house: although you count on it, you are still delighted when the invitation comes. I am pleased that *Language Power* has enough friends who keep inviting it back into their classrooms to justify bringing out a new edition.

Although sporting some new fashions, *Language Power*'s character—its purpose as a text—remains the same. *Language Power* is still a book about our language, a reader that illustrates through its selections and organization the flexibility and vitality of language that enable us to communicate with power whatever our writing purpose and whoever our audience. One goal of this reader is to develop students' sensitivity to words and their usage. But we know that good writing is not the result of language appreciation alone; it evolves from clear thinking. Thus *Language Power* is designed to develop the following analytical skills in conjunction with language skills:

1. Awareness of levels of usage and the importance of word choice
2. Recognition and use of rhetorical techniques for emphasis
3. A critical eye and ear for pompous writing
4. Recognition and avoidance of clichés and language that stereotypes
5. Discrimination between double-talk and plain talk, between propaganda and reality

To develop analytical skills, *Language Power* involves students in observing, analyzing, and writing about language. Throughout the text, the study of language use is closely tied to writing skills. As in the first edition, each chapter opens with a brief exercise or series of questions to start students thinking and often writing about the subject of that chapter. Each article in the book is followed by a word study list, questions on content and structure, and exercises for examining and writing about language. Many of these exercises can be developed into longer writing assignments. Chapters 1 through 4 include annotated student essays as models of the type of writing appropriate for the subject of the chapter. Chapter exercises and writing assignments complete each of the first seven chapters.

A closer look at the Table of Contents will reveal what is new about *Language Power,* as well as what remains unchanged. The most obvious change is the new length; *Language Power* has both more, and more varied, selections. The second most noticeable change is the addition of a new chapter (Chapter 2), one devoted to the whys and hows of the writing process, including attention paid to the problems of writing at all. Chapter 1 contains articles on word choice, usage, meaning, and clarity; it also considers what it means for human beings to use language. The old Chapter 2—now Chapter 3—covers various rhetorical or stylistic techniques—especially metaphor and connotation—used to shape our world through language. With Chapter 2's focus on the creative process, reasons for writing, and anxieties about writing added to the study of language development, word choice, and style, the first three chapters offer students a strong preparation for an analysis of the more specific uses of language described in Chapters 4 through 8.

The text maintains the same order of the first edition in its five chapters on different language uses, beginning in Chapter 4 with the language of advertising because it is the most familiar to students. A large, updated collection of advertisements is included in Chapter 4 to illustrate points made in the articles on advertising. From the clever, if tricky, world of advertising, the text moves to jargon, stereotyping, and political rhetoric in Chapters 5, 6, and 7. The exercises in Chapters 4 through 7 give students practice in distinguishing the subtle differences between effective and ineffective style and between appropriate and inappropriate wording for a given audience. Some exercises and writing assignments present methods for students to test the validity of ideas from the articles by gathering and analyzing additional evidence and by examining the author's logic. Other assignments sharpen students' reading skills by asking them to compare and contrast ideas and attitudes found in several selections.

The last chapter, Chapter 8, gives readers the opportunity to debate and research the controversial topic of the rights of a free press. To aid students in developing a documented paper, a list of suggested research topics and a bibliography conclude the chapter.

Although Carol Boltz did not participate in the preparation of this second edition, much of her work from the first edition remains, especially in the exercises in Chapters 1, 5, and 7. Responsibility for the choice of selections and the new and revised exercises is, for good or bad, entirely mine.

I continue to believe that the pursuit of language power is worthwhile, and that it can be fun. I hope you will enjoy using this new edition as much as I have enjoyed preparing it.

I wish to thank, once again, Richard Garretson for accepting our ideas for this text in its first edition, and the current Random House English editor, Steve Pensinger, who offered many fresh ideas for this edition. My research was greatly aided by Ruth Stanton, Jan Jeffries, and Marion Denton, members of the library staff at the Annandale Campus of Northern Virginia Community College. I also appreciate the many good suggestions from the following reviewers: Wayne Gunn, Texas A & I University; Teresita Sellers, Gulf Coast Community College; John Walsh, St. Peter's College; and Patricia Wiley, University of California at Davis. Finally, I want to thank our students, especially those whose papers have been included, for it was their curiosity, talents, and creativity that have led Carol and me to search for more and better ways to convey our love of language.

Dorothy U. Seyler
Annandale, Virginia

Contents

CHAPTER 1

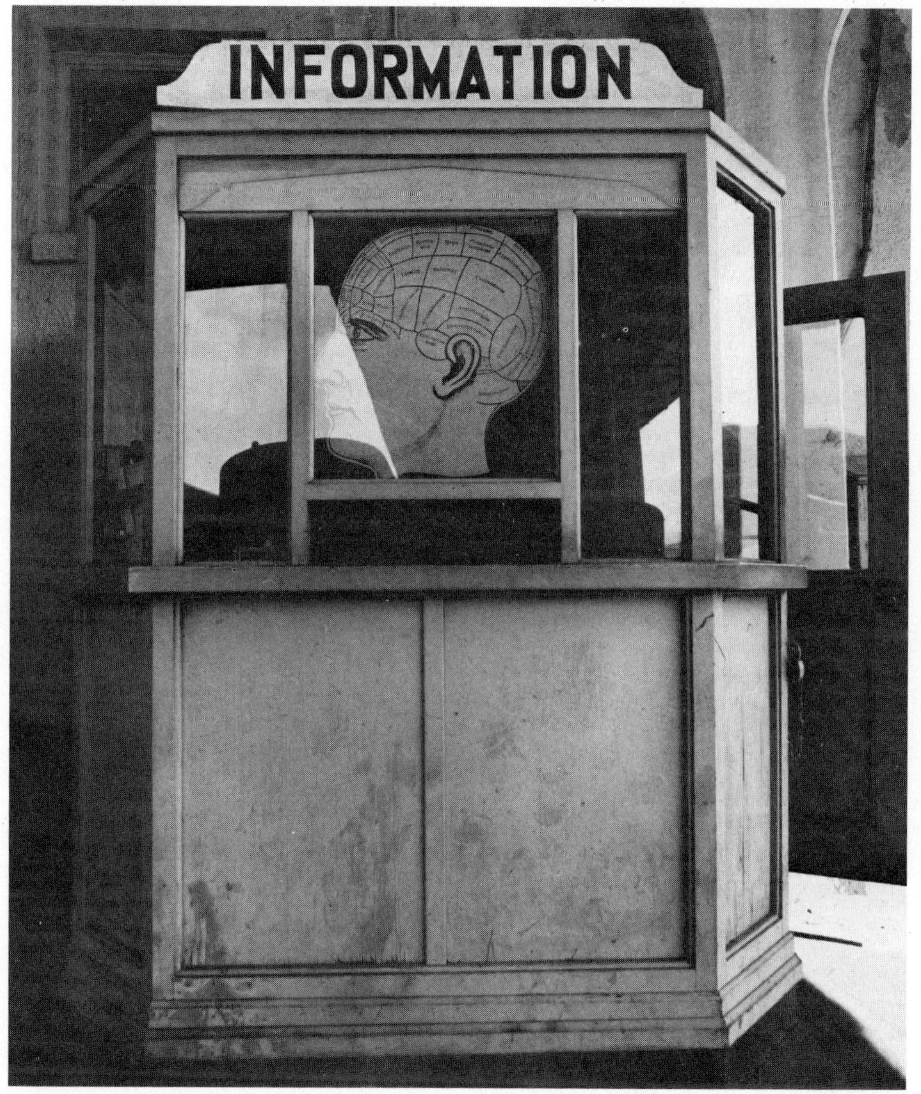

© Arthur Tress 1981/Woodfin Camp & Assoc.

Getting the Best of Words

GETTING STARTED
A Look at the Origin of Magic Words

All words can be powerful depending on the context and situation in which they are used, but some words are considered powerful, even magical, whatever their context. Check the origin of the following words in two desk dictionaries (see page 28 for recommendations).

1. hocus-pocus
2. abracadabra
3. amen
4. damn
5. goodby

Do the dictionaries agree on the origin of each one? If you find conflicting sources for any, consult the *Oxford English Dictionary,* a fourteen-volume historical dictionary located in the reference room of your college library. Is the word's origin any help in understanding how the word came to be associated with magical powers? In what context are these words used? Can you add any magical words to this list?

The Power of Words

Bergen Evans

Bergen Evans's (1904–1978) career included being master of ceremonies on network television and radio from the 1940s to the early 1960s and writing articles and books on language, including *A Dictionary of Contemporary American Usage.* "The Power of Words" is an excerpt from his book *The Word-a-Day Vocabulary Builder,* published in 1963.

Developing the metaphor of words as tools, Evans explains six ways that these powerful tools shape and clarify our experiences and ideas.

1 Words are the tools for the job of saying what you want to say. And what you want to say are your thoughts and feelings, your desires and your dislikes, your hopes and your fears, your business and your pleasure—almost everything, indeed, that makes up *you.* Except for our vegetablelike growth and our animallike impulses, almost all that we are is related to our use of words. Man has been defined as a tool-using animal, but his most important tool, the one that distinguishes him from all other animals, is his speech.

2 As with other tools, the number and variety of the words we know should meet our needs. Not that any man has ever had a vocabulary exactly fitted to his every need at all times. The greatest writers—those who have shown the rest of us how *in*adequate our command of words is—have agonized over their verbal shortcomings. But we can approach our needs. The more words we know, the closer we can come to expressing precisely what we want to.

3 We can, for instance, give clear instructions, and reduce misunderstandings. If we say, "See that he does it," we should make sure that the person spoken to knows what he is to do when he *sees,* that it is clear to him who *he* is and what *it* is and what must be accomplished to *do* it.

4 Some of history's great disasters have been caused by misunderstood directions. The heroic but futile charge of the Light Brigade at Balaclava in the Crimean War is a striking example. "Someone had blundered," Tennyson[1] wrote. That was true, and the blunder consisted of the confusion over one word, which meant one thing to the person speaking but another to the persons spoken to.

5 The brigade was ordered to charge "the guns." The man who gave the order was on a hilltop and had in mind a small battery which was very plain to him but was concealed from the soldiers in the valley by a slight rise. The only guns *they* could see were the main Russian batteries at the far end of the valley. Therefore they assumed that "the guns" referred to the batteries *they* saw. The command seemed utter madness, but it was a command and the leader of the brigade, after filing a protest, carried it out.

6 Fortunately, most misunderstandings don't have such diastrous consequences. But the continual confusion about such general terms as *thing, deal, it, fix,* and the like, certainly can be frustrating. Taken as a whole, the exasperation, humiliation, disappointment and quarreling caused by misunderstandings probably produce a thousand times the misery and suffering that the Light Brigade endured.

7 So the wise man, who wants peace of mind, and the efficient man, who wants to get on with the job, will take the trouble to use specific terms instead of doubtful ones.

8 Besides clarity, a large vocabulary provides variety. And that is useful; it is the basis for discrimination, since it provides a larger number of tools to choose from. A hammer won't do when a file is called for. Furthermore a large and varied vocabulary makes the speaker or writer more interesting. It allows him to avoid the dullness of repetition and to provoke attention. The interesting man is much more likely to be persuasive than the dull one. Dull people bore us. We don't listen to them. We hear them, but with a secret distaste. Instead of listening to them, we think only

---

[1]Alfred, Lord Tennyson (1809–1892) is a British poet who wrote "The Charge of the Light Brigade."—ED.

about getting away from them. Therefore a varied vocabulary is very useful for winning others to our point of view.

9 Thomas Wolfe[2] reveled in words with more glory and gusto than perhaps any man since Shakespeare or Rabelais. On seeing a shabby little man lying dead on a subway bench, Wolfe was struck with the thought of the dull and miserable existence such a man must have had because of the sterility of his speech. "Poor, dismal, ugly, sterile, shabby little man," Wolfe wrote in his essay, "Death the Proud Brother," "with your little scrabble of harsh oaths, and cries, and stale constricted words, your pitiful little designs and feeble purposes. . . . Joy, glory, and magnificence were here for you upon this earth, but you scrabbled along the pavements rattling a few stale words like gravel in your throat, and would have none of them."

10 When Caliban, the half-human monster in Shakespeare's last play, *The Tempest,* furiously denies that he owes any gratitude to his master, the magician Prospero, he demands to know what Prospero has ever done for him. The magician passes over all the many benefits he has conferred on the wretched creature, to stress only one: he has taught him to speak.

> I . . . took pains to make thee speak.
> When thou didst not, savage.
> Know thine own meaning, but wouldst gabble like
> A thing most brutish, I endow'd thy purposes
> With words that made them known.

11 The simple fact is that we all begin as Calibans—and do not know even our own purposes until we endow them with words. Do not, indeed, know ourselves. The pleasure you will feel as you develop your vocabulary is not solely the pleasure that comes with increased power; it is also the greater pleasure that comes with increased knowledge, especially of yourself. You will begin to appreciate expression as an art and to feel not only the advantage of commanding words but the satisfaction. You will notice that this or that phrase which someone utters in your hearing or which you see in the newspapers is very good.

12 And you will be pleased that it *is* good, just as you are pleased to see a forward pass completed, or a long putt holed, or a dance step gracefully executed. For words are to the mind what such actions are to the body.

13 You will see that the rightness of a well-chosen word is not merely a source of pleasure; it may provoke the most serious consequences or avoid the gravest danger. When, for example, America and Russia confronted each other during the Cuban crisis in 1962, and the world hovered for a few days on the brink of disaster, the use of the word *quarantine*

---

[2]Thomas Wolfe (1900–1938) is an American novelist known for his flowing, sometimes rambling, style.—ED.

instead of *blockade* was extremely important. A *blockade* is an act of war. No one knew quite what a *quarantine* meant, under the circumstances. But the very use of the word indicated that, while we were determined to protect ourselves, we wanted to avoid war. It was all a part of giving Russia some possibility of saving face. We wanted her missiles and planes out of Cuba and were prepared to fight even a nuclear war to get them out. But we certainly preferred to have them removed peacefully. We did not want to back Russia into a corner from which there could have been no escape except by violence.

14 Thus the use of *quarantine,* a purposefully vague word, was part of our strategy. Furthermore, it had other advantages over *blockade.* It is commonly associated with a restriction imposed by all civilized nations on people with certain communicable diseases to prevent them from spreading their disease throughout the community. It is a public health measure which, for all the inconvenience that it may impose on the afflicted individual, serves the public welfare. Thus, whereas a blockade would have been an announcement that we were proceeding aggressively to further our own interests, regardless of the rights of others, quarantine suggested a concern for the general welfare. In addition, it suggested that what was going on in Cuba was a dangerous disease which might spread.

15 So, as you develop a larger vocabulary you will be increasingly aware of what is going on. You will enjoy what you read more. New pleasures will be opened to you.

16 You will understand more. Difficult books whose meaning has been uncertain will become readable. The great poets who have enlarged our experience, the philosophers who have shaped our thoughts, the historians who have sought for patterns in the human story, the essayists whose observations have delighted men for centuries—all these and more will be available to you. And in sharing their thoughts your own world will expand. This particular benefit of an increased vocabulary is dramatically apparent in the strides that children make in comprehension as they progess in their use of language. Increased learning increases the child's word stock and the increased word stock makes learning easier. The National Conference on Research in English says "a child's ability to read, to speak, to write, and to think is inevitably conditioned by his vocabulary."

17 This goes for an adult too. Words cannot be separated from ideas. They interact. The words we use are so associated with our experiences and what the experiences mean to us that they cannot be separated. The idea comes up from our subconscious clothed in words. It can't come any other way.

18 We don't know how words are stored in our minds, but there does seem to be a sort of filing system. The filing system appears to be controlled by a perverse if not downright wacky filing clerk. Everyone has tried to remember a word and been unable to. Sometimes it is a common word, one that we *know* we know. Yet it won't come when we want it. It

can be almost a form of torture trying to recall it, but no amount of fuming or fretting helps. Then suddenly, usually some time later when it is no longer useful to us, it will come to mind readily. When we are searching for one of these words—often for a person's name—we will come up with other words or names that we know are close to but not exactly the one we want. This is curious in itself. For if we can't remember the word we want, how do we know the other word is very much like it? It's as though the filing clerk had seen the word we actually wanted or was even holding it in his hand but wouldn't give it to us.

19 Often we know that the unacceptable word has the same sound or begins with the same letter as the word we can't remember. And when we finally recall the word we wanted, we find this is so. It seems as though our mental filing systems were arranged alphabetically and cross-indexed for similarity of internal sound. If we are well-read, we can call up a host of synonyms (words that mean the same thing) for many words, which suggests more crossfiling. Furthermore, words have subtle and complex associations. The speech and writing of some people who have sustained brain injuries or suffered strokes indicate a curious kind of damage. Some injured people seem to lose all proper names, some all adjectives, and many mix up capitals and small letters. This indicates that the interlocking connections of words in our minds are more complex than we can imagine. The chances are that the most spectacular computer is a simple gadget compared to the human mind.

20 For our purposes, our ignorance of how this intricate filing system works does not matter. What matters to a person trying to enlarge his vocabulary is the many connections among the words he knows. Once we master a word, it is connected in our mind with scores of other words in what appears to be an infinite number of relationships and shades of meaning. A new word does not drop as a single addition into our word stock. Each new word learned enlarges a whole complex of thinking and is itself enlarged in meaning and significance.

21 A vocabulary is a tool which one uses in formulating the important questions of life, the questions which must be asked before they can be answered. To a large extent, vocabulary shapes all the decisions we make. Most decisions, of course, are shaped by our emotions, by circumstances, and by the forces which may hold us back or urge us on. These circumstances and forces are largely beyond our control. But our speech is a sort of searchlight that helps us to see these things more clearly and to see ourselves in relation to them. At least it helps us call things by their right names.

22 To a great extent our speech affects our judgments. We don't always—sometimes we can't—distinguish between words and things. A slogan, for example, especially if it rhymes, or is alliterative (that is, has a number of words that begin with the same sound), or has a strong rhythm, will move us to action. It convinces us that the action is necessary. "Motor-

ists wise Simonize" is far more effective in promoting sales than "Simonize, wise motorists" or "Wise motorists, Simonize" would have been. It's the witchery of rhythm, one of the most subtle and dangerous of unseen forces that move and muddle our minds. Seduced by "Fifty-four forty or fight," our great-grandfathers almost went to war in 1844. And there are historians who trace much of the misery of the modern world to the fascination that Grant's "Unconditional surrender" held for four generations of Americans.

23 Certainly anyone who develops the valuable habit of examining his own prejudices will find that many of them are, at bottom, verbal. A situation automatically calls forth a single word. The word is bathed in emotion. So whenever the situation is repeated, it produces the same emotional response. There is no effort to be rational, to see what is actually going on. The word triggers the response. But the more words one has at his command, the greater the possibility that he may be his own master. It takes words to free us from words. Removing an emotionally charged word from a phrase and substituting a neutral synonym often gives us an insight that nothing else can.

24 Speech is the means of relating our separate experiences and emotions, of combining them, reliving them and, as far as we can, understanding them. If we did not have the words *justice, equal, radiation*—and a thousand others like them—our minds and our whole lives would be much narrower. Each new word of this kind increases the scope of thought and adds its bit to humanity. Once we have the word, of course, it seems natural and it is an effort to imagine being without it.

25 Consider that remarkable British phrase which Lord Broughton invented during the reign of George IV (1820–1830): "His Majesty's opposition." Political parties rose in seventeenth-century England during a period of limited civil war and they behaved as if parliamentary victories were military ones. When one party gained power it immediately proceeded to impeach the leaders of the other party, demanding their very heads. But after a hundred and fifty years of peace and prosperity, men's tempers began to cool. A sense of fairness compelled them to grant their neighbor the right to a different opinion and even to grant that men who opposed them might still be loyal and honorable. But the atmosphere Lord Broughton described had to precede his phrase, just as the invention of the wheel had to precede the medieval concept of Fortune's wheel.

26 Once uttered, the phrase helped to further the idea it described. Men saw that criticism of an administration can be as much a part of good government as the government itself and that a man was not necessarily a traitor because he disagreed with the party in power.

27 Many studies have established the fact that there is a high correlation between vocabulary and intelligence and that the ability to increase one's vocabulary throughout life is a sure reflection of intellectual progress.

28 It is hard to stretch a small vocabulary to make it do all the things

that intelligent people require of words. It's like trying to plan a series of menus from the limited resources of a poverty-stricken, war-torn country compared to planning such a series in a prosperous, stable country. Words are one of our chief means of adjusting to all the situations of life. The better control we have over words, the more successful our adjustment is likely to be.

Word Study List

futile	4	subtle	19, 22
brigade	4	formulating	21
reveled	9	parliamentary	25
perverse	18	medieval	25

Questions

1. The short word study list above indicates that Evans has not used a sophisticated vocabulary in his article. What is the effect of his choosing a simple vocabulary to make his point about having a stock of words to "meet all our needs"?

2. Evans says that words and ideas are inseparable; to have ideas is to use words (paragraph 17). Try to do a simple task without thinking with words. What happened? What words crept into your consciousness by surprise? Why is it difficult to function without words, even to perform a routine task?

3. Evans reinforces his point, or thesis, about the advantages of a large vocabulary by comparing words to tools. Does the comparison make his ideas easier to grasp, more interesting, or both?

4. Evans supports his thesis with six advantages of having a good vocabulary. What are these six advantages, and how many paragraphs are used to develop each of the points? What techniques are used to connect the six points? (Consider repetition of key words and use of transitions.)

5. When have you had a misunderstanding with someone caused by confusion over the meaning of a word? Do you often use vague words such as *thing, deal* (as in "a great deal of"), or *it?* Why are such words more common in conversation than in writing?

6. Evans asserts that many prejudices are, on close examination, verbal. How do words create prejudice? Look at words such as *pig* for policeman, *playboy* for a man who dates many women, *Third World* countries for countries that are not industrialized, or *kid* for a child. Do new terms like *inner city* for the ghetto or *handicapped* for the disabled help to

erase prejudice? Why or why not? (See Chapter 6, "Subtle—and Not So Subtle—Stereotyping and Prejudice.")

7. You have probably discovered that most subjects in college require learning a specialized vocabulary. Can you explain why learning the vocabulary of economics, physics, or psychology helps you to succeed in these courses? In what way are you more intelligent for having learned the vocabulary?

Exercise

In paragraph 22 Evans discusses how speech affects our actions and reactions. What slogans have moved you to act? Consider bumper stickers, posters, advertisements, and slang expressions. Write a paragraph that explains the results of your reacting to a particular slogan or a paragraph that explains why you reacted to a slogan.

The Human Use of Language

Lawrence L. Langer

Lawrence Langer (b. 1929), professor of English at Simmons College in Boston, has written extensively on literature related to the horrors of World War II. Two of his books are *The Age of Atrocity: Death in Modern Literature* (1978) and *Versions of Survival: The Holocaust and the Human Spirit* (1982). The following essay was printed in *The Chronicle of Higher Education* in January 1977.

Writing with strong emotion, Langer encourages us to use language to understand and expose our feelings and to respond with feeling to others.

1 A friend of mine recently turned in a paper to a course on behavior modification. She had tried to express in simple English some of her reservations about this increasingly popular approach to education. She received it back with the comment: "Please rewrite this in behavioral terms."

2 It is little wonder that human beings have so much trouble saying what they feel, when they are told that there is a specialized vocabulary for saying what they think. The language of simplicity and spontaneity is forced to retreat behind the barricades of an official prose developed by a few experts who believe that jargon is the most precise means of com-

munication. The results would be comic, if they were not so poisonous; unfortunately, there is an attitude toward the use of language that is impervious to human need and drives some people back into silence when they realize the folly of risking human words on insensitive ears.

3 The comedy is easy to come by. Glancing through my friend's textbook on behavior modification, I happened on a chapter beginning with the following challenging statement: "Many of the problems encountered by teachers in the daily management of their classes could be resolved if. . . ." Although I was a little wary of the phrase "daily management," I was encouraged to plunge ahead, because as an educator I have always been interested in ideas for improving learning. So I plunged. The entire sentence reads: "Many of the problems encountered by teachers in the daily management of their classes could be resolved if the emission of desirable student behaviors was increased."

4 Emission? At first I thought it was a misprint for "omission," but the omission of desirable student behaviors (note the plural) hardly seemed an appropriate goal for educators. Then I considered the possibility of metaphor, both erotic and automotive, but these didn't seem to fit, either. A footnote clarified the matter: "'Emission' is a technical term used in behavioral analysis. The verb, 'to emit,' is used specifically with a certain category of behavior called 'operant behavior.' Operant behaviors are modified by their consequences. Operant behaviors correspond closely to the behavior colloquially referred to as voluntary." Voluntary? Is jargon then an attack on freedom of the will?

5 Of course, this kind of abuse of language goes on all the time—within the academic world, one regrets to say, as well as outside it. Why couldn't the author of this text simply say that we need to motivate students to learn willingly? The more I read such non-human prose, and try to avoid writing it myself, the more I am convinced that we must be in touch with ourselves before we can use words to touch others.

6 Using language meaningfully requires risk; the sentence I have just quoted takes no risks at all. Much of the discourse that poses as communication in our society is really a decoy to divert our audience (and often ourselves) from that shadowy plateau where our real life hovers on the precipice of expression. How many people, for example, have the courage to walk up to someone they like and actually *say* to them: "I'm very fond of you, you know"?

7 Such honesty reflects the use of language as revelation, and that sort of revelation, brimming with human possibilities, is risky precisely because it invites judgment and rebuff. Perhaps this is one reason why, especially in academe, we are confronted daily with so much neutral prose: Our students are not yet in touch with themselves; not especially encouraged by us, their instructors, to move in that direction; they are encouraged indeed to expect judgment and hence perhaps rebuff, too, in our evaluation of them. Thus they instinctively retreat behind the anonymity of

abstract diction and technical jargon to protect themselves against us—but also, as I have suggested, against themselves.

8 This problem was crystallized for me recently by an encounter only peripherally related to the issue. As part of my current research, I have been interviewing children of concentration-camp survivors. One girl I have been meeting with says that her mother does not like to talk about the experience, *except with other survivors.* Risk is diminished when we know in advance that our audience shares with us a sympathy for our theme. The nakedness of pain *and* the nakedness of love require gentle responses. So this survivor is reticent, except with fellow victims.

9 But one day a situation arose which tempted her to the human use of language although she could not be sure, in advance, of the reception her words would receive. We all recognize it. This particular woman, at the age of 40, decided to return to school to get a college degree. Her first assignment in freshman composition was to write a paper on something that was of great importance to her personally. The challenge was immense; the risk was even greater. For the first time in 20 years, she resolved to confront a silence in her life that she obviously needed to rouse to speech.

10 She was 14 when the Germans invaded Poland. When the roundup of the Jews began a year later, some Christian friends sent their young daughter to "call for her" one day, so that they might hide her. A half hour later, the friends went themselves to pick up her parents, but during that interval, a truck had arrived, loaded aboard the Jewish mother and father—and the daughter never saw them or heard from them again. Their fate we can imagine. The girl herself was eventually arrested, survived several camps, and after the war came to America. She married, had children of her own, and except for occasional reminiscences with fellow survivors, managed to live adequately without diving into her buried personal past. Until one day her instructor in English composition touched a well-insulated nerve, and it began to throb with a painful impulse to express. I present verbatim the result of that impulse, a paper called "People I Have Forgotten":

> 11 "Can you forget your own Father and Mother? If so—how or why?
>
> 12 "I thought I did. To mention their names, for me is a great emotional struggle. The brutal force of this reality shakes my whole body and mind, wrecking me into ugly splinters; each crying to be mended anew. So the silence I maintain about their memory is only physical and valid as such but not true. I could never forget my parents, nor do I want to do it. True, I seldom talk about them with my husband or my children. How they looked, who they were, why they perished during the war. The love and sacrifices they have made for me during their lifetime, never get told.
>
> 13 "The cultural heritage to which each generation is entitled to have access seems to be nonexistant [*sic*], since I dare not talk about anything relating to my past, my parents.

> 14 "This awful, awesome power of non-remembering, this heart-breaking sensation of the conspiracy of silence is my dilemma.
>
> 15 "Often, I have tried to break through my imprisoning wall of irrational silence, but failed: now I hope to be able to do it.
>
> 16 "Until now, I was not able to face up to the loss of my parents, much less talk about them. The smallest reminder of them would set off a chain reaction of results that I could anticipate but never direct. The destructive force of sadness, horror, fright would then become my master. And it was this subconscious knowledge that kept me paralyzed with silence, not a conscious desire to forget my parents.
>
> 17 "My silent wall, my locked shell existed only of real necessity; I needed time.
>
> 18 "I needed time to forget the tragic loss of my loved ones, time to heal my emotional wound so that there shall come a time when I can again remember the people I have forgotten."

19 The essay is not a confrontation, only a prelude, yet it reveals qualities which are necessary for the human use of language: In trying to reach her audience, the author must touch the deepest part of herself. She risks self-exposure—when we see the instructor's comment, we will realize how great was her risk—and she is prepared for judgment and perhaps even rebuff, although I doubt whether she was prepared for the form they took. This kind of prose, for all its hesitant phraseology, throws down a gauntlet to the reader, a challenge asking him to understand that life is pain as well as plenty, chaos as well as form. Its imagery of locked shells and imprisoning walls hints at a silent world of horror and sadness far less enchanting than the more familiar landscape of love where most of us dwell. Language is a two-edged tool, to pierce the wall which hides that world, or build high abstract barriers to protect us from its threats.

20 The instructor who graded the paper I have just read preferred walls to honest words. At the bottom of the last page she scrawled a large "D-minus," emphatically surrounded by a circle. Her only comment was: "Your theme is not clear—you should have developed your 1st paragraph. You talk around your subject." At this moment, two realms collide: a universe of unarticulated feeling seeking expression (and the courage and encouragement to express) and a nature made so immune to feeling by heaven-knows-what that she hides behind the tired, tired language of the professional theme-corrector.

21 Suddenly we realize that reading as well as writing requires risks, and that the metaphor of insulation, so central to the efforts of the Polish woman survivor to re-establish contact with her past, is a metaphor governing the response of readers, too. Some writing, like "the emission of desirable student behaviors," thickens the insulation that already separates the reader from the words that throw darts at his armor of indifference. But even when language unashamedly reveals the feeling that is hidden behind the words, it must contend with a different kind of barrier,

the one behind which our instructor lies concealed, unwilling or unable to hear a human voice and return a human echo of her own.

22 Ironically, the victor in this melancholy failure at communication is the villain of the piece, behavior modification. For the Polish survivor wrote her next theme on an innocuous topic, received a satisfactory grade, and never returned to the subject of her parents. The instructor, who had encountered a problem in the daily management of her class in the form of an essay which she could not respond to in a human way, altered the attitude of her student by responding in a non-human way, thus resolving her problem by increasing the emission of desirable student behavior. The student now knows how vital it is to develop her first paragraph, and how futile it is to reveal her first grief.

23 Even more, she has learned the danger of talking around her subject: She not only refuses to talk *around* it now, she refuses to talk *about* it. Thus the human use of language leads back to silence—where perhaps it should have remained in the first place.

Word Study List

jargon	2, 4, 7	reticent	8
discourse	6	verbatim	10
decoy	6	phraseology	19
academe	7	gauntlet	19
diction	7	insulation	21
peripherally	8	innocuous	22

Questions

1. What, for Langer, are human uses of language?
2. By contrast, what uses of language are nonhuman or inhuman?
3. What particular examples of inhuman language does Langer give? Can you provide other examples of inhuman language use?
4. Why, according to Langer, is the human use of language risky?
5. Langer never says what grade the student paper should have received. Why not? What is his chief objection to the instructor's response?
6. Do you think instructors should assign topics that require highly personal writing? When instructors give such assignments, by what standards should the student papers be judged? What roles do audience and purpose play when we write or evaluate personal essays?

Exercise

Placing yourself in the role of instructor, reread the student essay and write down the comments you would put on the student's paper. Then analyze your comments to decide if Langer would call them human or nonhuman uses of language.

Words to Live Without

Colman McCarthy

Colman McCarthy (b. 1938) is a syndicated columnist and member of the Washington Post Writer's Group. He is also author of *Disturbers of the Peace* (1973), *Inner Companions* (1975), and *The Pleasures of the Game* (1977). This editorial comment appeared in the February 6, 1972, issue of the *Washington Post.*

In contrast to the more general remarks on words that Evans makes, this piece focuses on a few specific words, such as *very* and *simply,* that clutter our writing. McCarthy says that good writing moves a reader's mind, but overused and misused words deaden thought.

1 The presidential candidates are already filtering into the small towns, making speeches to what they think are the common folks on themes they insist are common sense. Those who care about preserving the language while the light lasts look on darkly at the strains to which English is being put in the pursuit of votes. But the politicians are unfairly singled out. Their abuse of language—evasive words, dull metaphors, stale sentences—may be more depressing (because people still insist on believing big things will come from big talk), but it is not more harmful. Almost everyone is cutting up the language one way or another.

2 E. B. White,[1] co-author of the desktop classic *The Elements of Style,* has noted about language and usage that "everyone has his own prejudices, his own set of rules, his own list of horribles." Trouble appears when writers, editors, and readers no longer bother to work up a lively prejudice or carry around a strong shovel for burying dead words.

3 Most likely, they find it too much bother, considering all the other disasters to worry about. Yet if the language is not guarded—not necessarily by either the Nice Nellies[2] or Nervous Nellies but by everyone armed with a prejudice—we run the risk that a dying language can lead to a dying culture. Citizens careless with the tools of communication easily

[1]E. B. White (b. 1899) is an essayist, free-lance writer, and author of children's books.—Ed.

[2]Persons who use polite, even primly proper, expressions.—Ed.

leave out in the rain the tools for equal justice, health care, education, demilitarism and others. A connection exists between language and life.

DEAD WORDS

4 Even before a writer or reader compiles "a list of horribles," he must choose sides on the "dictionary issue." This is the well-known argument about whether the dictionary should be a standard or a reflection of usage. Should certain words or definitions be excluded because dictionary makers disapprove, or should words and meanings be included because the public uses them with increasing frequency? Each side in the argument is backed with sound opinions, but whatever camp one decides to settle in, there are still plenty of words and terms to live without.

5 "Very" is high on my own list of dead words. What does it mean? Almost nothing. To say "She is a very active woman" adds nothing to "She is an active woman." If the lady is furiously or feverishly active, as more women appear to be today, then her fury and fever deserve to be liberated by greater description than a "very." Others who put "very" on their list of horribles insist that they have never seen a case where the word added anything in either emphasis or style. Dictionaries trace "very" to the Latin *verac, verax,* meaning true or truthful, which gives almost a canonical importance to the word. Yet, the proof of "very's" deadness can be seen merely by deleting it whenever it appears.

6 One place where few "verys" are ever crossed out is in the columns of Joseph Alsop.[3] Alsop adores "very." He seldom misses a chance to squeeze it in. In fact, squeeze is hardly the word. It appears that prose holes as big as mine shafts are dug by Alsop just to fill in with "verys." He can put in three or four "verys" in a single column. In one recent stretch, when the fuse of Egyptians, Democrats or someone had apparently detonated his ire, Alsop's "very" production set what might be the indoor record: 13 in four columns. Strumming his "verys" as if they were banjo strings, the Alsop chord recently had three "verys" in consecutive sentences. It is not worth major study, but a pattern might exist: The "verys" pour out of Alsop often when he preaches sermons of faith likely to be doubted by liberal devils. Thus, in a column on Richard Nixon as "one of our better war presidents," three "verys" were jammed into the first three paragraphs. A column on how Vietnamization[4] will work needed four "verys."

7 It may be unfair to single out Alsop's prose. Few writers can throw stones at "very" users who do not live themselves in glass houses where a

---

[3]Joseph Alsop (b. 1910) is a newspaperman whose syndicated column "Matter of Fact" ran from 1958 to 1974 and with his brother as coauthor from 1945 to 1958.—Ed.

[4]Term coined in the late 1960s for the withdrawal of U.S. troops from Vietnam and the simultaneous build-up of South Vietnamese forces.—Ed.

"very" or two can be found in the panes. Even E. B. White, who advises that "very" be used sparingly, once admitted that he had occasionally slipped, although a White "very" is now a collector's item.

8 Occasionally, someone sees the body of language on the butcher table of poor writing and cries out, as though at the scene of a slaying, which it is. In a summer issue of *Saturday Review,* Ned O'Gorman, a craftsman poet and a master of the tongue, reviewed a book by a group of educators. Of all people, the teachers of our children would seem to be the most careful about English. No, says O'Gorman. "There are more gurus, leaders and silly prophets babbling on about education and children than there ought sanely to be. If these creatures could only write well; not brilliantly, not stylishly, but merely well. If they had just a little respect for the meanings of words. If they had mercy on syntax and loved a little less their foolish enthusiasms and neuroses, and cared a little more for meaning."

"MY GOD. IT'S SHE."

9 There is no shortage of dead words awaiting last rites. Newspaper offices are crowded with editors who, next to their opinions, will share nothing more eagerly than their lists of forbidden words. One editor at the *Washington Post,* for example, flushes red upon seeing "presently" used for "currently." *Wall Street Journal* reporters tell of one editor who considered "virtually" a felony; for years the word "practically" was substituted, though it is difficult to see how that improved any sentences.

10 Despite their undenied value, editors are occasionally too lacey in refining the prose of reporters. The story is told of a police line-up that contained a notorious murderess. A witness to her latest crime was brought in and, looking over the group, suddenly pointed and exclaimed, "My God. That's her." The reporter put this in the lead of his story, but the editor, a man of impeccable fuss, changed it: "My God. It's she."

11 Anyone can begin a list of words to live without. "Simply" would be a safe start. The word is all right in itself, if a fact or feeling of simplicity is meant—as in "He simply painted the room," meaning the room was painted with no frills or adornments. But simplicity is usually the last notion in the minds of "simply" users. "I simply can't go." "It's simply a matter of money." "She simply refused." In these usages, which some dictionaries have come to sanction, simply is used as a synonym for definitely, solely or emphatically. Why not use those words?

12 Dead expressions, as well as dead words, are also being kept alive. Among them are "a good deal," as in "A good deal of the season was dull." Does a bad deal of anything ever happen? Why not say "much of the season"? Another is "well aware," as in "We are well aware of the event." Is anyone ever unwell aware or bad aware? "Flatly rejected" is popular, as in "The idea was flatly rejected." Are ideas every bumpily rejected?

13 In much the way that we refuse to say a requiem for words and terms, we also insist on burying words that still rattle with life. Love is an example, perhaps one word that should be the most worried about. Here, the ad men are the happy pallbearers. In their pitches, people are made to "love" toothpaste, soups, cars, snacks, detergents and other treasures. A current television advertisement for Canada Dry ginger ale not only buries the word love but places over it a tombstone of absurdity. Canada Dry "tastes like love," the ad goes. Consumers know better. Canada Dry tastes not like love but like other ginger ales.

14 This ad is nothing in foolishness when compared to one for the National Biscuit Company's Milk-Bone dog food. A recent ad in *McCall's* shows a dog telling the reader, "I am a healthy dog with sound teeth but . . . I had dingy teeth. And doggy breath. Nobody kissed me twice." But then the dog took up with Milk-Bone and "got cleaner whiter teeth in just three weeks and found love."

15 The ad agencies have done their work well. Many citizens now speak of how much they "love" their pet, how much they "love" their new bucket seats. Whatever else may be said about it, the language is assuredly debased; in the basic meaning of both the word and the activity, whether emotional or physical, love can only happen between or among human beings. The rest—relationships between humans and their mutts, ginger ales, cars and gadgets—is something much less: attachment, attraction, habit. Fittingly, it was in Shakespeare's "Love's Labours Lost" where the lines are spoken: "They have been at a great feast of language, and stolen the scraps."

GUSHING IT ONTO PAPER

16 Can a respect for words be restored? It is possible, but the point-spread is wide on its happening soon. High school and college teachers speak in alarm about the first-draft mentality of their students. The kids think they must only write one draft and hand it in. Assignment papers are as thick as floured soup with clichés, hack words, dull phrases. A row of words—spread out any old way—is passed off as a sentence. Even correct spelling is rare. This is a double horror—not only mere stupidity, which can be corrected, but laziness in opening a dictionary, a deficiency less easy to correct because it involves the will.

17 A second unhopeful sign is that writing is now seen by many as a way of turning loose the emotions. Let it all come out. Gush it onto paper. How can word usage, spelling, and grammar be important against the mighty mission of saying What I Feel? I'm Sam or Sally Sensitive, so everyone listen. The trouble, as Sam or Sally may learn after the rejection slips or F grades in English mount, is that in communicating one's feelings, feelings alone are not enough. First, who cares about your tirade? Second, the final test of writing is not where it leaves the reader but where it takes him. If it takes him no further than the final period, then the writing has

low worth. If, instead, the reader is led to further exploration—into the outer world of everyone or into his own inner world—then this is everything and worthy of the bother to choose the best word at the best moment. The writer, through fine usage and clear style, has set something in motion—a mind, the most inert matter of all.

Word Study List

evasive	1	sanction	11
metaphors	1	requiem	13
demilitarism	3	debased	15
canonical	5	clichés	16
syntax	8	tirade	17

Questions

1. McCarthy's opening paragraph refers to the abuse of language by politicians. Is his article about politicians and their misuse of language? Why has he singled out politicians for criticism so early in his article?
2. After reading paragraphs 2 and 4, what do you think is McCarthy's opinion on standards of usage?
3. What is the subject of McCarthy's article, and what is his attitude toward this subject? What point is he making about this subject, or what is his thesis?
4. What examples of dead words does the writer give? Why do these words warrant our attention, according to McCarthy? Bring to class a paper you have recently written. What dead words do you find in it?
5. To emphasize words that have lost their punch or meaning and give coherence to his article, McCarthy develops an elaborate metaphor based on the word *dead.* Point out the paragraphs in which the metaphor or comparison is present and explain how, in each instance, it develops his thesis.
6. Check the meaning of *love* in your dictionary. Does that definition agree with McCarthy's? Do you speak of loving pets or objects? If so, think of a specific example of your using the word in this way and decide if you now think *love* was the appropriate word to use or if another word would have been more suitable.
7. McCarthy concludes his article with an explanation of students' inability to write—students tend to rely on feelings rather than precision in choosing words and shaping sentences. Is this an accurate explanation?
8. What, according to McCarthy, is the mark of effective writing?

Exercises

1. McCarthy writes that "anyone can begin a list of words to live without." Start your own list of dead words and add to it throughout the course. You might start with *pretty* and *nice* as in "It is a *pretty nice* day."

2. The author discusses in paragraph 5 how far removed the present usage of *very* is from the original meaning and root. Based on the root of *awful,* the definitions given, and the usage labels in your dictionary, what sentence below gives the current usage of the word? Which the oldest use of the word? Would McCarthy consider *awful* in its current use a dead word?
   a. The possibility of a third world war is too awful to contemplate.
   b. Awful were the words of God to Isaiah.
   c. Oversleeping is an awful way to begin the day.

Good Usage, Bad Usage, and Usage

Morris Bishop

Morris Bishop (1893–1973), professor of Romance languages and literature at Cornell University from 1926 until 1960, is widely known as a biographer of such varied men as Pascal, La Rochefoucauld, Petrarch, and Champlain, as well as a skillful writer of limericks and light verse.

In this essay from the preface to *The American Heritage Dictionary,* Bishop examines the question of what is proper and improper usage—a question that English speakers have debated without resolution for the past several hundred years.

1 The words of a living language are like creatures: they are alive. Each word has a physical character, a look and a personality, an ancestry, an expectation of life and death, a hope of posterity. Some words strike us as beautiful, some ugly, some evil. The word *glory* seems to shine; the common word for excrement seems to smell. There are holy words, like the proper name of God, pronounced only once a year in the innermost court of Jerusalem's Temple. There are magic words, spells to open gates and safes, summon spirits, put an end to the world. What are magic spells but magic spellings? Words sing to us, frighten us, impel us to self-immolation and murder. They belong to us; they couple at our order, to make what have well been called the aureate words of poets and the inkhorn words of pedants. We can keep our words alive, or at our caprice we can kill them—though some escape and prosper in our despite.

2 Thought makes the word; also the word makes thought. Some psychologists allege that explicit thought does not exist without verbalization. Thought, they say, emerges from our silent secret speech, from the tiny quivers of the speech organs, from the interior monologue we all carry on endlessly. Let us pause a moment and reflect on our thought; we reflect in words, on a surge of hurrying words.

3 Much of our formless, secret thought is, to be sure, idiotic. "We find it hard to believe that other people's thoughts are as silly as our own, but they probably are," said the American scholar James Harvey Robinson. Before we permit silent speech to emerge as spoken language, we must make choices and arrange words in patterns of sense and form, accessible to other people. These choices and patterns are usage. And usage is the ruler, the governor, the judge of language. Horace said it nearly two thousand years ago in his *Ars Poetica: "usus, Quem penes arbitrium est, et jus, et norma loquendi."* Or, in an old translation of the passage:

> Yes, words long faded may again revive;
> And words may fade now blooming and alive,
> If USAGE wills it so, to whom belongs
> The rule and law, the government of tongues.

4 Deferring to the rule and law of usage, we may yet order our words well or ill, thus creating Good Usage and Bad Usage.

5 Now the trouble begins. Whose usage is good, whose bad? Is not my usage good for me? May I not tell my own words what to do? Do you have authority over my usage? Does anyone have authority? And if authority exists, is it helpful or hurtful to usage?

6 We tend to demand freedom for our own usage, authority for others'. Yet we are not above seeking comfort and support from authority. One of our commonest phrases is "look it up in the dictionary." (Not any particular dictionary; just "the dictionary.") Every court of law has its big dictionary; the law settles cases, awards millions, rates crimes and misdemeanors, by quoting the definitions of some poor attic lexicographer, "a harmless drudge," as defined by lexicographer Samuel Johnson. We acclaim freedom, but we love the word *freedom* more than the fact. Most people most of the time would rather be secure than free; they cry for law and order. In this matter of usage, we suspect that complete freedom might outbabble Babel; without common agreement on the meaning of most words, communication would cease.

7 Who, then, shall wield authority? The King, perhaps? The phrase *the King's English* came in, we are told, with Henry VIII, who ruled from 1509 to 1547. He was a poet and a man of letters when he had the time. The King's English remained standard, even under George I, who could not speak English. Recent Kings and Queens of England have not been noteworthy for an exemplary style. In America the President's English has

never ruled the citizenry. The one notorious Presidential venture into lexicography was Harding's use of *normalcy.* But he said that he had looked it up in the dictionary.

8 The King's English was naturally identified with the spoken style of gentlemen and ladies of the English court. Similarly in France, the grammarian Vaugelas defined (in 1647) good usage as the speech habits of the sounder members of the court, in conformity with the practice in writing of the sounder contemporary authors. Good usage, then, would represent the practice of an elite of breeding, station, and intellect.

9 The idea of an elite with authority over language clearly needed delimitation. In France, Cardinal Richelieu, who piqued himself on his style in verse and prose, authorized in 1635 the formation of an *Académie française,* composed of writers, bookish nobles and magistrates, and amateurs of letters. The *Académie,* the supreme court of the French literary world, set itself the task of preparing a dictionary. It has been working at its dictionary, off and on, for over three hundred years. But England and America have always refused to constitute government-sponsored academies with power to regulate citizens' words.

10 Lacking an academy, Englishmen appealed to the practice of good writers to preserve or "fix" general usage. Thence more trouble. Who are the good writers? Shakespeare, no doubt. But Shakespeare, with his wild and carefree coinages, his cheery disregard for grammatical agreements, demands our admiration more than our imitation. In Latin, a fossilized tongue, the rule is simple: if a locution is in Cicero, it is correct. In English we have no Cicero. The only writers whom all critics would accept as "best" have been so long dead that their works are uncertain models for the living language of our times.

11 We should, perhaps, make the authority of the best writers defer to that of professional judges of language, the critics and grammarians. Quintilian, rhetorician of the first century A.D., appealed to the consensus of the *eruditi,* the scholarly, the well-informed. Ben Jonson said: "Custom is the most certain mistress of language, as the public stamp makes the current money . . . That I call custom of speech, which is the consent of the learned; as custom of life, which is the consent of the good." In the 17th and 18th centuries, the English grammarians appeared, devoting themselves to "refining, ascertaining, and fixing" the language. They were scholars. Aware of linguistic history, they conceived of English usage as a development from primitive barbarism to the harmonious perfection of their own times. They regarded the past as a preparation, the present as a glorious achievement, the future as a threatening decadence. Jonathan Swift was terrified of the coming corruption and invoked governmental authority to "fix" the language; else, he feared, within two centuries the literary works of his time, including his own, would be unreadable.

12 The grammarians justified their judgments by appealing not only to history but to reason. They strengthened the concepts of Good and Bad

to become Right and Wrong. They regarded language as something existing mysteriously apart from man, governed by a universal grammar waiting to be discovered by intrepid scholars. No doubt they were sympathetically fascinated by the story Herodotus tells of the king who isolated two small children with a deaf-and-dumb shepherd to find out what language they would learn to speak, thus to identify the original speech of mankind. (It was Phrygian.) Rightness was to be achieved by logical analysis of form and meaning, with much use of analogy. Popular usage was scouted, as of its nature corrupt. The grammarians made great play with Purity and Impurity. Pure English lived in perpetual danger of defloration by the impure.

13 The grammarians did some useful work in rationalizing the language. However, their precepts were often overlogical or based on faulty logic. From them derive many of the distinctions that have ever since tortured scholars young and old. The *shall/will, should/would* rules are said to be an invention of the 17th-century John Wallis. John Lowth, in 1762, first laid it down that two negatives are equivalent to an affirmative. It was Lowth who banned the use of the superlative to indicate one of two, as in Jane Austen's "the youngest of the two daughters of a most affectionate, indulgent father."

14 Samuel Johnson, whose epoch-making *A Dictionary of the English Language* appeared in 1755, shared many of the convictions of the grammarians. He was concerned to fix the language against lowering corruption, for, he said in his Preface, "Tongues, like governments, have a natural tendency to degeneration; we have long preserved our constitution, let us make some struggle for our language." He foresaw linguistic calamity. "The tropes of poetry will make hourly encroachments, and the metaphorical will become the current sense; pronunciation will be varied by levity or ignorance, and the pen must at length comply with the tongue; illiterate writers will at one time or other, by publick infatuation, rise into renown, who, not knowing the original import of words, will use them with colloquial licentiousness, confound distinction, and forget propriety." Those who knew better must fight on in the hopeless war: "we retard what we cannot repel, we palliate what we cannot cure."

15 One will have noticed, amid the funeral music of Dr. Johnson's Preface, the startling phrase: "the pen must at length comply with the tongue." This was a view already accepted more cheerfully by some other distinguished writers. Malherbe, 17th-century scholar-poet-critic and "legislator of Parnassus," said that he learned proper French by listening to the porters at the haymarket. Though Dr. Johnson deplored the fact, he recognized that speech, not writing, not grammatical logic, must in the end command usage. This idea took shape and found fuller expression in the work of Noah Webster (1758–1843).

16 Webster was a Connecticut farm boy with a Yale education, in a day when colleges did not teach English as a course. His series of spelling books and dictionaries actually went far toward "fixing" the American

language. His standard of correctness, however, was the usage of the enlightened members of each community, not just that of the "polite part" of city society, which he believed consisted largely of coxcombs. "General custom must be the rule of speaking," he said; and "it is always better to be *vulgarly* right than *politely* wrong." He was astonishingly liberal, even radical, in his acceptance of popular usage, giving his approval to *It is me, Who is she married to?* and *Them horses are mine.*

17 Thus, common usage began to assume dominance at the expense of formal grammar. The scholarly Irish archbishop Richard C. Trench in 1857 defined a dictionary as an inventory of the language: "It is no task of the maker of it to select the *good* words of a language . . . He is an historian of it, not a critic."

18 The view of language and its uses has prevailed to the 20th century and seems unlikely to fade. A school of linguistic scientists constituted itself, and in time found a place on most college faculties, ousting the old-fashioned philologists of the English and foreign-language departments. The descriptive or structural linguists, as they called themselves, would no more criticize a locution than a physicist would criticize an atom or an entomologist a cockroach.

19 The principles of descriptive linguistics have thus been simply put: (1) Language changes constantly; (2) Change is normal; (3) Spoken language is *the* language; (4) Correctness rests upon usage; (5) All usage is relative. This creed arouses indignation if not wrath in many people, including highly educated ones. But with the exception of number 3, which has been felt even by some linguists to be an overstatement on the part of gentlemen whose livelihood requires the written word, dispute about these principles seems to be nearly over among those who profess the study of English. The underlying assumption is that language, by its very nature, is a growing, evolving thing; and that whereas it may be cultivated, it cannot be "fixed" without killing it. Like any other fundamental social activity, it will undergo vicissitudes that to the older generation often seem regrettable; and indeed, some changes in language turn out to be empty fads that are soon forgotten, like some changes in fashions. Others are found to be enduringly useful, so that a generation later it becomes hard to imagine how we got along without them.

20 A descriptive linguist's lexicon can be expected to refrain from value judgments, from imposed pronunciations and spellings. It may classify usages as standard or nonstandard, formal, informal, or slang; but not right or wrong. It describes usage; it piously avoids prescribing it. Yet surely there is the possibility of self-deception here, of an objectivity more imaginary than real. By the very act of leaving *alrite* out of a dictionary, the lexicographer implies that that spelling—which does, after all, exist—is not all right. On the other hand, if he exhibits his scientific disinterest by reporting that "*ain't* is used orally in most parts of the United States by many cultivated speakers," the truth is that he is being inadequately descriptive with respect to contexts of usage. A reader who takes that

description seriously is likely to lay an egg *(slang)* at his next cocktail party unless he has the charm of Eliza Doolittle.

21 The makers of *The American Heritage Dictionary of the English Language* accept usage as the authority for correctness, but they have eschewed the "scientific" delusion that a dictionary should contain no value judgments. Some, to be sure, they have made merely implicit: the arrant solecisms of the ignoramus are here often omitted entirely, "irregardless" of how he may feel about this neglect. What is desirable is that when value judgments are explicit, they should be clearly attributed. Thus good usage can usually be distinguished from bad usage, even as good books can be distinguished from bad books. The present editors maintain that those best fitted to make such distinctions are, as Noah Webster said, the enlightened members of the community; not the scholarly theoreticians, not the instinctive verbalizers of the unlettered mass. The best authorities, at least for cultivated usage, are those professional speakers and writers who have demonstrated their sensitiveness to the language and their power to wield it effectively and beautifully.

22 The lexicographers of this Dictionary therefore commissioned a Usage Panel of about a hundred members—novelists, essayists, poets, journalists, writers on science and sports, public officials, professors. The panelists have in common only a recognized ability to speak and write good English. They accepted their task and turned to it with gusto. They revealed, often with passion, their likes and dislikes, their principles, and also their whims and crotchets. "We all get self-righteous in our judgments on language," Malcolm Cowley observes. As a matter of fact, many of them revealed, on particular questions, an attitude more reminiscent of Dr. Johnson than of the modern linguistic view; they tend to feel that the English language is going to hell if "we" don't do something to stop it, and they tend to feel that their own usage preferences are clearly *right.*

23 This does not mean for a moment that their preferences are invalid or negligible. Where this Dictionary differs notably from those that have preceded it, with regard to usage, is in exposing the lexical opinions of a larger group of recognized leaders than has heretofore been consulted, so that the ordinary user, looking up an expression whose social status is uncertain, can discover just how and to what extent his presumed betters agree on what he ought to say or write. Thus, he is not turned away uncounseled and uncomforted: he has before him an authoritative statement on a disputed issue; yet, he is left one of the most valuable of human freedoms, the freedom to say what he pleases.

24 It is significant that on specific questions, the Usage Panel disagreed more than they agreed, revealing a fact often conveniently ignored—that among those best qualified to know, there is a very considerable diversity of usage. Anyone surveying the panelists' various opinions is likely to conclude that good usage is indeed an elusive nymph, well worth pursuing but inconstant in shape and dress, and rather hard to back into a corner. In only one case did they agree 100 per cent—in disfavor of *simultaneous*

as an adverb ("the referendum was conducted *simultaneous* with the election"). Some other scores approached unanimity, as in the following:

Expression	Approved by	Disapproved by
ain't I? in writing		99%
between you and I in writing		99%
dropout used as a noun	97%	
thusly		97%
debut as a verb ("the company will debut its new models")		97%
slow as an adverb ("Drive Slow")	96%	
medias as a plural (instead of *media*)		95%
their own referring to the singular ("nobody thinks the criticism applies to their own work")		95%
but what ("There is no doubt but what he will try")		95%
myself instead of *me* in compound objects, in writing ("He invited Mary and myself to dinner")		95%
anxious in the sense of *eager*		72%
type for *type of* ("that type shrub")		94%
rather unique; most unique		94%

25 While the panelists tend toward conservatism, they try to avoid overniceness, prissiness. (*Was graduated,* says John Bainbridge contemptuously, is preferred "by all who write with a quill pen.") Sixty-one per cent of them feel bad about the expression *I feel badly* when they see it in writing; only 45 per cent object when they hear it in speech. More than most people, they know the history of words and have tested the value of idioms. More than most, they have grown tired of overused vogue words. They dislike *senior citizen* ("I'd as soon use *underprivileged* for *poor*—or any other social science Choctaw"—Berton Roueché). They are not concerned that senior citizens themselves seem to rejoice in the term and recoil at *old folks* and even at *old. Enthuse* finds little favor, and stirs preservative zeal in some: "By God, let's hold the line on this one!" cries Dwight Macdonald. *Finalize,* says Isaac Asimov, "is nothing more than bureaucratic illiteracy." But for the consensus, the reader is referred to the entries **enthuse** and **finalize,** each of which, like many other neologisms, is discussed in a Usage note.

26 The panelists are by no means opposed to all coinages. "I have great admiration," says Gilbert Highet, "for the American genius for creating short vivid words (often dissyllabic) to express complex ideas, for example, a collision between a vehicle and another object which is not direct but lateral or oblique, *sideswipe.*" In general, the jurymen are more cordial toward popular, low-level inventions than toward the pomposities of

professional jargons. John K. Sherman welcomes *rambunctious* as a "tangy Americanism." Forty per cent of the Panel are ready to accept the expression *not about,* used to express determination not to do something; but the other 60 per cent are not about to do so. None of them, however, likes Business English; and they betray a particular spite against the language of Madison Avenue, once a very respectable street, now an avenue of ill fame. Yet the advertisers are, after all, fecund creators languagewise.

27 It would seem that the panelists are often more attentive to the practice of their own social group than to grammatical logic or etymological precision. They are antipedantic, scornful of the grammarians' effort to ban *it's me.* Some, like Theodore C. Sorensen, would throw away the rule that the relative *that* must introduce restrictive clauses, *which* nonrestrictive. One or two would drop *whom* altogether, as a needless refinement. Ninety-one per cent of the panelists accept the use of *internecine* to mean "pertaining to civil war or to a struggle within a family, group, organization, nation, or the like." They know, of course, that the Latin *internecinus* just means mutually deadly, but they do not seem to care.

28 The Usage Panel has given us the enlightened judgments of a cultivated elite on a great many interesting and troublesome expressions. The very diversity of their response attests that language is alive and well in the United States, and that even the most descriptive of dictionaries could not succeed in reporting all of its shifting nuances.

29 Within their field, the determination of good current usage, the counselors found, as we have observed, no absolute standard of rightness. Though naturally believing in their own superiority, they do not presume to dictate. They seem to conclude, without explicit statement, that usage is our own affair, with due regard to the usage of other good writers and speakers. Let that be our conclusion. The duty of determination falls upon us all. By our choices we make usage, good or bad. Let us then try to make good choices, and guard and praise our lovely language and try to be worthy of her.

Word Study List

self-immolation	1	lexicon	20
aureate	1	eschewed	21
inkhorn	1	arrant	21
pedants	1	solecisms	21
caprice	1	crotchets	22
lexicographer	6	idioms	25
piqued	9	consensus	25
locution	10, 18	neologisms	25
linguistic	11, 14, 18	dissyllabic	26
intrepid	12	fecund	26
scouted	12	etymological	27
defloration	12	antipedantic	27
vicissitudes	19	nuances	28

Questions

1. Before examining the standards that determine good or bad usage, Bishop defines *usage*. What is his definition?

2. A number of questions are presented early in the article (paragraphs 1–7, especially paragraph 5). How do these questions attract our attention, influence our thinking, and establish Bishop's topic?

3. In paragraphs 7–18, Bishop gives a chronological survey of British and American attitudes toward usage, beginning with Henry VIII in the sixteenth century. Why does Bishop begin his look at usage in the sixteenth century? What purpose does this summary serve in developing the article? Does Bishop state his thesis before beginning the historical review or only state a problem to be resolved in the article?

4. In the seventeenth and eighteenth centuries there was a move to set the rules of English grammar, partly in an effort to model it after Latin, considered the purest of all languages. Why is it impossible to "fix" a language in current use with rules?

5. This article is part of the introductory material to *The American Heritage Dictionary*. Where does Bishop first mention the dictionary by name? Why does he delay a discussion of the dictionary and its Usage Panel until that point?

6. Compare the type of people selected to be on the Usage Panel by the editors of *The American Heritage Dictionary* with the type who in 1635 formed the *Académie française*.

7. What position on usage did the great English lexicographer Samuel Johnson hold? How does his view on usage compare with Jonathan Swift's? With the Usage Panel's view?

8. According to Bishop, what is bad usage?

9. What are the advantages of a dictionary that includes, as *The American Heritage* does, some explanation of why certain words are labeled as they are?

10. Bishop refers to many historical figures in his article, most of whom he briefly identifies (e.g., "Henry VIII, who ruled from 1509 to 1547"). But the following figures he does not identify in the context of the article:

    Shakespeare
    Cicero
    Ben Jonson
    Jonathan Swift
    Jane Austen

After looking over this list (and checking a dictionary for any who are not familiar to you), what can you infer about the audience that Bishop assumes will be reading this article?

Exercises

1. Check the sample usage problems (paragraph 24) considered by the Usage Panel in *Webster's New Collegiate Dictionary,* Eighth Edition. What labels does *Webster's,* noted for its linguistic approach to usage, give to these expressions? What similarities do you find in the labeling of these expressions? What differences?

2. Take a poll of your class on the usage that students would prefer in each of the following cases:
   a. (Fewer, Less) than half the registered voters of our city voted in the last election.
   b. It looks (like, as if) it will snow this afternoon.
   c. I read in the newspaper (that, where) the crime rate is up 5 percent over last month in the metropolitan area.
   d. The floor plan of our house is quite different (from, than) that of our neighbors.
   e. I have been (enthused, enthusiastic) about camping in the woods.

   Check your results against two desk dictionaries. Good desk dictionaries for this exercise and others in the chapter are *Webster's New World Dictionary of the American Language, The American Heritage Dictionary of the English Language, The Random House College Dictionary, The American College Dictionary, Webster's New Collegiate Dictionary,* Eighth Edition.

3. Give examples of situations in which a usage generally considered nonstandard (e.g., *ain't*) would be acceptable, even appropriate.

Contexts

S. I. Hayakawa

Linguist, college president, and politician, S. I. Hayakawa (b. 1906) is widely known both for his numerous works on language and for the term (1977–1983) he served as a United States senator from California. Prior to his election to Congress, he was president of San Francisco State College from 1969 to 1973 and professor of English there from 1955 to 1968. Hayakawa continues his interests in language and politics by his opposition to fostering bilingualism in the United States.

Hayakawa explains that we do not learn the meanings of most words from dictionaries but from hearing or seeing them used—that is, in verbal or physical contexts. He shows readers the connection between preparing dictionary definitions and learning word meanings.

HOW DICTIONARIES ARE MADE

1 It is widely believed that every word has a correct meaning, that we learn these meanings principally from teachers and grammarians (except that most of the time we don't bother to, so that we ordinarily speak "sloppy English"), and that dictionaries and grammars are the supreme authority in matters of meaning and usage. Few people ask by what authority the writers of dictionaries and grammars say what they say. I once got into a dispute with an Englishwoman over the pronunciation of a word and offered to look it up in the dictionary. The Englishwoman said firmly "What for? I am English. I was born and brought up in England. The way I speak *is* English." Such self-assurance about one's own language is not uncommon among the English. In the United States, however, anyone who is willing to quarrel with the dictionary is regarded as either eccentric or mad.

2 Let us see how dictionaries are made and how the editors arrive at definitions. What follows applies, incidentally, only to those dictionary offices where first-hand, original research goes on—not those in which editors simply copy existing dictionaries. The task of writing a dictionary begins with reading vast amounts of the literature of the period or subject that the dictionary is to cover. As the editors read, they copy on cards every interesting or rare word, every unusual or peculiar occurrence of a common word, a large number of common words in their ordinary uses, and also the sentences in which each of these words appears, thus

> pail
> The dairy *pails* bring home increase of milk
> KEATS, *Endymion*
> I, 44–45

3 That is to say, the context of each word is collected, along with the word itself. For a really big job of dictionary-writing, such as the *Oxford English Dictionary* (usually bound in about twenty-five volumes), millions of such cards are collected, and the task of editing occupies decades. As the cards are collected, they are alphabetized and sorted. When the sorting is completed, there will be for each word anywhere from two or three to several hundred illustrative quotations, each on its card.

4 To define a word, then, the dictionary-editor places before him the stack of cards illustrating that word; each of the cards represents an actual use of the word by a writer of some literary or historical importance. He reads the cards carefully, discards some, rereads the rest, and divides up the stack according to what he thinks are the several senses of the word. Finally, he writes his definitions, following the hard-and-fast rule that each definition *must* be based on what the quotations in front of him reveal

about the meaning of the word. The editor cannot be influenced by what *he* thinks a given word *ought* to mean. He must work according to the cards or not at all.

5 The writing of a dictionary, therefore, is not a task of setting up authoritative statements about the "true meanings" of words, but a task of *recording,* to the best of one's ability, what various words have *meant* to authors in the distant or immediate past. *The writer of a dictionary is a historian, not a lawgiver.* If, for example, we had been writing a dictionary in 1890, or even as late as 1919, we could have said that the word "broadcast" means "to scatter" (seed, for example), but we could not have decreed that from 1921 on, the most common meaning of the word should become "to disseminate audible messages, etc., by radio transmission." To regard the dictionary as an "authority," therefore, is to credit the dictionary-writer with gifts of prophecy which neither he nor anyone else possesses. In choosing our words when we speak or write, we can be *guided* by the historical record afforded us by the dictionary, but we cannot be *bound* by it, because new situations, new experiences, new inventions, new feelings are always compelling us to give new uses to old words. Looking under a "hood," we should ordinarily have found, five hundred years ago, a monk; today, we find a motorcar engine.[1]

VERBAL AND PHYSICAL CONTEXTS

6 The way in which the dictionary-writer arrives at his definitions merely systematizes the way in which we all learn the meanings of words, beginning at infancy and continuing for the rest of our lives. Let us say that we have never heard the word "oboe" before, and we overhear a conversation in which the following sentences occur:

> He used to be the best *oboe*-player in town. . . . Whenever they came to that *oboe* part in the third movement, he used to get very excited. . . . I saw him one day at the music shop, buying a new reed for his *oboe*. . . . He never liked to play the clarinet after he started playing the *oboe*. . . . He said it wasn't much fun, because it was too easy.

7 Although the word may be unfamiliar, its meaning becomes clear to us as we listen. After hearing the first sentence, we know that an "oboe" is "played," so that it must be either a game or a musical instrument. With the second sentence the possibility of its being a game is eliminated. With each succeeding sentence the possibilities as to what an "oboe" may be are narrowed down until we get a fairly clear idea of what is meant. This is how we learn by *verbal context.*

---

[1] *Webster's Third New International Dictionary* lists the word "hood" also as a shortened term of "hoodlum."

The time that elapsed between *Webster's Second Edition* (1934) and the *Third* (1961) indicates the enormous amount of reading and labor entailed in the preparation of a really thorough dictionary of a language as rapidly changing and as rich in vocabulary as English.

8 But even independently of this, we learn by physical and social context. Let us say that we are playing golf and that we have hit the ball in a certain way with certain unfortunate results, so that our companion says, "That's a bad *slice.*" He repeats this remark every time our ball fails to go straight. If we are reasonably bright, we learn in a very short time to say, when it happens again, "That's a bad slice." On one occasion, however, our friend says, "That's not a *slice* this time; that's a *hook.*" In this case we consider what has happened, and we wonder what is different about the last stroke from those previous. As soon as we make the distinction, we have added still another word to our vocabulary. The result is that after nine holes of golf, we can use both these words accurately—and perhaps several others as well, such as "divot," "number-five iron," "approach shot," *without ever having been told what they mean.* Indeed, we may play golf for years without ever being able to give a dictionary definition of "to slice": "To strike (the ball) so that the face of the club draws inward across the face of the ball, causing it to curve toward the right in flight (with a right-handed player)" *(Webster's New International Dictionary, Second Edition).* But even without being able to give such a definition, we should still be able to use the word accurately whenever the occasion demands.

9 We learn the meanings of practically all our words (which are, it will be remembered, merely complicated noises), not from dictionaries, not from definitions, but from hearing these noises as they accompany actual situations in life and then learning to associate certain noises with certain situations. Even as dogs learn to recognize "words," as for example by hearing "biscuit" at the same time as an actual biscuit is held before their noses, so do we all learn to interpret language by being aware of the happenings that accompany the noises people make at us—by being aware, in short, of contexts.

10 The definitions given by little children in school show clearly how they associate words with situations; they almost always define in terms of physical and social contexts: "Punishment is when you have been bad and they put you in a closet and don't let you have any supper." "Newspapers are what the paper boy brings and you wrap up the garbage with it." These are good definitions. They cannot be used in dictionaries mainly because they are too specific; it would be impossible to list the myriads of situations in which every word has been used. For this reason, dictionaries give definitions on a high level of abstraction, that is, with particular references left out for the sake of conciseness. This is another reason why it is a great mistake to regard a dictionary definition as telling us all about a word.

EXTENSIONAL AND INTENSIONAL MEANING

11 Dictionaries deal with the world of intensional meanings, but there is another world which a dictionary by its very nature ignores: the world of extensional meanings. *The extensional meaning of an utterance is that*

which it points to in the extensional (physical) world. That is to say, the extensional meaning cannot be expressed in words because it is that which words stand for. An easy way to remember this is *to put your hand over your mouth and point* whenever you are asked to give an extensional meaning.

12 Of course, we cannot always point to the extensional meanings of the words we use. Therefore, so long as we are *discussing* meanings, we shall refer to that which is being talked about as the *denotation* of an utterance. For example, the denotation of the word "Winnipeg" is the prairie city of that name in southern Manitoba; the denotion of the word "dog" is a class of animals which includes dog_1 (Fido), dog_2 (Rex), dog_3 (Rover) . . . dog_n.

13 The *intensional meaning* of a word or expression, on the other hand, is that which is *suggested* (connoted) inside one's head. Roughly speaking, whenever we express the meanings of words by uttering more words, we are giving intensional meanings or connotations. To remember this, put your hand over your eyes and let the words spin around in your head.

14 Utterances may have, of course, both extensional and intensional meaning. If they have no intensional meaning at all—that is,if they start no notions whatever spinning about in our heads—they are meaningless

noises, like foreign languages that we do not understand. On the other hand, it is possible for utterances to have no extensional meaning at all, in spite of the fact that they may start many notions spinning about in our heads. The statement, "Angels watch over my bed at night," is one that has intensional but no extensional meaning. This does not mean that there are no angels watching over my bed at night. When we say that the statement has no extensional meaning, we are merely saying that it is not operational, that we cannot see, touch, photograph, or in any scientific manner detect the presence of angels. The result is that, if an argument begins on the subject of whether or not angels watch over my bed, *there is no way of ending the argument to the satisfaction of all disputants,* the Christians and the non-Christians, the pious and the agnostic, the mystical and the scientific. Therefore, whether we believe in angels or not, knowing in advance that any argument on the subject will be both endless and futile, we can avoid getting into fights about it.

15 When, on the other hand, statements have extensional content, as when we say, "This room is fifteen feet long," arguments can come to a close. No matter how many guesses there are about the length of the room, all discussion ceases when someone produces a tape measure. This, then, is the important difference between extensional and intensional meanings: namely, when utterances have extensional meanings, discussion can be ended and agreement reached; when utterances have intensional meanings only and no extensional meanings, arguments may, and often do, go on indefinitely. Such arguments can result only in conflict. Among individuals, they may break up friendships; in society, they often split organizations into bitterly opposed groups; among nations, they may aggravate existing tensions so seriously as to become real obstacles to the peaceful settling of disputes.

16 Arguments of this kind may be termed "non-sense arguments," because they are based on utterances about which no sense data can be collected. Needless to say, there are occasions when the hyphen may be omitted—that depends on one's feelings toward the particular argument under consideration. The reader is requested to provide his own examples of "non-sense arguments." Even the foregoing example of the angels may give offense to some people, despite the fact that no attempt is made to deny or affirm the existence of angels. Imagine, then, the uproar that might result from giving a number of examples from theology, politics, law, economics, literary criticism, and other fields in which it is not customary to distinguish clearly sense from non-sense.

THE "ONE WORD, ONE MEANING" FALLACY

17 Everyone, of course, who has ever given any thought to the meanings of words has noticed that they are always shifting and changing in meaning. Usually, people regard this as a misfortune, because it "leads to

sloppy thinking" and "mental confusion." To remedy this condition, they are likely to suggest that we should all agree on "one meaning" for each word and use it only with that meaning. Thereupon it will occur to them that we simply cannot make people agree in this way, even if we could set up an ironclad dictatorship under a committee of lexicographers who would place censors in every newspaper office and microphones in every home. The situation, therefore, appears hopeless.

18 Such an impasse is avoided when we start with a new premise altogether—one of the premises upon which modern linguistic thought is based: namely, that *no word ever has exactly the same meaning twice.*[2] The extent to which this premise fits the facts can be demonstrated in a number of ways. First, if we accept the proposition that the contexts of an utterance determine its meaning, it becomes apparent that since no two contexts are ever *exactly* the same, no two meanings can ever be exactly the same. How can we "fix the meaning" even for so common an expression as "to believe in" when it can be used in such sentences as the following:

> I believe in you (I have confidence in you).
> I believe in democracy (I accept the principles implied by the term democracy).
> I believe in Santa Claus (It is my opinion that Santa Claus exists).

19 Second, we can take a word of "simple" meaning, like "kettle," for example. But when John says "kettle," its intensional meanings to him are the common characteristics of all the kettles John remembers. When Peter says "kettle," however, its intensional meanings to him are the common characteristics of all the kettles he remembers. *No matter how small or how negligible the differences may be between John's "kettle" and Peter's "kettle," there is some difference.*

20 Finally, let us examine utterances in terms of extensional meanings. If John, Peter, Harold, and George each say "my typewriter," we would have to point to four different typewriters to get the extensional meaning in each case: John's new Olivetti, Peter's old Remington, Harold's portable Smith-Corona, and the undenotable intended "typewriter" that George plans to buy someday: "My typewriter, when I buy it, will be an electric." Also, if John says "my typewriter" today, and again "my typewriter" tomorrow, the extensional meaning is different in the two cases, because the typewriter is not exactly the same from one day to the next (nor from one minute to the next): slow processes of wear, change, and decay are going on constantly. Although we can say, then, that the differences in the meanings of a word on one occasion, on another occasion a

---

[2]In the same vein, the Greek philosopher Heraclitus asserted that one cannot step into the same river twice.

minute later, and on still another occasion another minute later are negligible, we cannot say that the meanings are *exactly* the same.

21 To insist dogmatically that we know what a word means *in advance of its utterance* is nonsense. All we can know in advance is *approximately* what it will mean. After the utterance, we interpret what has been said in the light of both verbal and physical contexts and act according to our interpretation. An examination of the verbal context of an utterance, as well as the examination of the utterance itself, directs us to the intensional meanings; an examination of the physical context directs us to the extensional meanings. When John says to James, "Bring me that book, will you?" James looks in the direction of John's pointed finger (physical context) and sees a desk with several books on it (physical context); he thinks back over their previous conversation (verbal context) and knows which of those books is being referred to.

22 Interpretation *must* be based, therefore, on the totality of contexts. If it were otherwise, we should not be able to account for the fact that even if we fail to use the right (customary) words in some situations, people can very frequently understand us. For example:

A: Gosh, look at that second baseman go!

B: (looking): You mean the shortstop?

A: Yes, that's what I mean.

A: There must be something wrong with the oil line; the engine has started to balk.

B: Don't you mean "gas line"?

A: Yes—didn't I say "gas line"?

Contexts often indicate our meanings so clearly that we do not even have to say what we mean in order to be understood.

IGNORING CONTEXTS

23 It is clear, then, that the ignoring of contexts in any act of interpretation is at best a stupid practice. At its worst, it can be a vicious practice. A common example is the sensationalistic newspaper story in which a few words by a public personage are torn out of their context and made the basis of a completely misleading account. There is the incident of a Veterans Day speaker, a university teacher, who declared before a high-school assembly that the Gettysburg Address was "a powerful piece of propaganda." The context clearly revealed that "propaganda" was being used, not according to its popular meaning, but rather, as the speaker himself stated, to mean "explaining the moral purposes of a war." The

context also revealed that the speaker was a very great admirer of Lincoln. However, the local newspaper, ignoring the context, presented the account in such a way as to suggest that the speaker had called Lincoln a liar. On this basis, the newspaper began a campaign against the instructor. The speaker remonstrated with the editor of the newspaper, who replied, in effect, "I don't care what else you said. You said the Gettysburg Address was propaganda, didn't you?" This appeared to the editor complete proof that Lincoln had been maligned and that the speaker deserved to be discharged from his position at the university. Similar practices may be found in advertisements. A reviewer may be quoted on the jacket of a book as having said, "A brilliant work," while reading of the context may reveal that what he really said was, "It just falls short of being a brilliant work." There are some people who will always be able to find a defense for such a practice in saying, "But he did use the words 'a brilliant work,' didn't he?"

24 People in the course of argument very frequently complain about words being different things to different people. Instead of complaining, they should accept such differences as a matter of course. It would be startling indeed if the word "justice," for example, were to have the same meaning to each of the nine justices of the United States Supreme Court; we should get nothing but unanimous decisions. It would be even more startling if "justice" meant the same thing in the United States as it does in Russia. If we can get deeply into our consciousness the principle that no word ever has the same meaning twice, we will develop the habit of automatically examining contexts, and this will enable us to understand better what others are saying. As it is, however, we are all too likely, when a word sounds familiar, to assume that we understand it, even when we don't. In this way we read into people's remarks meanings that were never intended. Then we waste energy in angrily accusing people of "intellectual dishonesty" or "abuse of words," when their only sin is that they use words in ways unlike our own, as they can hardly help doing, especially if their background has been widely different from ours. There are cases of intellectual dishonesty and abuse of words, of course, but they do not always occur in the places where people think they do.

25 In the study of history or of cultures other than our own, contexts take on special importance. To say, "There was no running water or electricity in the house," does not condemn an English house in 1578 but says a great deal against a house in Chicago in 1978. Again, if we wish to understand the Constitution of the United States, it is not enough, as our historians now tell us, merely to look up all the words in the dictionary and to read the interpretations written by Supreme Court justices. We must see the Constitution in its historical context: the conditions of life, the state of the arts and industries and transportation, the climate of opinion of the time—all of which helped to determine what words went into the Constitution and what those words meant to those who wrote them.

After all, the words "United States of America" stood for quite a different-sized nation and a different culture in 1790 from what they stand for today. When it comes to very big subjects, the range of contexts to be examined—verbal, social, and historical—may become very large indeed.

26 In personal relations, furthermore, those who ignore psychological contexts often make the mistake of interpreting as insults remarks that are only intended in jest.

THE INTERACTION OF WORDS

27 All this is not to say, however, that the reader might just as well throw away his dictionary simply because contexts are so important. Any word in a sentence—any sentence in a paragraph, any paragraph in a larger unit—whose meaning is revealed by its context is itself part of the context of the rest of the text. To look up a word in a dictionary, therefore, frequently explains not only the word itself but the rest of the sentence, paragraph, conversation, or essay in which it is found. All words within a given context interact with one another.

28 Realizing, then, that a dictionary is a historical work, we should understand the dictionary thus: "The word *mother* has most frequently been used in the past among English-speaking people to indicate a female parent." From this we can safely infer, "If that is how it has been used, that is what it *probably* means in the sentence I am trying to understand." That is what we normally do, of course; after we look up a word in the dictionary, we reexamine the context to see if the definition fits. If the context reads, "Mother began to form in the bottle," one may have to look at the dictionary more carefully.

29 A dictionary definition, therefore, is an invaluable guide to interpretation. Words do not have a single "correct meaning"; they apply to *groups* of similar situations, which might be called *areas of meaning*. It is for defining these areas of meaning that a dictionary is useful. In each use of any word, we examine the particular context and the extensional events denoted (if possible) to discover the *point* intended within the area of meaning.

Word Study List

eccentric	1	non-sense	16
systematizes	6	lexicographers	17
myriads	10	negligible	20
intensional	11	dogmatically	21
extensional	11	propaganda	23
denotation	12	remonstrated	23
connotation	13	maligned	23
pious	14	psychological	26
agnostic	14	invaluable	29

Questions

1. Why does Hayakawa begin with a discussion of how dictionaries are made? Is this the subject of his chapter?

2. List the steps in the process of preparing a dictionary.

3. According to Hayakawa, we do not learn the meanings of a word from dictionaries but from hearing the word used. What examples does he use to support this point? Explain the verbal and/or physical contexts that provided the meanings for several words you have recently learned.

4. Why is the example of the university teacher whose reputation was jeopardized for describing the Gettysburg Address as "a powerful piece of propaganda" an effective one? How does it support Hayakawa's point?

5. How many different contexts does Hayakawa mention that can shape the meanings of words?

6. What is the dictionary useful for if all word meanings are dependent on context?

7. State Hayakawa's thesis in one sentence. Is it explicitly stated in the article? If so, how does your statement compare to his? Compare wording and word order to see if you have changed the meaning by changing the verbal context.

Exercises

1. Which of the following sentences would you label as "non-sense" statements? Why? What words, if any, need defining before you can make sense of the "non-sense" statements? Is there any context in which those you have labeled as "non-sense" statements would be acceptable?
   a. Love makes the world go round.
   b. A good citizen is one who stands by his country right or wrong.
   c. Marriage is no longer a workable institution.
   d. The poor in America are a politically disadvantaged minority.
   e. Faith is a more effective cure than any offered by medical science.
   f. Our society is decadent.

2. Why can a word never have exactly the same meaning twice? Explain how the meaning of *moment* shifts in the following sentences:
   a. I'll be there in just a moment.
   b. The moment that we've been waiting for has arrived.
   c. Moments like these will be with us always.

Discuss the shifts in the meaning of *right* in these statements:

a. It is the right of all citizens to vote.
b. Only one student had the right answer to the last question.
c. It isn't right to tattle on a friend.

3. Study the following paragraph and then see how many of the Old English words you can define from their context and vividness. You might start your search for meaning by figuring out what part of speech each new/old word is.

If you are nott-headed and have brown wink-a-peeps and murfles, it's nothing to be swerked about. But if an old trundle-tail snatched your belly-timber and dropped it into a drumbly glosh, you'd not only be swerked, but probably have the mumble-fumbles as well.

Clear Writing Means Clear Thinking Means . . .

Marvin H. Swift

Marvin H. Swift (b. 1923) is a professor of communications at the General Motors Institute, where he has taught in a variety of programs since 1954. *Harvard Business Review* published this article in its January/February 1973 issue.

Swift takes a hypothetical writing task and lets the reader follow the writer through the first draft, then the rethinking of purpose, and finally the revising of tone, content, and purpose. His goal is to show how thinking and writing interact.

1 If you are a manager, you constantly face the problem of putting words on paper. If you are like most managers, this is not the sort of problem you enjoy. It is hard to do, and time consuming; and the task is doubly difficult when, as is usually the case, your words must be designed to change the behavior of others in the organization.

2 But the chore is there and must be done. How? Let's take a specific case.

3 Let's suppose that everyone at X Corporation, from the janitor on up to the chairman of the board, is using the office copiers for personal matters; income tax forms, church programs, children's term papers, and God knows what else are being duplicated by the gross. This minor piracy costs the company a pretty penny, both directly and in employee time, and the general manager—let's call him Sam Edwards—decides the time has come to lower the boom.

4 Sam lets fly by dictating the following memo to his secretary:

> To: All Employees
> From: Samuel Edwards, General Manager
> Subject: Abuse of Copiers
>
> It has recently been brought to my attention that many of the people who are employed by this company have taken advantage of their positions by availing themselves of the copiers. More specifically, these machines are being used for other than company business.
>
> Obviously, such practice is contrary to company policy and must cease and desist immediately. I wish therefore to inform all concerned—those who have abused policy or will be abusing it—that their behavior cannot and will not be tolerated. Accordingly, anyone in the future who is unable to control himself will have his employment terminated.
>
> If there are any questions about company policy, please feel free to contact this office.

Now the memo is on his desk for his signature. He looks it over; and the more he looks, the worse it reads. In fact, it's lousy. So he revises it three times, until it finally is in the form that follows:

> To: All Employees
> From: Samuel Edwards, General Manager
> Subject: Use of Copiers
>
> We are revamping our policy on the use of copiers for personal matters. In the past we have not encouraged personnel to use them for such purposes because of the costs involved. But we also recognize, perhaps belatedly, that we can solve the problem if each of us pays for what he takes.
>
> We are therefore putting these copiers on a pay-as-you-go basis. The details are simple enough . . .
>
> Samuel Edwards

This time Sam thinks the memo looks good, and it *is* good. Not only is the writing much improved, but the problem should now be solved. He therefore signs the memo, turns it over to his secretary for distribution, and goes back to other things.

FROM VERBIAGE TO INTENT

5 I can only speculate on what occurs in a writer's mind as he moves from a poor draft to a good revision, but it is clear that Sam went through

several specific steps, mentally as well as physically, before he had created his end product:

- ☐ He eliminated wordiness.
- ☐ He modulated the tone of the memo.
- ☐ He revised the policy he stated.

Let's retrace his thinking through each of these processes.

ELIMINATING WORDINESS

6 Sam's basic message is that employees are not to use the copiers for their own affairs at company expense. As he looks over his first draft, however, it seems so long that this simple message has become diffused. With the idea of trimming the memo down, he takes another look at his first paragraph.

> It has recently been brought to my attention that many of the people who are employed by this company have taken advantage of their positions by availing themselves of the copiers. More specifically, these machines are being used for other than company business.

He edits it like this:

Item: "recently"

Comment to himself: Of course; else why write about the problem? So delete the word.

Item: "It has been brought to my attention"

Comment: Naturally. Delete it.

Item: "the people who are employed by this company"

Comment: Assumed. Why not just "employees"?

Item: "by availing themselves" and "for other than company business"

Comment: Since the second sentence repeats the first, why not coalesce?

And he comes up with this:

> Employees have been using the copiers for personal matters.

He proceeds to the second paragraph. More confident of himself, he moves in broader swoops, so that the deletion process looks like this:

> Obviously, such practice is contrary to company policy and must cease and desist immediately. I wish therefore to inform all concerned—those who have abused policy or will be abusing it—that their behavior cannot and will not be tolerated. Accordingly, anyone in the future who is unable to control himself will have his employment terminated. will result in dismissal.

The final paragraph, apart from "company policy" and "feel free," looks all right, so the total memo now reads as follows:

> To: All Employees
> From: Samuel Edwards, General Manager
> Subject: Abuse of Copiers
>
> Employees have been using the copiers for personal matters. Obviously, such practice is contrary to company policy and will result in dismissal.
>
> If there are any questions, please contact this office.

Sam now examines his efforts by putting these questions to himself:

Question: Is the memo free of deadwood?

Answer: Very much so. In fact, it's good, tight prose.

Question: Is the policy stated?

Answer: Yes—sharp and clear.

Question: Will the memo achieve its intended purpose?

Answer: Yes. But it sounds foolish.

Question: Why?

Answer: The wording is too harsh; I'm not going to fire anybody over this.

Question: How should I tone the thing down?

To answer this last question, Sam takes another look at the memo.

CORRECTING THE TONE

7 What strikes his eye as he looks it over? Perhaps these three words:

- ☐ Abuse . . .
- ☐ Obviously . . .
- ☐ . . . dismissal . . .

The first one is easy enough to correct: he substitutes "use" for "abuse." But "obviously" poses a problem and calls for reflection. If the policy is obvious, why are the copiers being used? Is it that people are outrightly dishonest? Probably not. But that implies the policy isn't obvious; and whose fault is this? Who neglected to clarify policy? And why "dismissal" for something never publicized?

8 These questions impel him to revise the memo once again:

> To: All Employees
> From: Samuel Edwards, General Manager
> Subject: Use of Copiers
>
> Copiers are not to be used for personal matters. If there are any questions, please contact this office.

REVISING THE POLICY ITSELF

9 The memo now seems courteous enough—at least it is not discourteous—but it is just a blank, perhaps overly simple, statement of policy. Has he really thought through the policy itself?

10 Reflecting on this, Sam realizes that some people will continue to use the copiers for personal business anyhow. If he seriously intends to enforce the basic policy (first sentence), he will have to police the equipment, and that raises the question of costs all over again.

11 Also the memo states that he will maintain an open-door policy (second sentence)—and surely there will be some, probably a good many, who will stroll in and offer to pay for what they use. His secretary has enough to do without keeping track of affairs of that kind.

12 Finally, the first and second sentences are at odds with each other. The first says that personal copying is out, and the second implies that it can be arranged.

13 The facts of organizational life thus force Sam to clarify in his own mind exactly what his position on the use of copiers is going to be. As he sees the problem now, what he really wants to do is put the copiers on a pay-as-you-go basis. After making that decision, he begins anew:

> To: All Employees
> From: Samuel Edwards, General Manager
> Subject: Use of copiers
>
> We are revamping our policy on the use of copiers . . .

This is the draft that goes into distribution and now allows him to turn his attention to other problems.

THE CHICKEN OR THE EGG?

14 What are we to make of all this? It seems a rather lengthy and tedious report of what, after all, is a routine writing task created by a problem of minor importance. In making this kind of analysis, have I simply labored the obvious?

15 To answer this question, let's drop back to the original draft. If you read it over, you will see that Sam began with this kind of thinking:

☐ "The employees are taking advantage of the company."
☐ "I'm a nice guy, but now I'm going to play Dutch uncle."
∴ "I'll write them a memo that tells them to shape up or ship out."

In his final version, however, his thinking is quite different:

☐ "Actually, the employees are pretty mature, responsible people. They're capable of understanding a problem."
☐ "Company policy itself has never been crystallized. In fact, this is the first memo on the subject."
☐ "I don't want to overdo this thing—any employee can make an error in judgment."
∴ "I'll set a reasonable policy and write a memo that explains how it ought to operate."

Sam obviously gained a lot of ground between the first draft and the final version, and this implies two things. First, if a manager is to write effectively, he needs to isolate and define, as fully as possible, all the critical variables in the writing process and scrutinize what he writes for its clarity, simplicity, tone, and the rest. Second, after he has clarified his thoughts on paper, he may find that what he has written is not what has to be said. In this sense, writing is feedback and a way for the manager to discover himself. What are his real attitudes toward that amorphous, undifferentiated gray mass of employees "out there"? Writing is a way of finding out. By objectifying his thoughts in the medium of language, he gets a chance to see what is going on in his mind.

16 In other words, *if the manager writes well, he will think well.* Equally, the more clearly he has thought out his message before he starts to dictate, the more likely he is to get it right on paper the first time round. In other words, *if he thinks well, he will write well.*

17 Hence we have a chicken-and-the-egg situation: writing and thinking go hand in hand; and when one is good, the other is likely to be good.

REVISION SHARPENS THINKING

18 More particularly, rewriting is the key to improved thinking. It demands a real openmindedness and objectivity. It demands a willingness

to cull verbiage so that ideas stand out clearly. And it demands a willingness to meet logical contradictions head on and trace them to the premises that have created them. In short, it forces a writer to get up his courage and expose his thinking process to his own intelligence.

19 Obviously, revising is hard work. It demands that you put yourself through the wringer, intellectually and emotionally, to squeeze out the best you can offer. Is it worth the effort? Yes, it is—if you believe you have a responsibility to think and communicate effectively.

Word Study List

gross	3	impel	8
verbiage	5, 18	tedious	14
speculate	5	crystallized	15
modulated	5	amorphous	15
diffused	6	cull	18
coalesce	6		

Questions

1. Swift points out at the end of this article that a writer learns from writing. Can you recall occasions when writing was a discovery process for you? Have you ever started a "Dear John" letter that turned out not to be one? Or did you finally see how some course material connected when you were writing an essay exam?

2. Some people say that letters reveal more about people than conversations with them. Based on what you have learned about writing from Swift's article, why would that be true?

3. What was the major fault of the first draft of the manager's memo?

4. What was wrong with the tone of the first draft? How would you react if you received this memo?

5. What did the writer discover after eliminating excess words from the first draft? Most writers are wordy and redundant in their first drafts. Do you usually read over your papers for excess words? Do you try to revise to improve content as well as to remove deadwood?

6. Swift says that "rewriting is the key to improved thinking." What does this statement suggest about the value of a composition course to your college education? Why would a course in grammar alone not be sufficient to develop your writing skills? Based on Swift's article, what can you list as the requirements of a good writing course?

Exercise

To practice handling audience, tone, and purpose, write a memo to your instructor that requests a change in some element of your course—perhaps course content, organization, classroom teaching techniques, or marking of papers. Think about exactly what change you want and how best to achieve your purpose through writing. Be prepared to try several drafts.

Clutter

William Zinsser

William Zinsser (b. 1922) has been on the English faculty at Yale and a free-lance contributor to magazines. He has written a number of books, both fiction and nonfiction, his most recent being *Writing with a Word Processor* (1983). "Clutter" is a chapter from his book *On Writing Well: An Informal Guide to Writing Nonfiction,* published in 1980.

Zinsser examines the clutter that mars writing and encourages us to prune the excess.

1 Fighting clutter is like fighting weeds—the writer is always slightly behind. New varieties sprout overnight, and by noon they are part of American speech. It only takes a John Dean[1] testifying on TV to have everyone in the country saying "at this point in time" instead of "now."

2 Consider all the prepositions that are routinely draped onto verbs that don't need any help. Head up. Free up. Face up to. We no longer head committees. We head them up. We don't face problems anymore. We face up to them when we can free up a few minutes. A small detail, you may say—not worth bothering about. It *is* worth bothering about. The game is won or lost on hundreds of small details. Writing improves in direct ratio to the number of things we can keep out of it that shouldn't be there. "Up," in "free up," shouldn't be there. It's not only unnecessary; it's silly. Can we picture anything being freed *up*? The writer of clean English must examine every word that he puts on paper. He will find a surprising number that don't serve any purpose.

3 Take the adjective "personal," as in "a personal friend of mine," "his personal feeling" or "her personal physician." It is typical of the words that can be eliminated nine times out of ten. The personal friend has come into the language to distinguish him from the business friend, thereby debasing not only language but friendship. Someone's feeling *is*

[1]A member of former President Nixon's staff who testified during the Watergate hearings.—ED.

his personal feeling—that's what "his" means. As for the personal physician, he is that man so often summoned to the dressing room of a stricken actress so that she won't have to be treated by the impersonal physician assigned to the theater. Someday I'd like to see him identified as "her doctor."

4 Or take those curious intervals of time like the short minute. "Twenty-two short minutes later she had won the final set." Minutes are minutes, physicians are physicians, friends are friends. The rest is clutter.

5 Clutter is the laborious phrase which has pushed out the short word that means the same thing. These locutions are a drag on energy and momentum. Even before John Dean gave us "at this point in time," people had stopped saying "now." They were saying "at the present time," or "currently," or "presently" (which means "soon"). Yet the idea can always be expressed by "now" to mean the immediate moment ("now I can see him"), or by "today" to mean the historical present ("today prices are high"), or simply by the verb "to be" ("it is raining"). There is no need to say "at the present time we are experiencing precipitation."

6 Speaking of which, we are experiencing considerable difficulty getting *that* word out of the language now that it has lumbered in. Even your dentist will ask if you are experiencing any pain. If he were asking one of his own children he would say, "Does it hurt?" He would, in short, be himself. By using a more pompous phrase in his professional role he not only sounds more important; he blunts the painful edge of truth. It is the language of the airline stewardess demonstrating the oxygen mask that will drop down if the plane should somehow run out of air. "In the extremely unlikely possibility that the aircraft should experience such an eventuality," she begins—a phrase so oxygen-depriving in itself that we are prepared for any disaster, and even gasping death shall lose its sting.

7 Clutter is the ponderous euphemism that turns a slum into a depressed socioeconomic area, a salesman into a marketing representative, a dumb kid into an underachiever and a bad kid into a pre-delinquent. (The Albuquerque public schools announced a program for "delinquent and pre-delinquent boys.")

8 Clutter is the official language used by the American corporation—in the news release and the annual report—to hide its mistakes. When a big company recently announced that it was "decentralizing its organizational structure into major profit-centered businesses" and that "corporate staff services will be aligned under two senior vice-presidents" it meant that it had had a lousy year.

9 Clutter is the language of the interoffice memo ("the trend to mosaic communication is reducing the meaningfulness of concern about whether or not demographic segments differ in their tolerance of periodicity") and the language of computers ("we are offering functional digital programming options that have built-in parallel reciprocal capabilities with compatible third-generation contingencies and hardware").

10 Clutter is the language of the Pentagon throwing dust in the eyes of the populace by calling an invasion a "reinforced protective reaction strike" and by justifying its vast budgets on the need for "credible second-strike capability" and "counterforce deterrence." How can we grasp such vaporous doubletalk? As George Orwell pointed out in "Politics and the English Language," an essay written thirty years ago but cited with amazing frequency during the Vietnam years of Johnson and Nixon, "In our time, political speech and writing are largely the defense of the indefensible. . . . Thus political language has to consist largely of euphemism, question-begging and sheer cloudy vagueness." Orwell's warning that clutter is not just a nuisance but a deadly tool did not turn out to be inoperative. By the 1960's his words had come true in America.

11 I could go on quoting examples from various fields—every profession has its growing arsenal of jargon to fire at the layman and hurl him back from its walls. Recently I received a brochure from a foundation which used the verb "potentialize." But the list would be depressing and the lesson tedious. The point of raising it now is to serve notice that clutter is the enemy, whatever form it takes. It slows the reader and robs the writer of his personality, making him seem pretentious.

12 Beware, then, of the long word that is no better than the short word: "numerous" (many), "facilitate" (ease), "individual" (man or woman), "remainder" (rest), "initial" (first), "implement" (do), "sufficient" (enough), "attempt" (try), "referred to as" (called), and hundreds more. Beware, too, of all the slippery new fad words for which the language already has equivalents: overview and quantify, optimize and maximize, parameter and interpersonal, input and throughput, peer group and paradigm, public sector and private sector. Avoid trendy words like "trendy." They are all weeds that will smother what you write.

13 Nor are all the weeds as obvious as these. Once alerted, anybody can see that compatible third-generation contingencies and reinforced protective reaction strikes are heavy weights to attach to any sentence. More insidious are the little growths of perfectly ordinary words with which we explain how we propose to go about our explaining, or which inflate a simple preposition or conjunction into a whole windy phrase.

14 "I might add," "It should be pointed out," "It is interesting to note that"—how many sentences begin with these dreary clauses announcing what the writer is going to do next? If you might add, add it. If it should be pointed out, point it out. If it is interesting to note, *make* it interesting. Being told that something is interesting is the surest way of tempting the reader to find it dull; are we not all stupefied by what follows when someone says, "This will interest you"? As for the inflated prepositions and conjunctions, they are the innumerable phrases like "with the possible exception of" (except), "for the reason that" (because), "he totally lacked the ability to" (he couldn't), "she was unable to give any information beyond the fact that" (she said).

15 Clutter takes more forms than you can shake twenty sticks at. Prune it ruthlessly. Be grateful for everything that you can throw away. Re-examine each sentence that you put on paper. Is every word doing new and useful work? Can any thought be expressed with more economy? Is anything pompous or pretentious or faddish? Are you hanging on to something useless just because you think it's beautiful? Remember Thoreau:

> Our life is frittered away by detail. . . . Instead of a million count half-a-dozen, and keep your accounts on your thumbnail. . . . Let us spend one day as deliberately as Nature and not be thrown off the track by every nutshell and mosquito's wing that falls on the rails.

16 Simplify, simplify.

Word Study List

debasing	3	demographic	9
laborious	5	parameter	12
locutions	5	paradigm	12
euphemism	7	insidious	13

Questions

1. Zinsser's piece is about bad writing, or about one characteristic of bad writing. What, then, is his view of good writing? What do we need to do to make our writing free from clutter?

2. Zinsser not only gives many examples of cluttered writing; he also groups examples into categories. Make a list of the *kinds* of clutter Zinsser examines.

3. Think about your writing. Does it frequently contain any of the types of clutter described by Zinsser? When you are having trouble writing, do you write a shorter piece or do you fill the "required" space with clutter?

4. Do you find it comforting to be told to write simply, without jargon or wordiness or faddish phrases? Do you believe that instructors want you to write simply? What evidence do you have to support your beliefs?

5. Notice that Zinsser opens with a metaphor. What is the metaphor? How does it effectively characterize Zinsser's view of cluttered writing?

6. How would you characterize Zinsser's writing? Is it simple? Is it simplistic? What is the difference between these terms?

Exercise

Take a recent piece of your writing and prune it of all the kinds of clutter Zinsser describes, circling every word or phrase that could be removed without loss. How much clutter did you find? How much has your piece improved just from one round of pruning? Switch pruned papers with a classmate to see if a fresh eye can spot additional clutter.

Student Essay: Definition

Gauging Gossip

Attention getter

Whenever my mother's two sisters visit from New York, the three of them ban everyone else from the kitchen and load the table with their Cokes and cake in preparation. With batteries charged, antennas raised, volumes adjusted, they begin. Their ritual is the prelude to none other than the art of gossip. The word *gossip* has had several unusual meanings in the past, but today it is included as an important part of conversation and amusement in our society.

Thesis

Origin of the term

For my mother and her sisters, gossip is the hit of the party, the star of the show, the bottle of fine wine to be sipped and savored. Gossip, however, used to have a much different meaning than it does today. The word originated from "God" and "sib," or related to God. It then evolved to mean a godparent or sponsor of a child. Later, dropping the "being related to" characteristic, it meant a familiar acquaintance or a gathering of females, taking on female connotations. Ultimately, gossip acquired the derogatory meaning of people (usually women) who fill their days with "idle chatter and groundless rumor." So today we relate to the word *gossip* as an act of talking behind someone's back with or without the facts, or of telling tall tales. Gossipers are often regarded as busybodies, tattlers, newsmongers, people who cannot mind their own business. Gossipry is considered a less-than-sophisticated and unsavory inclusion in our conversation.

Characteristics of gossip in contrast to conversation

Although gossip is a form of conversation, the two words have much different meanings. Gossip is the embroidering of a story, the relaying of tidbits, the passing on of hearsay or rumor. There is no genuine communication with gossip, only the superficial banter wrapped around the lives of other people. Gossip can be included in conversation, but it cannot be considered conversation on its own. Gossip is merely an additive, such as salt, to flavor the conversation. Conversation is the exchange of ideas, the exchange of opinions, the expression of feelings. Conversation is a learning, enlightening experience, a stimulation of thought. A discussion in which two or more people convey and connect their thoughts or feelings is a conversation. Do you want me to tell you what I know—or do you want gossip? For gossip is only the dash of Tabasco in the Bloody Mary, the between-meals snack, the dessert after dinner. It may be stimulating, but it is not the real thing.

Characteristics of gossip in contrast to conversation

Whether or not we realize it or like to admit it, gossip plays a part in just about everyone's daily life. Gossip seems to be everywhere, if not always at our own kitchen tables. If we don't get our fill at school or at the office, there are always television shows, newspapers, magazines, even enticing biographies. Many aging "show biz" personalities write their memoirs to keep from being forgotten or to make more money. Not-so-aging sons and daughters write *Mommy Dearest* and other revealing, sensationalist memoirs, trading on our love of gossip. Popular TV specials such as *Blood Feud,* a dramatization of the conflict between Robert Kennedy and Jimmy Hoffa, portray the personal lives of well-known figures. Gossip columns and tabloids thrive by filling in their readers on "exclusive" stories about the famous or infamous. Many Washingtonians are suffering withdrawal over the loss of the "Ear," a popular gossip column recently removed from *The Washington Post.* Editor Ben Bradlee of *The Post* has labeled gossip "the biggest industry in town." Gossip is the sole industry of *The National Enquirer.*

Examples of gossip

Gossip may not be the high priority for everyone that it is for addicts like my aunts, but we cannot deny that it is prevalent in our society. Gossip is easy to criticize but difficult to escape, for every now and then it catches our interest against our will, proving that none of us is totally immune to the seductive pleasures of "forbidden" news. Gossip does have its beneficial side, too. When approached by a friend who says she heard you were caught "driving under the influence," you can always reply: "Don't pay any attention to that; it was only gossip."

Conclusion emphasizing power or influence of gossip

Exercises

I. WORD MEANING AND USAGE

1. The English language has a wealth of words with similar meanings, but the key word here is *similar.* No two words ever mean exactly the same thing. List as many synonyms as you can for each of the following words. Allow yourself two minutes per word.
   a. sentimental
   b. strong
   c. dainty
   d. thin
   e. possible
   f. see
   g. burn
   h. laugh
   i. lift
   j. force

   When you have completed your brainstorming, take the word for which you generated the longest list of synonyms and explain the difference in the meaning of each synonym. Check a desk dictionary to see if it gives a discussion of synonyms for your word after the word's entry. How does knowing a range of synonyms help you in writing?
2. What labels (such as archaic, slang, colloquial, British, etc.) does your desk dictionary give the following words?
   a. quoth
   b. pone (meaning cornbread)
   c. enthuse
   d. gamp
   e. hoosegow
   f. ken

   Compare your answers with those of other class members. What differences in labeling do you note among dictionaries?
3. Define the *italicized* word in each group of sentences by studying the context or words around it.
   a. bag
      1. The grocery *bag* split as I lifted it from the trunk of my car.
      2. People who party late at night often have *bags* under their eyes the next morning.
      3. My beach *bag* is stuffed with toys and suntan lotion.
      4. Small leather *bags* in purple and plum are in fashion this year.
      5. We checked our *bags* at the Honolulu airport and then went sightseeing until our plane left.
   b. pin
      1. My grandmother always wore a small diamond *pin* on the collar of her dress.
      2. His last ball knocked down all ten *pins.*
      3. I spent the last of my *pin* money yesterday on a raspberry soda.
      4. Extra diaper *pins* are in the top drawer of the baby's dresser.
      5. Tom has been *pinned* to my sister for two months.
   c. state
      1. What is your home *state?*
      2. She was in a *state* of shock for several hours after the accident.

3. The building was a valuable piece of property despite its *state* of disrepair.
4. We learned in chemistry how to change nitrogen from its gaseous to its liquid *state.*
5. The president's *State* of the Union Address was delayed a half hour.

Write five sentences for each of the following words: *play, take, open, plain,* and *fine.* Use a different meaning of the word in each sentence.

4. Lack of clarity often results from unintentional ambiguity, or two or more possible meanings for a word in a certain context. Deliberate ambiguity can enrich our writing by suggesting multiple meanings (as in puns or double-entendres), but unintentional ambiguity causes confusion. Identify the ambiguity in each of the following statements:
   a. She appealed to him.
   b. Mrs. Smith is a poor school teacher.
   c. The secretary said that she could retype the report in an hour.
   d. Mr. Brown pressed his suit.

   Revise each sentence, expanding the context in order to clear up the ambiguity.
5. The origins of words are often interesting, as the student who wrote about gossip learned. In a desk dictionary check the origin (or etymology) of these popular items of apparel:
   a. pants
   b. trousers
   c. slacks
   d. dungarees
   e. jeans
   f. Levi's

II. TONE, AUDIENCE, AND WORD CHOICE

Tone in writing, like a speaker's tone of voice, expresses your feelings toward your audience and your subject. Any adjectives used to describe tone of voice—angry, casual, naive or childish, sophisticated, sarcastic, formal—apply to tone in writing.

1. Describe the appropriate tone to use in responding to each of the following situations:
   a. Third request to correct charge on computerized billing statement from a local department store
   b. Letter of application for a job as a camp counselor
   c. Letter to your Representative asking for an explanation of the high interest rates on home mortgages and car loans
   d. Essay describing your goals and beliefs in support of your application to a church-supported college
   e. Letter to the editor of your local newspaper in reply to an editorial arguing against tax credit for installation of solar heating
   f. Guide to your campus written for incoming freshmen and their parents

g. Research paper on an unsolved engineering problem and possible ways to solve it

2. Choose one of the following topics and write one descriptive paragraph appropriate in tone and content for each of the three audiences listed. Avoid vague nouns such as *thing, aspect, quality, kind,* and *type.* Avoid meaningless modifiers such as *very, simply, pretty, nice,* and *so.*
   a. Your home (where you or your parents live)
      1. To a friend who is going to spend a holiday with you
      2. For a real estate agent
      3. For the city (or county) tax assessor
   b. An old girl or boy friend from high school
      1. To a friend who wants a blind date
      2. To your sister (or brother) who is considering her (or him) for a roommate
      3. To your diary
   c. Your college's snack bar or cafeteria
      1. For a booklet written to incoming freshmen
      2. In a letter to the Dean of Student Services asking for improved facilities
      3. To a friend at another college
3. Based on what you have read about words, usage, meaning, and context and remarks that have been made on your papers in the past, freewrite for ten minutes on how to write an F paper. Revise your draft, selecting the tone, details, and organization that would be appropriate for your instructor. Write another version appropriate for a fellow classmate. Compare the two papers. What differences in word choice, tone, and content do you find?

Writing Assignments

1. Choose one pair of words from the list below and brainstorm on the one of the pair that you know best, listing everything that comes to mind about the word. Consider whether or not the paired word is opposite in every way to what you have listed. From the ideas you now have about the differences in the two words, write a paper that contrasts the two words to stress the important differences as well as the perhaps surprising ways in which the words overlap somewhat in meaning.
   a. patriot and traitor
   b. sanity and madness
   c. work and play
   d. professional and amateur

   Look over your first draft to see if you have used some of the following methods of definition: by classification (or dictionary definition), by comparison (both direct and metaphoric), by function, by description, and by example. If necessary, revise your paper to include several of these methods.

2. Choose one pair of words from the list below and write a paper that defines the two words by comparing them. Start by brainstorming on the word you know best. Compare your second word to your list of ideas to see in what ways it is similar and different. Your paper should point out the subtle but important distinction that you see between them.
   a. tolerance and compassion
   b. wisdom and knowledge
   c. pride and arrogance
   d. house and home

   Revise your first draft to include as many methods of definition as you find useful to prove your thesis. See assignment 1 above for methods of defining.
3. Examine the vocabulary of a familiar group such as your family, roommates, classmates, instructors, people you work with, or members of a club or team. Note the words or phrases that are repeated often. Review what various authors such as Evans, Langer, and McCarthy say about how words define who we are and give purpose to our existence. Group the words that characterize your chosen group in some significant way (words of greeting, farewell, approval, disapproval, etc.) and then explain, using examples, how these words or phrases limit or control relationships or make conversations within the group dull and repetitive.
4. You probably know the frustration of being unable to complete a project because of poorly written instructions. Find such a set of inadequate or inaccurate instructions and write a paper explaining what the task is, what the instructions say, what was either omitted or explained ambiguously or incorrectly in the instructions, what happened as a result of the poor directions, and what revisions you would make.

CHAPTER 2

Writing: The Struggle for Language

GETTING STARTED: A Writer's List of First Questions

We are familiar with the reporter's litany of questions: who, what, where, when, and why. But all writers, not just reporters covering an event, need to answer some key questions before they can plan their writing and execute those plans successfully. Having specific answers to the following questions before you jump into any writing assignment is guaranteed to improve your work. Knowing that professional writers have also answered these questions will help you analyze the works you read. In addition to answering the specific questions following each article in this text, answer these general questions for every article you read.

I. Type
   What kind of writing do I want to produce?
   What is the appropriate format?
   What is the appropriate length?

II. Purpose
   Beyond completing an assignment, what is my purpose in writing?
   What do I want my readers to know, to feel, or to do after reading my piece?

III. Subject
   What is my specific topic?
   What main point or thesis do I want to establish?
   Does my choice of topic fit into the broad subject area and meet the guidelines of purpose and format that have been established for this piece of writing?

IV. Audience
   Who is my audience?
   What do they already know about my topic?
   What are their interests and values? What attitudes toward my subject are they likely to hold?
   How should answers to these questions guide my choice of approach and tone?

The Word

Pablo Neruda

A Chilean Marxist, Pablo Neruda (1904–1973) has written many volumes of poetry and prose, relatively little of which has been translated into English, partly because his poetry is difficult to translate, partly because of his politics. In a checkered political career, Neruda served in the Chilean Senate, lived in exile, and was ambassador to France. His greatest recognition as a writer came in 1971 when he won the Nobel prize for literature. "The Word" was first published in *Plenos poderes* (1962). The volume, translated by Alastair Reid, was printed in English, as *Fully Empowered,* in 1975.

In his poem, Neruda speaks to the power, the miracle, of the word, of human language.

LA PALABRA

Nació
la palabra en la sangre,
creció en el cuerpo oscuro, palpitando,
y voló con los labios y la boca.

Más lejos y más cerca 5
aún, aún venía
de padres muertos y de errantes razas,
de territorios que se hicieron piedra,
que se cansaron de sus pobres tribus,
porque cuando el dolor salió al camino 10
los pueblos anduvieron y llegaron
y nueva tierra y agua reunieron
para sembrar de nuevo su palabra.
Y así la herencia es ésta:
éste es el aire que nos comunica 15
con el hombre enterrado y con la aurora
de nuevos seres que aún no amanecieron.

Aún la atmósfera tiembla
con la primera palabra
elaborada 20
con pánico y gemido.
Salió
de las tinieblas
y hasta ahora no hay trueno
que truene aún con su ferretería 25
como aquella palabra,
la primera
palabra pronunciada:
tal vez sólo un susurro fue, una gota,
y cae y cae aún su catarata. 30

Luego el sentido llena la palabra.
Quedó preñada y se llenó de vidas,
Todo fue nacimientos y sonidos:
la affirmación, la claridad, la fuerza,
la negación, la destrucción, la muerte: 35
el verbo asumió todos los poderes
y se fundió existencia con esencia
en la electricidad de su hermosura.

Palabra humana, sílaba, cadera
de larga luz y dura platería, 40
hereditaria copa que recibe
las communicaciones de la sangre:
he aquí que el silencio fue integrado
por el total de la palabra humana

THE WORD

The word
was born in the blood,
grew in the dark body, beating,
and took flight through the lips and the mouth.

Farther away and nearer 5
still, still it came
from dead fathers and from wandering races,
from lands which had turned to stone,
lands weary of their poor tribes,
for when grief took to the roads 10
the people set out and arrived
and married new land and water
to grow their words again.
And so this is the inheritance;
this is the wavelength which connects us 15
with dead men and the dawning
of new beings not yet come to light.

Still the atmosphere quivers
with the first word uttered
dressed up 20
in terror and sighing.
It emerged
from the darkness
and until now there is no thunder
that ever rumbles with the iron voice 25
of that word,
the first
word uttered—
perhaps it was only a ripple, a single drop,
and yet its great cataract falls and falls. 30

Later on, the word fills with meaning.
Always with child, it filled up with lives.
Everything was births and sounds—
affirmation, clarity, strength,
negation, destruction, death— 35
the verb took over all the power
and blended existence with essence
in the electricity of its grace.

Human word, syllable, flank
of extending light and solid silverwork, 40
hereditary goblet which receives
the communications of the blood—
here is where silence came together with
the wholeness of the human word,

y no hablar es morir entre los seres: 45
se hace lenguaje hasta la cabellera,
habla la boca sin mover los labios:
los ojos de repente son palabras.

Yo tomo la palabra y la recorro
como si fuera sólo forma humana, 50
me embelesan sus líneas y navego
en cada resonancia del idioma:
pronuncio y soy y sin hablar me acerca
el fin de las palabras al silencio.

Bebo por la palabra levantando 55
una palabra o copa cristalina,
en ella bebo
el vino del idioma
o el agua interminable,
manantial maternal de las palabras, 60
y copa y agua y vino
originan mi canto
porque el verbo es origen
y vierte vida: es sangre,
es la sangre que expresa su substancia 65
y está dispuesto así su desarrollo:
dan cristal al cristal, sangre a la sangre,
y dan vida a la vida las palabras.

Word Study List

cataract	l. 30	resonance	l. 52
essence	l. 37		

Questions

1. What is Neruda's attitude toward language? What words and images help to convey his attitude? When we "drink to" or toast someone or something, what is the purpose of our action?

2. Early in the poem Neruda says that the word is born in blood and grows in the body; later he says it passes through our senses, and he repeats its connection with our blood. What do these images suggest about the relationship between humans and language? How central is speech to human existence?

3. What connections does language make possible for humans?

4. Sometimes Neruda speaks of "the word," sometimes specifically of verbs. Why does he give special attention to verbs?

and, for human beings, not to speak is to die— 45
language extends even to the hair,
the mouth speaks without the lips moving,
all of a sudden, the eyes are words.

I take the word and pass it through my senses
as though it were no more than a human shape; 50
its arrangements awe me and I find my way
through each resonance of the spoken word—
I utter and I am and, speechless, I approach
across the edge of words silence itself.

I drink to the word, raising 55
a word or a shining cup;
in it I drink
the pure wine of language
or inexhaustible water,
maternal source of words, 60
and cup and water and wine
give rise to my song
because the verb is the source
and vivid life—it is blood,
blood which expresses its substance 65
and so ordains its own unwinding.
Words give glass quality to glass, blood to blood,
and life to life itself.

---

5. In his connecting of "the word" with "the blood" and "the dark body," the poet alludes to what Biblical passage?
6. Neruda gives expression to language's power primarily through what dominant image in the poem? Look especially at lines 60–66.

Exercises

1. If there is someone in your class who speaks Spanish, have that person read aloud the Spanish version of the poem. Then have someone read aloud the English version. What differences in sounds and rhythms are found in the two versions? How do those sounds and rhythms affect your response to the poem?
2. If you know Spanish, put aside the English version of the poem and, working only with the Spanish version, make your own translation. Compare your translation to the translation in the text and note the sections that differ. What have you learned about the task of translating poetry? Be prepared to discuss the issue with your class.

The Watcher at the Gates

Gail Godwin

Gail Godwin (b. 1937), with a Ph.D. and several grants and fellowships to her credit, is best known for her collection of short stories (*Dream Children,* 1976) and her novels, including *Glass People* (1972), *The Odd Woman* (1974), and the best seller *A Woman and Two Daughters* (1982). The following article was printed on January 9, 1977, in the *New York Times Book Review.*

Giving life to the concept of writer's block in the figure of a Watcher at the Gates, Godwin helps us see the problem more clearly and see some solutions to the problem.

1 I first realized I was not the only writer who had a restraining critic who lived inside me and sapped the juice from green inspirations when I was leafing through Freud's "Interpretation of Dreams" a few years ago. Ironically, it was my "inner critic" who had sent me to Freud. I was writing a novel, and my heroine was in the middle of a dream, and then I lost faith in my own invention and rushed to "an authority" to check whether she could have such a dream. In the chapter on dream interpretation, I came upon the following passage that has helped me free myself, in some measure, from my critic and has led to many pleasant and interesting exchanges with other writers.

2 Freud quotes Schiller,[1] who is writing a letter to a friend. The friend complains of his lack of creative power. Schiller replies with an allegory. He says it is not good if the intellect examines too closely the ideas pouring in at the gates. "In isolation, an idea may be quite insignificant, and venturesome in the extreme, but it may acquire importance from an idea which follows it. . . . In the case of a creative mind, it seems to me, the intellect has withdrawn its watchers from the gates, and the ideas rush in pell-mell, and only then does it review and inspect the multitude. You are ashamed or afraid of the momentary and passing madness which is found in all real creators, the longer or shorter duration of which distinguishes the thinking artist from the dreamer . . . you reject too soon and discriminate too severely."

3 So that's what I had: a Watcher at the Gates. I decided to get to know him better. I discussed him with other writers, who told me some of the quirks and habits of their Watchers, each of whom was as individual as his host, and all of whom seemed passionately dedicated to one goal: rejecting too soon and discriminating too severely.

4 It is amazing the lengths a Watcher will go to keep you from pursuing the flow of your imagination. Watchers are notorious pencil sharpeners, ribbon changers, plant waterers, home repairers and abhorrers of

[1]A German poet and dramatist (1759–1805).—Ed.

messy rooms or messy pages. They are compulsive looker-uppers. They are superstitious scaredy-cats. They cultivate self-important eccentricities they think are suitable for "writers." And they'd rather die (and kill your inspiration with them) than risk making a fool of themselves.

5 My Watcher has a wasteful penchant for 20-pound bond paper above and below the carbon of the first draft. "What's the good of writing out a whole page," he whispers begrudgingly, "if you just have to write it over again later? Get it perfect the first time!" My Watcher adores stopping in the middle of a morning's work to drive down to the library to check on the name of a flower or a World War II battle or a line of metaphysical poetry. "You can't possibly go on till you've got this right!" he admonishes. I go and get the car keys.

6 Other Watchers have informed their writers that:

7 "Whenever you get a really good sentence you should stop in the middle of it and go on tomorrow. Otherwise you might run dry."

8 "Don't try and continue with your book till your dental appointment is over. When you're worried about your teeth, you can't think about art."

9 Another Watcher makes his owner pin his finished pages to a clothesline and read them through binoculars "to see how they look from a distance." Countless other Watchers demands "bribes" for taking the day off: lethal doses of caffeine, alcoholic doses of Scotch or vodka or wine.

10 There are various ways to outsmart, pacify or coexist with your Watcher. Here are some I have tried, or my writer friends have tried, with success:

11 Look for situations when he's likely to be off-guard. Write too fast for him in an unexpected place, at an unexpected time. (Virginia Woolf[2] captured the "diamonds in the dustheap" by writing at a "rapid haphazard gallop" in her diary.) Write when very tired. Write in purple ink on the back of a Master Charge statement. Write whatever comes into your mind while the kettle is boiling and make the steam whistle your deadline. (Deadlines are a great way to outdistance the Watcher.)

12 Disguise what you are writing. If your Watcher refuses to let you get on with your story or novel, write a "letter" instead, telling your "correspondent" what you are going to write in your story or next chapter. Dash off a "review" of your own unfinished opus. It will stand up like a bully to your Watcher the next time he throws obstacles in your path. If you write yourself a good one.

13 Get to know your Watcher. He's yours. Do a drawing of him (or her). Pin it to the wall of your study and turn it gently to the wall when necessary. Let your Watcher feel needed. Watchers are excellent critics after inspiration has been captured; they are dependable, sharp-eyed readers of things already set down. Keep your Watcher in shape and he'll have

---

[2]A British novelist and essayist (1882–1941).—Ed.

less time to keep you from shaping. If he's really ruining your whole working day sit down, as Jung did with his personal demons, and write him a letter. On a very bad day I once wrote my Watcher a letter. "Dear Watcher," I wrote, "What is it you're so afraid I'll do?" Then I held his pen for him, and he replied instantly with a candor that has kept me from truly despising him.

14 "Fail," he wrote back.

Word Study List

allegory	2	penchant	5
notorious	4	admonishes	5
abhorrers	4	opus	12
eccentricities	4		

Questions

1. Godwin's piece is a good example of a personal essay: she writes of her own experience in an informal manner. Still she has a clear and specific subject and a main point or thesis. What is her subject? What is her thesis?

2. Where did Godwin find the idea of a Watcher at the Gates? What are the two problem traits found in most Watchers?

3. What are some of the gimmicks Watchers use to keep us from writing? Can you add to Godwin's list from your own experience?

4. What are some of the ways writers can outsmart their Watchers? Again, can you add to Godwin's list those techniques that have worked for you?

5. What, ultimately, do all Watchers, not just Godwin's, seem to fear? Why, in other words, do we have writer's block?

6. Does it help you to know that most people share, to some degree or at some times, the experience of writing anxiety? Why or why not? Why do you suppose so many people have writing anxiety?

Exercise

Godwin suggests that we get to know our Watcher at the Gates. If you are more adept at drawing than writing, begin by drawing a picture of your Watcher. Then write a brief description of him or her. If writing comes more easily than drawing, write first and then draw or sketch, as best you can, the person you have described.

Silences

Tillie Olsen

Tillie Olsen (b. 1913) made her reputation as a writer with a highly praised collection of short stories, *Tell Me a Riddle,* published in 1961 when she was in her late forties. She has since held visiting professorships and writer-in-residence positions at several colleges and has won fellowships and awards. *Silences* was first an unwritten talk, then an essay published in *Harper's* in 1965, and finally a book printed in 1978.

Her interest in writers who do not write—those who publish late in life, who publish one good work and no more, or who endure a dry period—the subject of this shortened version of her essay, is not surprising, given her own painful experience with silence.

1 Literary history and the present are dark with silences: some the silences for years by our acknowledged great; some silences hidden; some the ceasing to publish after one work appears; some the never coming to book form at all.

2 What is it that happens with the creator, to the creative process, in that time? What *are* creation's needs for full functioning? Without intention of or pretension to literary scholarship, I have had special need to learn all I could of this over the years, myself so nearly remaining mute and having to let writing die over and over again in me. . . .

3 Now, what *is* the work of creation and the circumstances it demands for full functioning—as told in the journals, letters, notes, of the practitioners themselves: Henry James, Katherine Mansfield, André Gide, Virginia Woolf; the letters of Flaubert, Rilke, Joseph Conrad; Thomas Wolfe's *Story of a Novel,* Valéry's *Course in Poetics.* What do they explain of the silences?

4 "Constant toil is the law of art, as it is of life," says (and demonstrated) Balzac:[1]

> To pass from conception to execution, to produce, to bring the idea to birth, to raise the child laboriously from infancy, to put it nightly to sleep surfeited, to kiss it in the mornings with the hungry heart of a mother, to clean it, to clothe it fifty times over in new garments which it tears and casts away, and yet not revolt against the trials of this agitated life—this unwearying maternal love, this habit of creation—this is execution and its toils.

5 "Without duties, almost without external communication," Rilke[2] specifies, "unconfined solitude which takes every day like a life, a spaciousness which puts no limit to vision and in the midst of which infinities surround."

---

[1]French novelist and short-story writer (1799–1850)—Ed.

[2]Austrian poet (1875–1926).—Ed.

6 Unconfined solitude as Joseph Conrad[3] experienced it:

> For twenty months I wrestled with the Lord for my creation . . . mind and will and conscience engaged to the full, hour after hour, day after day . . . a lonely struggle in a great isolation from the world. I suppose I slept and ate the food put before me and talked connectedly on suitable occasions, but I was never aware of the even flow of daily life, made easy and noiseless for me by a silent, watchful, tireless affection.

7 So there is a homely underpinning for it all, the even flow of daily life made easy and noiseless.

8 "The terrible law of the artist"—says Henry James[4]—"the law of fructification, of fertilization. The old, old lesson of the art of meditation. To woo combinations and inspirations into being by a depth and continuity of attention and meditation."

9 "That load, that weight, that gnawing conscience," writes Thomas Mann[5]—

> That sea which to drink up, that frightful task . . . The will, the discipline and self-control to shape a sentence or follow out a hard train of thought. From the first rhythmical urge of the inward creative force towards the material, towards casting in shape and form, from that to the thought, the image, the word, the line, what a struggle, what Gethsemane.

10 Does it become very clear what Melville's Pierre[6] so bitterly remarked on, and what literary history bears out—why most of the great works of humanity have come from lives (able to be) wholly surrendered and dedicated? How else sustain the constant toil, the frightful task, the terrible law, the continuity? Full self: this means full time as and when needed for the work. (That time for which Emily Dickinson[7] withdrew from the world.)

11 But what if there is not that fullness of time, let alone totality of self? What if the writers, as in some of these silences, must work regularly at something besides their own work—as do nearly all in the arts in the United States today.

12 I know the theory (kin to "starving in the garret makes great art") that it is this very circumstance which feeds creativity. I know, too, that for the beginning young, for some who have such need, the job can be

---

[3]Polish-born English novelist and short-story writer (1857–1924)—Ed.

[4]Prolific American-born novelist, short-story writer, and critic (1843–1916) who lived most of his adult life in England.—Ed.

[5]German novelist (1875–1955) and Nobel prize winner (1929) who became an American citizen in 1940.—Ed.

[6]Main character in a novel by Herman Melville (1819–1891), the American writer best known for *Moby Dick*.—Ed.

[7]American poet (1830–1886) whose creative skills were not recognized until after her death.—Ed.

valuable access to life they would not otherwise know. A few (I think of the doctors, the incomparables: Chekhov[8] and William Carlos Williams[9]) for special reasons sometimes manage both. But the actuality testifies: substantial creative work demands time, and with rare exceptions only full-time workers have achieved it. Where the claims of creation cannot be primary, the results are atrophy; unfinished work; minor effort and accomplishment; silences. (Desperation which accounts for the mountains of applications to the foundations for grants—undivided time—in the strange bread-line system we have worked out for our artists.)

13 Twenty years went by on the writing of *Ship of Fools,* while Katherine Anne Porter,[10] who needed only two, was "trying to get to that table, to that typewriter, away from my jobs of teaching and trooping this country and of keeping house." "Your subconscious needed that time to grow the layers of pearl," she was told. Perhaps, perhaps, but I doubt it. Subterranean forces can make you wait, but they are very finicky about the kind of waiting it has to be. Before they will feed the creator back, they must be fed, passionately fed, what needs to be worked on. "We hold up our desire as one places a magnet over a composite dust from which the particle of iron will suddenly jump up," says Paul Valéry.[11] A receptive waiting, that means, not demands which prevent "an undistracted center of being." And when the response comes, availability to work must be immediate. If not used at once, all may vanish as a dream; worse, future creation be endangered—for only the removal and development of the material frees the forces for further work.

14 There is a life in which all this is documented: Franz Kafka's.[12] For every one entry from his diaries here, there are fifty others that testify as unbearably to the driven stratagems for time, the work lost (to us), the damage to the creative powers (and the body) of having to deny, interrupt, postpone, put aside, let work die.

15 "I cannot devote myself completely to my writing," Kafka explains (in 1911). "I could not live by literature if only, to begin with, because of the slow maturing of my work and its special character." So he worked as an official in a state insurance agency, and wrote when he could.

> These two can never be reconciled. . . . If I have written something one evening, I am afire the next day in the office and can bring nothing to completion. Outwardly I fulfill my office duties satisfactorily, not my inner duties however, and every unfulfilled inner duty becomes a misfortune that never leaves. What strength it will necessarily drain me of.

---

[8]Russian dramatist and short-story writer (1860–1904) who was also a physician.—Ed.

[9]American poet and physician (1883–1963).—Ed.

[10]American writer (1890–1980) of short stories and one novel, *Ship of Fools.*—Ed.

[11]French poet (1871–1945).—Ed.

[12]Austrian novelist (1883–1924).—Ed.

1911

> No matter how little the time or how badly I write, I feel approaching the imminent possibility of great moments which could make me capable of anything. But my being does not have sufficient strength to hold this to the next writing time. During the day the visible world helps me; during the night it cuts me to pieces unhindered. . . . In the evening and in the morning, my consciousness of the creative abilities in me then I can encompass. I feel shaken to the core of my being. Calling forth such powers which are then not permitted to function.

. . . which are then not permitted to function . . .

1911

> I finish nothing, because I have no time, and it presses so within me.

1912

> When I begin to write after such a long interval, I draw the words as if out of the empty air. If I capture one, then I have just this one alone, and all the toil must begin anew.

1914

> Yesterday for the first time in months, an indisputable ability to do good work. And yet wrote only the first page. Again I realize that everything written down bit by bit rather than all at once in the course of the larger part is inferior, and that the circumstances of my life condemn me to this inferiority.

1915

> My constant attempt by sleeping before dinner to make it possible to continue working [writing] late into the night, senseless. Then at one o'clock can no longer fall asleep at all, the next day at work insupportable, and so I destroy myself.

1917

> Distractedness, weak memory, stupidity. Days passed in futility, powers wasted away in waiting. . . . Always this one principal anguish—if I had gone away in 1911 in full possession of all my powers. Not eaten by the strain of keeping down living forces.

16 Eaten into tuberculosis. By the time he won through to himself and time for writing, his body could live no more. He was forty-one.

17 I think of Rilke who said, "If I have any responsibility, I mean and desire it to be responsibility for the deepest and innermost essence of the loved reality [writing] to which I am inseparably bound"; and who also

said, "Anything alive that makes demands, arouses in me an infinite capacity to give it its due, the consequences of which completely use me up." These were true with Kafka, too, yet how different their lives. When Rilke wrote that about responsibility, he is explaining why he will not take a job to support his wife and baby, nor live with them (years later will not come to his daughter's wedding nor permit a two-hour honeymoon visit lest it break his solitude where he awaits poetry). The "infinite capacity" is his explanation as to why he cannot even bear to have a dog. Extreme—and justified. He protected his creative powers.

18 Kafka's, Rilke's "infinite capacity," and all else that has been said here of the needs of creation, illuminate women's silence of centuries. I will not repeat what is in Virginia Woolf's *A Room of One's Own,*[13] but talk of this last century and a half in which women have begun to have voice in literature. (It has been less than that time in Eastern Europe, and not yet, in many parts of the world.)

19 In the last century, of the women whose achievements endure for us in one way or another,* nearly all never married (Jane Austen, Emily Brontë, Christina Rossetti, Emily Dickinson, Louisa May Alcott, Sarah Orne Jewett) or married late in their thirties (George Eliot, Elizabeth Barrett Browning, Charlotte Brontë, Olive Schreiner). I can think of only four (George Sand, Harriet Beecher Stowe, Helen Hunt Jackson, and Elizabeth Gaskell) who married and had children as young women.** All had servants.

20 In our century, until very recently, it has not been so different. Most did not marry (Selma Lagerlof, Willa Cather, Ellen Glasgow, Gertrude Stein, Gabriela Mistral, Elizabeth Madox Roberts, Charlotte Mew, Eudora Welty, Marianne Moore) or, if married, have been childless (Edith Wharton, Virginia Woolf, Katherine Mansfield, Dorothy Richardson, H. H. Richardson, Elizabeth Bowen, Isak Dinesen, Katherine Anne Porter, Lillian Hellman, Dorothy Parker). Colette had one child (when she was forty). If I include Sigrid Undset, Kay Boyle, Pearl Buck, Dorothy Canfield Fisher, that will make a small group who had more than one child. All had household help or other special circumstances.

21 Am I resaying the moldy theory that women have no need, some say no capacity, to create art, because they can "create" babies? And the additional proof is precisely that the few women who have created it are nearly all childless? No.

22 The power and the need to create, over and beyond reproduction,

---

[13]A long essay, published in 1929 by British novelist and essayist Virginia Woolf (1882–1941), that examines the problems of being a woman and a writer.—Ed.

*"One Out of Twelve" has a more extensive roll of women writers of achievement.

**I would now add a fifth—Kate Chopin—also a foreground silence.

is native in both women and men. Where the gifted among women *(and men)* have remained mute, or have never attained full capacity, it is because of circumstances, inner or outer, which oppose the needs of creation.

23 Wholly surrendered and dedicated lives; time as needed for the work; totality of self. But women are traditionally trained to place others' needs first, to feel these needs as their own (the "infinite capacity"); their sphere, their satisfaction to be in making it possible for others to use their abilities. This is what Virginia Woolf meant when, already a writer of achievement, she wrote in her diary:

> Father's birthday. He would have been 96, 96, yes, today; and could have been 96, like other people one has known; but mercifully was not. His life would have entirely ended mine. What would have happened? No writing, no books—inconceivable.

24 It took family deaths to free more than one woman writer into her own development.* Emily Dickinson freed herself, denying all the duties expected of a woman of her social position except the closest family ones, and she was fortunate to have a sister, and servants, to share those. How much is revealed of the differing circumstances and fate of their own as-great capacities, in the diaries (and lives) of those female bloodkin of great writers: Dorothy Wordsworth,[14] Alice James,[15] Aunt Mary Moody Emerson.[16]

25 And where there is no servant or relation to assume the responsibilities of daily living? Listen to Katherine Mansfield[17] in the early days of her relationship with John Middleton Murry, when they both dreamed of becoming great writers:**

---

[14]Sister (1771–1855) of British poet William Wordsworth. She traveled with him, and her journal was included in his guide to the English Lake District.—ED.

[15]The only sister (1848–1892) of the novelist Henry and philosopher William James. An intelligent and sensitive woman, she struggled unsuccessfully to find an identity and purpose in her life.—ED.

[16]The aunt (1774–1863) of Ralph Waldo Emerson and a writer of extensive journals from which Emerson borrowed for his own writings.—ED.

[17]A British poet and short-story writer (1888–1923) who married editor, literary critic, and political activist John Middleton Murry (1889–1957).—ED.

*Among them: George Eliot, Helen Hunt Jackson, Mrs. Gaskell, Kate Chopin, Lady Gregory, Isak Dinesen. Ivy Compton-Burnett finds this the grim reason for the emergence of British women novelists after World War I: " . . . The men were dead, you see, and the women didn't marry so much because there was no one for them to marry, and so they had leisure, and, I think, in a good many cases they had money because their brothers were dead, and all that would tend to writing, wouldn't it, being single, and having some money, and having the time—having no men, you see."

**Already in that changed time when servants were not necessarily a part of the furnishings of almost anyone well educated enough to be making literature.

> The house seems to take up so much time. . . . I mean when I have to clean up twice over or wash up extra unnecessary things, I get frightfully impatient and want to be working [writing]. So often this week you and Gordon have been talking while I washed dishes. Well someone's got to wash dishes and get food. Otherwise "there's nothing in the house but eggs to eat." And after you have gone I walk about with a mind full of ghosts of saucepans and primus stoves and "will there be enough to go around?" And you calling, whatever I am doing, writing, "Tig, isn't there going to be tea? It's five o'clock."
>
> I loathe myself today. This woman who superintends you and rushes about slamming doors and slopping water and shouts "You might at least empty the pail and wash out the tea leaves." . . . O Jack, I wish that you would take me in your arms and kiss my hands and my face and every bit of me and say, "It's all right, you darling thing, I understand."

A long way from Conrad's favorable circumstances for creation: the flow of daily life made easy and noiseless.

26 And, if in addition to the infinite capacity, to the daily responsibilities, there are children?

27 Balzac, you remember, described creation in terms of motherhood. Yes, in intelligent passionate motherhood there are similarities, and in more than the toil and patience. The calling upon total capacities; the reliving and new using of the past; the comprehensions; the fascination, absorption, intensity. All almost certain death to creation—(so far).

28 Not because the capacities to create no longer exist, or the need (though for a while, as in any fullness of life, the need may be obscured), but because the circumstances for sustained creation have been almost impossible. The need cannot be first. It can have at best, only part self, part time. (Unless someone else does the nurturing. Read Dorothy Fisher's "Babushka Farnham" in *Fables for Parents.*) More than in any other human relationship, overwhelmingly more, motherhood means being instantly interruptable, responsive, responsible. Children need one *now* (and remember, in our society, the family must often try to be the center for love and health the outside world is not). The very fact that those are real needs, that one feels them as one's own (love, not duty); *that there is no one else responsible for these needs,* gives them primacy. It is distraction, not meditation, that becomes habitual; interruption, not continuity; spasmodic, not constant toil. The rest has been said here. Work interrupted, deferred, relinquished, makes blockage—at best, lesser accomplishment. Unused capacitites atrophy, cease to be.

29 When H. H. Richardson,[18] who wrote the Australian classic *Ultima*

---

[18]The pseudonym of Ethel Florence Richardson (1870–1946), an Australian novelist, translator, and short-story writer.—Ed.

Thule, was asked why she—whose children, like all her people, were so profoundly written—did not herself have children, she answered: "There are enough women to do the childbearing and childrearing. I know of none who can write my books." I remember thinking rebelliously, yes, and I know of none who can bear and rear my children either. But literary history is on her side. Almost no mothers—as almost no part-time, part-self persons—have created enduring literature . . . so far.

30 If I talk now quickly of my own silences—almost presumptuous after what has been told here—it is that the individual experience may add.

31 In the twenty years I bore and reared my children, usually had to work on a paid job as well, the simplest circumstances for creation did not exist. Nevertheless writing, the hope of it, was "the air I breathed, so long as I shall breathe at all." In the hope, there was conscious storing, snatched reading, beginnings of writing, and always "the secret rootlets of reconnaissance."

32 When the youngest of our four was in school, the beginnings struggled toward endings. This was a time, in Kafka's words, "like a squirrel in a cage: bliss of movement, desperation about constriction, craziness of endurance."

33 Bliss of movement. A full extended family life; the world of my job (transcriber in a dairy-equipment company); and the writing, which I was somehow able to carry around within me through work, through home. Time on the bus, even when I had to stand, was enough; the stolen moments at work, enough; the deep night hours for as long as I could stay awake, after the kids were in bed, after the household tasks were done, sometimes during. It is no accident that the first work I considered publishable began: "I stand here ironing, and what you asked me moves tormented back and forth with the iron."

34 In such snatches of time I wrote what I did in those years, but there came a time when this triple life was no longer possible. The fifteen hours of daily realities became too much distraction for the writing. I lost craziness of endurance. What might have been, I don't know; but I applied for, and was given, eight months' writing time. There was still full family life, all the household responsibilities, but I did not have to hold an eight-hour job. I had continuity, three full days, sometimes more—and it was in those months I made the mysterious turn and became a writing writer.

35 Then had to return to the world of work, someone else's work, nine hours, five days a week.

36 This was the time of festering and congestion. For a few months I was able to shield the writing with which I was so full, against the demands of jobs on which I had to be competent, through the joys and responsibilities and trials of family. For a few months. Always roused by the writing, always denied. "I could not go to write it down. It convulsed and died in me. I will pay."

37 My work died. What demanded to be written, did not. It seethed, bubbled, clamored, peopled me. At last moved into the hours meant for sleeping. I worked now full time on temporary jobs, a Kelly, a Western Agency girl (girl!), wandering from office to office, always hoping to manage two, three writing months ahead. Eventually there was time.

38 I had said: always roused by the writing, always denied. Now, like a woman made frigid, I had to learn response, to trust this possibility for fruition that had not been before. Any interruption dazed and silenced me. It took a long while of surrendering to what I was trying to write, of invoking Henry James's "passion, piety, patience," before I was able to re-establish work.

39 When again I had to leave the writing, I lost consciousness. A time of anesthesia. There was still an automatic noting that did not stop, but it was as if writing had never been. No fever, no congestion, no festering. I ceased being peopled, slept well and dreamlessly, took a "permanent" job. The few pieces that had been published seemed to have vanished like the not-yet-written. I wrote someone, unsent: "So long they fed each other—my life, the writing—; —the writing or hope of it, my life—; but now they begin to destroy." I knew, but did not feel the destruction.

40 A Ford grant in literature, awarded me on nomination by others, came almost too late. Time granted does not necessarily coincide with time that can be most fully used, as the congested time of fullness would have been. Still, it was two years.

41 Drowning is not so pitiful as the attempt to rise, says Emily Dickinson. I do not agree, but I know whereof she speaks. For a long time I was that emaciated survivor trembling on the beach, unable to rise and walk. Said differently, I could manage only the feeblest, shallowest growth on that devastated soil. Weeds, to be burned like weeds, or used as compost. When the habits of creation were at last rewon, one book went to the publisher, and I dared to begin my present work. It became my center, engraved on it: "Evil is whatever distracts." (By now had begun a cost to our family life, to my own participation in life as a human being.) I shall not tell the "rest, residue, and remainder" of what I was "leased, demised, and let unto" when once again I had to leave work at the flood to return to the Time-Master, to business-ese and legalese. This most harmful of all my silences has ended, but I am not yet recovered; may still be a one-book silence.

42 However that will be, we are in a time of more and more hidden and foreground silences, women *and* men. Denied full writing life, more may try to "nurse through night" (that part-time, part-self night) "the ethereal spark," but it seems to me there would almost have had to be "flame on flame" first; and time as needed, afterwards; and enough of the self, the capacities, undamaged for the rebeginnings on the frightful task. I would like to believe this for what has not yet been written into literature. But it cannot reconcile for what is lost by unnatural silences.

Word Study List

fructification	8	reconnaissance	31
Gethsemane	9	anesthesia	39
atrophy	12, 28	emaciated	41
stratagems	14	ethereal	42
presumptuous	30		

Questions

1. Why is Olsen particularly interested in the silences—the periods of non-creativity—in the lives of writers?

2. What question does she seek to answer in her exploration of the lives, journals, and letters of certain writers?

3. Express in your own words the circumstances and environment needed for writing as explained by Balzac, Rilke, Conrad, James, and Kafka. How does Olsen's life demonstrate the wisdom of their observations?

4. How have the circumstances needed for full creativity particularly affected women? What changes in life style in the twentieth century have made a female writer's life even more difficult?

5. Why does Olsen call these silences "unnatural"? What, then, would constitute natural silences?

6. What is the attitude toward the writing task held by Olsen and those she quotes? That is, do they see the task as easy or hard? As pleasurable or painful?

7. What can we, as part-time writers, learn from Olsen and the writers she discusses?

Exercises

1. What kind of environment do you seek for your periods of writing? Do you write in your room? In the library? At a friend's place? Do you work in silence? With music? Do you tolerate—or seek—interruptions? Do you usually write in the same place? Give some thought to the characteristics of your writing environment and then, in a paragraph, explain why you think it is—or is not—conducive to "full creation."

2. Olsen mentions many important and some lesser-known writers. Select one writer you do not know and find a biographical essay on him or her.

(For dead British writers, use the *Dictionary of National Biography;* for dead American writers, use the *Dictionary of American Biography;* for living writers, use *Who's Who* (British), *Who's Who in America,* or *Contemporary Authors.* You will find these volumes in the reference area of your library.) Be prepared to report to the class on the most significant facts of the writer's life and works.

Why I Write

Joan Didion

A prolific author of both fiction and nonfiction, Joan Didion (b. 1934) has written several novels, including *Play It as It Lays* (1970) and *Democracy* (1984), and a work of political analysis, *Salvador* (1983). She is also well known for her essays, many of which have been collected in *The White Album* (1979) and *Slouching Towards Bethlehem* (1968). The following essay, adapted from a lecture delivered at Berkeley, was first published on December 6, 1976, in the *New York Times Book Review* section.

Through a forceful expression of her reasons for being a writer, Didion gives us insight into a writer's ways of thinking and feeling.

1 Of course I stole the title for this talk, from George Orwell. One reason I stole it was that I like the sound of the words: Why I Write. There you have three short unambiguous words that share a sound, and the sound they share is this:

I
I
I

2 In many ways writing is the act of saying *I,* of imposing oneself upon other people, of saying *listen to me, see it my way, change your mind.* It's an aggressive, even a hostile act. You can disguise its aggressiveness all you want with veils of subordinate clauses and qualifiers and tentative subjunctives, with ellipses and evasions—with the whole manner of intimating rather than claiming, of alluding rather than stating—but there's no getting around the fact that setting words on paper is the tactic of a secret bully, an invasion, an imposition of the writer's sensibility on the reader's most private space.

3 I stole the title not only because the words sounded right but because they seemed to sum up, in a no-nonsense way, all I have to tell you. Like many writers I have only this one "subject," this one "area": the act of writing. I can bring you no reports from any other front. I may have other interests: I am "interested," for example, in marine biology,

but I don't flatter myself that you would come out to hear me talk about it. I am not a scholar. I am not in the least an intellectual, which is not to say that when I hear the word "intellectual" I reach for my gun, but only to say that I do not think in abstracts. During the years when I was an undergraduate at Berkeley I tried, with a kind of hopeless late-adolescent energy, to buy some temporary visa into the world of ideas, to forge for myself a mind that could deal with the abstract.

4 In short I tried to think. I failed. My attention veered inexorably back to the specific, to the tangible, to what was generally considered, by everyone I knew then and for that matter have known since, the peripheral. I would try to contemplate the Hegelian dialectic[1] and would find myself concentrating instead on a flowering pear tree outside my window and the particular way the petals fell on my floor. I would try to read linguistic theory and would find myself wondering instead if the lights were on in the bevatron up the hill. When I say that I was wondering if the lights were on in the bevatron you might immediately suspect, if you deal in ideas at all, that I was registering the bevatron as a political symbol, thinking in shorthand about the military-industrial complex and its role in the university community, but you would be wrong. I was only wondering if the lights were on in the bevatron, and how they looked. A physical fact.

5 I had trouble graduating from Berkeley, not because of this inability to deal with ideas—I was majoring in English, and I could locate the house-and-garden imagery in *The Portrait of a Lady*[2] as well as the next person, "imagery" being by definition the kind of specific that got my attention—but simply because I had neglected to take a course in Milton.[3] For reasons which now sound baroque I needed a degree by the end of that summer, and the English department finally agreed, if I would come down from Sacramento every Friday and talk about the cosmology of *Paradise Lost,* to certify me proficient in Milton. I did this. Some Fridays I took the Greyhound bus, other Fridays I caught the Southern Pacific's City of San Francisco on the last leg of its transcontinental trip. I can no longer tell you whether Milton put the sun or the earth at the center of his universe in *Paradise Lost,* the central question of at least one century and a topic about which I wrote 10,000 words that summer, but I can still recall the exact rancidity of the butter in the City of San Francisco's dining car, and the way the tinted windows on the Greyhound bus cast the oil refineries around Carquinez Straits into a grayed and obscurely sinister light. In short my attention was always on the periphery, on what I could see and taste and touch, on the butter, and the Greyhound bus. During those years I was traveling on what I knew to be a very shaky passport,

---

[1]A process whereby a higher form of truth is obtained by the synthesis of an idea with its opposite, according to the German philosopher Hegel (1770–1831).—ED.

[2]A novel by Henry James.—ED.

[3]Seventeenth-century English poet.—ED.

forged papers: I knew that I was no legitimate resident in any world of ideas. I knew I couldn't think. All I knew then was what I couldn't do. All I knew then was what I wasn't, and it took me some years to discover what I was.

6 Which was a writer.

7 By which I mean not a "good"writer or a "bad" writer but simply a writer, a person whose most absorbed and passionate hours are spent arranging words on pieces of paper. Had my credentials been in order I would never have become a writer. Had I been blessed with even limited access to my own mind there would have been no reason to write. I write entirely to find out what I'm thinking, what I'm looking at, what I see and what it means. What I want and what I fear. Why did the oil refineries around Carquinez Straits seem sinister to me in the summer of 1956? Why have the night lights in the bevatron burned in my mind for twenty years? *What is going on in these pictures in my mind?*

8 When I talk about pictures in my mind I am talking, quite specifically, about images that shimmer around the edges. There used to be an illustration in every elementary psychology book showing a cat drawn by a patient in varying stages of schizophrenia. This cat had a shimmer around it. You could see the molecular structure breaking down at the very edges of the cat: the cat became the background and the background the cat, everything interacting, exchanging ions. People on hallucinogens describe the same perception of objects. I'm not a schizophrenic, nor do I take hallucinogens, but certain images do shimmer for me. Look hard enough, and you can't miss the shimmer. It's there. You can't think too much about these pictures that shimmer. You just lie low and let them develop. You stay quiet. You don't talk to many people and you keep your nervous system from shorting out and you try to locate the cat in the shimmer, the grammar in the picture.

9 Just as I meant "shimmer" literally I mean "grammar" literally. Grammar is a piano I play by ear, since I seem to have been out of school the year the rules were mentioned. All I know about grammar is its infinite power. To shift the structure of a sentence alters the meaning of that sentence, as definitely and inflexibly as the position of a camera alters the meaning of the object photographed. Many people know about camera angles now, but not so many know about sentences. The arrangement of the words matters, and the arrangement you want can be found in the picture in your mind. The picture dictates the arrangement. The picture dictates whether this will be a sentence with or without clauses, a sentence that ends hard or a dying-fall sentence, long or short, active or passive. The picture tells you how to arrange the words and the arrangement of the words tells you, or tells me, what's going on in the picture. *Nota bene:*[4]

10 It tells you.

---

[4]Latin phrase meaning "note well."—ED.

11 You don't tell it.

12 Let me show you what I mean by pictures in the mind. I began *Play It as It Lays* just as I have begun each of my novels, with no notion of "character" or "plot" or even "incident." I had only two pictures in my mind, more about which later, and a technical intention, which was to write a novel so elliptical and fast that it would be over before you noticed it, a novel so fast that it would scarcely exist on the page at all. About the pictures: the first was of white space. Empty space. This was clearly the picture that dictated the narrative intention of the book—a book in which anything that happened would happen off the page, a "white" book to which the reader would have to bring his or her own bad dreams—and yet this picture told me no "story," suggested no situation. The second picture did. This second picture was of something actually witnessed. A young woman with long hair and a short white halter dress walks through the casino at the Riviera in Las Vegas at one in the morning. She crosses the casino alone and picks up a house telephone. I watch her because I have heard her paged, and recognize her name: she is a minor actress I see around Los Angeles from time to time, in places like Jax and once in a gynecologist's office in the Beverly Hills Clinic, but have never met. I know nothing about her. Who is paging her? Why is she here to be paged? How exactly did she come to this? It was precisely this moment in Las Vegas that made *Play It as It Lays* begin to tell itself to me, but the moment appears in the novel only obliquely, in a chapter which begins:

13 "Maria made a list of things she would never do. She would never: walk through the Sands or Caesar's alone after midnight. She would never: ball at a party, do S-M unless she wanted to, borrow furs from Abe Lipsey, deal. She would never: carry a Yorkshire in Beverly Hills."

14 That is the beginning of the chapter and that is also the end of the chapter, which may suggest what I meant by "white space."

15 I recall having a number of pictures in my mind when I began the novel I just finished, *A Book of Common Prayer.* As a matter of fact one of these pictures was of that bevatron I mentioned, although I would be hard put to tell you a story in which nuclear energy figures. Another was a newspaper photograph of a hijacked 707 burning on the desert in the Middle East. Another was the night view from a room in which I once spent a week with paratyphoid, a hotel room on the Colombian coast. My husband and I seemed to be on the Colombian coast representing the United States of America at a film festival (I recall invoking the name "Jack Valenti"[5] a lot, as if its reiteration could make me well), and it was a bad place to have fever, not only because my indisposition offended our hosts but because every night in this hotel the generator failed. The lights went out. The elevator stopped. My husband would go to the event of the

---

[5]President, since 1966, of the Motion Picture Association of America.—Ed.

evening and make excuses for me and I would stay alone in this hotel room, in the dark. I remember standing at the window trying to call Bogotá (the telphone seemed to work on the same principle as the generator) and watching the night wind come up and wondering what I was doing eleven degrees off the equator with a fever of 103. The view from that window definitely figures in *A Book of Common Prayer,* as does the burning 707, and yet none of these pictures told me the story I needed.

16 The picture that did, the picture that shimmered and made these other images coalesce, was the Panama airport at 6 A.M. I was in this airport only once, on a plane to Bogotá that stopped for an hour to refuel, but the way it looked that morning remained superimposed on everything I saw until the day I finished *A Book of Common Prayer.* I lived in that airport for several years. I can still feel the hot air when I step off the plane, can see the heat already rising off the tarmac at 6 A.M. I can feel my skirt damp and wrinkled on my legs. I can feel the asphalt stick to my sandals. I remember the big tail of a Pan American plane floating motionless down at the end of the tarmac. I remember the sound of a slot machine in the waiting room. I could tell you that I remember a particular woman in the airport, an American woman, a *norteamericana,* a thin *norteamericana* about forty who wore a big square emerald in lieu of a wedding ring, but there was no such woman there.

17 I put this woman in the airport later. I made this woman up, just as I later made up a country to put the airport in, and a family to run the country. This woman in the airport is neither catching a plane nor meeting one. She is ordering tea in the airport coffee shop. In fact she is not simply "ordering" tea but insisting that the water be boiled, in front of her, for twenty minutes. Why is this woman in this airport? Why is she going nowhere, where has she been? Where did she get that big emerald? What derangement, or disassociation, makes her believe that her will to see the water boiled can possibly prevail?

18 "She had been going to one airport or another for four months, one could see it, looking at the visas on her passport. All those airports where Charlotte Douglas's passport had been stamped would have looked alike. Sometimes the sign on the tower would say "Bienvenidos" and sometimes the sign on the tower would say "Bienvenue," some places were wet and hot and others dry and hot, but at each of these airports the pastel concrete walls would rust and stain and the swamp off the runway would be littered with the fuselages of cannibalized Fairchild F-227's and the water would need boiling.

19 "I knew why Charlotte went to the airport even if Victor did not.

20 "I knew about airports."

21 These lines appear about halfway through *A Book of Common Prayer,* but I wrote them during the second week I worked on the book, long before I had any idea where Charlotte Douglas had been or why she went to airports. Until I wrote these lines I had no character called "Victor" in

mind: the necessity for mentioning a name, and the name "Victor," occurred to me as I wrote the sentence. *I knew why Charlotte went to the airport* sounded incomplete. *I knew why Charlotte went to the airport even if Victor did not* carried a little more narrative drive. Most important of all, until I wrote these lines I did not know who "I" was, who was telling the story. I had intended until that that the "I" be no more than the voice of the author, a nineteenth-century omniscient narrator. But there it was:

22 "I knew why Charlotte went to the airport even if Victor did not.

23 "I knew about airports."

24 This "I" was the voice of no author in my house. This "I" was someone who not only knew why Charlotte went to the airport but also knew someone called "Victor." Who was Victor? Who was this narrator? Why was this narrator telling me this story? Let me tell you one thing about why writers write: had I known the answer to any of these questions I would never have needed to write a novel.

Word Study List

ellipses	2	rancidity	5
intimating	2	hallucinogens	8
inexorably	4	elliptical	12
peripheral	4	obliquely	12
linguistic	4	paratyphoid	15
bevatron	4	coalesce	16
baroque	5		

Questions

1. What kind of act, according to Didion, is the act of writing?

2. Why is Didion not an intellectual? What gets her attention?

3. What is Didion's definition of a writer? Are you surprised by her definition? How would you have defined a writer?

4. By discussing parts of her novels, Didion reveals her writing process. What does she start with? Why does she want to arrange words into sentences? What questions does she want to answer?

5. Although Didion apparently begins her novels with a cluster of images, we know from writers' notebooks available to us that some novelists do begin with character or plot. How might what a writer starts with affect the kind of novel (or short story or poem) that is written? What differences in emphasis or focus might result from differences in the writer's point of departure?

6. When discussing getting her pictures into words, Didion draws an effective comparison. Differing arrangements of words in a sentence are compared to what? How does this comparison help us understand the importance of sentence structure?

7. Didion says that the picture in the writer's mind should determine the wording of the sentence designed to describe it. But is writing that uncomplicated a process? What else determines the words we choose and the ways we arrange them in sentences?

Exercise

Didion knows herself as a writer; how well do you know yourself as a writer? For ten or fifteen minutes, brainstorm about yourself, using the following questions as guidelines:

1. On what occasions and for what reasons do you most frequently write?

2. What is most important to you when you write? To persuade others to your way of thinking? To express feelings? To capture an image? To learn about yourself?

3. Does the process of writing give you pleasure, or do you get more pleasure from finishing, from having written?

4. Do you prefer writing description? Developing an idea logically? Pleading forcefully for a cause?

The Exact Location of the Soul

Richard Selzer

In private practice in general surgery since 1960, Richard Selzer (b. 1928) has also received attention for his short stories (*Rituals of Surgery,* 1974) and essays (*Mortal Lessons,* 1976, and *Letters to a Young Doctor,* 1982). While continuing to write essays and stories, he is at work as well on a mythological treatment of the Civil War. The following essay is from *Mortal Lessons.*

1 Someone asked me why a surgeon would write. Why, when the shelves are already too full? They sag under the deadweight of books. To add a single adverb is to risk exceeding the strength of the boards. A sur-

geon should abstain. A surgeon, whose fingers are more at home in the steamy gullies of the body than they are tapping the dry keys of a typewriter. A surgeon, who feels the slow slide of intestines against the back of his hand and is no more alarmed than were a family of snakes taking their comfort from such an indolent rubbing. A surgeon, who palms the human heart as though it were some captured bird.

2 Why should he write? Is it vanity that urges him? There is glory enough in the knife. Is it for money? One can make too much money. No. It is to search for some meaning in the ritual of surgery, which is at once murderous, painful, healing, and full of love. It is a devilish hard thing to transmit—to find, even. Perhaps if one were to cut out a heart, a lobe of the liver, a single convolution of the brain, and paste it to a page, it would speak with more eloquence than all the words of Balzac. Such a piece would need no literary style, no mass of erudition or history, but in its very shape and feel would tell all the frailty and strength, the despair and nobility of man. What? Publish a heart? A little piece of bone? Preposterous. Still I fear that is what it may require to reveal the truth that lies hidden in the body. Not all the undressings of Rabelais,[1] Chekhov,[2] or even William Carlos Williams[3] have wrested it free, although God knows each one of those doctors made a heroic assault upon it.

3 I have come to believe that it is the flesh alone that counts. The rest is that with which we distract ourselves when we are not hungry or cold, in pain or ecstasy. In the recesses of the body I search for the philosophers' stone. I know it is there, hidden in the deepest, dampest cul-de-sac. It awaits discovery. To find it would be like the harnessing of fire. It would illuminate the world. Such a quest is not without pain. Who can gaze on so much misery and feel no hurt? Emerson[4] has written that the poet is the only true doctor. I believe him, for the poet, lacking the impediment of speech with which the rest of us are afflicted, gazes, records, diagnoses, and prophesies.

4 I invited a young diabetic woman to the operating room to amputate her leg. She could not see the great shaggy black ulcer upon her foot and ankle that threatened to encroach upon the rest of her body, for she was blind as well. There upon her foot was a Mississippi Delta brimming with corruption, sending its raw tributaries down between her toes. Gone were all the little web spaces that when fresh and whole are such a delight to loving men. She could not see her wound, but she could feel it. There is no pain like that of the bloodless limb turned rotten and festering. There

[1]A satirical French writer and physician (1494?–1553).—ED.

[2]A Russian dramatist and short-story writer (1860–1904) who was also a physician.—ED.

[3]American poet and physician (1883–1963).—ED.

[4]American poet and essayist (1803–1882). He was chief spokesman for American transcendentalism.—ED.

is neither unguent nor anodyne to kill such a pain yet leave intact the body.

5 For over a year I trimmed away the putrid flesh, cleansed, anointed, and dressed the foot, staving off, delaying. Three times each week, in her darkness, she sat upon my table, rocking back and forth, holding her extended leg by the thigh, gripping it as though it were a rocket that must be steadied lest it explode and scatter her toes about the room. And I would cut away a bit here, a bit there, of the swollen blue leather that was her tissue.

6 At last we gave up, she and I. We could no longer run ahead of the gangrene. We had not the legs for it. There must be an amputation in order that she might live—and I as well. It was to heal us both that I must take up knife and saw, and cut the leg off. And when I could feel it drop from her body to the table, see the blessed *space* appear between her and that leg, I too would be well.

7 Now it is the day of the operation. I stand by while the anesthetist administers the drugs, watch as the tense familiar body relaxes into narcosis. I turn then to uncover the leg. There, upon her kneecap, she has drawn, blindly, upside down for me to see, a face; just a circle with two ears, two eyes, a nose, and a smiling upturned mouth. Under it she has printed SMILE, DOCTOR. Minutes later I listen to the sound of the saw, until a little crack at the end tells me it is done.

8 So, I have learned that man is not ugly, but that he is Beauty itself. There is no other his equal. Are we not all dying, none faster or more slowly than any other? I have become receptive to the possibilities of love (for it is love, this thing that happens in the operating room), and each day I wait, trembling in the busy air. Perhaps today it will come. Perhaps today I will find it, take part in it, this love that blooms in the stoniest desert.

9 All through literature the doctor is portrayed as a figure of fun. Shaw[5] was splenetic about him; Molière[6] delighted in pricking his pompous medicine men, and well they deserved it. The doctor is ripe for caricature. But I believe that the truly great writing about doctors has not yet been done. I think it must be done *by* a doctor, one who is through with the love affair with his technique, who recognizes that he has played Narcissus, raining kisses on a mirror, and who now, out of the impacted masses of his guilt, has expanded into self-doubt, and finally into the high state of wonderment. Perhaps he will be a nonbeliever who, after a life-

[5]An Irish-born English dramatist (1856–1950) who satirized the medical profession in *The Doctor's Dilemma.*—ED.

[6]The pen name of Jean-Baptiste Poquelin (1622–1673), a French dramatist who satirizes doctors in *The Physician in Spite of Himself.*—ED.

time of grand gestures and mighty deeds, comes upon the knowledge that he has done no more than meddle in the lives of his fellows, and that he has done at least as much harm as good. Yet he may continue to pretend, at least, that there is nothing to fear, that death will not come, so long as people depend on his authority. Later, after his patients have left, he may closet himself in his darkened office, sweating and afraid.

10 There is a story by Unamuno[7] in which a priest, living in a small Spanish village, is adored by all the people for his piety, kindness, and the majesty with which he celebrates the Mass each Sunday. To them he is already a saint. It is a foregone conclusion, and they speak of him as Saint Immanuel. He helps them with their plowing and planting, tends them when they are sick, confesses them, comforts them in death, and every Sunday, in his rich, thrilling voice, transports them to paradise with his chanting. The fact is that Don Immanuel is not so much a saint as a martyr. Long ago his own faith left him. He is an atheist, a good man doomed to suffer the life of a hypocrite, pretending to a faith he does not have. As he raises the chalice of wine, his hands tremble, and a cold sweat pours from him. He cannot stop for he knows that the people need this of him, that their need is greater than his sacrifice. Still . . . still . . . could it be that Don Immanuel's whole life is a kind of prayer, a paean to God?

11 A writing doctor would treat men and women with equal reverence, for what is the "liberation" of either sex to him who knows the diagrams, the inner geographies of each? I love the solid heft of men as much as I adore the heated capaciousness of women—women in whose penetralia is found the repository of existence. I would have them glory in that. Women are physics and chemistry. They are matter. It is their bodies that tell of the frailty of men. Men have not their cellular, enzymatic wisdom. Man is albuminoid, proteinaceous, laked pearl; woman is yolky, ovoid, rich. Both are exuberant bloody growths. I would use the defects and deformities of each for my sacred purpose of writing, for I know that it is the marred and scarred and faulty that are subject to grace. I would seek the soul in the facts of animal economy and profligacy. Yes, it is the exact location of the soul that I am after. The smell of it is in my nostrils. I have caught glimpses of it in the body diseased. If only I could tell it. Is there no mathematical equation that can guide me? So much pain and pus equals so much truth? It is elusive as the whippoorwill that one hears calling incessantly from out the night window, but which, nesting as it does low in the brush, no one sees. No one but the poet, for he sees what no one else can. He was born with the eye for it.

12 Once I thought I had it: Ten o'clock one night, the end room off a long corridor in a college infirmary, my last patient of the day, degree of

[7]Spanish philosopher, poet, and essayist (1864–1936).—Ed.

exhaustion suitable for the appearance of a vision, some manifestation. The patient is a young man recently returned from Guatemala, from the excavation of Mayan ruins. His left upper arm wears a gauze dressing which, when removed, reveals a clean punched-out hole the size of a dime. The tissues about the opening are swollen and tense. A thin brownish fluid lips the edge, and now and then a lazy drop of the overflow spills down the arm. An abscess, inadequately drained. I will enlarge the opening to allow better egress of the pus. Nurse, will you get me a scalpel and some . . . ?

13 What happens next is enough to lay Francis Drake[8] avomit in his cabin. No explorer ever stared in wilder surmise than I into that crater from which there now emerges a narrow gray head whose sole distinguishing feature is a pair of black pincers. The head sits atop a longish flexible neck arching now this way, now that, testing the air. Alternately it folds back upon itself, then advances in new boldness. And all the while, with dreadful rhythmicity, the unspeakable pincers open and close. Abscess? Pus? Never. Here is the lair of a beast at whose malignant purpose I could but guess. A Mayan devil, I think, that would soon burst free to fly about the room, with horrid blanket-wings and iridescent scales, raking, pinching, injecting God knows what acid juice. And even now the irony does not escape me, the irony of my patient as excavator excavated.

14 With all the ritual deliberation of a high priest I advance a surgical clamp toward the hole. The surgeon's heart is become a bat hanging upside down from his rib cage. The rim achieved—now thrust—and the ratchets of the clamp close upon the empty air. The devil has retracted. Evil mocking laughter bangs back and forth in the brain. More stealth. Lying in wait. One must skulk. Minutes pass, perhaps an hour. . . . A faint disturbance in the lake, and once again the thing upraises, farther and farther, hovering. Acrouch, strung, the surgeon is one with his instrument; there is no longer any boundary between its metal and his flesh. They are joined in a single perfect tool of extirpation. It is just for this that he was born. Now—thrust—and clamp—and *yes.* Got him!

15 Transmitted to the fingers comes the wild thrashing of the creature. Pinned and wriggling, he is mine. I hear the dry brittle scream of the dragon, and a hatred seizes me, but such a detestation as would make of Iago[9] a drooling sucktit. It is the demented hatred of the victor for the vanquished, the warden for his prisoner. It is the hatred of fear. Within the jaws of my hemostat is the whole of the evil of the world, the dark concentrate itself, and I shall kill it. For mankind. And, in so doing, will open the way into a thousand years of perfect peace. Here is Surgeon as Savior indeed.

---

[8]English navigator (1540?–1596) who sailed around the world.—Ed.

[9]A cruelly evil character in Shakespeare's *Othello.*—Ed.

16 Tight grip now . . . steady, relentless pull. How it scrabbles to keep its tentacle-hold. With an abrupt moist plop the extraction is complete. There, writhing in the teeth of the clamp, is a dirty gray body, the size and shape of an English walnut. He is hung everywhere with tiny black hooklets. Quickly . . . into the specimen jar of saline . . . the lid screwed tight. Crazily he swims round and round, wiping his slimy head against the glass, then slowly sinks to the bottom, the mass of hooks in frantic agonal wave.

17 "You are going to be all right," I say to my patient. "We are *all* going to be all right from now on."

18 The next day I take the jar to the medical school. "That's the larva of the botfly," says a pathologist. "The fly usually bites a cow and deposits its eggs beneath the skin. There, the egg develops into the larval form which, when ready, burrows its way to the outside through the hide and falls to the ground. In time it matures into a full-grown botfly. This one happened to bite a man. It was about to come out on its own, and, of course, it would have died."

19 The words *imposter, sorehead, servant of Satan* spring to my lips. But now he has been joined by other scientists. They nod in agreement. I gaze from one gray eminence to another, and know the mallet-blow of glory pulverized. I tried to save the world, but it didn't work out.

20 No, it is not the surgeon who is God's darling. He is the victim of vanity. It is the poet who heals with his words, stanches the flow of blood, stills the rattling breath, applies poultice to the scalded flesh.

21 Did you ask me why a surgeon writes? I think it is because I wish to be a doctor.

Word Study List

convolution	2	albumenoid	11
erudition	2	proteinaceous	11
impediment	3	ovoid	11
unguent	4	egress	12
anodyne	4	ratchets	14
narcosis	7	extirpation	14
Narcissus	9	sucktit	15
paean	10	hemostat	15
capaciousness	11	agonal	16
penetralia	11	poultice	20

Questions

1. What is Selzer's reason for writing? (See paragraph 2.) What, exactly, is he looking for? (See paragraph 11.)

2. What reasons for writing does he reject?

3. Who, for Selzer, best understands the meaning of life?

4. Selzer is right in saying that writers have satirized doctors in literature. Why do you suppose doctors have often been ridiculed? What seems to be our attitude toward doctors today? Can you account for this attitude?

5. Selzer sees irony in the young man who has been excavating Mayan ruins having a "Mayan devil" or botfly in his arm. Explain the irony of the "excavator excavated."

6. Why does Selzer experience the "mallet-blow of glory pulverized"?

7. Explain Selzer's concluding statement.

Exercise

Not all writers write for the same reasons. Read Didion's "Why I Write" (pp. 77–82) and be prepared to explain how Didion's and Selzer's reasons for writing differ. Also, decide which writer's reasons seem closer to your reasons for writing and be prepared to explain why you identify more closely with one than the other.

On Being Female, Black, and Free

Margaret Walker

A professor of English at Jackson State College since 1949, Margaret Walker (b. 1915) has been awarded honorary degrees and awards in recognition of her writing, especially her poetry. Collections of her poems include *Prophets for a New Day* (1970) and *October Journey* (1973). The following piece was written for a collection of essays, *The Writer on Her Work,* edited by Janet Sternburg and published in 1980.

In her article, Walker shares with us the joy and the pain of being a black female writer in America.

1 My birth certificate reads female, Negro, date of birth and place. Call it fate or circumstance, this is my human condition. I have no wish to change it from being female, black, and free. I like being a woman. I have a proud black heritage, and I have learned from the difficult exigencies of life that freedom is a philosophical state of mind and existence.

The mind is the only place where I can exist and feel free. In my mind I am absolutely free.

2 My entire career of writing, teaching, lecturing, yes, and raising a family is determined by these immutable facts of my human condition. As a daughter, a sister, a sweetheart, a wife, a mother, and now a grandmother, my sex or gender is preeminent, important, and almost entirely deterministic. Maybe my glands have something to do with my occupation as a creative person. About this, I am none too sure, but I think the cycle of life has much to do with the creative impulse and the biorhythms of life must certainly affect everything we do.

3 Creativity cannot exist without the feminine principle, and I am sure God is not merely male or female but He-She—our Father-Mother God. All nature reflects this rhythmic and creative principle of feminism and femininity: the sea, the earth, the air, fire, and all life whether plant or animal. Even as they die, are born, grow, reproduce, and grow old in their cyclic time, so do we in lunar, solar, planetary cycles of meaning and change.

4 Ever since I was a little girl I have wanted to write and I have been writing. My father told my mother it was only a puberty urge and would not last, but he encouraged my early attempts at rhyming verses just the same, and he gave me the notebook or daybook in which to keep my poems together. When I was eighteen and had ended my junior year in college, my father laughingly agreed it was probably more than a puberty urge. I had filled the 365 pages with poems.

5 Writing has always been a means of expression for me and for other black Americans who are just like me, who feel, too, the need for freedom in this "home of the brave, and land of the free." From the first, writing meant learning the craft and developing the art. Going to school had one major goal, to learn to be a writer. As early as my eighth year I had the desire, at ten I was trying, at eleven and twelve I was learning, and at fourteen and fifteen I was seeing my first things printed in local school and community papers. I have copies of a poem published in 1930 and an article with the caption, "What Is to Become of Us?" which appeared in 1931 or 1932. All of this happened before I went to Northwestern.

6 I spent fifteen years becoming a poet before my first book appeared in 1942. I was learning my craft, finding my voice, seeking discipline as life imposes and superimposes that discipline upon the artist. Perhaps my home environment was most important in the early stages—hearing my mother's music, my sister and brother playing the piano, reading my father's books, hearing his sermons, and trying every day to write a poem. Meanwhile, I found I would have to start all over again and learn how to write prose fiction in order to write the novel I was determined to create to the best of my ability and thus fulfill my promise to my grandmother. A novel is not written exactly the same way as a poem, especially a long novel and a short poem. The creative process may be basically the

same—that is, the thinking or conceptualization—but the techniques, elements, and form or craft are decidely and distinctively different.

7 It has always been my feeling that writing must come out of living, and the writer is no more than his personality endures in the crucible of his times. As a woman, I have come through the fires of hell because I am a black woman, because I am poor, because I live in America, and because I am determined to be both a creative artist and maintain my inner integrity and my instinctive need to be free.

8 I don't think I noticed the extreme discrimination against women while I was growing up in the South. The economic struggle to exist and the racial dilemma occupied all my thinking until I was more than an adult woman. My mother had undergone all kinds of discrimination in academia because of her sex; so have my sisters. Only after I went back to school and earned a doctorate did I begin to notice discrimination against me as a woman. It seems the higher you try to climb, the more rarefied the air, the more obstacles appear. I realize I had been naïve, that the issues had not been obvious and that as early as my first employment I felt the sting of discrimination because I am female.

9 I think it took the women's movement to call my attention to cases of overt discrimination that hark back to my WPA days on the Writer's Project. It did not occur to me that Richard Wright[1] as a supervisor on the project made $125 per month and that he claimed no formal education, but that I had just graduated from Northwestern University and I was a junior writer making $85 per month. I had no ambitions to be an administrator; I was too glad to have a job; I did not think about it. Now I remember the intense antagonism on the project toward the hiring of a black woman as a supervisor, none other than the famous Katherine Dunham,[2] the dancer, but it never occurred to me then that she was undergoing double discrimination.

10 When I first went to Iowa and received my master's degree that year there were at least five or six women teaching English in the university. When I returned to study for the doctorate, not a single woman was in the department. At Northwestern my only woman teacher had taught personal hygiene. I did not expect to find women at Yale, but it slowly dawned on me that black women in black colleges were more numerous than white women in coed white universities.

11 And then I began looking through the pages of books of American and English literature that I was teaching, trying in vain to find the works of many women writers. I have read so many of those great women writers of the world—poets, novelists, and playwrights: Sigrid Undset[3] and Selma

---

[1]Black American novelist, short-story writer, poet, (1908–1960); author of *Native Son.*—Ed.

[2]Black American professional dancer and director of schools of dance (b. 1910).—Ed.

[3]Prominent Scandinavian novelist (1882–1949).—Ed.

Lagerlof,[4] Jane Austen,[5] George Sand,[6] George Eliot,[7] and Colette.[8] All through the ages women have been writing and publishing, black and white women in America and all over the world. A few women stand out as geniuses of their times, but those are all too few. Even the women who survive and are printed, published, taught and studied in the classroom fall victim to negative male literary criticism. Black women suffer damages at the hands of every male literary critic, whether he is black or white. Occasionally a man grudgingly admits that some woman writes well, but only rarely.

12 Despite severe illness and painful poverty, and despite jobs that always discriminated against me as a woman—never paying me equal money for equal work, always threatening or replacing me with a man or men who were neither as well educated nor experienced but just men—despite all these examples of discrimination I have managed to work toward being a self-fulfilling, re-creating, reproducing woman, raising a family, writing poetry, cooking food, doing all the creative things I know how to do and enjoy. But my problems have not been simple; they have been manifold. Being female, black, and poor in America means I was born with three strikes against me. I am considered at the bottom of the social class-caste system in these United States, born low on the totem pole. If "a black man has no rights that a white man is bound to respect," what about a black woman?

13 Racism is so extreme and so pervasive in our American society that no black individual lives in an atmosphere of freedom. The world of physical phenomena is dominated by fear and greed. It consists of pitting the vicious and the avaricious against the naïve, the hunted, the innocent, and the victimized. Power belongs to the strong, and the strong are BIG in more ways than one. No one is more victimized in this white male American society than the black female.

14 There are additional barriers for the black woman in publishing, in literary criticism, and in promotion of her literary wares. It is an insidious fact of racism that the most highly intellectualized, sensitized white person is not always perceptive about the average black mind and feeling, much less the creativity of any black genius. Racism forces white humanity to underestimate the intelligence, emotion, and creativity of black humanity. Very few white Americans are conscious of the myth about race that includes the racial stigmas of inferiority and superiority. They do not understand its true economic and political meaning and therefore fail to

---

[4]Swedish writer (1858–1940) who was important in the revival of romantic literature in Sweden and the first woman to win the Nobel prize for literature.—ED.

[5]English novelist (1775–1817); author of *Pride and Prejudice.*—ED.

[6]Pen name of the French novelist Amandine Aurore Lucie Dupin, Baroness Dudevant (1804–1876).—ED.

[7]Pen name of English novelist Mary Ann Evans (1819–1880).—ED.

[8]French novelist Sidonie Gabrielle Colette (1873–1954).—ED.

understand its social purpose. A black, female person's life as a writer is fraught with conflict, competitive drives, professional rivalries, even danger, and deep frustrations. Only when she escapes to a spiritual world can she find peace, quiet, and hope of freedom. To choose the life of a writer, a black female must arm herself with a fool's courage, foolhardiness, and serious purpose and dedication to the art of writing, strength of will and integrity, because the odds are always against her. The cards are stacked. Once the die is cast, however, there is no turning back.

15 In the first place, the world of imagination in which the writer must live is constantly being invaded by the enemy, the mundane world. Even as the worker in the fires of imagination finds that the world around her is inimical to intellectual activity, to the creative impulse, and to the kind of world in which she must daily exist and also thrive and produce, so, too, she discovers that she must meet that mundane world head-on every day on its own terms. She must either conquer or be conquered.

16 A writer needs certain conditions in which to work and create art. She needs a piece of time; a peace of mind; a quiet place; and a private life.

17 Early in my life I discovered I had to earn my living and I would not be able to eke out the barest existence as a writer. Nobody writes while hungry, sick, tired, and worried. Maybe you can manage with one of these but not all four at one time. Keeping the wolf from the door has been my full-time job for more than forty years. Thirty-six of those years I have spent in the college classroom, and nobody writes to full capacity on a full-time teaching job. My life has been public, active, and busy to the point of constant turmoil, tumult, and trauma. Sometimes the only quiet and private place where I could write a sonnet was in the bathroom, because that was the only room where the door could be locked and no one would intrude. I have written mostly at night in my adult life and especially since I have been married, because I was determined not to neglect any members of my family; so I cooked every meal daily, washed dishes and dirty clothes, and nursed sick babies.

18 I have struggled against dirt and disease as much as I have against sin, which, with my Protestant and Calvinistic background, was always to be abhorred. Every day I have lived, however, I have discovered that the value system with which I was raised is of no value in the society in which I must live. This clash of my ideal with the real, of my dream world with the practical, and the mystical inner life with the sordid and ugly world outside—this clash keeps me on a battlefield, at war, and struggling, even tilting windmills. Always I am determined to overcome adversity, determined to win, determined to be me, myself at my best, always female, always black, and everlastingly free. I think this is always what the woman writer wants to be, herself, inviolate, and whole. Shirley Chisholm,[9] who

[9]Former member of the United States House of Representatives from Brooklyn, New York.—ED.

is also black and female, says she is unbossed and unbought. So am I, and I intend to remain that way. Nobody can tell me what to write because nobody owns me and nobody pulls my strings. I have not been writing to make money or earn my living. I have taught school as my vocation. Writing is my life, but it is an avocation nobody can buy. In this respect I believe I am a free agent, stupid perhaps, but *me* and still free.

19 When I was younger I considered myself an emancipated woman, freed from the shackles of mind and body that typified the Victorian woman, but never would I call myself the liberated woman in today's vernacular; never the bohemian; never the completely free spirit living in free love; never the lesbian sister; always believing in moderation and nothing to excess; never defying convention, never radical enough to defy tradition; not wanting to be called conservative but never moving beyond the bounds of what I consider the greatest liberty within law, the greatest means of freedom with control. I have lived out my female destiny within the bonds of married love. For me, it could not have been otherwise. In the same way I refuse to judge others, for if tolerance is worth anything, love is worth everything. Everyone should dare to love.

20 I am therefore fundamentally and contradictorily three things. I am religious almost to the point of orthodoxy—I go to church, I pray, I believe in the stern dogma and duty of Protestant Christianity; I am radical but I wish to see neither the extreme radical left nor the radical right in control. And I am like the astrological description of a crab, a cancer—quick to retreat into my shell when hurt or attacked. I will wobble around circuitously to find another way out when the way I have chosen has been closed to me. I believe absolutely in the power of my black mind to create, to write, to speak, to witness truth, and to be heard.

21 Enough for a time about being female and black. What about freedom? The question of freedom is an essential subject for any writer. Without freedom, personal and social, to write as one pleases and to express the will of the people, the writer is in bondage. This bondage may seem to be to others outside oneself but closely related by blood or kinship in some human fashion; or this bondage may appear to be to the inimical forces of the society that so impress or repress that individual.

22 For the past twenty years or longer I have constantly come into contact with women writers of many different races, classes, nationalities, and degrees. I look back on more than forty years of such associations. Whether at a cocktail party for Muriel Rukeyser[10] at *Poetry* magazine or at Yaddo where Carson MacCullers,[11] Jean Stafford,[12] Karen Blixen,[13] Car-

---

[10]American poet of social protest (1913–1980) and the author of children's books.—Ed.

[11]American novelist (1917–1967) and the author of *The Heart Is a Lonely Hunter*.—Ed.

[12]American novelist and short-story writer (1915–1979). She won the Pulitzer prize in 1970 for her collected short stories.—Ed.

[13]Danish novelist, short-story writer, and essayist (1885–1962) who published in English under the pseudonym of Isak Dinesen.—Ed.

oline Slade,[14] and Katherine Anne Porter[15] were guests; or meeting Adrienne Rich[16] and Erica Jong[17] in Massachusetts at Amherst, or having some twenty-five of my black sister-poets at a Phillis Wheatley poetry festival here in Mississippi, including many of the young and brilliant geniuses of this generation; or here in Mississippi where I have come to know Eudora Welty[18] and Ellen Douglas,[19] or having women from foreign countries journey to Jackson to see me, women like Rosey Pool[20] from Amsterdam and a young woman writer a few weeks ago from Turkey or Bessie Head[21] from South Africa—all these experiences have made me know and understand the problems of women writers and our search for freedom.

23 For the nonwhite woman writer, whether in Africa, Asia, Latin America, the islands of the Caribbean, or the United States, her destiny as a writer has always seemed bleak. Women in Africa and Asia speak of hunger and famine and lack of clean water at the same time that their countries are riddled with warfare. Arab women and Jewish women think of their children in a world that has no hope of peace. Irish women, Protestant and Catholic, speak of the constant threat of bombs and being blown to bits. The women of southern Africa talk of their lives apart from their husbands and their lives in exile from their homelands because of the racial strife in their countries. A Turkish woman speaks of the daily terrorism in her country, of combing the news each evening to see if there are names known on the list of the murdered.

24 I have read the works of scores of these women. I saw Zora Neale Hurston[22] when I was a child and I know what a hard life she had. I read the words of a dozen black women in the Harlem Renaissance, who despite their genius received only a small success. Langston Hughes[23] translated Gabriela Mistral,[24] and I read her before she won the Nobel Prize for Literature. Hualing Nieh Engle[25] tells of her native China, and my friends in Mexico speak of the unbelievable poverty of their people. Each of these internationally known women writers is my sister in search of an island of freedom. Each is part of me and I am part of her.

---

[14]American novelist (1886–1975).—ED.

[15]American short-story writer (1890–1980) who also wrote the novel *Ship of Fools*.—ED.

[16]Contemporary American poet (b. 1929).—ED.

[17]Contemporary American novelist and poet (b. 1942).—ED.

[18]Southern regional writer of novels, short stories, and poems (b. 1909).—ED.

[19]Twentieth-century American writer of mostly nonfiction.—ED.

[20]A Dutch teacher (1905–1971) who translated and published many black American poets and maintained an extensive correspondence with many who, like Walker, have become famous.—ED.

[21]Contemporary South African novelist (b. 1937), living in Botswana.—ED.

[22]Black American novelist, short-story writer, and folklorist (1903–1968).—ED.

[23]Black American poet, short-story writer, and novelist (1902–1967).—ED.

[24]Chilean poet (1889–1957). She was the first South American to win the Nobel prize for literature.—ED.

[25]Chinese-American author (b. 1925?); wife of the poet Paul Engle.—ED.

25 Writing is a singularly individual matter. At least it has historically been so. Only the creative, original individual working alone has been considered the artist working with the fire of imagination. Today, this appears no longer to be the case. In America, our affluent, electronic, and materalistic society does not respect the imaginative writer regardless of sex, race, color, or creed. It never thought highly of the female worker, whether an Emily Dickinson[26] or Amy Lowell,[27] Phillis Wheatley,[28] or Ellen Glasgow.[29] Our American society has no respect for the literary values of intellectual honesty nor for originality and creativity in the sensitive individual. Books today are managed, being written by a committee and promoted by the conglomerate, corporate structures. Best sellers are designed as commodities to sell in the marketplace before a single word is written. Plastic people who are phony writers pretending to take us into a more humanistic century are quickly designated the paper heroes who are promoted with super-HYPE. Do I sound bitter? A Black Woman Writer who is free? Free to do what? To publish? To be promoted? Of what value is freedom in a money-mad society? What does freedom mean to the racially biased and those bigots who have deep religious prejudices? What is my hope as a woman writer?

26 I am a black woman living in a male-oriented and male-dominated white world. Moreover, I live in an American Empire where the financial tentacles of the American Octopus in the business-banking world extend around the globe, with the multinationals and international conglomerates encircling everybody and impinging on the lives of every single soul. What then are my problems? They are the pressures of a sexist, racist, violent, and most materialistic society. In such a society life is cheap and expendable; honor is a rag to be scorned; and justice is violated. Vice and money control business, the judicial system, government, sports, entertainment, publishing, education, and the church. Every other arm of this hydra-headed monster must render lip service and yeoman support to extend, uphold, and perpetuate the syndicated world-system. The entire world of the press, whether broadcast or print journalism, must acquiesce and render service or be eliminated. And what have I to do with this? How do I operate? How long can I live under fear before I too am blown to bits and must crumble into anonymous dust and nonentity?

27 Now I am sixty-three. I wish I could live the years all over. I am sure I would make the same mistakes and do all the things again exactly the same way. But perhaps I might succeed a little more; and wistfully I hope, too, I might have written more books.

28 What are the critical decisions I must make as a woman, as a writer?

---

[26]American poet (1830–1886).—Ed.

[27]American poet (1874–1925).—Ed.

[28]African-born American slave and poet (1753?–1784).—Ed.

[29]American novelist and short-story writer (1874–1945).—Ed.

They are questions of compromise, and of guilt. They are the answers to the meaning and purpose of all life; questions of the value of life lived half in fear and half in faith, cringing under the whip of tyranny or dying, too, for what one dares to believe and dying with dignity and without fear. I must believe there is more wisdom in a righteous path that leads to death than an ignominious path of living shame; that the writer is still in the avant-garde for Truth and Justice, for Freedom, Peace, and Human Dignity. I must believe that women are still in that humanistic tradition and I must cast my lot with them.

29 Across the world humanity seems in ferment, in war, fighting over land and the control of people's lives; people who are hungry, sick, and suffering, most of all fearful. The traditional and historic role of womankind is ever the role of the healing and annealing hand, whether the outworn modes of nurse, and mother, cook, and sweetheart. As a writer these are still her concerns. These are still the stuff about which she writes, the human condition, the human potential, the human destiny. Her place, let us be reminded, is anywhere she chooses to be, doing what she has to do, creating, healing, and always being herself. Female, Black, and Free, this is what I always want to be.

Word Study List

exigencies	1	vernacular	19
immutable	2	bohemian	19
preeminent	2	conglomerate	25, 26
rarefied	8	expendable	26
avaricious	13	hydra-headed	26
inimical	15, 21	ignominious	28
inviolate	18	annealing	29

Questions

1. Like Godwin, Didion, and Selzer, Walker writes a personal essay, but from her experiences she draws conclusions about our times and about being a writer. What are her three topics? How does she organize her essay around them?

2. What is the connection, according to Walker, between creativity and being female?

3. When did Walker first experience sex discrimination? What is her explanation for her "delayed" experience with this type of discrimination? What attitudes toward women writers has Walker found? Do you think these attitudes continue today? What are your attitudes toward women writers?

4. What conditions are necessary for writing? Did Walker have these conditions? How similar is her list to Tillie Olsen's? (See "Silences," p. 67.)

5. In paragrah 13, Walker writes—in 1980—that "racism is so extreme and so pervasive in our American society that no black individual lives in an atmosphere of freedom." Does this surprise you? Walker says that being female, black, and poor places one at the bottom of the social heap. Does your experience support this observation?

6. What relationship does Walker see between being a female writer, or a minority writer, and freedom? What kind of freedom is Walker talking about? What does she think women, especially, can offer our times?

Exercise

Like Tillie Olsen, Walker refers to many writers, some well known, others obscure. Select one writer you do not know and prepare a class report on the significant facts of that writer's life and works. See page 77 for advice on completing this assignment.

Student Essay: Personal Experience

Writer's Paralysis

Attention-getting opening

Many people experience sheer panic when they sit down to write. One blank piece of paper has more power to induce terror than a dozen horror movies. They stare at the paper. The paper stares back. The paper wins. At this point, they do one of two things—leave the field of battle to do nearly anything else (the Great Wall of China and the Egyptian pyramids were probably built by people who were putting off writing an essay) or sit, unable to move or write. In either case, the writing never begins.

Thesis

This problem is not limited to student writers, but also afflicts professionals. It's called writer's paralysis. Fortunately, writer's paralysis is not incurable, and there are effective techniques to help you successfully cope with it.

Causes of writer's paralysis

What causes writer's paralysis? Perhaps if you view the question in a more general way, you will discover that you already have the answer. Why do people hesitate on the edge of a diving board? Why do people stop before entering a crowded room? Why do they put off talking to teachers about completing missed assignments? Nervousness and fear usually cause the reluctance. The water seems impossibly far away, the party is doing well without you, the teacher has all the warmth and sympathy of a barracuda.

Causes of writer's paralysis

Notice particularly when freezing occurs: people do not stop mid-dive or mid-writing. Paralysis sets in as we anticipate the activity, and we are unable to begin. Once we do launch into the action, the fear and nervousness usually disappear. The remedy for the paralysis lies in making yourself begin. So, how do you get started? Here are some suggestions.

Timing of paralysis

Free writing exercises will help familiarize you with the process of thinking on paper. A free writing is writing without restrictions on any subject, expressing any thoughts, using any words. It is not necessary to conform to the rules of spelling, grammar, or punctuation. In free writing, you must begin to write immediately and continue through the alloted time, usually five or ten minutes. The important thing is to write. If your mind is a blank, write, "My mind is a blank." If you despise what you're doing, write, "I hate this." Just follow your thoughts on paper. Write down what you're thinking without worrying about its making sense or following the last thought, or being in correct form. At the end of the time you have given yourself, stop writing. Set your writing aside for a while, come back to it later, and read what you have written. At this point, if your experience is like mine, you will have enough raw material with which to work.

Solutions to writer's paralysis: (1) free writing

Brainstorming is an activity which, like free writing, aims at rapid production of words and ideas. Although originally designed as a group activity, brainstorming can be adapted to individuals needs. Here's how to do it: first, put yourself in the frame of mind that you would be in if you were in a group of congenial, intelligent people. Next, take pencil in hand and let your mind wander, unrestricted, over the topic. Write down every idea that comes to you. Be imaginative. Don't hold anything back. The goal is mental thunder and lightning, producing a rich flow of open-ended, daring, even outrageous, seemingly crazy ideas. Don't evaluate, interpret, criticize, or judge. There will be time for that later, after you have produced the ideas. Reject nothing! Now read back over the list of

(2) brainstorming

ideas you have generated and begin to outline and shape the material.

(3) knowing when to write and when to relax

It's also important to know when to push (as in free writing exercises) and when to let up. Get in touch with your own creative rhythm. Sometimes letting up means getting up from your desk and doing something entirely different—walking around the block, going to a movie, or even watching an ant disappear into a crevice. Of course, you can't get an essay written by continually interrupting yourself, but you can get the most out of your working periods by alternating them with periods of relaxation. When wrestling with a problem, if you can set it aside for a while, you will often find when you return to your desk that your subconscious has been working for you during the break. That is when inspiration may strike. But you have to earn those magic moments by periods of conscious, concentrated effort.

Final advice, with upbeat closing

There you have it—a few techniques used by writers to combat writer's paralysis. Unfortunately, they are not guaranteed cures, only suggestions. What works for others may not work for you. Just do your best; and if it doesn't turn out exactly as you wish, do better next time. But at least you've begun. One thing is certain—as you become more accustomed to expressing yourself on paper, the tendency to freeze diminishes. If you are a victim of writer's paralysis, practice will help more than anything else. So, the next time you find yourself staring at that blank piece of paper and beginning to carry on a two-way discussion with yourself, one worthy of any split personality, stating all the reasons why you can't get started, just shrug impatiently, tell yourself you have heard all those excuses before, and begin writing.

Exercises

I. GETTING BACK AT THE WATCHER—FINDING ANSWERS TO TYPICAL EXCUSES

Listed below are excuses we've all heard, and probably used, for avoiding writing tasks. Practice avoiding these roadblocks by listing two or three ways of coping for each excuse. For example, in response to 1, you can tell yourself to write at least three paragraphs today—set a shorter goal than finishing.

1. I don't have time to finish today, so I won't start.
2. I promised I would go out with a friend, whom I can't let down.
3. I'm out of typing paper, so there is no point in starting on the draft.
4. I can only write in the library, but I don't feel like going there now.
5. I can't start until I can think of a clever opening paragraph.

II. SEEING PICTURES INTO WORDS

Joan Didion (see "Why I Write," pp. 77–82) stresses the importance of writers having pictures in their minds and then shaping them into words. Concentrate on finding three pictures: one natural scene, one picture of a single person, one brief action scene. To find your pictures, take a walk, look out your window, or go where you will find a group of people. When you have found your three pictures, capture them in no more than two sentences for each. Try at least three versions of each picture and decide which version you prefer. Bring your versions to class, switch papers with a classmate, and get another's selection of the best version. Discuss reasons for any differences of opinion.

III. WORKING ON SENTENCE STYLE

Joan Didion also talks about letting the pictures in your mind determine the best kind of sentence pattern. Practice revising the following selections, listening for the best rhythms, the most effective emphasis, for conveying each picture. (Each selection below is an altered version of sentences from three novels. Your instructor will be able to tell you if any of your revisions recreate the author's original lines.)

1. Altered from Joan Didion's *Run River:*

   Lily heard the shot at seventeen minutes to one. She knew the time precisely because she continued fastening the clasp on the diamond wrist watch Everett had given her on their seventeenth anniversary two years before, looked at it on her wrist for a long time, and then began winding it, sitting on the edge of the bed without looking out the window into the dark where the shot reverberated.

2. Altered from William Kennedy's *Ironweed:*

   As he flew and then fell in a broken pile, Francis, running to him, was the first at his side. After looking for a way to straighten the angular body but fearing any move, Francis pulled off his own sweater, pillowing his father's head with it.

3. Altered from Iris Murdoch's *Nuns and Soldiers:*

   Here of a sudden the canal curved to the right and became narrower. It was now enclosed by beautiful walls of hard neatly cut grey stone. The stone gave a clean stony footway at the top. Tim walked on upon the stone edge and looked down. The water was becoming more turbulent and more noisy and swifter. It rose up into a curling wave on the inside of the curve.

Writing Assignments

1. Have you had difficulty with writing in the past, or do you feel anxious about this writing course? If so, explain in an essay why you have anxiety about writing. Is it hard to get started? Do you worry about grammar or spelling? Do you feel that you express yourself better when you talk than when you write? Be specific, using your past writing experiences as examples.
2. How have you learned to fool your "Watcher at the Gates" (see Gail Godwin, pp. 64–66) so that you can write? Based on techniques that have worked for you, in an essay give your advice to would-be writers for avoiding writer's block.
3. Richard Selzer writes because he believes that only in writing, not in dealing with life and death as a surgeon, can he begin to understand life's meaning. Why do you think you, given your career plans, should write? In an essay explain why an engineer, or a banker, or a teacher—or whatever you plan to be—should write. You can focus either on the practical considerations of the job or on more philosophical concerns such as those Selzer discusses.
4. Margaret Walker asserts that "our American society has no respect for the literary values of intellectual honesty nor for originality and creativity in the sensitive individual." Agree or disagree with this assertion, supporting your position with evidence, not generalities.

CHAPTER 3

Pablo Picasso, *Les Demoiselles d'Aignon,* 1907. Oil on canvas, 8' x 7'8".
Courtesy of Collection. The Museum of Modern Art, New York. Acquired through the Lillie P. Bliss Bequest.

Style: The Shaping of Reality

GETTING STARTED: Words Shape Reality

The words we choose not only describe reality as we perceive it but also shape and control our readers' perception of reality. Robert Graves, understanding the power of words to shape our perceptions, enjoys playing with the connotative differences between naked and nude.

THE NAKED AND THE NUDE
Robert Graves

For me, the naked and the nude
(By lexicographers construed
As synonyms that should express
The same deficiency of dress
Or shelter) stand as wide apart 5
As love from lies, or truth from art.

Lovers without reproach will gaze
On bodies naked and ablaze;
The Hippocratic eye will see
In nakedness, anatomy; 10
And naked shines the Goddess when
She mounts her lion among men.

The nude are bold, the nude are sly
To hold each treasonable eye.
While draping by a showman's trick 15
Their dishabille in rhetoric,
They grin a mock-religious grin
Of scorn at those of naked skin.

The naked, therefore, who compete
Against the nude may know defeat; 20
Yet when they both together tread
The briary pastures of the dead,
By Gorgons with long whips pursued,
How naked go the sometime nude!

☐ What, according to Graves, is the difference in connotation between *naked* and *nude*? What do the examples of *naked* in stanza 2 have in common? What do the examples of *nude* in stanza 3 have in common?

☐ Think of synonyms for *gaze* (line 7), *bold* (line 13), *sly* (line 13), and *grin* (line 17). How would substituting your synonyms change the effect of Graves's lines and hence change the connotation of *nude*?

☐ Can you think of contexts in which the term *nude* does not have the negative connotations given to it by Graves? How, for example, would you describe the figures in Picasso's *Les Demoiselles D'Avignon?*

SENSUAL AND SENSUOUS: A PAIR FOR YOU TO CONSIDER

Define, briefly, the words *sensual* and *sensuous*, focusing on the subtle differences in meaning or connotation. Use your dictionary if necessary. Consider: Are you more likely to perceive yourself as sensual or sensuous? How do you want to be perceived by someone of the opposite sex?

Silent Questions

Neil Postman

Neil Postman (b. 1931) is a professor of media ecology at New York University and author of books and articles on teaching, language, and contemporary culture, including *The Disappearance of Childhood* (1982) and *Teaching as a Conserving Activity* (1979). "Silent Questions" is a chapter from his book *Crazy Talk, Stupid Talk,* published in 1976.

In his direct and entertaining style, Postman examines the confusions and distortions of reality that arise from the way we ask certain questions.

1 I cannot vouch for the story, but I have been told that once upon a time, in a village in what is now Lithuania, there arose a most unusual problem. A curious disease afflicted many of the townspeople. It was mostly fatal (although not always), and its onset was signaled by the victim's lapsing into a deathlike coma. Medical science not being quite so advanced as it is now, there was no definite way of knowing if the victim was actually dead when it appeared seemly to bury him. As a result, the townspeople feared that several of their relatives had already been buried alive and that a similar fate might await them—a terrifying prospect, and not only in Lithuania. How to overcome this uncertainty was their dilemma.

2 One group of people suggested that the coffins be well stocked with water and food and that a small air vent be drilled into them just in case one of the "dead" happened to be alive. This was expensive to do, but seemed more than worth the trouble. A second group, however, came up with an inexpensive and more efficient idea. Each coffin would have a twelve-inch stake affixed to the inside of the coffin lid, exactly at the level of the heart. Then, when the coffin was closed, all uncertainty would cease.

3 There is no record as to which solution was chosen, but for my pur-

poses, whichever it was is irrelevant. What is mostly important here is that the two different solutions were generated by two different questions. The first solution was an answer to the question, How can we make sure that we do not bury people who are still alive? The second was an answer to the question, How can we make sure that everyone we bury is dead?

4 The point is that all the answers we ever get are responses to questions. The questions may not be evident to us, especially in everyday affairs, but they are there nonetheless, doing their work. Their work, of course, is to design the form that our knowledge will take and therefore determine the direction of our actions. A great deal of stupid and/or crazy talk is produced by bad, unacknowledged questions which inevitably produce bad and all-too-visible answers.

5 As far as I can determine, there are at least four important reasons why question-asking language causes us problems. The first is that our questions are sometimes formed at such a high level of abstraction that we cannot answer them at all. "Why am I a failure?" and "What is the meaning of life?" are typical examples. The connection between a question of this form and the "IFD disease"[1] is fairly obvious: The key words in the questions are so vague that it is a mystery to know where to begin looking for answers. For example, in trying to respond helpfully to a troubled questioner who asks, Why am I a failure?, a sensible person would have to ask several more pointed questions to get within answering range: What do you mean by "failure"? What specifically have you "failed" at? When have these "failures" taken place? In what circumstances? What do you mean by "success," when and where have you experienced it, and how many "successes" have you had? What needs to be done with such questions is to "operationalize" them, to restate them in forms that will allow for concrete, reality-oriented answers. In the process of doing this, one may discover that the question being asked was not so much, "Why am I a failure?" but, "Why did my marriage end in divorce?" "Why did I lose my job?" or even something as relatively simple as, "Why did I fail advanced calculus?"

6 I do not say that questions about one's dead marriage or lost job are easy ones; only that they are more approachable than loose-ended questions that imply one's nature is marred by some nondefinable affliction called *failure*.

7 It is characteristic of the talk of troubled people that they will resist bringing their questions down to a level of answerability. If fanaticism is falling in love with an irrefutable answer, then a neurosis is falling in love with an unanswerable question. "Why are people always trying to cheat me?" or "When will the breaks start to come my way?" is the sort of ques-

---

[1]Stands for idealization/frustration/demoralization. Postman argues that frustration and despair follow from establishing vague, abstract goals such as "success" or "happiness."—ED.

tion that can be treacherously endearing. As it stands, there is no answer to it, and perhaps that is why some people choose to ask it and ask it repeatedly. It is, in fact, not so much a question as a kind of assertion that the responsibility for one's life lies entirely outside oneself. But because it has the *form* of a question, one may well be deceived into trying to answer it, which will lead to continuous frustration and demoralization.

8 Of course, questions of this type are not confined to one's personal relationship to the cosmos but are also used, unfortunately, as an instrument for discovering "facts." And they produce the same unsatisfying results. "Who is the best President that America has ever had?" is the sort of commonplace, completely unanswerable question which results in no knowledge at all. The conversation between Stupid Talk and Sensible Talk usually goes something like this:

Stupid Talk: Who's the best President we ever had?

Sensible Talk: What do you mean by "best"?

Stupid Talk: What do you mean "What do I mean?"? Best means "the best," "the most excellent," "tops."

Sensible Talk: "Tops" in what respect? Most votes? Least criticized? Most well-read? Richest?

Stupid Talk: What do those things have to do with it? I mean "the best"—all around.

Sensible Talk: Using what criteria for which aspects of his performance?

Stupid Talk: Why are you making this so complicated? You mean to tell me you don't know what "best" means?

Sensible Talk: Right.

Stupid Talk: Jeez!

9 Now, it is possible I am being unfair to Stupid Talk here, in that he may have asked the question only in order to get some diversion at a rather dull party. If that was his intention, then you should reverse the names of the characters in my scene. Sensible Talk is simply being obnoxious or has misunderstood the purpose of the semantic environment he is in. But if the question was asked to start a serious conversation, resulting in the development and expression of informed opinion, then the names of my characters must stand as they are. The question as originally posed will not produce a discussable answer. I might add, as well, that even a seemingly specific question, such as Who discovered oxygen?, is unanswerable except insofar as it implies a somewhat longer and more detailed question. For example, if the question means to say, "According to the *Encyclopaedia Britannica,* who is credited with the discovery of oxygen?," it is certainly answerable. But that is really quite a different ques-

tion from "Who discovered oxygen?" and the difference, I would insist, is not "mere semantics." I have not verified it, but my guess is that textbooks in the Soviet Union do not credit Joseph Priestley and Karl Wilhelm Scheele with discovering oxygen and may not even credit Lavoisier with coining the word. I do not say "they" are right and "we" are wrong. But in such matters as who did what and when, there are always lively and even legitimate disputes, and if you do not take into account *in your question* the source of the knowledge you are seeking, there is bound to be trouble.

10 The first problem, then, in question-asking language may be stated in this way: The type of words used in a question will determine the type of words used in the answer. In particular, question-words that are vague, subjective, and not rooted in any verifiable reality will produce their own kind in the answer.

11 A second problem arises from certain structural characteristics, or grammatical properties, of sentences. For example, many questions seem almost naturally to imply either-or alternatives. "Is that good?" (as against "bad"), "Is she smart?" (as against "dumb"), "Is he rich?" (as against "poor"), and so on. The English language is heavily biased toward "either-or-ness," which is to say that it encourages us to talk about the world in polarities. We are inclined to think of things in terms of their singular opposites rather than as part of a continuum of multiple alternatives. *Black* makes us think of *white, rich* of *poor, smart* of *dumb, fast* of *slow,* and so on. Naturally, when questions are put in either-or terms, they will tend to call forth an either-or answer. "This is bad," "She's dumb," "He's poor," etc. There are many situations in which such an emphatic answer is all that is necessary, since the questioner is merely seeking some handy label, to get a "fix" on someone, so to speak. But, surprisingly and unfortunately, this form of question is also used in situations where one would expect a more serious and comprehensive approach to a subject. For example, in Edwin Newman's popular book, *Strictly Speaking,* he asks in his subtitle, "Will America Be the Death of English?" The form of the question demands either a *yes* or *no* for its answer. (Newman, by the way, says yes, and for no particular reason, so far as I could tell.) Had the question been phrased as, "To what extent will English be harmed (impoverished, diminished, etc.) by Americans?" you would have had a very boring subtitle but, in my opinion, a much more serious book, or at least the possibility of one. Questions which ask, "To what extent" or "In what manner" invite a more detailed, qualified look at a problem than questions which ask, "Is it this or that?" The latter divide the universe into two possibilities; the former allow one to consider the multiple possibilities inherent in a problem. "Is America an imperial power?" "Have we lost our faith in democracy?" "Are our taxes too high?"—these are some questions which insinuate that a position must be taken; they do not ask that thought be given.

12 A similar structural problem in our questions is that we are apt to

use singular forms instead of plural ones. What is the cause of . . . ? What is the reason for . . . ? What is the result of . . . ? As with either-or questions, the form of these questions limits our search for answers and therefore impoverishes our perceptions. We are not looking for cause*s*, reason*s*, or result*s*, but for *the* cause, *the* reason, and *the* result. The idea of multiple causality is certainly not unfamiliar, and yet the form in which we habitually ask some of our most important questions tends to discourage our thinking about it: What is the reason we don't get along? What is the cause of your overeating? What will be the effect of school integration? What is the problem that we face? I do not say that a question of this sort rules out the possibility of our widening our inquiries. But to the extent that we allow the form of such questions to go unchallenged, we are in danger of producing shallow and unnecessarily restricted answers.

13 This is equally true of the third source of problems in question-asking language, namely, the assumptions that underlie it. Unless we are paying very close attention, we can be led into accepting as fact the most precarious and even preposterous ideas. Perhaps the two most famous assumption-riddled questions are, Have you stopped beating your wife? and How many angels can dance on the head of a pin? But in almost every question, there lurks at least one assumption which may slip by if we are not accustomed to looking for it. By an assumption, I mean a belief that is not subject to scrutiny because it is so deeply embedded in the question that we are hardly even aware of its presence. Consider, for instance, such questions as these, which I have recently heard discussed on television: Why is America losing its moral direction? When will we achieve equality of opportunity? How does the white power structure operate? The first question assumes that there is such a thing as a "moral direction," that a country can have one, that America once did, and, of course, that we are presently losing it. I do not say that these assumptions are untenable, but each one of them is surely worth inquiring into before proceeding to the question. In fact, once you start discussing these assumptions, you may never get back to the original question, and may even find it has disappeared, to everyone's relief.

14 The second question assumes that there is such a thing as equality of opportunity; that it is, in some sense, "achievable" by society; that it is worth achieving; and that some effort is being made to achieve it—all extremely arguable assumptions in my opinion. I have, for example, long suspected that the phrase "equality of opportunity" is a kind of semantic fiction, not unlike the legal term "a reasonable and prudent man"; that is to say, one is free to give it almost any meaning that suits one's purpose in a given situation. In any case, I should want the term carefully defined before listening to a discussion of when "it" will be achieved.

15 The third question, of course, assumes the existence of a white power structure, as well as mechanisms through which it operates. Given the rather bumbling, haphazard ways of American business and govern-

ment, I am inclined to be at least suspicious of this assumption, although I would like to hear it defended.

16 The point is that if you proceed to answer questions without reviewing the assumptions implicit in them, you may end up in never-never land without quite knowing how you got there. My favorite invitation to never-never land, incidentally, was extended to me by a young woman who asked, "Why do you think the extraterrestrials are coming in such large numbers to Earth?" You might expect that a person who would ask such a question also would have an answer to it—which was, you will be happy to know, "to help Earth people develop an effective World Organization."

17 The fourth source of difficulty in question-asking language is that two people in the same semantic environment may ask different questions about a situation, but without knowing it. For example, in a classroom, the teacher may be asking himself, "How can I get the students to learn this?" But it is almost certain that the students are asking, "How can I get a good grade in this course?" Naturally, two different questions will generate two different approaches to the situation and may be the source of great frustration for everyone concerned. There are many situations where it is well understood that different "roles" are required to ask different questions, and this in itself is not necessarily a source of trouble. In business transactions, for instance, buyers and sellers are almost always asking different questions. That is inherent in their situation. I have never heard of a buyer, for example, who has asked himself, "How can I make sure this man makes the largest possible profit from this sale?" (The reason, incidentally, that used-car salesmen have such low credibility is that they are inclined to pretend that they are asking the same question as the potential car buyer, namely, "How can I get this car at the lowest possible price?" Since the buyer knows that the dealer cannot possibly be interested in this question, he is rightfully suspicious.) But in situations where it is assumed that different people will be asking roughly the same question—and they are not—we are faced with problems that are sometimes hard to discern. I have recently heard of a situation where a family vacation was marred because, without their knowing it, wife and husband were seeking answers to two quite different questions. The wife was asking, "How can we have a good time?" The husband was asking, "How can we get through this without spending too much money?" Two administrators who were trying to avoid bankruptcy provide another example: The first was asking, "How can we cut our staff?" The second, "How can we increase our income?" Naturally, their solutions moved in different directions. Finally, a pregnant woman and her obstetrician: The woman is asking, "How can I have my baby safely and with no unnecessary pain?" The doctor is asking, "How can this baby get born in time for me to have a full two-week vacation?"

18 I do not say that different questions are always incompatible in such situations. But they do have considerable potential for confusion if we are ignorant of their existence.

Word Study List

abstraction	5	semantic	9, 14, 17
marred	6, 17	polarities	11
affliction	6	inherent	11, 17
fanaticism	7	insinuate	11
irrefutable	7	impoverishes	12
neurosis	7	precarious	13
demoralization	7	preposterous	13
diversion	9	scrutiny	13
obnoxious	9	untenable	13

Questions

1. How does Postman's opening story relate to his subject? Did you find the story an effective attention getter? If so, why?

2. What is Postman's main idea or thesis? Where does he state it?

3. What is the relationship between the words used in a question and the answer it generates?

4. List the four types of questions that can create problems and explain what kinds of problems each type can cause.

5. When Postman writes of confusion in a semantic environment, he is referring to a contemporary concept of language use. Can you explain Postman's concept of the communication process?

6. Postman says that one of his favorite unanswerable questions is "Why do you think the extraterrestrials are coming in such large numbers to Earth?" List all the assumptions underlying this question that make it "an invitation to never-never land."

Exercises

1. Think of at least one new sample question for each of Postman's four types and bring them to class. Swap questions with a classmate and practice explaining why these questions cause confusion or distortions of reality.

2. Select one of the following questions to experiment with. Direct your question to at least five people and carefully record their responses. After studying the responses, decide if your question generated confused, distorted, or unrealistic answers. Report your results in a short essay.

a. Why is life such a struggle?
b. Which is the greatest American novel?
c. Are you a good swimmer/dancer/student?
d. What caused the Soviet Union to decide not to participate in the 1984 Olympics?
e. How many angels can dance on the head of a pin?
f. Will the Moral Majority win its fight to restore prayer to public schools?
g. Did you get your good grades by cheating or buttering-up your instructor?

Watching Out for Loaded Words

Frank Trippett

Frank Trippett (b. 1926), a free-lance writer who has twice shared the National Headliner Award and has written such diverse books as *The United States: United They Fell* (1967), a study of state legislatures, and *The First Horsemen* (1974), one of the Time-Life Emergence of Man series, is currently a senior writer with *Time* magazine. His article on loaded words was published May 24, 1982, in *Time.*

Selecting a style that illustrates his subject, Trippett explains the effect of loaded words and techniques for creating them.

1 Via eye and ear, words beyond numbering zip into the mind and flash a dizzy variety of meaning into the mysterious circuits of knowing. A great many of them bring along not only their meanings but some extra freight—a load of judgment or bias that plays upon the emotions instead of lighting up the understanding. These words deserve careful handling—and minding. They are loaded.

2 Such words babble up in all corners of society, wherever anybody is ax-grinding, arm-twisting, back-scratching, sweet-talking. Political blather leans sharply to words *(peace, prosperity)* whose moving powers outweigh exact meanings. Merchandising depends on adjectives *(new, improved)* that must be continually recharged with notions that entice people to buy. In casual conversation, emotional stuffing is lent to words by inflection and gesture: the innocent phrase, "Thanks a lot," is frequently a vehicle for heaping servings of irritation. Traffic in opinion-heavy language is universal simply because most people, as C. S. Lewis puts it, are "more anxious to express their approval and disapproval of things than to describe them."

3 The trouble with loaded words is that they tend to short-circuit

thought. While they may describe something, they simultaneously try to seduce the mind into accepting a prefabricated opinion about the something described. The effect of one laden term was incidentally measured in a recent survey of public attitudes by the Federal Advisory Commission on Intergovernmental Relations. The survey found that many more Americans favor governmental help for the poor when the programs are called "aid to the needy" than when they are labeled "public welfare." And that does not mean merely that some citizens prefer H_2O to water. In fact, the finding spotlights the direct influence of the antipathy that has accumulated around the benign word *welfare.*

4 Every word hauls some basic cargo or else can be shrugged aside as vacant sound. Indeed, almost any word can, in some use, take on that extra baggage of bias or sentiment that makes for the truly manipulative word. Even the pronoun *it* becomes one when employed to report, say, that somebody has what *it* takes. So does the preposition *in* when used to establish, perhaps, that zucchini quiche is *in* this year: used just so, *in* all but sweats with class bias. The emotion-heavy words that are easiest to spot are epithets and endearments: *blockhead, scumbum, heel, sweetheart, darling, great human being* and the like. All such terms are so full of prejudice and sentiment that S. I. Hayakawa, a semanticist before he became California's U.S. Senator, calls them "snarl-words and purr-words."

5 Not all artfully biased terms have been honored with formal labels. Word loading, after all, is not a recognized scholarly discipline, merely a folk art. Propagandists and advertising copywriters may turn it into a polished low art, but it is usually practiced—and witnessed—without a great deal of deliberation. The typical person, as Hayakawa says in *Language in Thought and Action,* "takes words as much for granted as the air."

6 Actually, it does not take much special skill to add emotional baggage to a word. Almost any noun can be infused with skepticism and doubt through the use of the word *so-called.* Thus a friend in disfavor can become a *so-called friend,* and similarly the nation's leaders can become *so-called leaders.* Many other words can be handily tilted by shortening, by prefixes and suffixes, by the reduction of formal to familiar forms. The word *politician,* which may carry enough downbeat connotation for most tastes, can be given additional unsavoriness by truncation: *pol.* By prefacing liberal and conservative with *ultra* or *arch,* both labels can be saddled with suggestions of inflexible fanaticism. To speak of a pacifist or peacemaker as a *peacenik* is, through a single syllable, to smear someone with the suspicion that he has alien loyalties. The antifeminist who wishes for his (or her) prejudice to go piggyback on his (or her) language will tend to speak not of feminists but of *fem-libbers.* People with only limited commitments to environmental preservation will tend similarly to allude not to environmentalists but to *eco-freaks.*

7 Words can be impregnated with feeling by oversimplification. People who oppose all abortions distort the position of those favoring freedom of private choice by calling them *pro-abortion.* And many a progressive or

idealist has experienced the perplexity of defending himself against one of the most peculiar of all disparaging terms, *do-gooder*. By usage in special contexts, the most improbable words can be infused with extraneous meaning. To speak of the "truly needy" as the Administration habitually does is gradually to plant the notion that the unmodified *needy* are falsely so. Movie Critic Vincent Canby has noticed that the word *film* has become imbued with a good deal of snootiness that is not to be found in the word *movie*. *Moderate* is highly susceptible to coloring in many different ways, always by the fervid partisans of some cause: Adlai Stevenson, once accused of being too *moderate* on civil rights, wondered whether anyone wished him to be, instead, immoderate.

8 The use of emotional vocabularies is not invariably a dubious practice. In the first place, words do not always get loaded by sinister design or even deliberately. In the second, that sort of language is not exploited only for mischievous ends. The American verities feature words—*liberty, equality*—that, on top of their formal definitions, are verily packed with the sentiments that cement U.S. society. The affectionate banalities of friendship and neighborliness similarly facilitate the human ties that bind and support. The moving vocabularies of patriotism and friendship are also subject to misuse, of course, but such derelictions are usually easy to recognize as demagoguery or hypocrisy.

9 The abuse and careless use of language have been going on for a long time; witness the stern biblical warnings such as the one in *Matthew 12: 36:* "Every idle word that men shall speak, they shall give account thereof in the day of judgment." Yet the risks of biased words to the unwary must be greater today, in an epoch of propagandizing amplified by mass communications. "Never," Aldous Huxley said, "have misused words—those hideously efficient tools of all the tyrants, warmongers, persecutors and heresy hunters—been so widely and disastrously influential." In the two decades since that warning, the practice of bamboozlement has, if anything, increased. The appropriate response is not a hopeless effort to cleanse the world of seductive words. Simple awareness of how frequently and variously they are loaded reduces the chances that one will fall out of touch with so-called reality.

Word Study List

inflection	2	disparaging	7
antipathy	3	extraneous	7
benign	3	verities	8
semanticist	4	banalities	8
infused	6, 7	derelictions	8
prefixes	6	demagoguery	8
suffixes	6	propagandizing	9
truncation	6	bamboozlement	9

Questions

1. How does Trippett define loaded words?

2. Although Trippett acknowledges that most words carry some emotion or bias, he still considers loaded words a problem. Why?

3. What people are mentioned as users of loaded words? Are there others who could be mentioned?

4. What are some techniques for adding emotional baggage to a word?

5. Trippett suggests that some loaded words are advantageous, not threatening. What kinds receive his approval? Do you agree that we easily recognize the misuse of words that stir political and personal feelings? Should Trippett have given evidence to support his assertion? Why or why not?

6. What advice does Trippett offer for coping with loaded words? Based on what you have learned about language, do you think that "simple awareness" of language use is really so simple?

Exercises

1. With considerable cleverness Trippett spices his own style with loaded words in addition to the specific examples he provides. List all the loaded words you can find in the article and briefly explain the emotional impact or bias in each one.

2. Some loaded words Trippett does not mention are the words we use to "dress up" or "cover up" those people, places, situations, or actions that we have difficulty referring to with more precision. These words are called *euphemisms.* For example, to describe a seriously ill person as "under the weather" is to use a euphemism. List all the euphemisms you can think of for *toilet* and for *death* or *dying.* What might your lists tell us about the society we live in?

Metaphors: Live, Dead, and Silly

Roger Sale

Author of articles, reviews, and books, Roger Sale (b. 1932) is a professor of English at the University of Washington. Two of his recent books are *Seattle,*

Past to Present (1976) and *Fairy Tales and After: From Snow White to E. B. White* (1978). The following selection is reprinted from *On Writing* (1970).

In his chapter on metaphors, Sale illustrates the pervasiveness of metaphors in our speech and explains the reality—or absurdities—conveyed by particular metaphors.

1 I may only be betraying my own ignorance, but the way metaphor usually is taught seems to invite my students to think of it as an ornament to their style, an effect achieved in poetry but not really necessary for any decent, hard-working plain style. As a result, most students seem unaware of the way metaphor pervades even the plainest and most hard-working of styles, and is the dominant feature of almost all our speech. Students seem to feel that metaphor is something they can "use" or not "use" as they wish, and so when they decide to use metaphors, they become wildly self-conscious and liable to cliché. When asked, they speak of metaphor as something different from a simile. "The moon was a ghostly galleon tossed upon stormy seas," they have learned, is a metaphor, and "My love is like a red, red rose" is a simile. Their examples, as I say, come from poems; metaphors are what you learn about in English classes, nowhere else.

2 The definition of metaphor most students have carried with them from English class to English class, however, can serve a wider purpose than it usually does. A metaphor is a comparison in which one thing is said to *be* another thing, as opposed to a simile, which is a comparison in which one thing is said to be *like* another thing. The distinction may have its purpose, but a moment's reflection will show that when one thing is said to *be* another thing, that does not mean that it in fact *is* that other thing but only that it is *like* that thing; metaphors and similes do exactly the same thing. When I say, in the first sentence of this paragraph, that students "have carried" a definition of metaphor from class to class, I do not mean that this carrying is literally the same carrying one might do if the subject were a ball of twine, but only that what students do with their definition of metaphor is *like* what they might do with a ball of twine. The word "carry" is a metaphor here, then. Look at the words "show" and "do" in the third sentence of this paragraph. These are obviously not felt as metaphors, yet they obviously are not meant to be taken literally; a moment's reflection cannot "show," a metaphor cannot "do" or be "felt" except metaphorically.

3 You can take almost any passage and treat it like the pictures in which you try to find the hidden animals. How many metaphors can you find in the following:

> Sure, I see Joe Fisher every morning. He comes in after class, scrounges around until he finds someone with a dime, buys his coffee and then he parks himself off in the corner. Within five minutes the son-of-a-bitch is holding court with a bunch of women. It's incredible. He sits back, pounds

> his spoon on the table, blows smoke down their throat, looks bored, yet somehow he manages it all so as to seem the biggest thing in their world. I've seen girls who wouldn't give me the time of day and to whom I've been princely treat him like some guru. It's as though he digs some language or tunes in on some obscure wave length made just for Joe Fisher and women.

Without stretching the idea of a metaphor very much, I count nineteen: scrounges, parks, son-of-a-bitch, holding court, bunch, incredible, pounds, blows smoke down their throat, manages, biggest thing, world, seen, give me the time of day, princely, guru, digs some language, tunes in on some wave length, obscure, made. And that doesn't count those that are like metaphors, even if one doesn't want to call them that: every morning, someone with a dime, within five minutes, all, treat. Within a hundred words Joe Fisher is a rodent, a car, a male offspring of a female dog, a king, a stage director, a wise man, a mystic, a favored child of nature for whom things are "made."

4 Granted that an unprepared speech in conversation has the highest metaphorical density of any language we use, the game can be played even in conversations where everything is short bursts, with newspapers, with dialogue in movies. Our sense of the world involves us so constantly and completely in metaphors that there is little exaggeration in saying that all our speech and writing approaches metaphor; for example, you can hear many people who don't know what a metaphor is make one out of "literally" when they say, "He literally brought the house down," by which, of course, it is not to be understood that that is what he literally did.

5 Given the way metaphors pervade our speech, a few statements are perhaps in order. A metaphor is a kind of lie or untruth: something is said to be something that it is not. "He parks himself in the corner" compares Joe to an automobile. Unpacking the metaphor, we can say, "Joe is like an automobile in the way he finds his place of rest," or, simply, "Joe is an automobile," or, "Joe is an automobile in this respect." We cannot, nor do we want to, say, "An automobile is Joe." If a metaphor were not a metaphor, it would be an identity and therefore reversible, as in "Sunrise is the beginning of day" and "The beginning of day is sunrise." There is a kind of magic in our key verb "to be," such that it cannot only make equalities and definitions but can also state or imply likenesses between two things that aren't each other and do not, in most respects, resemble each other, like Joe and an automobile. Likewise, metaphors are not capable of replacing each other; "Joe parks himself in the corner" is okay, and so is "The car parks hard," but "Joe parks hard" won't do. All this is perhaps elementary enough, but it can have consequences that are not always easy to determine, so it is best to get the elementary things straight. One of the basic tasks of intelligent living is to understand the extent to which certain statements which use some form of "to be" are statements of identity: "God is . . . ," "My country is . . . ," "You are. . . . " Most

really important statements about the human condition or the nature of the universe are of the form "x is y," and if "You are the promised kiss of springtime" is only a rather pretty and confused pile-up of metaphors, what are we to say of "God is the Father Almighty"? In any event, we must see that though many metaphors do not take the grammatical form of "x is y," all metaphors can be transformed into statements of that pattern and often can best be understood and evaluated when this transformation is made. This is especially true when the metaphor lies in a verb—"Joe scrounged," "Joe parked," "Joe held court"—and the fact that the statement is metaphorical is apt to pass unnoticed. It is often possible to examine the implications of one's own statements by taking all the metaphors and turning them into the "x is y" form, and quite often writers gain a much better grip on their writing when they practice doing this. If nothing else, to take a paragraph of one's own writing and to unpack and rephrase all its metaphors is to see what a strange and wonderful instrument the language is and how much control it is possible to exert over one's use of it.

6 Here, for instance, is a paragraph with some rather interesting metaphors that its author probably was unaware he was using:

> In Sherwood Anderson's "I Want to Know Why," only one of the characters is described in depth. Here we see a boy whose entire life has but one goal, to be a trainer or a jockey. His dreams are the dreams of a young boy, not those of a grown man. Hopping freights, exploring strange places, living only for his moments at the stables and the track—these are described so vividly the reader can feel them. The boy's life centers around the track, and as long as this is so, the boy's world is secure. The races are always there, along with the parade of new colts. The boy depends heavily on the horses for this way of life.

Let's again list the metaphors: in depth, see, entire life, dreams, grown man, hopping freights, exploring strange places, moments, feel, centers around, world, secure, always there, parade, depends heavily, way of life. What I want to look at especially are those which are so much a part of the way we speak that the metaphorical quality of the phrase is not easy to see. First, though, a word about "centered around," which must be the commonest mixed metaphor in the present use of the language. A mixed metaphor is not simply two consecutive metaphors; "That man is a snake, a rat" is simply a change of metaphor. A mixed metaphor is an absurdity that arises when someone is not aware that he is using a metaphor: "We pulverized them into sending up the white flag" is such a mix, because to pulverize something is to leave it in no condition to send up white flags; "The foundation of his position must flounder" is mixed because, of the many wonderful things metaphorical foundations can do, floundering is not one. The term "centered around" is, in this sense, self-contradictory, because to center on something is to be, metaphorically, at the one point incapable of motion—around, through, by, or any other way. What happens, of course, is that people forget that "to center" is a metaphor in itself and so demands a preposition appropriate to the action of centering.

7 Mixed metaphors, however, are really an interesting sidelight, and most writers learn early to avoid them. More important are the metaphors in this paragraph that silently construct this writer's "world": in depth, world, secure. The questions raised by metaphors of depth and shallowness really ask us who we think we are and how we see others. The writer here says that only the boy in this story "is described in depth." One way of stating the curiosity of the problem is to point out that almost certainly this writer means that the boy is the only character described "at length." Surely, "in depth" and "at length" should not mean the same thing, but the fact that they do tells us something. Most studies that are carried on in depth are carried on longer than other studies, but whatever else is implied by "in depth" is seldom made clear. Presumably, to be deep is not to be shallow, and a study in depth would explore the deeps, the profundities, the complexities, of a person or a problem. Presumably, also, one could carry on at great length, that is, for a long time, about a problem and never explore its depths. The difficulty is that no one will ever confess this, because if an analysis that takes five minutes is not deep, no one expected it could be, but an analysis that takes far longer ought to be far deeper. So it is that we presume, or let others presume for us, that length makes depth. It is possible, though in our world it is not allowed to be possible, that someone can be deep about someone else in a single sentence, and it is not only possible but likely that most people can go on at length about a problem without ever being deep. As long as length and depth are allowed to measure the same things, however, no one is apt to find this out, and the confusion of metaphorical reality can only be a really long and deep confusion.

8 Now, "world," that most fashionable of metaphors. "The boy's world is secure," says the passage; professional football or fashion or Henry Orient or youth or marijuana or almost everything else one can name is said to have its own "world," or "sphere" (it used to be only a "niche"). In James Baldwin's world, in the world of Harlem, in the modern world, in my world, and each time the metaphor is used the implication grows stronger that each item that has a world is isolated from everything else in creation. "This is my Father's world," says the hymn, but that is not the way the term is used now; the metaphor says that it is not all of us, or the physical body known as the earth, but some small segment thereof, that is its world. If someone tells me that I do not live in his world, he implies that the gap between my world and his is so great that I cannot possibly know what his life is like. It is as though there were no common inheritance of humanity, of a Western tradition, of American life, that is shared; each lives in his own world, each peers out onto a

universe of strangers, each finds his own world made up of himself and a few other like-minded people. I have spoken as though the classroom were a separate world, and have constantly deplored the fact that the metaphor may speak truly. It is a common metaphor, and if what it implies is true, then it is hard to know how we are going to get along in "the world."

9 Finally, "secure" and "security." My dictionary does not really think that the word as it is used in this sentence is metaphorical any longer: "The boy's world is secure," and "secure" here means "free from or not exposed to danger." What is interesting here is the way in which the term so often is used in a context that implies transience, fragility, and danger. The writer here says: "The boy's life centers around the track, and as long as this is so, the boy's world is secure." We know, thus, that the security is temporary. It is a word most often used by or about people who do not feel in the least safe; or, it may be said, people who live in their own "world" tend to use the word "secure" but seldom feel as the word or metaphor implies they do. Here are some common usages:

> I don't ever feel very secure when called upon to speak. [Here "secure" means comfortable or relaxed.]
>
> She needs more security than he will ever be able to give her. [Here "security" means steadiness.]
>
> If he gets the best job, he will feel secure. [Here "secure" almost means valuable.]
>
> The moment he gets outside the security of the classroom, he fumbles and feels lost. [Here "security" means protection.]

What we have here is a spectrum of meanings for "secure," no one clearly literal or metaphorical, no one quite like any of the others, so that the word has a solidity of tone but no solidity of meaning. Such a word is harder to use than "in depth" or "world" when what one needs is a sense that the word *is* a metaphor. The word "security," like the word "real," can be used well only by someone who is fully aware of its different shadings and nuances. It is a word that has come to prominence precisely because what it describes or implies is so seldom felt, and the word often seems like a cry for help from someone who knows there is no help. "If he gets that job, he will feel secure" is a harmless enough sentence, but the "he" it describes is no fun to contemplate at all, for any "he" that needs this or that job to feel secure is quite obviously never going to feel secure, no matter what job he gets. "She needs more security than he will ever be able to give her" means "She must marry a rock, nothing else will save her." "I don't ever feel secure when called upon to speak" means, really, "I don't ever feel secure." As a result, though "secure" and "security" themselves are not, in the strict sense, metaphors as used most of the time, they can be used as a means of avoiding a gnawing sense of pathos, loneliness, and insecurity when their potential meanings are clear to both user and reader or listener.

10 I have concentrated on the three words discussed above because they were the ones the paragraph offered, and I have done so only to show the kind of awareness about metaphor that any concentrated thought about writing can provoke. Three other words would call for a quite different discussion but not for a different awareness. Metaphor is how we live because it is the way we relate what we see to what we know: this is like that. The only sentences we can construct that are really without metaphors are those we construct just to prove we can do it. Care in the use of metaphor is tantamount to careful writing; sloppiness in the use of metaphor is the same thing as sloppy writing. The best and only way I know to become aware of this is to perform exercises like those I've been doing in the last few pages. Take something you have written that you are rather proud of, or maybe just something that seems all right but from which you don't see how to go on. List its metaphors, unpack a few of the obvious ones, then a few of the hidden ones that may or may not seem like metaphors to you. All of a sudden, instead of being a great writer or a drudge, you are aware of yourself for what, most importantly, you are—a user of words.

Word Study List

simile	1	profundities	7
density	4	spectrum	9
grammatical	5	nuances	9
transformed	5	tantamount	10
mixed metaphor	6		

Questions

1. Define the term *metaphor*. How is a simile different from a metaphor? How are they the same?

2. Based on your experience, do you think Sale's analysis of student attitudes about metaphors is accurate? How does his introduction help to establish his purpose in writing?

3. State Sale's thesis.

4. Sale provides many examples of metaphors from conversations, student papers, and ads to demonstrate their central place in our language use. Why is it difficult to speak or write for long without using metaphors?

5. Explain the process of "unpacking" metaphors. List and unpack the metaphors in paragraph 10.

6. What do we call overworked metaphors such as "the rat race," "as smart as a whip," "a stitch in time"? How many of the following clichés can you complete?
   dead as a _______
   hare-brained _______
   brown as a _______
   warm as _______
   cool as a _______
   a stiff upper _______
   slow as _______
   Which clichés in the list are expressed as metaphors? Which are expressed as similes?

Exercises

1. Because we can fill in the blanks in question 6 easily, clichés, or dead metaphors, no longer have the power to make us see or think. If they do make us "see," often what we see is not what a writer using a cliché intends. Write a brief description of what the following clichés make you see.
   splitting hairs
   tongue lashing
   as right as rain
   a brown study
2. Select a recent paper of yours, list all the metaphors it contains, and then "unpack" the metaphors. How many metaphors did you have in the paper? Are you surprised at how many—or how few—you have? What have you learned from this exercise about your ways of looking at life and your writing style?

3. Unpack the metaphors in paragraph 9 of Bradley Miller's essay "Cutesy," page 157.

Metaphor and Social Belief

Weller Embler

Author of many articles on language, literature, and the fine arts, and the book *Metaphor and Meaning* (1966), Weller Embler (b. 1906) is Emeritus Professor of English and former head of the Humanities Department at the

Cooper Union in New York City. He is currently at work on an informal history of the arts in America during the 1930s. "Metaphor and Social Belief" was printed in the Fall 1983 issue of *ETC,* a journal devoted to language.

Demonstrating his great breadth of knowledge through the essay's many examples, Embler argues that powerful metaphors of great writers and thinkers influence as well as reflect the philosophies of their times.

1 Grammarians have often busied themselves defining what a metaphor *is.* But it is more meaningful in our day to find out what a metaphor *does.* The little words 'like' and 'as' exert an enormous influence over our thoughts and our behavior; and there is vastly more to figurative language than the customary pedagogical distinctions between similes and metaphors. Our behavior is a function of the words we use. More often than not, our thoughts do not select the words we use; instead, words determine the thoughts we have. We can say with some assurance that language develops out of social conditions and in turn influences social behavior.

2 Modern rhetorics and grammar books insist that written and spoken English shall avoid the hackneyed figure of speech. Triteness, they say, is 'evidence of a failure to attain animation and originality in expression.' But the trite figure is worn-out not because it has been used often before, but because it cannot bear the burden of new attitudes. Consider the following extended figure of speech from the novel *Young Man with a Horn* by Dorothy Baker.

> Fortune, in its workings, has something in common with a slot-machine. There are those who can bait it forever and never get more than an odd assortment of lemons for their pains; but once in a while there will come a man for whom all the grooves will line up, and when that happens there's no end to the showering down.

3 Fortune (or the more common 'Fate') is a concept for which the only referent in the external world is a series of observable events without an assignable cause, and creative writers in all ages have sought analogies which will force the concept of fate, for the time being, at least, to accept a local habitation and a name.[1] For instance, to the Elizabethans, it was quite believable that the capricious order of happenings should be governed by malicious creatures who looked like very old women. When the fantastical Witches appear before Macbeth and Banquo announcing Macbeth's ascendancy from Glamis to Cawdor to King, it appeared to Shake-

---

[1]A phrase from Shakespeare's *A Midsummer Night's Dream:*

The poet's eye, in a fine frenzy rolling,
Doth glance from heaven to earth, from earth to heaven;
And, as imagination bodies forth
The forms of things unknown the poet's pen
Turns them to shapes and gives to airy nothing
A local habitation and a name.—ED.

speare's audience that the course of Macbeth's life was chargeable to the whims of the horrid sisters. What is important is not the originality of the metaphors 'invented' by Dorothy Baker and William Shakespeare but the relationship which their figures of speech bear to their times. If we think of events of our lives as controlled by witches or even controlled by some force known only to witches, we shall behave in one way; if we think that the course of our experience is a matter of statistical probabilities, we shall behave in quite another way.

4 A whole philosophy of life is often implicit in the metaphors of creative writers, the philosophy of an entire generation, indeed, even of an entire civilization. In the great tradition of the western world, it has been common to liken (in some essential respects) men to gods. Classical man so loved the gods he had created that he wished to emulate them and to be like them. Ulysses[2] was not a god, but he had many things in common with the classical divinities, and it was fair to call him god-like. In other words, it was important to the social attitudes of Homer's Greece to believe that some men at least were 'like' gods; and it is common knowledge that this belief in the divinity of man was responsible for much that was fairest and best in the classical civilization. The statues of Phidias[3] are metaphors inspired by this ideal; the temples and the great dramas and the noble philosophies all testify to the comparison.

5 By way of contrast to the Greek, consider the figurative language of a modern novelist. In one of John Steinbeck's short stories, 'The Leader of the People,' the old grandfather of the story had at one time been a man of the frontier world of Indians and buffalo. But it wasn't Indians that were important, he tells his grandson, Jody, 'nor adventures, nor even getting out here. It was a whole bunch of people made into one big crawling beast. . . . Every man wanted something for himself, but the big beast that was all of them wanted only westering.' And while Jody thinks of 'the wide plains and of the wagons moving across like centipedes,' his grandfather continues, saying 'We carried life out here and set it down the way those ants carry eggs. And I was the leader.'

6 We must remember that Steinbeck matured as a writer during the depression era[4] and that his social philosophy grew out of the social problems of the 1930s. In his search for a social philosophy which could meet the problems of his day, he turned for assistance to the biological sciences. In these he found sound method, tested hypotheses, and, if it could be translated into language descriptive of human behavior, a body of usable information about subhuman life. Steinbeck was one of the first American

---

[2]Latin spelling of Odysseus, a main character in *The Iliad* and *The Odyssey,* narrative poems ascribed to the ancient Greek poet Homer.—ED.

[3]Greek sculptor of the fifth century B.C.—ED.

[4]Period of severe economic decline in America from 1929 through the 1930s.—ED.

novelists to think consistently and seriously, but not always clearly, and mostly with a political purpose in mind, of men as something other than men. And it became Steinbeck's habit to compare human beings with marine animals, with land animals, and with insects. It may be fairly said that Steinbeck's dramatic similarities between mice and men, between fish and men (*Sea of Cortez*), between centipedes and men, whether drawn from observation or embedded within the firm system of ecology, have changed the social thinking of many readers.

7 To future generations, an age may be known by the metaphors it chose to express its ideals. Between 1798 and 1859 a good deal happened to change men's minds about the world they lived in. Among other revolutions in thought not the least effective was the change in attitude toward nature. Wordsworth[5] had said that nature was full of consolation, of joy, and of wisdom. Presently, however, as a result of geological and biological investigations, nature ceased to be regarded as 'Wordsworthian' and came to be thought of as 'Darwinian.'[6] The theory of natural selection brought about a new attitude toward nature that had perforce to be expressed and communicated in new figures of speech. Tennyson[7] was not simply striving to attain animation and originality in expression when he described nature as 'red in tooth and claw.' The association of abstract nature with tigers was striking, but for the Victorians it was also to become 'true.' *In Memoriam* anticipated the *Origin of Species* by nearly a decade, but its representation of nature as a tiger was subsequently to assist in the firm entrenchment of the Darwinian hypothesis; in fact, I suspect that it did more to consolidate the philosophy of struggle than did the *Origin of Species* itself.

8 As a force behind nineteenth-century socialism, Edward Bellamy's[8] famous stagecoach metaphor in his *Looking Backward* had an effect that was immense. Its pertinence to the social conditions of the time, and the 'rightness' of its phrasing gave verbal form to many an inarticulated thought. The analogy of the watch in eighteenth-century Deism[9] was so befitting the ideas of the scientists, poets, and philosophers of the age that the analogy became a 'truth' and God a cosmic clockmaker. When an age abandons its attitudes, it will exile its figures to the limbo for clichés, and new metaphors will take the place of the old. T. S. Eliot[10] inspired a whole generation with the image of the wasteland; and in 1935 Horace

[5]British poet (1770–1850) of the Romantic era.—Ed.

[6]Concepts of evolution by natural selection and survival of the fittest associated with the work of Charles Darwin (1809–1882), author of *On the Origin of Species*.—Ed.

[7]British poet (1809–1892) of the Victorian period.—Ed.

[8]American socialist thinker and writer of utopian literature (1850–1890).—Ed.

[9]Religious belief that emphasizes reason and recognition of God as creator of a world that runs according to natural laws without divine intervention.—Ed.

[10]American-born poet and playwright (1888–1965).—Ed.

Gregory's[11] poetic picture of a chorus of men joining hands to make a new world supplanted, for a time, the figure of the wasteland.

METAPHOR AS STATEMENT OF FACT

9 But it is here that we must observe an important linguistic and social phenomenon. It will be noted that Homer does not say that men *are* gods but only that in certain aspects they resemble gods. Wordsworth does not say that nature *is* a teacher, but only that nature is like a teacher. Yet when metaphor is new, those who find their attitudes implicit in the metaphor construe the metaphor to be a statement of identity, that is, a statement of fact. Figures of speech, when they are fitting and felicitous, and especially when they occur in print, give poetic sanction, as it were, to hitherto dimly felt, inarticulated beliefs. When metaphor is new, and when the reader does not enjoy the perspective vouchsafed by time, the metaphor is taken literally, and its function is not that of rhetorical device, but of statement of fact, *prescribing* certain kinds of behavior. *Indeed, it may be said that the habit which sees the germane metaphor as a statement of identity is a habit which changes the character of civilizations.*

10 Iago[12] is a villain, but a clever one, and he says many things which were pleasing to an Elizabethan ear. For instance:

> 'Tis in ourselves that we are thus or thus. Our bodies are our gardens, to which our wills are gardeners; so that if we will plant nettles, or sow lettuce, set hyssop and weed up thyme, supply it with one gender of herbs, or district it with many, either to have it sterile with idleness, or manured with industry, why, the power and corrigible authority of this lies in our wills.

We may find Shakespeare's figure entertainingly turned, and we may even agree with the sentiment expressed, but in the twentieth century we shall hardly be aware of more than a casual similarity between ourselves and gardens. But when my friend explains to me that life is like a pin-ball machine—that we are little balls shot out through an alley, kicked around from place to place, sometimes ringing a bell or flashing a light, and eventually falling into a trough and rolling out of sight—when he says this, I inquire whether his figure is not perhaps the perfect analogy. His figure has a lively meaning for us today because we believe in the laws of probability, and half suspect the aimlessness of our existence. For all practical purposes, I am well prepared to think of life and pin-ball machines as identities, of taking my friend's metaphor as a statement of fact about human experience.

---

[11]American poet and critic (1898–1983) influenced by Marxist theory and more positive about the future than Eliot.—ED.

[12]Character in Shakespeare's tragedy *Othello.*—ED.

11 When we read in Friedrich von Schelling[13] that 'architecture is frozen music,' we are charmed with the originality and neatness of the analogy. But when James Johnson Sweeney in describing Piet Mondrian's painting *Victory Boogie-Woogie* says the 'The eye is led from one group of color notes to another at varying speeds; at the same time contrasted with this endless change in the minor motives we have a constant repetition of the right angle theme like a persistent bass chord sounding through a sprinkle of running arpeggios and grace notes from the treble,' we are convinced for the moment that the canvas *is* music.

12 The figure of Socrates[14] as a gadfly is interesting but seldom taken literally. Yet when the villain in the cinema is called a 'rat' and shot thrice in the abdomen forthwith, it is a nice question whether the villain was a man or a rat. We know that Grieg's[15] music is not pink bonbons stuffed with snow, although we rather admire the aptness of the similarity and the sensuousness of the image. Yet when someone says of the music of Shostakovich[16] that it is the 'cacophonous scream of a communist manifesto,' we wonder if that is not perhaps 'true.' We are delighted with the little girl who said that carbonated water tastes 'like my foot's asleep,' but when we say a dish we don't like is 'garbage,' it is indeed! When Byron[17] says of poetry that it is the lava of the imagination which prevents an eruption, the metaphor strikes us as an amusing romantic definition of poetry; but when a contemporary writer (I have forgotten who) says that a poem is the sublimation of the social irritant which troubled the poet, just as a pearl is the 'higher order' of the speck which irritated the oyster, we accept the metaphor as a statement of fact about all poetry.

13 The intricate and highly complex network making up the human nervous system has often been likened to a telephonic organization in which messages are sent out from central offices over the 'wires' of the system to all areas of the organism. The analogy is a picturesque explanation of the way the human nervous system 'seems to work.' At the moment, the telephone metaphor is being supplanted by an electronic metaphor in a new system of efficiency called Cybernetics. In this system the mind is likened to a communication system which has its own 'feedback,' making possible automatic adjustments between what it imagines to be 'out there' and what is really out there. But what the human nervous system will be likened to a century from now is unpredictable. New analogies will depend on future neurological theories and on future social, moral, and technological developments.

---

[13]German philosopher (1775–1854).—ED.

[14]Greek philosopher (470?–399 B.C.) best known for the technique of eliciting philosophical truths through a question/answer dialogue.—ED.

[15]Norwegian composer (1843–1907).—ED.

[16]Contemporary Soviet composer (b. 1906).—ED.

[17]British Romantic poet (1788–1824).—ED.

14 Most figurative language is not dangerous in its effects. It is when we take political and social metaphors literally, as statements of identities, that we must proceed with caution. Far more than we are aware, the way we use language determines what the social philosophy of our society shall be. When we take figurative language literally, we are in danger of behaving as if something were true which is manifestly not true *unless we proceed to make it so.* Orators disturbed with social conditions will see new relationships and will express them with vigor. The figure of the 'brotherhood of man' arose out of the way the Age of Reason[18] chose to look at its political situation; the figure was unusually far-reaching in its political effect.

EFFECT OF METAPHOR ON MODERN BEHAVIOR

15 Let us examine several current metaphors, stated or felt, which express 'truths' of modern social beliefs and which, because they are often taken as identities, are in many ways responsible for modern social behavior.

16 1. Murray Schumach's extended figure of speech which appeared on the front page of the *New York Times* for February 26, 1946, is, to be sure, innocuous enough; moreover, it is an analogy which occurs to us as rather common, one which would seem to most people living in New York City to bear itself out in many exact ways:

> Complete shutdown of the city's subways would be almost as disastrous to the city as a serious circulatory ailment to a human being. For New York's subways are her main veins and arteries, distributing her human corpuscles throughout the municipal body twenty-four hours a day.

Mr. Schumach had no ulterior motive, I am sure, in describing New York City in this fashion. I do not want to be misunderstood in what follows as saying that the authors of social metaphors are each and all conspirators against the public morale. Nor do I suggest that Mr. Schumach has caused the inhabitants of New York City to think of themselves as corpuscles. The idea had probably occurred to some people before. But I do suggest that the author of this figure has himself seen New York City in this way and that henceforth some of his readers will unconsciously identify *other* people in New York City as corpuscles. The effect of such metaphors is subtle. If the city is personified as a monstrous human being, and its inhabitants think of themselves as red and white corpuscles, presently, from their understanding of what red and white corpuscles do, they may be inclined to act as if they were, and that might or might not be a good thing; but if

---

[18]Term for the eighteenth century. The period's political philosophy shaped the American and French revolutions.—ED.

carried to extremes, the habit of behaving like a red corpuscle within a monstrous body will change the culture patterns of a society.

17 2. If it were not for the fact that a colleague of mine brought the following parallel to my attention, as a parallel that came spontaneously to his mind, I should consider it rather too far-fetched for inclusion in this essay. In the December 28, 1942 issue of *Life,* there is printed an extraordinary picture of Field Marshal Rommel's[19] army retreating westward along the Mediterranean coast. The picture was photographed from a British plane, and it strongly resembles a slide of bacteria as seen under a microscope. New instruments, new inventions cause us to 'see' things differently. In the *Life* picture we see thousands of men who look 'exactly' *like* bacteria. The resemblance is so striking that for a moment we suspect an identity. If we say enough times that men are like or look like bacteria, and if we see enough pictures showing the resemblance, we shall soon begin to behave toward men as we behave toward bacteria. (One is reminded here, for example, of the rather widespread use of the phrase 'to be immunized against totalitarian philosophies.') Most important of all, from the social point of view, is the fact that our world is prepared in a great variety of ways to think of men as bacteria. Was it Robert Louis Stevenson[20] who referred to humanity as a disease on the face of the earth? In any event, more than one sensitive person has taken Stevenson's metaphor literally and despaired.

18 3. I have often heard large cities referred to as jungles. The main characteristics of a jungle in darkest Africa, as I have read, are an amoral attitude toward all creatures outside the family, the need for alertness in order to survive, the constant feeling of insecurity, and the value of certain traits such as strength, cunning, and agility. Now it is quite possible that these are characteristics of modern city life, and in these respects, therefore, life in a city is like life in a jungle. This is, if true, and we suspect it is, unfortunate, for no one whom I know wants to live in a jungle. It is perfectly natural to think of a city as a jungle, perhaps, but the more we think of it in that way and the more we extend the analogy, the more likely it is that the city will *be* a jungle. At the moment, at any rate, a large city is not a 'jungle,' it is only in some respects like a jungle, and presumably the differences can be pointed out. When, therefore, we insist that the city *is* a jungle, we are no longer speaking figuratively, we are making a statement of moral fact; indeed, we are issuing (as did Upton Sinclair[21]) a moral ultimatum.

19 4. Oswald Spengler[22] was a master of intellectual analogy, perhaps

---

[19]German army officer (1891–1944) of World War II.—Ed.

[20]British novelist (1850–1894), author of *Treasure Island.*—Ed.

[21]American novelist and social reformer (1873–1968), author of *The Jungle.*—Ed.

[22]German philosopher (1880–1936) best known for *The Decline of the West.*—Ed.

the greatest of all time, certainly second to none in the modern world. *The Decline of the West* foretells the eventual demise of the western world, but the entire structure of Spengler's thesis rests on a metaphor. The organic theory of history is a figure of speech, which, simply put, says that a civilization is *like* a living creature—it is born, it grows, and it decays. But Spengler's book is no cause for pessimism, for a civilization is not identical with a living being, as will be seen when Spengler is as old as Homer. A civilization seems to be in some (pertinent, we admit) respects like a living being. But it should have occurred to someone long ago, and perhaps it did, that to take Spengler literally is to put all one's faith in the logic of 'if.' If one believes that the western world has entered upon a stage of decline, then what Spengler says about the western world is 'true.' If there were to take place an historical experience such as a 'decline,' it would perhaps happen as Spengler has described it. In fact, so long as we understand Spengler's analogies to be identities, so long shall we believe in, *and perhaps assist in,* the inevitable decline of the western world.[23]

20 5. One of the most pertinent of modern metaphors, one that seems to many young people to be an accurate description of our modern world, is the analogy of the myth of Sisyphus with contemporary experience. Sisyphus was the mortal condemned by the gods for his sins to roll a stone to the top of a mountain from which the stone falls back down the mountain of its own weight, and Sisyphus must again roll it to the top. The labor of Sisyphus goes on endlessly forever. Albert Camus, contemporary French novelist, and expositor of the 'philosophy of the absurd,' has written a philosophical work entitled *The Myth of Sisyphus,* and in this work he says, 'The gods thought with some reason that there was no punishment more awful than useless and hopeless labor.' Although Camus thinks of Sisyphus as a tragic hero, noble in his scorn of the gods, he also thinks of him as the absurd hero, and he likens the worker of today to Sisyphus. 'The worker of today labors every day of his life at the same tasks and his destiny is no less absurd.'

21 But the myth of Sisyphus is a story, as a moving picture is a story, as a ballad is a story as an epic or a novel is a story. We often think of ourselves as 'like' a character out of a novel or story. In fact, a whole nation of people (generally speaking) thought of themselves as 'like' the Siegfried or Brunhild[24] of Teutonic mythology. It is pleasant to some people to suspect that they have something in common with Siegfried, but if we say we *are* Siegfried, unless the whole world agrees with us, we are in trouble. We

---

[23]Talking about a 'possible' future event will in itself tend to bring the event to pass. And the evidence selected to anticipate the event will direct the event to take the form foreseen. That people often behave according to the way they have expressed their expectations is brilliantly discussed by Robert K. Merton in his article 'The Self-Fulfilling Prophecy,' *Antioch Review,* 8.193ff (1948).

[24]Principal heroic characters of medieval Germanic stories.—ED.

are not less in error if we take the myth of Sisyphus literally and say that we are Sisyphus, that we are absurd heroes engaged in 'useless and hopeless labor.' It is only too patently true that our world seems to be 'like' the Hell of Sisyphus. But that our world *is* the Hell of Sisyphus and that we *are* doomed to hopeless labor is a fiction evolving out of an inferred identity which simply does not exist. Camus has used his parallel as a device for illuminating and criticizing the social world of today. If we take his figure literally, and especially if we take it without an understanding of its 'tragic' implications, we are likely to be very unhappy if nothing more.

22 6. A good deal of theoretical discourse is diagrammatic in character. The Ptolemaic cosmology[25] in the form of a diagram says only that as far as can be observed and inferred, the universe is 'like' the diagram. Diagrammatic representations which are the results of inference and imaginative picturing forth of an idea cannot be tested empirically, and we must beware of seeing identities where they do not exist.[26]

23 To take the most illustrious modern example, I turn to the popularized psychology of Sigmund Freud.[27] (But first I should like to point out that I have the greatest respect for Freud, and I should be the last to choose to discredit psychoanalysis. Only provincial prejudice finds Freud ridiculous and offensive.) Freud was a poet and a philosopher. Freud's work is one long extended figure of speech, as is the *Divine Comedy* of Dante.[28] Both Dante and Freud have written allegories of the spiritual life. If there were a Hell, it might be 'like' Dante's. I think it was Waldo Frank who said somewhere that if you believe in Hell, it makes a great deal of difference to you how many circles there 'really are.' If you take Freud literally, the true nature and character of 'complexes' make a great deal of difference; but what the analyst says in effect is that we act 'as if' we had an Oedipus complex,[29] supposing there were such a thing as an Oedipus complex, just as a physician might have said in the seventeenth century that his patient behaved as if he were a witch, supposing that there were such things as witches. But the 'cure' for witches was different.

24 Freud was a philosopher whom many people have taken literally, assuming that the subconscious as Freud describes it is *identical* with some 'part' of our 'self.' Freud's diagram of the Id, the Ego, and the Super Ego

---

[25]Cosmology of the second-century Greek astronomer Ptolemy, who depicted the earth as the center of the universe.—ED.

[26]For an analysis of schematic, symbolic, and tropic 'fictions' see Hans Vaihinger, *The Philosophy of 'As if'* (London 1949), 24ff. In fact, Vaihinger's work is throughout a painstaking study of the consciously false assumptions which are implicit in most if not all metaphorical expressions. In many respects, my 'Metaphor and Social Belief' is a kind of extended footnote to *The Philosophy of 'As if.'*

[27]Austrian physician and founder of psychoanalysis (1856–1939).—ED.

[28]Italian poet (1265–1321) most famous for his long narrative poem *Divine Comedy*.—ED.

[29]Sexual feelings in a male child for his mother together with feelings of resentment toward the father.—ED.

is a schema which is a metaphor useful merely in discussion. In *An Autobiographical Study* Freud warned against taking his schematic representations literally. 'The subdivision of the unconscious is part of an attempt to picture the apparatus of the mind as being built up of a number of *functional systems* whose interrelations may be expressed in spatial terms, without reference, of course, to the actual anatomy of the brain.' But many readers will take the image of the subconscious literally. We imagine the Id as a murky 'depth' of turbulence somewhere at the bottom of the 'mind,' its poisonous fumes rising up from deep upon deep of mystery through the trap door of the censor at night when the censor is 'asleep.' The Ego, our every-day consciousness, lives on the first-floor of the mind, looks out of its windows, and conforms to the customs of the every-day world—the bewildered little man of the cartoon who always stands between two opposing forces. Above, at the 'top' of our mind, is the Super-Ego, a kind of stern father who looks down upon our conscious behavior and issues commands.

25 Even professional analysts sometimes 'think' in this manner; and amateur psychologists, as I have discovered, almost invariably do. It is impossible to know how much such a 'metaphor' has affected the common reader in his attitudes toward life, but it is fairly certain that many have taken the figure of the subconscious literally, saying that this is the way the mind works. On the contrary, we should say that our inner life seems only in some respects to be *like* the Freudian description.

26 7. Drawing analogies between the subject-matter of zoology and biology and the subject-matter of the social sciences has been very popular in recent years among some social thinkers. It has been fashionable to think of men as animals and even as insects. One of the most common parallels drawn by fascist theorizers is the parallel between men and ants. I recall magazine articles describing Nazi scientists observing ant societies in order to discover how human society may most easily be converted into a society similar to (or identical with) that of the white ant of Africa.

27 The propagandistic use of the ant metaphor has been most vividly described by a character in Arthur Koestler's[30] novel *Arrival and Departure.* In the enthusiasm with which Koestler's Nazi speaks, we see among other things that the language he uses has convinced him beyond any doubt of the desirability of understanding that ants and men are, for political purposes, identical. When, as in Nazi Germany, men are likened to ants, then beyond question men will be treated as though they were ants. Whatever is thinkable is also possible in the world of today.

---

[30]Hungarian-born British novelist (b. 1905) who was imprisoned in France during World War II.—Ed.

> Absolute conditioning must finally result in the creation of a collective consciousness in the full biological sense of the term. Nature has a perfect working model for it in the city-states of the African white ant. They each embrace several million members of the race, they cover areas up to fifty square miles and function with absolute expediency. They have perfect division of labor; they control highly complicated technical devices including a system of heating by vegetable fermentation which keeps the temperature in their vaults constant through all seasons; they enforce a mathematically perfect birthrate policy. And yet they have no planning body, no blueprints, no governing administration, not even the means of written communication. How is this possible? The answer usually given is 'by instinct'; but such a highly differentiated instinct which is shared by, and limited to, members of one city-state amounts to nothing less than a collective brain-function of the state organism. In a similar way, and probably helped by artificially-produced biological mutations, the individuals in the suprastate will become mere cells in an organism of a higher order—a million-legged, million-armed cyclopean colossus. . . .

28 8. It is apparent from the illustrations I have used that our contemporary social similitudes are often drawn from the biological sciences. The master metaphor of the modern world, however, is drawn from technology and is the identification of men with machines.

29 In our thinking we often, nay almost invariably, make the distinguished blunder of supposing that the human body is a machine, that it works as a machine works, according to the laws of mechanics. *Why* we prefer to 'think' in this way about ourselves is open to speculation. In any event, that we should be unaware of the simple fact that men are only in a few unimportant respects like machines, but that machines are, *as far as they go,* in all respects like men is the supreme misunderstanding of our time and accounts almost exclusively for our lack, just when we need it most, of a real humanistic philosophy. The obvious fact is that machines are like men for the simple reason that man made the machine, as far as he could, *in his own image.* It would be unpleasing to some ears to have it said that man left out a soul when he made the machine, but that, or something very like that, is precisely what happened.

30 In recent years the machine has been perfected to perform uncanny tasks, the most striking being the calculation and solution of involved mathematical problems. The electronic brain has its place in the imaginations of men as the Most High. Presently we shall wish that our nerve cells were as clever as electron tubes, quite forgetting that it was our nerve cells that had the wit to create electron tubes.

31 Make no mistake about it, we think more highly of our machines than we do of ourselves. We try to live up to the machine, to learn from the machine, to be more nearly machines, because we think they are better

than we are.[31] It appears that our dearest wish is to *be* machines and to function wholly as they do. This wish will strike future ages as the dominating feature of a lost society, of a deluded people who worshipped their engines more than their gods, to say nothing of themselves.

32 But creative writers and some social philosophers have been saying all this for more than a hundred years. There is little excuse for me to labor the point. All I wish to insist upon is that the way we use language may account in part for our madness. The moment we say that the human being *is* a machine, at that moment we shall believe that the human being can be conditioned to behave in a perfectly predictable way with admirable regularity. Then it is that we shall have made of ourselves something less, ever so much less, than we are. But if we speak with caution to the effect that machines are *in some respects* like human beings, we can put the machine to its good use and still keep our self-respect and our humanity.

33 If ever we needed to think of man as man, as unique, identical with nothing else in the world, it is today. Contemporary imagery is blurred and confused. Our hardest intellectual task is to keep things apart, to separate out issues and ideas from one another. Our present efforts are to see all particulars as alike, and we tend to force identities where only similarities exist. No two things are identical, although we seem to want to think so. We have abandoned the exact and differentiated in favor of mingled associations and blurred relationships. The use of analogy in all branches of human thought is indispensable; but the making of nice distinctions is equally important and has ever been a leading characteristic of the human mind. The knowledge of subtle differences—as between people of different cultures, between one human being and another, or even between brands of coffee, kinds of perfumes, vintages in wines, spoiled food and edible food, poison and medicine, beauty and ugliness, justice and injustice—is a knowledge invaluable to mankind. What is more, the knowledge of differences leads to an understanding of relationships. We are more likely to be at home in our world not so much by striving to cut each particular to the same pattern, as by studying to understand the tenuous, the subtle, the often beautiful relationships which are the foundations of human society and to a great extent the joy of life. The knowledge of just and workable relationships among dissimilars is what every philosopher, every artist, and every statesman has longed to attain.

---

[31] While preparing this article for publication, the writer was introduced to *Dianetics* by L. Ronald Hubbard (New York 1950). In this 'modern science of mental health' would appear to be the most appalling example yet of the identification of men with machines. Constructed in the name of efficiency, the central theme of *Dianetics* depends on the fiction that a human being is a calculating machine capable of functioning in a 100 per cent mechanical fashion.

Word Study List

pedagogical	1	neurological	13
hackneyed	2	innocuous	16
capricious	3	amoral	18
emulate	4	pertinent	19
embedded	6	discourse	22
perforce	7	diagrammatic	22
inarticulated	8, 9	empirically	22
linguistic	9	schema	24
implicit	9	fascist	26
construe	9	similitudes	28
vouchsafed	9	deluded	31
rehtorical	9	differentiated	33
germane	9	tenuous	33

Questions

1. Embler says that what a metaphor *does* is more important than what a metaphor *is*. What do metaphors do? Why does Embler think they are so important?

2. Why, according to Embler, are trite figures or clichés to be avoided? Why have they become worn out?

3. How do the metaphors of Baker and Shakespeare (paragraphs 2 and 3) illustrate the importance of metaphors?

4. Briefly describe the metaphor of the following writers that is mentioned by Embler: Homer, Steinbeck, Wordsworth, Tennyson, T. S. Eliot, Horace Gregory, Shakespeare.

5. How might readers respond to metaphors that seem "right" for their time? When can metaphors have dangerous consequences?

6. List the eight contemporary metaphors Embler mentions as affecting modern social behavior. Which do you think most affect our time? Which one do you find most "truthful"?

Exercise

In what ways has the metaphor you find most meaningful affected your values and behavior? Think, for example, about your political views, your social relationships, your behavior with strangers, your concepts of human development. (Are individuals responsible for what they do with their lives?) Bring to class a list of the specific ways "your" metaphor has affected you.

The Gettysburg Address

Abraham Lincoln

Our sixteenth president, Abraham Lincoln (1809–1865) was first elected in 1860 and reelected in 1864. Although he did not speak or write extensively, Lincoln's two inaugural addresses, the Gettysburg Address, and his last speech, delivered on April 11, 1865, all deserve study as examples of effective oratory. The Gettysburg Address was delivered on November 19, 1863.

Fourscore and seven years ago our fathers brought forth on this continent a new nation, conceived in liberty and dedicated to the proposition that all men are created equal. Now we are engaged in a great civil war, testing whether that nation, or any nation so conceived and so dedicated, can long endure. We are met on a great battlefield of that war. We have come to dedicate a portion of that field as a final resting place for those who here gave their lives that that nation might live. It is altogether fitting and proper that we should do this. But, in a larger sense, we cannot dedicate—we cannot consecrate—we cannot hallow—this ground. The brave men, living and dead, who struggled here have consecrated it far above our poor power to add or to detract. The world will little note nor long remember what we say here, but it can never forget what they did here. It is for us, the living, rather to be dedicated here to the unfinished work which they who fought here have thus far so nobly advanced. It is rather for us to be here dedicated to the great task remaining before us—that from these honored dead we take increased devotion to that cause for which they gave the last full measure of devotion; that we here highly resolve that these dead shall not have died in vain; that this nation, under God, shall have a new birth of freedom; and that government of the people, by the people, for the people shall not perish from the earth.

Word Study List

conceived	consecrate
proposition	hallow

Questions

1. Probably no speech by any American president is better known than Lincoln's Gettysburg Address, perhaps because many school children are required to memorize it. But being familiar with a piece, we sometimes forget to concentrate on its meaning. In no more than three sentences, summarize the main point of Lincoln's address.

2. The journalist Henry Fairlie, in a defense of rhetoric (the art of speaking and writing effectively), asserts that "to think of politics without rhetoric is to deny politics its very existence" because politics is "the art of moving people by language . . . and its main instrument is rhetoric." How does Lincoln's speech demonstrate the connection between rhetoric and politics described by Fairlie?

The Gettysburg Address

Gilbert Highet

Gilbert Highet (1906–1978) was long head of the Department of Greek and Latin at Columbia University. He wrote on literary and intellectual topics for both the scholar and the nonscholar. Two of his books are *The Classical Tradition* (1949) and *Poets in a Landscape* (1957). Highet's analysis of Lincoln's Gettysburg Address was printed in a collection of essays entitled *A Clerk of Oxenford: Essays on Literature and Life* (1954).

In his analysis Highet begins by placing the address in its historical context and then reminding us of those elements of Lincoln's education that prepared him for great oratory. Highet then examines each stylistic or rhetorical technique used in the speech.

1 *Fourscore and seven years ago . . .*

2 These five words stand at the entrance to the best-known monument of American prose, one of the finest utterances in the entire language, and surely one of the greatest speeches in all history. Greatness is like granite: it is molded in fire, and it lasts for many centuries.

3 Fourscore and seven years ago . . . It is strange to think that President Lincoln was looking back to the 4th of July 1776, and that he and his speech are now further removed from us than he himself was from George Washington and the Declaration of Independence. Fourscore and seven years before the Gettysburg Address, a small group of patriots signed the Declaration. Fourscore and seven years after the Gettysburg

Address, it was the year 1950,[1] and that date is already receding rapidly into our troubled, adventurous, and valiant past.

4 Inadequately prepared and at first scarcely realized in its full importance, the dedication of the graveyard at Gettysburg was one of the supreme moments of American history. The battle itself had been a turning point of the war. On the 4th of July 1863, General Meade repelled Lee's invasion of Pennsylvania. Although he did not follow up his victory, he had broken one of the most formidable aggressive enterprises of the Confederate armies. Losses were heavy on both sides. Thousands of dead were left on the field, and thousands of wounded died in the hot days following the battle. At first, their burial was more or less haphazard; but thoughtful men gradually came to feel that an adequate burying place and memorial were required. These were established by an interstate commission that autumn, and the finest speaker in the North was invited to dedicate them. This was the scholar and statesman Edward Everett of Harvard. He made a good speech—which is still extant: not at all academic, it is full of close strategic analysis and deep historical understanding.

5 Lincoln was not invited to speak, at first. Although people knew him as an effective debater, they were not sure whether he was capable of making a serious speech on such a solemn occasion. But one of the impressive things about Lincoln's career is that he constantly strove to *grow.* He was anxious to appear on that occasion and to say something worthy of it. (Also, it has been suggested, he was anxious to remove the impression that he did not know how to behave properly—an impression which had been strengthened by a shocking story about his clowning on the battlefield of Antietam[2] the previous year.) Therefore when he was invited he took considerable care with his speech. He drafted rather more than half of it in the White House before leaving, finished it in the hotel at Gettysburg the night before the ceremony (not in the train, as sometimes reported), and wrote out a fair copy next morning.

6 There are many accounts of the day itself, 19 November 1863. There are many descriptions of Lincoln, all showing the same curious blend of grandeur and awkwardness, or lack of dignity, or—it would be best to call it humility. In the procession he rode horseback: a tall lean man in a high plug hat, straddling a short horse, with his feet too near the ground. He arrived before the chief speaker, and had to wait patiently for half an hour or more. His own speech came right at the end of a long and exhausting ceremony, lasted less than three minutes, and made little impression on the audience. In part this was because they were tired, in part because (as eyewitnesses said) he ended almost before they knew he had begun, and in part because he did not speak the Address, but read it, very slowly, in

---

[1]In November 1950 the Chinese had just entered the war in Korea.

[2]A village near Harpers Ferry, West Virginia, scene of a Civil War battle in 1862.—Ed.

a thin high voice, with a marked Kentucky accent, pronouncing 'to' as 'toe' and dropping his final R's.

7 Some people of course were alert enough to be impressed. Everett congratulated him at once. But most of the newspapers paid little attention to the speech, and some sneered at it. The *Patriot and Union* of Harrisburg wrote, 'We pass over the silly remarks of the President; for the credit of the nation we are willing . . . that they shall no more be repeated or thought of'; and the London *Times* said, 'The ceremony was rendered ludicrous by some of the sallies of that poor President Lincoln,' calling his remarks 'dull and commonplace.' The first commendation of the Address came in a single sentence of the Chicago *Tribune,* and the first discriminating and detailed praise of it appeared in the Springfield *Republican,* the Providence *Journal,* and the Philadelphia *Bulletin.* However, three weeks after the ceremony and then again the following spring, the editor of *Harper's Weekly* published a sincere and thorough eulogy of the Address, and soon it was attaining recognition as a masterpiece.

8 At the time, Lincoln could not care much about the reception of his words. He was exhausted and ill. In the train back to Washington, he lay down with a wet towel on his head. He had caught smallpox. At that moment he was incubating it, and he was stricken down soon after he reentered the White House. Fortunately it was a mild attack, and it evoked one of his best jokes: he told his visitors, 'At last I have something I can give to everybody.'

9 He had more than that to give to everybody. He was a unique person, far greater than most people realize until they read his life with care. The wisdom of his policy, the sources of his statesmanship—these were things too complex to be discussed in a brief essay. But we can say something about the Gettysburg Address as a work of art.

10 A work of art. Yes: for Lincoln was a literary artist, trained both by others and by himself. The textbooks he used as a boy were full of difficult exercises and skillful devices in formal rhetoric, stressing the qualities he practiced in his own speaking: antithesis, parallelism, and verbal harmony. Then he read and reread many admirable models of thought and expression: the King James Bible, the essays of Bacon,[3] the best plays of Shakespeare. His favorites were *Hamlet, Lear, Macbeth, Richard III,* and *Henry VIII,* which he had read dozens of times. He loved reading aloud, too, and spent hours reading poetry to his friends. (He told his partner Herndon that he preferred getting the sense of any document by reading it aloud.) Therefore his serious speeches are important parts of the long and noble classical tradition of oratory which begins in Greece, runs through Rome to the modern world, and is still capable (if we do not neglect it) of producing masterpieces.

---

[3]A British philosopher (1561–1626) and author. Bacon and Shakespeare were contemporaries who lived when the much admired King James Bible was printed in 1611.—Ed.

11 The first proof of this is that the Gettysburg Address is full of quotations—or rather of adaptations—which give it strength. It is partly religious, partly (in the highest sense) political: therefore it is interwoven with memories of the Bible and memories of American history. The first and the last words are Biblical cadences. Normally Lincoln did not say 'fourscore' when he meant eighty; but on this solemn occasion he recalled the important dates in the Bible—such as the age of Abram when his first son was born to him, and he was 'fourscore and six years old.'[4] Similarly he did not say there was a chance that democracy might die out: he recalled the somber phrasing of the Book of Job—where Bildad speaks of the destruction of one who shall vanish without a trace, and says that 'his branch shall be cut off; his remembrance shall perish from the earth.'[5] Then again, the famous description of our State as 'government of the people, by the people, for the people' was adumbrated by Daniel Webster[6] in 1830 (he spoke of 'the people's government, made for the people, made by the people, and answerable to the people') and then elaborated in 1854 by the abolitionist Theodore Parker[7] (as 'government of all the people, by all the people, for all the people'). There is good reason to think that Lincoln took the important phrase 'under God' (which he interpolated at the last moment) from Weems,[8] the biographer of Washington; and we know that it had been used at least once by Washington himself.

12 Analyzing the Address further, we find that it is based on a highly imaginative theme, or group of themes. The subject is—how can we put it so as not to disfigure it?—the subject is the kinship of life and death, that mysterious linkage which we see sometimes as the physical succession of birth and death in our world, sometimes as the contrast, which is perhaps a unity, between death and immortality. The first sentence is concerned with birth:

> Our *fathers brought forth* a *new* nation, *conceived* in liberty.

The final phrase but one expresses the hope that

> this nation, under God, shall have a *new birth* of freedom.

And the last phrase of all speaks of continuing life as the triumph over death. Again and again throughout the speech, this mystical contrast and kinship reappear: 'those who *gave their lives* that that nation might *live,*'

---

[4]Gen. 16.16; cf. Exod. 7.7.

[5]Job 18.16–17; cf. Jer. 10.11, Micah 7.2.

[6]An American statesman (1782–1852) and orator.—Ed.

[7]A Unitarian clergyman (1810–1860), popular lecturer, essayist, and strong supporter of abolition.—Ed.

[8]An American clergyman (1759–1825) and biographer who first wrote the story of George Washington cutting down the cherry tree.—Ed.

'the brave men *living* and *dead,'* and so in the central assertion that the dead have already consecrated their own burial place, while 'it is for us, the *living,* rather to be dedicated . . . to the great task remaining.' The Gettysburg Address is a prose poem; it belongs to the same world as the great elegies, and the adagios of Beethoven.

13 Its structure, however, is that of a skillfully contrived speech. The oratorical pattern is perfectly clear. Lincoln describes the occasion, dedicates the ground, and then draws a larger conclusion by calling on his hearers to dedicate themselves to the preservation of the Union. But within that, we can trace his constant use of at least two important rhetorical devices.

14 The first of these is *antithesis:* opposition, contrast. The speech is full of it. Listen:

> The world will little *note*
> nor long *remember* what *we say* here
> but it can never *forget* what *they did* here.

And so in nearly every sentence: 'brave men, *living* and *dead';* 'to *add* or *detract.'* There is the antithesis of the Founding Fathers and the men of Lincoln's own time:

> Our *fathers brought forth* a new nation . . .
> now *we* are testing whether that nation . . . can *long endure.*

And there is the more terrible antithesis of those who have already died and those who still live to do their duty. Now, antithesis is the figure of contrast and conflict. Lincoln was speaking in the midst of a great civil war.

15 The other important pattern is different. It is technically called *tricolon*—the division of an idea into three harmonious parts, usually of increasing power. The most famous phrase of the Address is a tricolon:

> government of the people
> by the people
> and for the people.

The most solemn sentence is a tricolon:

> we cannot dedicate
> we cannot consecrate
> we cannot hallow this ground.

And above all, the last sentence (which has sometimes been criticized as too complex) is essentially two parallel phrases, with a tricolon growing out of the second and then producing another tricolon: a trunk, three branches, and a cluster of flowers. Lincoln says that it is for his hearers to be dedicated to the great task remaining before them. Then he goes on,

> that from these honored dead

—apparently he means 'in such a way that from these honored dead'—

> we take increased devotion to that cause.

Next, he restates this more briefly:

> that we here highly resolve . . .

And now the actual resolution follows, in three parts of growing intensity:

> that these dead shall not have died in vain
> that this nation, under God, shall have a new birth
> of freedom

and that (one more tricolon)

> government of the people
> by the people
> and for the people.

> shall not perish from the earth.

Now, the tricolon is the figure which, through division, emphasizes basic harmony and unity. Lincoln used antithesis because he was speaking to a people at war. He used the tricolon because he was hoping, planning, praying for peace.

16 No one thinks that when he was drafting the Gettysburg Address, Lincoln deliberately looked up these quotations and consciously chose these particular patterns of thought. No, he chose the theme. From its development and from the emotional tone of the entire occasion, all the rest followed, or grew—by that marvelous process of choice and rejection which is essential to artistic creation. It does not spoil such a work of art to analyze it as closely as we have done; it is altogether fitting and proper that we should do this: for it helps us to penetrate more deeply into the rich meaning of the Gettysburg Address, and it allows us the very rare privilege of watching the workings of a great man's mind.

Word Study List

extant	4	adumbrated	11
eulogy	7	interpolated	11
rhetoric	10	elegies	12
antithesis	10, 14, 15	adagios	12

Questions

1. What is Highet's thesis? Where is it stated?

2. What is the purpose of the first eight paragraphs?

3. List the three characteristics of Lincoln's address that make it a great speech.

4. What two rhetorical devices used by Lincoln does Highet analyze in detail? Why are they especially appropriate choices for shaping the style of the speech?

5. Analyze Highet's style. Consider the length and structure of his sentences, the structure of the essay as a whole, and his use of specific rhetorical devices such as repetition, parallelism, antithesis, metaphor, and tricolon.

6. What generalization can you make about the aptness of Highet's style, given his subject and purpose?

Exercise

Practice using tricolon, coordination, and antithesis, writing one or two of your own sentences for each of the models.

MODEL TRICOLON:	"Reading maketh a full man, conference a ready man, and writing an exact man." (Bacon)
SAMPLE STUDENT TRICOLON:	Walking makes a relaxed man, jogging makes a healthy man, and running makes a robust man.
MODEL TRICOLON:	" . . . we cannot dedicate—we cannot consecrate—we cannot hallow this ground." (Lincoln)
MODEL TRICOLON:	"Crafty men condemn studies, simple men admire them, and wise men use them." (Bacon)
MODEL COORDINATION:	Sleep is the only state of mind without either a purpose or a destination.
MODEL COORDINATION:	I have neither the patience for most hobbies nor the athletic ability for most sports.
MODEL ANTITHESIS:	"Children sweeten labors, but they make misfortunes more bitter." (Bacon)
MODEL ANTITHESIS:	Love brightens the night, but its loss darkens the day.

How *Time* Stereotyped Three U.S. Presidents

John C. Merrill

A professor of journalism at Louisana State University, John C. Merrill (b. 1924) is the author of numerous books on the media, including *Journalistic Autonomy: A Philosophy of Press Freedom* (1974) and *Basic Issues in Mass Communication* (1984). This essay appeared in *Journalism Quarterly* in Autumn 1965.

Merrill's study of *Time*'s techniques for creating bias provides both a good example of careful scholarly analysis and useful "bias categories" that can serve as guidelines for other style analyses. Merrill's examination of particular uses of connotation and other techniques for slanting the news reaffirms the power of language to shape a reader's perceptions of reality.

1 The suggestion that *Time* magazine selects, aligns and explains (*i.e.,* "subjectivizes") information will certainly not startle many persons. In fact, its editors have insisted from the magazine's founding in 1923 that objectivity in news presentation is impossible and that *Time* writers should "make a judgment" in their articles.[1] This study investigates some of the techniques used by the publication to subjectivize its news and to try to determine what stereotyped pictures of three American Presidents were presented. The study is not concerned with the "ethics" of a news magazine's "subjectivizing" its news content, although some writers have been critical in this respect.[2]

2 This study[3] was undertaken primarily to answer this question: What kind of stereotyped image of each of the Presidents—Truman, Eisenhower, and Kennedy—was presented by the magazine? Rather cursory and nonanalytical reading of *Time* had given the impression that the magazine was anti-Truman and pro-Eisenhower. And during the Kennedy administration, there were many surface indications that *Time* was at least more objective (or neutral) toward the late President. What would be the stereotypes of the three Presidents presented by *Time* and how would the magazine go about creating them?

---

[1]John Kobler, "Luce: The First Tycoon and the Power of His Press," *Saturday Evening Post* (Jan. 16, 1965), pp. 28–45. Cf. James Playsted Wood, *Magazines in the United States* (New York: Ronald Press, 1956), pp. 205–6, and *The Story of an Experiment* (New York: Time, Inc., 1948).

[2]Almost the entire first issue of *FACT* (Jan.–Feb., 1964) was devoted to a series of highly critical essays by important personages, all deploring the practices of *Time*. Another criticism of *Time,* even more harsh, perhaps, was the entire issue of *UAW Ammunition* (Dec. 1956). Yet another, couched in more intellectual though hardly less cutting language, was "Time: the Weekly Fiction Magazine" by Jigs Gardner in *The Nation* (Aug. 15, 1959), pp. 65–67.

[3]Sponsored in part by the Fund for Organized Research, Texas A&M University.

3 Would the "newsstories" in the magazine indicate political bias? Would the stories provide clear-cut examples of subjective, judgmental or opinionated reporting? If so, what were these techniques of subjectivizing? This study would at least be a beginning in a systemized critique.

THE METHOD

4 Ten consecutive issues of *Time* were chosen for study from each of the three Presidential administrations. The beginning date of each consecutive issue period was chosen by the random method of selection. First, the years of each administration were chosen; for Truman, 1951; for Eisenhower, 1955; for Kennedy, 1962. Successive procedures determined the month and the week which would be used as the beginning date for the 10 issues in each administration. The Truman beginning date was April 2, 1951; the Eisenhower date was January 24, 1955, and the Kennedy beginning date was November 23, 1962.

5 It was decided that there was no need to compare space treatment given the three Presidents, since space in itself has no necessary bearing on subjectivity or bias. What was considered important was the language used to describe each President, with special emphasis on the presence or absence of "loaded" words and expressions and on general contextual impressions presented.

6 Six *bias categories* were set up: 1) attribution bias, 2) adjective bias, 3) adverbial bias, 4) contextual bias, 5) outright opinion, and 6) photographic bias. In considering these categories, as they related to the 30 issues of *Time* studied, instances of bias were noted either as *positive* (favorable) or as *negative* (unfavorable). Advanced journalism students served as an evaluative panel. Indications of bias (either positive or negative) thought dubious (borderline cases) were not counted as bias in this study.

THE BIAS CATEGORIES

7 *Attribution Bias* designates bias which stems from the magazine's means of attributing information to the President. In other words, this is bias which is contained in the synonym for the word "said" used by the magazine. An attribution verb such as "said" is neutral (not opinionated and evokes no emotional response) and was ignored in the study. An attribution verb such as "snapped" (negatively affective) is a word designed to appeal to the reader's emotions, to give a judgmental stimulus. An attribution verb such as "smiled" is counted as a "favorable" term, for it is positively affective.

8 *Adjective Bias* is a type which, like attribution bias, attempts to build up an impression of the person described; this is accomplished by using adjectives, favorable or unfavorable, in connection with the person. While use of adjectives is quite common in news reporting, they must be used

with extreme care or subjectivity will creep in and the mere use of the adjectives will create a favorable or unfavorable impression. Or, as Rudolf Flesch points out, "the little descriptive adjectives" of *Time* "tend to blot out" the other words because of their "overpotency." This results, says Flesch, in the reader getting "a wrong impression or, at least, an emphasis that isn't there."[4]

9 An example of "favorable" bias in adjective use: "*serene* state of mind." An example of "unfavorable" bias in adjective use: "*flat, monotonous* voice." Not only do these adjectives tend to prejudice the reader for or against the person described, but they are actually *subjective* in nature; they are opinions of the writer. They might be called "judgmental" adjectives; at any rate they are quite different from adjectives which might be called "neutral" or "objective"—such as "the *blue* sky."

10 *Adverbial Bias* depends on qualifiers or magnifiers—adverbs—to create an impression in the reader's mind. Often this adverbial bias is a sort of reinforcing of another bias expression already present (*e.g.*, when an adverb reinforces an attribution bias as in this case: "He barked *sarcastically*"). This is a technique by which the magazine creates a favorable or unfavorable impression in the mind of the reader by generally telling *how* or *why* a person said or did something.

11 *Contextual Bias* cannot be notated in neat lists. It is the bias in whole sentences or paragraphs or in other (and larger) units of meaning, even an entire story. The purpose is to present the person reported on in a favorable or an unfavorable light by the overall meaning or innuendo of the report, not by specific words and phrases alone. The whole context must be considered. Since one's own biases or interpretations might very well determine what he considers contextually biased, it was necessary to get the opinions of a panel.[5] Contextual bias was counted *only* when there was agreement among the panelists.

12 *Outright Opinion,* of course, is the most blatant and obvious type of bias or subjectivity in newswriting. The expression of opinion by the publication might be called "presenting a judgment," which S. I. Hayakawa says should be kept out of reports.[6] Dr. Hayakawa defines "judgments" as "all expressions of the writer's approval or disapproval of the occurrences, persons, or objects he is describing." Readers do not expect to

---

[4]*How to Write, Speak and Think More Effectively* (New York: Signet Books, 1963), pp. 68–9. Dr. Flesch says that these adjectives, according to *Time* editors, help the reader get a better picture of what's going on. Dr. Flesch takes issue with this and says that it is "quite obvious that *Time* readers are apt to learn a lot about the faces, figures, hands, lips and eyes of world leaders, but are liable to misread or skip what these people do" (p. 69).

[5]Six advanced journalism students at Texas A&M composed the panel to decide on these cases of possible contextual bias.

[6]*Language In Thought and Action* (New York: Harcourt, Brace and Company, 1940), pp. 38, 42–44.

find the judgments or opinions of the writer in a newspaper or a newsmagazine except in a signed column or editorial. *Time* does use outright opinion. Examples: "His (Eisenhower's) powers of personal persuasion are strong" and "He has an aversion to stirring up unnecessary national crises."

13 The expression of opinion is sometimes disguised. In other words, through semantic tricks *Time* permits someone else (or the whole United States) to say or believe something about the President, thus presenting its own opinion indirectly. Example: "Few at home in the U.S. seemed to begrudge the President his trip, however inauspicious the timing." In addition, *Time* projects its opinion by explaining *why* people in the news do as they do. As one writer puts it: "*Time* reads men's motives—good for friends, bad for enemies—with that Olympian supremacy and aloofness which prompted Commager to speak of the period 'before Time became omniscient.'"[7]

14 *Photographic Bias,* it is granted, might possibly result from inability to get other photographs or from no real desire to prejudice the reader. In other words, it could be unintentional. However, intention is not considered in the treatment of this or any other category, for there is no real way to know intent. These questions were asked in trying to determine this bias: What overall impression does the photograph give? How is the President presented in the picture—dignified, undignified; angry, happy; calm, nervous, etc.? What does the caption say/imply?

A SELECTED WEEK: TRUMAN

15 *Issue of April 23, 1951:* Of the 10 weeks of *Time* studied from the Truman administration, this issue of April 23 contains more obvious indications of bias and subjectivity than any of the others. It is one of the several issues which dealt with Truman's relieving General MacArthur of his post as Supreme Commander in the Far East. *Time* is obviously in sympathy with the general, and in this week's issue makes some of its more biased statements. Some examples of the magazines's opinions can be seen in the following paragraph (p. 24):

> Seldom had a more unpopular man fired a more popular one. Douglas MacArthur was the personification of the big man, with the many admirers who look to the great man for leadership, with the few critics who distrust and fear a big man's domineering ways. Harry Truman was almost a professional little man, with admirers who like the little man's courage, with the many critics who despise a little man's inadequacies.

16 Not satisfied with the then-current issue, *Time* quickly and in broad strokes presents the readers with a "flash-back" to an administration filled

---

[7]Garry Wills, "Timestyle," *National Review* (Aug. 3, 1957), p. 130.

with six years of "shabby politicking and corruption" and "doubts about his State Department" coupled with "distaste for his careless government-by-crony."

17 *Time* in this issue, *however,* does not stop here; it goes further and gives the impression that the nation shares its opinions of President Truman. Says *Time* (p. 25): "A few days later, over the morning coffee, the nation read of Harry Truman's reply and fumed." (This followed a report by the magazine that Truman had "replied curtly" to a critic of his MacArthur action.) Also in this issue readers were reminded that "probers were still unearthing new evidence of skulduggery in the RFC" and that Truman was a President who "stubbornly protected shoddy friends."

A SELECTED WEEK: EISENHOWER

18 *Issue of Feb. 7, 1955:* In this week's issue, *Time* quite typically provides vivid examples of subjective and biased reporting and evidences a strong pro-Eisenhower slant. According to the magazine: "The strong leadership of President Eisenhower and the near-unanimity of the Congress in backing him in the Formosa resolution undoubtedly retrieved much of the U.S. prestige and influence that had been recently lost in Asia." As described by *Time,* Ike's resolution that the U.S. would fight was "evidence of the President's patience and peacefulness" (p. 9).

19 A few further quotes from this story might serve to indicate the magazine's bias toward *Eisenhower* and give good examples of subjective reporting:

> A few days before the President's message to Congress last week, the whole anti-Communist position in the Far East seemed to be coming apart. Ike stopped the rot, and the U.S. emerged in a better light than it had enjoyed in several weeks. (p. 9)
>
> He (Eisenhower) wanted to demonstrate national unity behind the policy: he wanted to keep his 1952 campaign promise that he would submit to Congress any proposed steps to use U.S. forces in combat. (p. 10)
>
> For Dwight Eisenhower, the week's events were demonstration of forceful and skillful presidential leadership. He had used his prestige to score a political and policy victory, and placed Capitol Hill—its Republicans and Democrats alike—in the position of sharing the decision. (p. 10)

A SELECTED WEEK: KENNEDY

20 *Issue of Dec. 28, 1962:* Again in this issue *Time* presented the President as a confident person, one who "bluntly voiced his growing impatience with British and European bellyaching about U.S. contributions to the common defense," one who was behind the ransom payments to Castro's government, and one whose TV interview "from the rocking chair" showed the President "at his informal confident best" (pp. 13–15). Over in the "Business" section (pp. 50–55), the Presidential image turned more

unpleasant. Recounting the business year of 1962, *Time* dealt at some length with JFK's part in the steel crisis. The magazine referred to "John F. Kennedy's hasty and whitelipped counterattack" against U.S. Steel Chairman Roger Blough, who was trying to raise steel prices $6 a ton. According to *Time,* "virtually all U.S. businessmen were outraged by the tactics Kennedy used against Blough." But, added the magazine later in the story, "in board rooms around the country, businessmen were impressed that President Kennedy had talked even tougher to Khrushchev than to Roger Blough" (p. 62).

THE PRESIDENTIAL STEREOTYPES

21 It was found in this study that from week to week *Time,* through the skillful use of devices described earlier, creates and reinforces a stereotype of the President in office. The personality of the President gets more emphasis through the colorful and subjective language of the magazine than does his news activities. As Jigs Gardner wrote in *The Nation,* it is the "reduction of news to emotional conflicts of personalities."[8] One reason for this, obviously, is that "conflicts of personalities" make strong appeal to emotions. This appeal is far greater for the general reader than is the appeal of straight, neutralist reporting.

22 The following paragraph from *Time* (June 16, 1952) serves as an example:

> They saw Ike, and liked what they saw. They liked him for his strong, vigorous manner of speech . . . and for an overriding innate kindliness and modesty. But most of all, they liked him in a way they could scarcely explain. They liked Ike because, when they saw him and heard him talk, he made them proud of themselves and all the half-forgotten best that was in them and the nation.

23 This example is typical of the way *Time* creates and develops its presidential images or stereotypes. Below, in brief profiles taken from *Time*-treatment, are re-created the stereotypes of the three Presidents which the reader of the magazine had developed for him week by week during the three administrations. These stereotypes, although naturally abstractions even of *Time*-images, picture each president as seen through the verbal lenses of the "weekly newsmagazine."

> *Truman:* A bouncy man, sarcastic and shallow. A very unpopular man, a "little" man with many inadequacies. A President who condoned all types of "shabby politicking and corruption" in his administration. A man who practiced "careless government-by-crony." A petulant President who "stubbornly protected shoddy friends," one who had "grown too touchy to make

---

[8]Gardner, *op. cit.,* p. 66.

judicious decisions." A President who failed to give firm leadership to the country. A man whose State Department was full of homosexuals. A man who evaded issues and refused to face an argument. A President who "breathed cocky belligerence," and bounced on his heels while he launched off-the-cuff oratory. A President whose every action was motivated by shabby politics. A President, who when he spoke, generally sputtered, barked, cracked, droned, or "popped a gasket." A person who "grinned slyly," and "preached the Truman sermon" and "probed with a blunt finger." A man whose speeches had a "thin, overworked and flat quality" as he spoke with a "flat, monotonous voice." A man who stirred up national crises and who left the nation's nervous system "jangled and jumpy." A man who was blunt, sarcastic, belligerent, cocky, petulant, irascible, harried, lazy, vain, angry, sly, curt, and cold.

Eisenhower: A smiling, warm-hearted, sincere leader. A man of "earnest demeanor." A President whose strong leadership brought united determination. A patient and peaceful man, and one who wanted to keep his campaign promises. A skillful leader who was a statesman rather than a politician. One who was humble and who took his duties very seriously. One who was "on top of his job." A President who when he moved, moved "quietly." One who was sensitive to "the mood of the nation," and who did not like to stir up crises. A person who loved children, one who was forgiving and religious. One who brushed away misunderstandings and insisted on facts and the truth. A President who was cautious, warm, charitable, modest, happy, amiable, firm, cordial, effective, serene, frank, calm, skillful, and earnest. A person who talked with a happy grin, who pointed out cautiously, spoke warmly, and chatted amiably.

Kennedy: A President who was wealthy but generous in charity. A man who liked much social life in the White House, and who travelled extensively. A versatile man—who wore "many hats." A President who fostered a kind of "forced togetherness of New Frontier society." A man whose mistake it was not to censor the press, but "to talk out loud" about it. A confident person, usually pleasant. A happy man with a "cheery look." A man who seldom showed irritation, but who could launch a "hasty and white-lipped counterattack." A President who would bring full force of his power to bear to get his way. A President who talked tough to Khrushchev. A man whose presence had great impact on crowds, one who was willing to take risks, who had a "conviction of correctness." A speaker who, when he spoke, said, reaffirmed, announced, promised, concluded, and insisted. He usually simply "said." A man who was usually confident, informed, emphatic, cheery, social, versatile, energetic, youthful, impressive, determined, and well-informed.

EXAMPLES AND COMMENTARY

24 Following is a group of selected examples of subjective and biased reportorial quotations taken from the sample study periods. After each

example is the author's comment[9] on the example. These examples offer insight into the kind of techniques used by *Time* in its reporting during the periods studied:

If the Administration had ever toyed with the idea of appeasement, it had been forced to a public renunciation. (May 21, 1951, p. 19.)

Here is the case of implicating somebody of something where nothing—so far as Time *knew—really existed. This is possibly the most questionable type of reporting used by the magazine.*

Harry Truman had worn a harried and rumpled air during General MacArthur's three days of testimony before Congress. (May 21, 1951, p. 19.)

Here there is an insinuation of a guilty conscience, of someone afraid something unpleasant will leak out about him. A case of implication by appearance.

History would remember this day and this man, and mark him large. (April 30, 1951, p. 23.)

Here is a case of pure opinion and doubtful syntax. The quote relates to MacArthur.

It was a neat bit of off-the-cuff campaigning, and was calculated—like his "hope" of making a cross-country give-'em-hell speaking tour this spring or summer—to gladden the hearts of Democrat bigwigs who met in Denver last week to beat the drums for '52. (June 4, 1951, p. 19.)

Here is the case of Time *telling the reader why Truman greeted a group of young people at the White House; this is purely the magazine's conjecture stated as fact.*

TABLE 1

Bias Category Breakdown for the Three Presidents in Each 10-Issue Period

Bias Category	*Truman*	*Eisenhower*	*Kennedy*
Attribution Bias	9	11	5
Adjective Bias	21	22	3
Adverbial Bias	17	7	4
Contextual Bias	33	20	13
Outright Opinion	8	17	12
Photographic Bias	5	5	8
Total Bias	93	82	45
Total Positive Bias	1	81	31
Total Negative Bias	92	1	14

[9]These comments by the author dealing with the examples from *Time* are certainly themselves "subjective." But there is one thing in their favor: they are *said to be comments* and are not hidden in a factual context.

TABLE 2

Subjective Expressions Used by Time *in Reporting Speeches of the Three Presidents*

Truman:

“said curtly”
“said coldly”
“barked Harry S Truman”
“cracked Harry Truman”
“with his voice heavy with sarcasm”
“preached the Truman sermon”
“flushed with anger”
“grinning slyly”
“petulant, irascible President”
“had worn a harried and rumpled air”
“made his familiar, chopping motions”
“cocky as ever”
“publicly put his foot in his mouth”
“with a blunt finger he probed”

Eisenhower:

“said with a happy grin”
“cautiously pointed out”
“chatted amiably”
“said warmly”
“paused to gather thought”
“equanimity and inner ease”
“sensitive to the mood of the nation”
“devastatingly effective”
“serene state of mind”
“calm and confident”
“frankness was the rule”
“skillfully refused to commit himself”
“obviously a man with a message”
“brushing aside misunderstanding”

Kennedy:

“President Kennedy said” (10 t.)
“President Kennedy announced”
“Concluded the President”
“stated the case in plain terms”
“the President urged”
“Kennedy argued”
“concluded Kennedy”
“he suggested”
“President Kennedy recommended”
“Kennedy insisted”
“Kennedy contended”
“Kennedy maintained”
“The President promised”

The State Department was still clearing homosexuals out of its woodwork. . . . Total number of homosexuals dismissed as bad security risks since 1947: 146 men and two women. (May 7, 1951, p. 26.)

Here is a case of imputing corruption to an administration by pointing out and playing up a certain "scandal" in one department.

A few days later, over the morning coffee, the nation read of Harry Truman's reply and fumed. (April 23, 1951, p. 25.)

Time *here projects its omniscience over the entire nation and tells the reader what the country read and even how it reacted after reading it.*

The strong leadership of President Eisenhower and the near-unaminity of the Congress in backing him in the Formosa resolution undoubtedly retrieved much of the U.S. prestige and influence that had been recently lost in Asia. (Feb. 7, 1955, p. 9.)

This example is interesting not only for the clever way positive bias is packed in, but for the use of the subjective key-word "undoubtedly."

He (Eisenhower) has an aversion to stirring up unnecessary national crises, has deliberately tried to soothe the nation's nervous system—left jangled and jumpy by an unbroken procession of Truman crises. (Feb. 28, 1955, p. 13.)

Here is the implication that other presidents might like to stir up trouble, but not Ike. Also Truman's "crises" are dragged in and the reader is informed that this is the reason for the "nation's nervous system" being "jumpy."

CONCLUSIONS

25 Because of its racy style, its clever use of captions and pictures and its smooth integration of separated (in space and time) incidents and speeches, *Time* is understandably a popular publication for the general reader. However, the careful and thoughtful reader who is looking for proper perspective and serious backgrounding instead of entertainment and polemic will probably not find the magazine very satisfying.[10] This is not to imply that *Time* contains no *facts;* certainly its pages abound with facts. But it is the popularization of these facts, the constant weaving of these facts into semi-fictionalized language patterns and the constant evidence of preferential or prejudicial treatment of news subjects that would probably be unpalatable to the reader seeking the "true picture."

26 This study indicated that *Time* editorialized in its regular "news" col-

[10]It should be noted, however, that some critics seem to feel that *Time* in 1965 has become more responsible in its news reporting; see, for example, William Forbis, "The March of Time; Curt, Clear and More Complete," *Montana Journalism Review* (Spring 1965), pp. 6–8. This article contrasts sharply with the negative criticism about *Time* made by David Halberstam in his *The Making of a Quagmire* (New York: Random House, 1964), pp. 35–37.

umns to a great extent, and that it used a whole series of tricks to bias the stories and to lead the reader's thinking. Mostly, in its Presidential treatment, the magazine presented the reader with highly loaded essays of a subjective type.

27 In addition to isolating several interesting types of subjectivizing procedure, the study showed that *Time* 1) was clearly anti-Truman, 2) was strongly pro-Eisenhower, and 3) was neutral or certainly moderate toward Kennedy. Stereotypes of the three Presidents built up by the magazine during the periods studied were quite vivid—especially in the cases of Truman and Eisenhower.

28 By way of summary, the following principal techniques were used by *Time* in subjectivizing its reports: 1) deciding which incidents, which remarks etc., to play up and which ones to omit completely or to play down; 2) failing to tell the whole story; 3) weaving opinion into the story; 4) imputing wisdom and courage and other generally admired qualities by use of adjectives, adverbs and general context and by quoting some friend of the person; 5) dragging into the story past incidents unnecessary to the present report; 6) using one person's opinion to project opinion to this person's larger group—the "one-man cross-section device."

29 7) Imputing wide acceptance, such as "the nation believed" without presenting any evidence at all; 8) transferring disrepute to a person by linking him or his group to some unpopular person, group, cause or idea; 9) playing up certain phrases or descriptions which tend to point out possible weaknesses, paint a derogatory picture or create a stereotype (e.g., "small-town boy," "off-the-cuff oratory").

30 10) Creating an overall impression of a person by words, an impression which is reinforced from issue to issue (e.g., to show an active and healthy President when the nation was concerned about his health, *Time* would have him "yelling tirelessly," "playing a wicked game of golf," "enjoying himself tremendously," "waving happily," and "stepping lightly"); 11) explaining motives for Presidential actions, and 12) telling the reader what "the people" think or what the nation or public thinks about almost anything.

Word Study List

cursory	2	inauspicious	13
critique	3	Olympian	13
random	4	skulduggery	17
contextual	5, 6, 11	reportorial	24
attribution	6, 7, 8, 10	conjecture	24
notated	11	omniscience	24
innuendo	11	polemic	25
semantic	13	imputing	28

Questions

1. How has Merrill's audience of professional journalists and instructors in journalism helped to shape the style of his article?

2. What is Merrill's statement of purpose? What is his thesis? What is the difference between the two?

3. What does Merrill gain by using subtitles? What other elements of style and organization give the essay the form of a scientific report?

4. List and explain in your own words each of Merrill's bias categories.

5. Does Merrill approve of biased news reporting? How do you know?

6. Are the editors of *Time* right in asserting that "objectivity in news presentation is impossible"? What are you learning about language that can help to answer that question?

Exercise

A specific audience and purpose will influence a writer's selection of a voice and style for a particular article. In a paragraph, contrast Merrill's style and voice with Gilbert Highet's ("The Gettysburg Address," page 137) to show the effect of audience and purpose on each writer's essay. Contrast specific characteristics of organization, sentence structure, word choice, and tone that were dictated, at least in part, by each writer's audience and purpose.

Cutesy

Bradley Miller

Bradley Miller (b. 1951), who holds degrees in philosophy and journalism, is a columnist and editorial writer for the *Dallas Morning News*. His essays have appeared in various newspapers, including the *Los Angeles Times* and the *Boston Globe*. "Cutesy" was published in the *Washington Post* on March 23, 1980.

Perceiving that a cloying cutesiness is the characteristic style of today, Miller calls for a "revolution" against this sickening sweetness.

1 How could any middle-aged man of the slightest dignity, or even a self-respecting schoolboy, write the following lyric: "When you give me

that pretty little pout/You turn me inside-out"? Let alone sing it before crowds. James Taylor,[1] being but sweet and 30 when he wrote it, is a spring chicken compared to many of the cutesy pies fluttering and cooing across America. Probably a majority of them are over 40, and many of them are even worse than Sweet Baby James (the title of one of Taylor's albums). They make millions, some of them. Their spiritual guidance is sought. One of them is president of the United States.

2 To go by "Jimmy"—not James or Jim but Jimmy—is perhaps the most cutesy act ever committed by a sitting president. Well, why not? What could be more in tune with the spirit of our age? For that spirit, unless my eyes and ears deceive me, is not primarily hedonism or narcissism, but cutesiness. The business of America may still be business, but the business of business has become cutesiness, i.e., an amazingly prevalent form of adult childishness, not to be confused with sentimentality or affection, though the similarities are obvious.

3 Cutesiness usually takes the form of an affected archness that in certain susceptible roles—those assumed by Avon[2] saleswomen and game-show hosts, for example—can easily flare up into cutesy-wootsiness, or the advanced stage of cutesiness. The cutesy-wootsy are not merely inane; they are infuriating.

4 If they were condemned to death—and at the least they should be taken off the streets—they would walk to the gallows wearing a fixed smile and a Have a Nice Day button. They honk because they love Jesus, but I doubt that Jesus is amused. I dare say He's as revolted as any other genuine adult. So, despite more wars and rumors of wars, expect no Second Coming until society deals with this criminally inane class.

5 My point is that, far from trying to rid our society of this strain, we are simpering toward making it the ideal. Why the hell does cutesiness sell? To be sure, some adults have always remained children intellectually and emotionally, as everyone knows, and some have always simpered and postured for money and attention. But have so many ever simpered so much, or adopted postures that should revolt the instincts of even a politician and be psychologically impossible to anyone else? Surely not. Even the enormous appeal of smut palls in comparison. The cutesy pies, far from feeling ridiculous by what they do, leap at every chance to blabber away on talk shows about how wonderful and neat they consider one of their latest pieces of wit.

6 Let us not pistol whip Poppin' Fresh, the Pillsbury doughboy—he's genuinely cute. Let us not pie the face of Joe Namath[3] on account of his

---

[1]A contemporary folk singer and songwriter.—Ed.

[2]A brand of cosmetics sold in the home, not in stores.—Ed.

[3]A former pro football quarterback, also known as a ladies' man, who has starred in several TV commercials.—Ed.

panty hose ad, because Joe, compared to the true cutesy pies, is almost refreshing. And let us show restraint even in poking fun at the innocent doltishness of a born-again Sunday-school teacher.

7 For cutesiness is not quite any of those things. It is the artificially soft voices of mellow-music deejays, it is touchy-feeling psychologists, the schoolboy naughtiness that tries to add spice to TV talk shows, John Denver,[4] moviemakers trying to be morally instructive, movie critics who feel morally instructed, Playboy bunnies thinking somebody cares that there are really so many things they really want to do, Cosmopolitan articles telling women how they can really do a lot of things and still look yummy, presidents of student bodies, Suzanne Somers,[5] banquet speakers who try to be funny, banquet speakers who don't try to be funny, Paul Anka,[6] grinning yaps on TV commercials who love to eat biscuits, hillbilly guitar players, the Dallas Cowboy cheerleaders, a commercial for U.S. Savings Bonds urging Americans to "invest in the United States—for sugar and spice and everything nice" (because bonds can pay for your daughter's wedding).

8 If TV advertising isn't the worst offender it is certainly the most visible. The TV blats seven hours a day in the average American home and is probably as responsible as anything for the impression, voiced so often by foreign visitors, that we're a nation of simpering mules, fat and happy perhaps, but unbelievably dumb. I cannot believe that we're the dumbest people in the world, yet why else would some ad agency assume that a good number of us fret that mouthwash might be "too mediciney"? The assumption is doubtless correct: not for nothing are millions spent in market research both to discover and to stimulate such things. The assumption, indeed, seems to be that the imbecility of the audience is illimitable. Consider the ad in which a bulwark of a Babbitt[7] of a husband beams into the camera and purrs and coos, "My wife—I think I'll keep her," as the oh-so-sweet sweetie purrs and coos her gratitude. Is that off the air? Then consider the heroic character who now grins and chirps, "Squeeze and go from flat to fluffy!" The idea behind these things is that Americans not only won't retch and rage at them but will actually be inspired by them to buy the products being pushed. As I say, consider it, and see if it doesn't confirm P. T. Barnum's[8] observation on the birth rate.

9 We ignore what we constantly inhale, but all the same it transforms us, and to live in America today is to constantly inhale cutesiness. For too

---

[4]A contemporary folk singer and songwriter best known for "Rocky Mountain High."—ED.

[5]An actress who played a "sexy, dumb blond" on a TV situation comedy.—ED.

[6]A contemporary singer and songwriter.—ED.

[7]Allusion to the main character in a Sinclair Lewis novel, a "solid" businessman of limited ethical and social awareness; the term is derogatory.—ED.

[8]American showman and master of publicity who asserted that there is a sucker born every minute.—ED.

long I too tried to ignore it, until it dawned on me that unless I actively opposed it I could soon lose the capacity to distinguish cutesiness from genuine emotion, and could become cutesy myself. Something as superficially harmless as joining a poetry-reading circle could be the start of a subtle corruption of the soul and psyche that would end with me going on a game show to smirk about my sex life in the hope of winning a washing machine.

10 Laying it to greed merely begs the question of why cutesiness is so lucrative. I suggest the prime wellspring of cutesiness is the desire for attention, almost regardless of what kind of attention. A child will keep provoking his parents despite repeated punishment if punishment is the only attention he gets. The same motive, I fear, explains much of what Americans do as adults. The nature of most jobs makes it necessary for most of us to look for attention outside our jobs; the egalitarian orchestrators convince us that everyone, no matter how arrant a nitwit, is owed a share of the spotlight; finally, the worthies already in the spotlight prove to us that the more arrant one's nitwittery the larger one's share.

11 I don't presume to be able to trace all the cause-effect development of cutesiness. It's enough to warn that the thing is snowballing, that more and more of us are becoming either inane posturers or their devotees. Already we are a nation of people who don't have to be drunk to like "Little House on the Prairie."[9]

12 The real peril is that emotion that is mature, honest and honorable will drown in the sugar. At the least, passion will yield to giggles, and one will always need the sneer or snicker, or perhaps an impersonation of Richard Nixon, to indicate that, after all, one is not so unworldly as to be *serious;* at worst, nothing seriously describable as passion will even exist. Whose love letters, even now, would be worth reading? Certainly no cutesy pie's. Rod McKuen's?[10] Those of the PR wonder who thought up "Reach out, reach out and touch someone,/Reach out, call up and just say 'Hi.'"? Is there a difference?

13 For the letters of the man who best represents our era, I'd choose, besides President Jimmy's, those of Alex Comfort, MB, PhD, editor of "The Joy of Sex" and "More Joy of Sex," for Alex's advice to lovers is oh so precious that I quote from it:

14 "So let him be a Roman or a dog or a woman or a gangster, and let her be a virgin, or a slave, or a Sultana, or Lolita, or someone you're trying to rape, or indeed anything which turns either of you on. You weren't self-conscious about this when you were 3—grow backward again

---

[9]A top-rated TV show, a romantic portrayal of frontier family life based on a series of novels by Laura Ingalls Wilder.—ED.

[10]A contemporary songwriter and poet whose works are viewed by many to be sweetly romantic and sentimental.—ED.

in an adult context. The rules are only those of childplay—if it gets nasty or spiteful or unhappy, stop the game: while it stays wild and exciting, it has a climax children's [sic] games lack; that is the privilege of adult play."

15 But beneath the sugar, concealed from Alex's glance, rage and rebellion are simmering and congealing into an army of rebel roughnecks who envision a climax rather different from Alex's. Some in this army want to attack the Pepsi Generation and Coke-Adds-Lifers right now, and maybe even hold the gee-whiz kids hostage and puncture their volleyballs right before their eyes. For it can hardly be disputed anymore that cutesiness causes crime, especially violent crime by the young. Of course, it's not the chief cause, but there is no doubt that in violence, no less than in drugs, rock and sex, the young seek release from the sickly sweet smiles that confront them at all turns. After constant exposure to all the gagging cutesiness of television, radio, movies, magazines and billboards, the young are soaked in the unctuous fuddy-duddyism of their parents and teachers. Unable to run away from cutesiness, they are run amok by it. Properly channeled, their natural rebelliousness could begin to clear cutesiness off the scene. The torch is theirs.

Word Study List

hedonism	2	imbecility	8
narcissism	2	illimitable	8
sentimentality	2	psyche	9
affectation	2	egalitarian	10
inane	3, 4, 11	arrant	10
doltishness	6	unctuous	15

Questions

1. Once Miller establishes his thesis—the spirit of our age is cutesiness—he commits himself, as a writer, to two tasks: to define the term *cutesy* and to demonstrate that it is an accurate label for our time. What does Miller mean by the term *cutesy?* How does he develop his essay to demonstrate the term's appropriateness?

2. Do you agree that our age is appropriately defined as cutesy? if you agree with Miller, did you agree before reading the essay, or did he convince you?

3. What stylistic techniques used by Miller are his most persuasive? What makes them effective? (Consider his examples, word choice, metaphors, sentence structure, tone, and use of the label *cutesy.*)

4. Do you find any elements of Miller's style to be ineffective? Why? (Consider use of fragments, repetition, the number of negative words.)

5. At the end of his essay, Miller calls for a rebellion against cutesiness, a rebellion led primarily by young people, but he does not offer specific suggestions for staging this rebellion. What can we do, specifically, to help get rid of cutesiness?

Exercise

The 1970s has been called the "me decade," a period of self-centeredness and self-indulgence. List as many examples as you can of popular people, popular activities, TV ads, national fads and fashions, popular books, records, and movies that could perhaps be used to support this assertion. Share lists in class, debating one another's examples as necessary. As a result of discussion, compile a class list of examples and then consider whether or not the evidence is significant enough, central enough to the period, to justify the "me decade" label for the 1970s.

Student Essay: Style Analysis

Miller's Assault on Cutesy Pies

Attention getter that mirrors Miller's style and attitude

There are those times when we are once again astounded at how doltish our friends or co-workers can be, a price they feel they must pay for acceptance. At least as often, we cringe before cathode ray tubes that suffer automatic volume increases several times each hour, as a favorite actor or athlete decomposes into a loathsome heap of Madison Avenue idiocy in as little as sixty seconds.

Subject introduced

Bradley Miller's essay, "Cutesy," is one man's attempt to express his revulsion at this assault on our sense of good taste. It is a thought-provoking piece that causes the reader to pause and reflect on behavior patterns observed

Thesis

in both daily social contacts and mass media. Miller's success with this essay is achieved through efficient word choice, adroit use of metaphor, and an effective organizational pattern.

In the second paragraph, Miller presents a clever series of images that indicate just how serious he feels the problem of cutesiness is. The use of the name "Jimmy" for President Carter is referred to as an act which is "committed." The choice of the word "commit" brings forth all manner of grave thoughts: murderers who commit homicide, the dejected who commit suicide, the infidels who commit adultery. Commission of cutesiness by a president is no less serious to Miller than commission of a capital crime. This belief is further evidenced in the fourth paragraph when he relishes the idea of cutesy pies being executed for their heinous crimes. Finally one finds the reference to the "criminally inane" cutesies, obviously negative because we stumble, here, sobered, wondering if he meant the more familiar phrase, criminally insane.

Analysis of Miller's word choice

Miller's use of some metaphors is particularly derogatory when he discusses the cutesy pies and those who are influenced by them. In the fifth paragraph the antics of the cutesy are compared to those "of even a politician." By his use of this comparison, Miller reveals his awareness of his audience, whose memory of political capers is still fresh, scarred with the easily-lanced wounds of Watergate-like affairs. The image of a cutesy pie becomes something worse than that of the ever smiling, two-faced, insincere politican whose livelihood often depends on the extremes to which he will go to appear to please the most voters. Those of us who are taken in by the cutesy pies, who believingly purchase the products they promote on commercial television, are likened to "simpering mules, fat and happy perhaps, but unbelievably dumb." Since none of Miller's readers wants to be included in such a group, the intended effect, that they will share his low opinion of cutesy pies, is achieved.

Analysis of Miller's metaphors

Student uses an effective metaphor

However, "Cutesy" is an effective essay primarily because Miller, through careful organization, is able to befriend his audience and gain our confidence, before shaking us by the lapels, forcing us to look at ourselves and witness what we are becoming.

Transition paragraph

Miller first draws us to his side, gaining our confidence through his use of examples. His barrage of examples from popular music and TV sitcoms pervades the first half of the essay, occasionally providing us a chance to chuckle along with the author. In doing this, Miller hopes that we are able to say to ourselves, "Yeah, I've seen that myself. I know exactly what he's talking about." Paragraph seven is the most obvious in this attempt, shotgun-like in its spray of various examples that would surely strike anyone who has ever watched commercial television, listened to the radio, or read a magazine.

Analysis of Miller's organizational pattern

Student uses another effective metaphor

In paragraphs nine through eleven, having captured the audience he desires, Miller continues to build our confidence in himself by leading us, as a friendly scientist would allow us to look at the latest findings under a microscope, into a brief discussion of the reasons for the contagious nature of cutesiness. Beneath it all he suggests that it is not really our fault and that where the fault lies is not important. In paragraph eleven Miller subordinates the discussion on the origins of cutesiness in preparation for the impact he hopes to achieve in the final paragraphs.

Summary of analysis of Miller's organizational pattern

In the last four paragraphs Miller makes his strongest point. After gaining our confidence and our belief that he knows what he is talking about, he slaps us as though he is saying, "Never mind all that, look at what you are becoming!" The potential for the loss of the ability to feel and express real emotions, first mentioned in paragraph nine, is Miller's strongest point. He successfully uses the organizational formula: important, least important, most important, where the least important information is buried in the middle, followed by the most important points at the end. The potential for long-term psychological effects from cutesiness stands out in the reader's mind because of its position at the end of the essay.

Conclusion that restates the thesis

"Cutesy" illustrates how a writer, by skillful creation of images properly orchestrated for impact, can successfully project an attitude to the point that his readers rally to his side.

Exercises

I. DEVELOPING AN AWARENESS OF CONNOTATION

To convey attitude and control tone in our writing, we need to be sensitive to connotations. Here are some exercises to increase your awareness of connotative language.

1. List all the words you can think of for "human female" and for "human male." Group the words in each list into three categories: those with a positive connotation, those that are neutral, those with a negative connotation. Compare your groupings with those of your classmates and discuss reasons for any disagreements.
2. For each of the following words, list at least two synonyms that have more positive connotations than the given word.
   a. politician   d. old (person)
   b. crazy (person)   e. maid
   c. garbage   f. drunk
3. For each of the following words, list at least two synonyms that have more negative connotations than the given word.
   a. associates   d. plump
   b. willowy   e. fastidious
   c. average   f. large group
4. All of the following words have a degree of similarity. Describe the situation that each word suggests to you to see how each differs in connotation. When you need help, consult a good desk dictionary.
   a. brawl   e. hubbub
   b. fracas   f. squabble
   c. row   g. fling down the gauntlet
   d. tiff   h. ballyhoo

   Which fight is the least serious? Which the most physical? Which the most romantic?

II. THINKING AND WRITING METAPHORICALLY

For our writing to be effective, we need to be in control of style, conscious of word choice and sentence structure. We also need to develop control over metaphors, avoiding those that are dead or dying, selecting those that are consistent with writing purpose, chosen style, and our perceptions of life. Here are opportunities for practice.

1. Compare a person you know to an object and develop the metaphor into a paragraph. Your topic sentence should be: "If __________ were an object, he or she would be a __________." Examine as many characteristics of the object as you can, developing the metaphor to describe several of the person's traits.

2. In a paragraph, describe an activity you like or dislike without including a direct statement of your attitude. Convey your attitude by your word choice and selection of metaphors.

Writing Assignments

1. Responding to an essay selected by you or your instructor (a possible choice is Miller's essay "Cutesy"), analyze some elements of style to demonstrate their effectiveness in conveying the writer's attitude and supporting the writer's purpose. You can examine some combination of the following: word choice (connotative language, level of vocabulary, use of metaphors), types of paragraph development, overall organization, and rhetorical devices such as repetition, antithesis, and parallelism. Focus on the elements of style that seem most significant in conveying attitude.
2. Embler says that the dominant metaphor of our time is the comparison of humans with machines. Miller characterizes our time as "cutesy." How would you characterize our time? How would you characterize your neighborhood? Your school? Think of a word, a phrase, or a metaphor that best describes our society, the dominant element in your neighborhood, or the nature of your school. Whichever you pick—society, neighborhood, school—explain in an essay the appropriateness of your descriptive word or metaphor and illustrate with examples.
3. Select a painting, print, or photograph and consider its effect. What attitude, feeling, or mood does it convey? Show how the details (figures, color, light/shadow, arrangement) in the work create its effect.
4. Choose a political figure of recent years (e.g., Ford, Carter, Thatcher, Reagan, Mondale) and select a year during which he or she was regularly in the news. Then find at least five articles from one of the major weekly newsmagazines *(Newsweek, U.S. News & World Report, Time)* and analyze them for bias, applying Merrill's five bias categories (see pp.145–147) to your analysis. Write an essay in which you demonstrate that the newsmagazine has—or has not—slanted its coverage of the political figure you selected.

CHAPTER 4

ADVERTISING MAKES YOU WONDER...

... why your choice of deli products should be influenced by what an inarticulate three-year-old on TV tells you he prefers to eat!

Wanted: Words and Images to Sell!

GETTING STARTED: Analyzing Ads—Some Questions to Ask

Nine ads illustrating a variety of appeals and selling techniques are grouped at the end of this chapter. Study each ad, using the following general questions as guidelines for analysis. Then, after reading an article in the chapter, study the ads again to see which ones best illustrate the observations about advertising made by the writer.

1. What are the ad's purposes? To sell a product? An idea? An image of the company?
2. What audience is the ad designed to reach?
3. What kind of relationship does it establish with its audience?
4. What social values does it express?
5. To what degree are those values held by the target audience? To what degree are they the values of a different social class or group?
6. Does the ad use metaphors? Puns? Rhyme? Does the company establish and repeat a logo or slogan for the product? How effectively do these techniques work?
7. Does the ad use symbols? To what extent do the symbols help express the ad's social values? How effective are the symbols? Does their association with the product seem appropriate?
8. Is the ad's appeal primarily direct and explicit or indirect and associative? That is, is the message stated or implied, or is one message stated while others are implied?
9. In what sense can the language of advertising be "true"? By what standards can we judge its truth?
10. Should a company be responsible only for the truth of its literal language, or for the truth of the ad's implications as well?

Weasel Words: God's Little Helpers

Paul Stevens

A former advertising copyeditor, Paul Stevens (b. 1937) is the author of a book on advertising language, *I Can Sell You Anything,* published in 1972 under the pseudonym Carl P. Wrighter. What follows is a chapter from his book.

In his chapter on weasel words, Stevens lists the ad writer's favorite words and explains how their deceptive qualities give them selling power.

1 First of all, you know what a weasel is, right? It's a small, slimy animal that eats small birds and other animals, and is especially fond of devouring vermin. Now, consider for a moment the kind of winning personality he must have. I mean, what kind of a guy would get his jollies eating rats and mice? Would you invite him to a party? Take him home to meet your mother? This is one of the slyest and most cunning of all creatures; sneaky, slippery, and thoroughly obnoxious. And so it is with great and warm personal regard for these attributes that we humbly award this King of All Devious the honor of bestowing his name upon our golden sword: the weasel word.

2 A weasel word is "a word used in order to evade or retreat from a direct or forthright statement or position" (Webster). In other words, if we can't say it, we'll weasel it. And, in fact, a weasel word has become more than just an evasion or retreat. We've trained our weasels. They can do anything. They can make you hear things that aren't being said, accept as truths things that have only been implied, and believe things that have only been suggested. Come to think of it, not only do we have our weasels trained, but they, in turn, have got you trained. When *you* hear a weasel word, you automatically hear the implication. Not the real meaning, but the meaning *it* wants *you* to hear. So if you're ready for a little re-education, let's take a good look under a strong light at the two kinds of weasel words.

1. WORDS THAT MEAN THINGS THEY REALLY DON'T MEAN

3 *Help* That's it. "Help." It means "aid" or "assist." Nothing more. Yet, "help" is the one single word which, in all the annals of advertising, has done the most to say something that couldn't be said. Because "help" is the great qualifier; once you say it, you can say almost anything after it. In short, "help" has helped help us the most.

Helps keep you young
Helps prevent cavities
Helps keep your house germ-free

4 "Help" qualifies everything. You've never heard anyone say, "This product will keep you young," or "This toothpaste will positively prevent cavities for all time." Obviously, we can't say anything like that, because there aren't any products like that made. But by adding that one little word, "help," in front, we can use the strongest language possible afterward. And the most fascinating part of it is, you are immune to the word. You literally don't hear the word "help." You only hear what comes after it. And why not? That's strong language, and likely to be much more important to you than the silly little word at the front end.

5 I would guess that 75 percent of all advertising uses the word "help." Think, for a minute, about how many times each day you hear these phrases:

Helps stop . . .
Helps prevent . . .
Helps fight . . .
Helps overcome . . .
Helps you feel . . .
Helps you look . . .

I could go on and on, but so could you. Just as a simple exercise, call it homework if you wish, tonight when you plop down in front of the boob tube for your customary three and a half hours of violence and/or situation comedies, take a pad and pencil, and keep score. See if you can count how many times the word "help" comes up during the commercials. Instead of going to the bathroom during the pause before Marcus Welby operates, or raiding the refrigerator prior to witnessing the Mod Squad wipe out a nest of dope pushers, stick with it. Count the "helps," and discover just how dirty a four-letter word can be.

6 *Like* Coming in second, but only losing out by a nose, is the word "like," used in comparison. Watch:

It's like getting one bar free
Cleans like a white tornado
It's like taking a trip to Portugal

7 Okay. "Like" is a qualifier, and is used in much the same way as "help." But "like" is also a comparative element, with a very specific purpose; we use "like" to get you to stop thinking about the product per se, and to get you thinking about something that is bigger or better or different from the product we're selling. In other words, we can make you believe that the product is more than it is by likening it to something else.

8 Take a look at that first phrase, straight out of recent Ivory Soap

advertising. On the surface of it, they tell you that four bars of Ivory cost about the same as three bars of most other soaps. So, if you're going to spend a certain amount of money on soap, you can buy four bars instead of three. Therefore, it's like getting one bar free. Now, the question you have to ask yourself is, "Why the weasel? Why do they say 'like'? Why don't they just come out and say, 'You get one bar free'?" The answer is, of course, that for one reason or another, you really don't. Here are two possible reasons. One: sure, you get four bars, but in terms of the actual amount of soap that you get, it may very well be the same as in three bars of another brand. Remember, Ivory has a lot of air in it—that's what makes it float. And air takes up room. Room that could otherwise be occupied by more soap. So, in terms of pure product, the amount of actual soap in four bars of Ivory may be only as much as the actual amount of soap in three bars of most others. That's why we can't—or won't—come out with a straightforward declaration such as, "You get 25 percent more soap," or "Buy three bars, and get the fourth one free."

9 Reason number two: the actual cost and value of the product. Did it ever occur to you that Ivory may simply be a cheaper soap to make and, therefore, a cheaper soap to sell? After all, it doesn't have any perfume, or hexachlorophene, or other additives that can raise the cost of manufacturing. It's plain, simple, cheap soap, and so it can be sold for less money while still maintaining a profit margin as great as more expensive soaps. By way of illustrating this, suppose you were trying to decide whether to buy a Mercedes-Benz or a Ford. Let's say the Mercedes cost $7,000, and the Ford $3,500. Now the Ford salesman comes up to you with this deal: as long as you're considering spending $7,000 on a car, buy my Ford for $7,000 and I'll give you a second Ford, free! Well, the same principle can apply to Ivory: as long as you're considering spending 35 cents on soap, buy my cheaper soap, and I'll give you more of it.

10 I'm sure there are other reasons why Ivory uses the weasel "like." Perhaps you've thought of one or two yourself. That's good. You're starting to think.

11 Now, what about that wonderful white tornado? Ajax pulled that one out of the hat some eight years ago, and you're still buying it. It's a classic example of the use of the word "like" in which we can force you to think, not about the product itself, but about something bigger, more exciting, certainly more powerful than a bottle of fancy ammonia. The word "like" is used here as a transfer word, which gets you away from the obvious—the odious job of getting down on your hands and knees and scrubbing your kitchen floor—and into the world of fantasy, where we can imply that this little bottle of miracles will supply all the elbow grease you need. Isn't that the name of the game? The whirlwind activity of the tornado replacing the whirlwind motion of your arm? Think about the swirling of the tornado, and all the work it will save you. Think about the power of that devastating windstorm; able to lift houses, overturn cars, and now,

pick the dirt up off your floor. And we get the license to do it simply by using the word "like."

12 It's a copywriter's dream, because we don't have to substantiate anything. When we compare our product to "another leading brand," we'd better be able to prove what we say. But how can you compare ammonia to a windstorm? It's ludicrous. It can't be done. The whole statement is so ridiculous it couldn't be challenged by the government or the networks. So it went on the air, and it worked. Because the little word "like" lets us take you out of the world of reality, and into your own fantasies.

13 Speaking of fantasies, how about that trip to Portugal? Mateus Rosé is actually trying to tell you that you will be transported clear across the Atlantic Ocean merely by sipping their wine. "Oh, come on," you say. "You don't expect me to believe that." Actually, we don't expect you to believe it. But we do expect you to get our meaning. This is called "romancing the product," and it is made possible by the dear little "like." In this case, we deliberately bring attention to the word, and we ask you to join us in setting reality aside for a moment. We take your hand and gently lead you down the path of moonlit nights, graceful dancers, and mysterious women. Are we saying that these things are all contained inside our wine? Of course not. But what we mean is, our wine is part of all this, and with a little help from "like," we'll get you to feel that way, too. So don't think of us as a bunch of peasants squashing a bunch of grapes. As a matter of fact, don't think of us at all. Feel with us.

14 "Like" is a virus that kills. You'd better get immune to it.

OTHER WEASELS

15 "Help" and "like" are the two weasels so powerful that they can stand on their own. There are countless other words, not quite so potent, but equally effective when used in conjunction with our two basic weasels, or with each other. Let me show you a few.

16 *Virtual or Virtually* How many times have you responded to an ad that said:

> Virtually trouble-free . . .
> Virtually foolproof . . .
> Virtually never needs service . . .

Ever remember what "virtual" means? It means "in essence or effect, but not in fact." Important—"but not in fact." Yet today the word "virtually" is interpreted by you as meaning "almost or just about the same as. . . . " Well, gang, it just isn't true. "Not," in fact, means not, in fact. I was scanning, rather longingly I must confess, through the brochure Chevrolet publishes for its Corvette, and I came to this phrase: "The seats in the 1972 Corvette are virtually handmade." They had me, for a minute. I almost took the bait of that lovely little weasel. I almost decided that those seats were just about completely handmade. And then I remembered.

Those seats were not, *in fact,* handmade. Remember, "virtually" means "not, in fact," or you will, in fact, get sold down the river.

17 *Acts or Works* These two action words are rarely used alone, and are generally accompanied by "like." They need help to work, mostly because they are verbs, but their implied meaning is deadly, nonetheless. Here are the key phrases:

Acts like . . .
Acts against . . .
Works like . . .
Works against . . .
Works to prevent (or help prevent) . . .

You see what happens? "Acts" or "works" brings an action to the product that might not otherwise be there. When we say that a certain cough syrup "acts on the cough control center," the implication is that the syrup goes to this mysterious organ and immediately makes it better. But the implication here far exceeds what the truthful promise should be. An act is simply a deed. So the claim "acts on" simply means it performs a deed on. What that deed is, we may never know.

18 The rule of thumb is this: if we can't say "cures" or "fixes" or use any other positive word, we'll nail you with "acts like" or "works against," and get you thinking about something else. Don't.

MISCELLANEOUS WEASELS

19 *Can Be* This is for comparison, and what we do is to find an announcer who can really make it sound positive. But keep your ears open, "Crest can be of significant value when used in . . . ," etc., is indicative of an ideal situation, and most of us don't live in ideal situations.

20 *Up To* Here's another way of expressing an ideal situation. Remember the cigarette that said it was aged, or "cured for up to eight long, lazy weeks"? Well, that could, and should, be interpreted as meaning that the tobaccos used were cured anywhere from one hour to eight weeks. We like to glamorize the ideal situation; it's up to you to bring it back to reality.

21 *As Much As* More of the same. "As much as 20 percent greater mileage" with our gasoline again promises the ideal, but qualifies it.

22 *Refreshes, Comforts, Tackles, Fights, Comes On* Just a handful of the same action weasels, in the same category as "acts" and "works," though not as frequently used. The way to complete the thought here is to ask the simple question, "How?" Usually, you won't get an answer. That's because, usually, the weasel will run and hide.

23 *Feel or The Feel Of* This is the first of our subjective weasels. When we deal with a subjective word, it is simply a matter of opinion. In our opinion, Naugehyde has the feel of real leather. So we can say it. And, indeed, if you were to touch leather, and then touch Naugehyde, you may

very well agree with us. But that doesn't mean it is real leather, only that it feels the same. The best way to handle subjective weasels is to complete the thought yourself, by simply saying, "But it isn't." At least that way you can remain grounded in reality.

24 *The Look Of or Looks Like* "Look" is the same as "feel," our subjective opinion. Did you ever walk into a Woolworth's and see those $29.95 masterpieces hanging in their "Art Gallery"? "The look of a real oil painting," it will say. "But it isn't," you will reply. And probably be $29.95 richer for it.

2. WORDS THAT HAVE NO SPECIFIC MEANING

25 If you have kids, then you have all kinds of breakfast cereals in the house. When I was a kid, it was Rice Krispies, the breakfast cereal that went snap, crackle, and pop. (One hell of a claim for a product that is supposed to offer nutritional benefits.) Or Wheaties, the breakfast of champions, whatever that means. Nowadays, we're forced to a confrontation with Quisp, Quake, Lucky Stars, Cocoa-Puffs, Clunkers, Blooies, Snarkles and Razzmatazz. And they all have one thing in common: they're all "fortified." Some are simply "fortified with vitamins," while others are specifically "fortified with vitamin D," or some other letter. But what does it all mean?

26 "Fortified" means "added on to." But "fortified," like so many other weasel words of indefinite meaning, simply doesn't tell us enough. If, for instance, a cereal were to contain one unit of vitamin D, and the manufacturers added some chemical which would produce two units of vitamin D, they could then claim that the cereal was "fortified with twice as much vitamin D." So what? It would still be about as nutritional as sawdust.

27 The point is, weasel words with no specific meaning don't tell us enough, but we have come to accept them as factual statements closely associated with some good that has been done to the product. Here's another example.

28 *Enriched* We use this one when we have a product that starts out with nothing. You mostly find it in bread, where the bleaching process combined with the chemicals used as preservatives render the loaves totally void of anything but filler. So the manufacturer puts a couple of drops of vitamins into the batter, and presto! It's enriched. Sounds great when you say it. Looks great when you read it. But what you have to determine is, is it really great? Figure out what information is missing, and then try to supply that information. The odds are, you won't. Even the breakfast cereals that are playing it straight, like Kellogg's Special K, leave something to be desired. They tell you what vitamins you get, and how much of each in one serving. The catch is, what constitutes a serving? They say, one ounce. So now you have to whip out your baby scale and weigh one serving. Do you have any idea how much that is? Maybe you do. Maybe

you don't care. Okay, so you polish off this mound of dried stuff, and now what? You have ostensibly received the minimum, repeat, minimum dosage of certain vitamins for the day. One day. And you still have to go find the vitamins you didn't get. Try looking it up on a box of frozen peas. Bet you won't find it. But do be alert to "fortified" and "enriched." Asking the right questions will prove beneficial.

29 Did you buy that last sentence? Too bad, because I weaseled you, with the word "beneficial." Think about it.

30 *Flavor and Taste* These are two totally subjective words that allow us to claim marvelous things about products that are edible. Every cigarette in the world has claimed the best taste. Every supermarket has advertised the most flavorful meat. And let's not forget "aroma," a subdivision of this category. Wouldn't you like to have a nickel for every time a room freshener (a weasel in itself) told you it would make your home "smell fresh as all outdoors"? Well, they can say it, because smell, like taste and flavor, is a subjective thing. And, incidentally, there are no less than three weasels in that phrase. "Smell" is the first. Then, there's "as" (a substitute for the ever-popular "like"), and, finally, "fresh," which, in context, is a subjective comparison, rather than the primary definition of "new."

31 Now we can use an unlimited number of combinations of these weasels for added impact. "Fresher-smelling clothes." "Fresher-tasting tobacco." "Tastes like grandma used to make." Unfortunately, there's no sure way of bringing these weasels down to size, simply because you can't define them accurately. Trying to ascertain the meaning of "taste" in any context is like trying to push a rope up a hill. All you can do is be aware that these words are subjective, and represent only one opinion—usually that of the manufacturer.

32 *Style and Good Looks* Anyone for buying a new car? Okay, which is the one with the good looks? The smart new styling? What's that you say? All of them? Well, you're right. Because this is another group of subjective opinions. And it is the subjective and collective opinion of both Detroit and Madison Avenue that the following cars have "bold new styling": Buick Riviera, Plymouth Satellite, Dodge Monaco, Mercury Brougham, and you can fill in the spaces for the rest. Subjectively, you have to decide on when bold new styling is, indeed, bold new styling. Then, you might spend a minute or two trying to determine what's going on under that styling. The rest I leave to Ralph Nader.

33 *Different, Special, and Exclusive* To be different, you have to be not the same as. Here, you must rely on your own good judgment and common sense. Exclusive formulas and special combinations of ingredients are coming at you every day, in every way. You must constantly assure yourelf that, basically, all products in any given category are the same. So when you hear "special," "exclusive," or "different," you have to establish two things: on what basis are they different, and is that difference an important one? Let me give you a hypothetical example.

34 All so-called "permanent" antifreeze is basically the same. It is made from a liquid known as ethylene glycol, which has two amazing properties: It has a lower freezing point than water, and a higher boiling point than water. It does not break down (lose its properties), nor will it boil away. And every permanent antifreeze starts with it as a base. Also, just about every antifreeze has now got antileak ingredients, as well as antirust and anticorrosion ingredients. Now, let's suppose that, in formulating the product, one of the companies comes up with a solution that is pink in color, as opposed to all the others, which are blue. Presto—an exclusivity claim. "Nothing else looks like it, nothing else performs like it." Or, how about, "Look at ours, and look at anyone else's. You can see the difference our exclusive formula makes." Granted, I'm exaggerating. But did I prove a point?

A FEW MORE GOODIES

35 At Phillips 66, it's performance that counts
Whisk puts its strength where the dirt is
At Bird's Eye, we've got quality in our corner
Delicious and long-lasting, too

Very quickly now, let's deflate those four lines. First, what the hell does "performance" mean? It means that this product will do what any other product in its category will do. Kind of a back-handed reassurance that this gasoline will function properly in your car. That's it, and nothing more. To perform means to function at a standard consistent with the rest of the industry. All products in a category are basically the same.
36 Second line: What does "strength" or "strong" mean? Does it mean "not weak"? Or "superior in power"? No, it means consistent with the norms of the business. You can bet your first-born that if Whisk were superior in power to other detergents, they'd be saying it, loud and clear. So strength is merely a description of a property inherent in all similar products in its class. If you really want to poke a pin in a bubble, substitute the word "ingredients" for the word "strength." That'll do it every time.
37 Third line: The old "quality" claim, and you fell for it. "Quality" is not a comparison. In order to do that, we'd have to say, "We've got better quality in our corner than any other frozen food." Quality relates only to the subjective opinion that Bird's Eye has of its own products, and to which it is entitled. The word "quality" is what we call a "parity" statement; that is, it tells you that it is as good as any other. Want a substitute? Try "equals," meaning "the same as."
38 Fourth line: How delicious is delicious? About the same as good-tasting is good-tasting, or fresher smelling is fresher smelling. A subjective opinion regarding taste, which you can either accept or reject. More fun, though, is "long-lasting." You might want to consider writing a note to Mr. Wrigley, inquiring as to the standard length of time which a piece of gum is supposed to last. Surely there must be a guideline covering it. The

longest lasting piece of gum I ever encountered lasted just over four hours, which is the amount of time it took me to get it off the sole of my shoe. Try expressing the line this way: "It has a definite taste, and you may chew it as long as you wish." Does that place it in perspective?

39 There are two other aspects of weasel words that I should mention here. The first one represents the pinnacle of the copywriter's craft, and I call it the "Weasel of Omission." Let me demonstrate:

> Of America's best-tasting gums, Trident is sugar-free

40 Disregard, for a moment, the obvious subjective weasel "best-tasting." Look again at the line. Something has been left out. Omitted very deliberately. Do you know what that word is? The word that's missing is the word "only," which should come right before the name of the product. But it doesn't. It's gone. Left out. And the question is, why? The answer is, the government wouldn't let them. You see, they start out by making a subjective judgment, that their gum is among the best-tasting. That's fine, as far as it goes. That's their opinion. But it is also the opinion of every other maker of sugar-free gum that his product is also among the best-tasting. And, since both of their opinions must be regarded as having equal value, neither one is allowed the superiority claim, which is what the word "only" would do. So Trident left it out. But the sentence is so brilliantly constructed, the word "only" is so heavily implied, that most people hear it, even though it hasn't been said. That's the Weasel of Omission. Constructing a set of words that forces you to a conclusion that otherwise could not have been drawn. Be on the lookout for what isn't said, and try to fill the gaps realistically.

41 The other aspect of weasels is the use of all those great, groovy, swinging, wonderful, fantastic, exciting and fun-filled words known as adjectives. Your eyes, ears, mind, and soul have been bombarded by adjectives for so long that you are probably numb to most of them by now. If I were to give you a list of adjectives to look out for, it would require the next five hundred pages, and it wouldn't do you any good, anyway. More important is to bear in mind what adjectives do, and then to be able to sweep them aside and distinguish only the facts.

42 An adjective modifies a noun, and is generally used to denote the quality or a quality of the thing named. And that's our grammar lesson for today. Realistically, an adjective enhances or makes more of the product being discussed. It's the difference between "Come visit Copenhagen," and "Come visit beautiful Copenhagen." Adjectives are used so freely these days that we feel almost naked, robbed, if we don't get at least a couple. Try speaking without adjectives. Try describing something; you can't do it. The words are too stark, too bare-boned, too factual. And that's the key to judging advertising. There is a direct, inverse proportion between the number of adjectives and the number of facts. To put it succinctly, the more adjectives we use, the less we have to say.

43 You can almost make a scale, based on that simple mathematical

premise. At one end you have cosmetics, soft drinks, cigarettes, products that have little or nothing of any value to say. So we get them all dressed up with lavish word and thought images, and present you with thirty or sixty seconds of adjectival puffery. The other end of the scale is much harder to find. Usually, it will be occupied by a new product that is truly new or different. The first Pampers advertising I mentioned earlier might have gone there, but interestingly enough, it didn't work. Our craving for adjectives has become so overriding that we simply cannot listen to what is known as "nuts and bolts" advertising. The rest falls somewhere in the middle; a combination of adjectives, weasels, and semitruths. All I can tell you is, try to brush the description aside, and see what's really at the bottom.

SUMMARY

44 A weasel word is a word that's used to imply a meaning that cannot be truthfully stated. Some weasels imply meanings that are not the same as their actual definition, such as "help," "like," or "fortified." They can act as qualifiers and/or comparatives. Other weasels, such as "taste" and "flavor," have no definite meanings, and are simply subjective opinions offered by the manufacturer. A weasel of omission is one that implies a claim so strongly that it forces you to supply the bogus fact. Adjectives are weasels used to convey feelings and emotions to a greater extent than the product itself can.

45 In dealing with weasels, you must strip away the innuendos and try to ascertain the facts, if any. To do this, you need to ask questions such as: How? Why? How many? How much? Stick to basic definitions of words. Look them up if you have to. Then, apply the strict definition to the text of the advertisement or commercial. "Like" means similar to, but not the same as. "Virtually" means the same in essence, but not in fact.

46 Above all, never underestimate the devious qualities of a weasel. Weasels twist and turn and hide in dark shadows. You must come to grips with them, or advertising will rule you forever.

47 My advice to you is: Beware of weasels. They are nasty and untrainable, and they attack pocketbooks.

Word Study List

immune	4	ostensibly	28
per se	7	hypothetical	33
hexachlorophene	9	inherent	36
odious	11	succinctly	42
substantiate	12	puffery	43
potent	15	bogus	44
subjective	23, 30, 31, 32, 37, 38, 40, 44	innuendos	45

Questions

1. What is the definition of a weasel word? Why is the weasel an appropriate image for the language of advertising?

2. Into what two categories can weasel words be divided? List the key examples of weasel words in each category.

3. Why are adjectives used so often in ads? How do they help to sell the product?

4. What techniques for limiting the power of weasel words does Stevens suggest? What kinds of questions should we ask ourselves?

5. Can you complete the following statement: Instead of describing _________, weasel words create _________.

6. Analyzing Stevens's writing style can make us aware of the elements that create tone. Are Stevens's sentences generally long or short? Simple or complex? Do his sentences generally start with the subject or with introductory modifiers? What is the effect of his use of questions and sentence fragments?

7. Is Stevens's word choice formal, colloquial, technical? How does his use of slang affect the essay's tone? How would you describe the essay's tone?

8. What kind of audience does Stevens seem to be writing to?

Exercises

1. Complete the experiment Stevens suggests in paragraph 5, counting the number of times the word *help* is used in the commercials you hear during one evening of television.

2. List all the weasel words that appear in the following ad copy and explain, briefly, why each word "weasels."

> Sunbeam has a Mixmaster Mixer for any and all foods you'd like to whip up. Sunbeam makes a complete line of excellent mixers. Complete with the features to help you make it right. Just look at the Power Plus Mixmaster Mixer. It's one of the most powerful mixers ever to wear the Sunbeam name, thanks to a 335 watt motor with precision controls. It can help you prepare anything from fluffy egg whites to heavy yeast dough. It comes with deep, tapered stainless steel bowls to concentrate the ingredients into the beaters. So it mixes like no ordinary mixer can.

Advertising's Fifteen Basic Appeals

Jib Fowles

An associate professor at the University of Houston, Jib Fowles (b. 1940) teaches courses on mass media and advertising. His books include *Mass Advertising as Social Forecast* (1976) and *Television Viewers vs. Media Snobs* (1982). This article was published in the Fall 1982 issue of *ETC*, a journal devoted to semantics.

In an analytic rather than judgmental manner, Fowles explains and illustrates the major emotional or psychological appeals used by advertisers.

EMOTIONAL APPEALS

1 The nature of effective advertisements was recognized full well by the late media philosopher Marshall McLuhan. In his *Understanding Media,* the first sentence of the section on advertising reads, "The continuous pressure is to create ads more and more in the image of audience motives and desires."

2 By giving form to people's deep-lying desires, and picturing states of being that individuals privately yearn for, advertisers have the best chance of arresting attention and affecting communication. And that is the immediate goal of advertising: to tug at our psychological shirt sleeves and slow us down long enough for a word or two about whatever is being sold. We glance at a picture of a solitary rancher at work, and "Marlboro" slips into our minds.

3 Advertisers (I'm using the term as a shorthand for both the products' manufacturers, who bring the ambition and money to the process, and the advertising agencies, who supply the know-how) are ever more compelled to invoke consumers' drives and longings; this is the "continuous pressure" McLuhan refers to. Over the past century, the American marketplace has grown increasingly congested as more and more products have entered into the frenzied competition after the public's dollars. The economies of other nations are quieter than ours since the volume of goods being hawked does not so greatly exceed demand. In some economies, consumerwares are scarce enough that no advertising at all is necessary. But in the United States, we go to the other extreme. In order to stay in business, an advertiser must strive to cut through the considerable commercial hub-bub by any means available—including the emotional appeals that some observers have held to be abhorrent and underhanded.

4 The use of subconscious appeals is a comment not only on conditions among sellers. As time has gone by, buyers have become stoutly resistant to advertisements. We live in a blizzard of these messages and have learned to turn up our collars and ward off most of them. A study

done a few years ago at Harvard University's Graduate School of Business Administration ventured that the average American is exposed to some 500 ads daily from television, newspapers, magazines, radio, billboards, direct mail, and so on. If for no other reason than to preserve one's sanity, a filter must be developed in every mind to lower the number of ads a person is actually aware of—a number this particular study estimated at about seventy-five ads per day. (Of these, only twelve typically produced a reaction—nine positive and three negative, on the average.) To be among the few messages that do manage to gain access to minds, advertisers must be strategic, perhaps even a little underhanded at times.

5 There are assumptions about personality underlying advertisers' efforts to communicate via emotional appeals, and while these assumptions have stood the test of time, they still deserve to be aired. Human beings, it is presumed, walk around with a variety of unfulfilled urges and motives swirling in the bottom half of their minds. Lusts, ambitions, tendernesses, vulnerabilities—they are constantly bubbling up, seeking resolution. These mental forces energize people, but they are too crude and irregular to be given excessive play in the real world. They must be capped with the competent, sensible behavior that permits individuals to get along well in society. However, this upper layer of mental activity, shot through with caution and rationality, is not receptive to advertising's pitches. Advertisers want to circumvent this shell of consciousness if they can, and latch on to one of the lurching, subconscious drives.

6 In effect, advertisers over the years have blindly felt their way around the underside of the American psyche, and by trial and error have discovered the softest points of entree, the places where their messages have the greatest likelihood of getting by consumers' defenses. As McLuhan says elsewhere, "Gouging away at the surface of public sales resistance, the ad men are constantly breaking through into the *Alice in Wonderland* territory behind the looking glass, which is the world of subrational impulses and appetites."

7 An advertisement communicates by making use of a specially selected image (of a supine female, say, or a curly-headed child, or a celebrity) which is designed to stimulate "subrational impulses and desires" even when they are at ebb, even if they are unacknowledged by their possessor. Some few ads have their emotional appeal in the text, but for the greater number by far the appeal is contained in the artwork. This makes sense, since visual communication better suits more primal levels of the brain. If the viewer of an advertisement actually has the importuned motive, and if the appeal is sufficiently well-fashioned to call it up, then the person can be hooked. The product in the ad may then appear to take on the semblance of gratification for the summoned motive. Many ads seem to be saying, "If you have this need, then this product will help satisfy it." It is a primitive equation, but not an ineffective one for selling.

8 Thus, most advertisements appearing in national media can be

understood as having two orders of content. The first is the appeal to deep-running drives in the minds of consumers. The second is information regarding the good or service being sold: its name, its manufacturer, its picture, its packaging, its objective attributes, its functions. For example, the reader of a brassiere advertisement sees a partially undraped but blandly unperturbed woman standing in an otherwise commonplace public setting, and may experience certain sensations; the reader also sees the name "Maidenform," a particular brassiere style, and, in tiny print, words about the material, colors, price. Or, the viewer of a television commercial sees a demonstration with four small boxes labelled 650, 650, 650, and 800; something in the viewer's mind catches hold of this, as trivial as thoughtful consideration might reveal it to be. The viewer is also exposed to the name "Anacin," its bottle, and its purpose.

9 Sometimes there is an apparently logical link between an ad's emotional appeal and its product information. It does not violate common sense that Cadillac automobiles be photographed at country clubs, or that Japan Air Lines be associated with Orientalia. But there is no real need for the linkage to have a bit of reason behind it. Is there anything inherent to the connection between Salem cigarettes and mountains, Coke and a smile, Miller Beer and comradeship? The link being forged in minds between product and appeal is a pre-logical one.

10 People involved in the advertising industry do not necessarily talk in the terms being used here. They are stationed at the sending end of this communications channel, and may think they are up to any number of things—Unique Selling Propositions, explosive copywriting, the optimal use of demographics or psychographics, ideal media buys, high recall ratings, or whatever. But when attention shifts to the receiving end of the channel, and focuses on the instant of reception, then commentary becomes much more elemental: an advertising message contains something primary and primitive, an emotional appeal, that in effect is the thin end of the wedge, trying to find its way into a mind. Should this occur, the product information comes along behind.

11 When enough advertisements are examined in this light, it becomes clear that the emotional appeals fall into several distinguishable categories, and that every ad is a variation on one of a limited number of basic appeals. While there may be several ways of classifying these appeals, one particular list of fifteen has proven to be especially valuable.

Advertisements can appeal to:

1. The need for sex
2. The need for affiliation
3. The need to nurture
4. The need for guidance
5. The need to aggress

6. The need to achieve
7. The need to dominate
8. The need for prominence
9. The need for attention
10. The need for autonomy
11. The need to escape
12. The need to feel safe
13. The need for aesthetic sensations
14. The need to satisfy curiosity
15. Physiological needs: food, drink, sleep, etc.

MURRAY'S LIST

12 Where does this list of advertising's fifteen basic appeals come from? Several years ago, I was involved in a research project which was to have as one segment an objective analysis of the changing appeals made in post-World War II American advertising. A sample of magazine ads would have their appeals coded into the categories of psychological needs they seemed aimed at. For this content analysis to happen, a complete roster of human motives would have to be found.

13 The first thing that came to mind was Abraham Maslow's famous four-part hierarchy of needs. But the briefest look at the range of appeals made in advertising was enough to reveal that they are more varied, and more profane, than Maslow had cared to account for. The search led on to the work of psychologist Henry A. Murray, who together with his colleagues at the Harvard Psychological Clinic had constructed a full taxonomy of needs. As described in *Explorations in Personality,* Murray's team had conducted a lengthy series of depth interviews with a number of subjects in order to derive from scratch what they felt to be the essential variables of personality. Forty-four variables were distinguished by the Harvard group, of which twenty were motives. The need for achievement ("to overcome obstacles and obtain a high standard") was one, for instance; the need to defer was another; the need to aggress was a third; and so forth.

14 Murray's list had served as the groundwork for a number of subsequent projects. Perhaps the best-known of these was David C. McClelland's extensive study of the need for achievement, reported in his *The Achieving Society.* In the process of demonstrating that a people's high need for achievement is predictive of later economic growth, McClelland coded achievement imagery and references out of a nation's folklore, songs, legends, and children's tales.

15 Following McClelland, I too wanted to cull the motivational appeals from a culture's imaginative product—in this case, advertising. To develop categories expressly for this purpose, I took Murray's twenty motives and added to them others he had mentioned in passing in *Explo-*

rations in Personality but not included on the final list. The extended list was tried out on a sample of advertisements, and motives which never seemed to be invoked were dropped. I ended up with eighteen of Murrays' motives, into which 770 print ads were coded. The resulting distribution is included in the 1976 book *Mass Advertising as Social Forecast.*

16 Since that time, the list of appeals has undergone refinements as a result of using it to analyze television commercials. A few more adjustments have stemmed from the efforts of students in my advertising classes to decode appeals; tens of term papers surveying thousands of advertisements have caused some inconsistencies in the list to be hammered out. Fundamentally, though, the list remains the creation of Henry Murray. In developing a comprehensive, parsimonious inventory of human motives, he pinpointed the subsurface mental forces that are the least quiescent and the most susceptible to advertising's entreaties.

FIFTEEN APPEALS

17 1. *Need for sex.* Let's start with sex, because this is the appeal which seems to pop up first whenever the topic of advertising is raised. Whole books have been written about this one alone, to find a large audience of mildly titillated readers. Lately, due to campaigns to sell blue jeans, concern with sex in ads has redoubled.

18 The fascinating thing is not how much sex there is in advertising, but how little. Contrary to impressions, unambiguous sex is rare in these messages. Some of this surprising observation may be a matter of definition: the Jordache ads with the lithe, blouse-less female astride a similarly clad male is clearly an appeal to the audience's sexual drives, but the same cannot be said about Brooke Shields in the Calvin Klein commercials. Directed at young women and their credit-card carrying mothers, the image of Miss Shields instead invokes the need to be looked at. Buy Calvins and you'll be the center of much attention, just as Brooke is, the ads imply; they do not primarily inveigle their target audience's need for sexual intercourse.

19 In the content analysis reported in *Mass Advertising as Social Forecast,* only two percent of ads were found to pander to this motive. Even *Playboy* ads shy away from sexual appeals: a recent issue contained eighty-three full-page ads, and just four of them (or less than five percent) could be said to have sex on their minds.

20 The reason this appeal is so little used is that it is too blaring and tends to obliterate the product information. Nudity in advertising has the effect of reducing brand recall. The people who do remember the product may do so because they have been made indignant by the ad; this is not the response most advertisers seek.

21 To the extent that sexual imagery is used, it conventionally works better on men than women; typically a female figure is offered up to the

male reader. A Black Velvet liquor advertisement displays an attractive woman wearing a tight black outfit, recumbent under the legend, "Feel the Velvet." The figure does not have to be horizontal, however, for the appeal to be present, as National Airlines revealed in its "Fly me" campaign. Indeed, there does not even have to be a female in the ad: "Flick my Bic" was sufficient to convey the idea to many.

22 As a rule, though, advertisers have found sex to be a tricky appeal, to be used sparingly. Less controversial and equally fetching are the appeals to our need for affectionate human contact.

23 2. *Need for affiliation.* American mythology upholds autonomous individuals, and social statistics suggest that people are ever more going it alone in their lives, yet the high frequency of affiliative appeals in ads belies this. Or maybe it does not: maybe all the images of companionship are compensation for what Americans privately lack. In any case, the need to associate with others is widely invoked in advertising and is probably the most prevalent appeal. All sorts of goods and services are sold by linking them to our unfulfilled desires to be in good company.

24 According to Henry Murray, the need for affiliation consists of desires "to draw near and enjoyably cooperate or reciprocate with another; to please and win affection of another; to adhere and remain loyal to a friend." The manifestations of this motive can be segmented into several different types of affiliation, beginning with romance.

25 Courtship may be swifter nowadays, but the desire for pair-bonding is far from satiated. Ads reaching for this need commonly depict a youngish male and female engrossed in each other. The head of the male is usually higher than the female's, even at this late date; she may be sitting or leaning while he is standing. They are not touching in the Smirnoff vodka ads, but obviously there is an intimacy, sometimes frolicsome, between them. The couple does touch for Martell Cognac when "The moment was Martell." For Wind Song perfume they have touched, and "Your Wind Song stays on his mind."

26 Depending on the audience, the pair does not absolutely have to be young—just together. He gives her a DeBeers diamond, and there is a tear in her laugh lines. She takes Geritol and preserves herself for him. And numbers of consumers, wanting affection too, follow suit.

27 Warm family feelings are fanned in ads when another generation is added to the pair. Hallmark Cards brings grandparents into the picture, and Johnson and Johnson Baby Powder has Dad, Mom, and baby, all fresh from the bath, encircled in arms and emblazoned with "Share the Feeling." A talc has been fused to familial love.

28 Friendship is yet another form of affiliation pursued by advertisers. Two women confide and drink Maxwell House coffee together; two men walk through the woods smoking Salem cigarettes. Miller Beer promises that afternoon "Miller Time" will be staffed with three or four good buddies. Drink Dr. Pepper, as Mickey Rooney is coaxed to do, and join in

with all the other Peppers. Coca-Cola does not even need to portray the friendliness; it has reduced this appeal to "a Coke and a smile."

29 The warmth can be toned down and disguised, but it is the same affiliative need that is being fished for. The blonde has a direct gaze and her friends are firm businessmen in appearance, but with a glass of Old Bushmill you can sit down and fit right in. Or, for something more upbeat, sing along with the Pontiac choirboys.

30 As well as presenting positive images, advertisers can play to the need for affiliation in negative ways, by invoking the fear of rejection. If we don't use Scope, we'll have the "Ugh! Morning Breath" that causes the male and female models to avert their faces. Unless we apply Ultra-Brite or Close-Up to our teeth, it's goodbye romance. Our family will be cursed with "House-a-tosis" if we don't take care. Without Dr. Scholl's anti-perspirant foot spray, the bowling team will keel over. There go all the guests when the supply of Dorito's nacho cheese chips is exhausted. Still more rejection if our shirts have ring-around-the-collar, if our car needs to be Midasized. But make a few purchases, and we are back in the bosom of human contact.

31 As self-directed as Americans pretend to be, in the last analysis we remain social animals, hungering for the positive, endorsing feelings that only those around us can supply. Advertisers respond, urging us to "Reach out and touch someone," in the hopes our monthly bills will rise.

32 3. *Need to nurture.* Akin to affiliative needs is the need to take care of small, defenseless creatures—children and pets, largely. Reciprocity is of less consequence here, though; it is the giving that counts. Murray uses synonyms like "to feed, help, support, console, protect, comfort, nurse, heal." A strong need it is, woven deep into our genetic fabric, for if it did not exist we could not successfully raise up our replacements. When advertisers put forth the image of something diminutive and furry, something that elicits the word "cute" or "precious," then they are trying to trigger this motive. We listen to the childish voice singing the Oscar Mayer weiner song, and our next hot-dog purchase is prescribed. Aren't those darling kittens something, and how did this Meow Mix get into our shopping cart?

33 This pitch is often directed at women, as Mother Nature's chief nurturers. "Make me some Kraft macaroni and cheese, please," says the elfin preschooler just in from the snowstorm, and mothers' hearts go out, and Kraft's sales go up. "We're cold, wet, and hungry," whine the husband and kids, and the little woman gets the Manwiches ready. A facsimile of this need can be hit without children or pets: the husband is ill and sleepless in the television commercial, and the wife grudgingly fetches the NyQuil.

34 But it is not women alone who can be touched by this appeal. The father nurses his son Eddie through adolescence while the John Deere lawn tractor survives the years. Another father counts pennies with his

young son as the subject of New York Life Insurance comes up. And all over America are businessmen who don't know why they dial Qantas Airlines when they have to take a trans-Pacific trip; the koala bear knows.

35 4. *Need for guidance.* The opposite of the need to nurture is the need to be nurtured: to be protected, shielded, guided. We may be loath to admit it, but the child lingers on inside every adult—and a good thing it does, or we would not be instructable in our advancing years. Who wants a nation of nothing but flinty personalities?

36 Parent-like figures can successfully call up this need. Robert Young recommends Sanka coffee, and since we have experienced him for twenty-five years as television father and doctor, we take his word for it. Florence Henderson as the expert mom knows a lot about the advantages of Wesson oil.

37 The parent-ness of the spokesperson need not be so salient; sometimes pure authoritativeness is better. When Orson Wells scowls and intones, "Paul Masson will sell no wine before its time," we may not know exactly what he means, but we still take direction from him. There is little maternal about Brenda Vaccaro when she speaks up for Tampax, but there is a certainty to her that many accept.

38 A celebrity is not a necessity in making a pitch to the need for guidance, since a fantasy figure can serve just as well. People accede to the Green Giant, or Betty Crocker, or Mr. Goodwrench. Some advertisers can get by with no figure at all: "When E. F. Hutton talks, people listen."

39 Often it is tradition or custom that advertisers point to and consumers take guidance from. Bits and pieces of American history are used to sell whiskeys like Old Crow, Southern Comfort, Jack Daniels. We conform to the traditional male/female roles and age-old social norms when we purchase Barclay cigarettes, which informs us "The pleasure is back."

40 The product itself, if it has been around for a long time, can constitute a tradition. All those old labels in the ad for Morton salt convince us that we should continue to buy it. Kool-Aid says, "You loved it as a kid. You trust it as a mother," hoping to get yet more consumers to go along.

41 Even when the product has no history at all, our need to conform to tradition and to be guided are strong enough that they can be invoked through bogus nostalgia and older actors. Country-Time lemonade sells because consumers want to believe it has a past they can defer to.

42 So far the needs and the ways they can be invoked which have been looked at are largely warm and affiliative; they stand in contrast to the next set of needs, which are much more egoistic and assertive.

43 5. *Need to aggress.* The pressures of the real world create strong retaliatory feelings in every functioning human being. Since these impulses can come forth as bursts of anger and violence, their display is normally tabooed. Existing as harbored energy, aggressive drives present a large, tempting target for advertisers. It is not a target to be aimed at thoughtlessly, though, for few manufacturers want their products associated with

destructive motives. There is always the danger that, as in the case of sex, if the appeal is too blatant, public opinion will turn against what is being sold.

44 Jack-in-the-Box sought to abruptly alter its marketing by going after older customers and forgetting the younger ones. Their television commercials had a seventy-ish lady command, "Waste him," and the Jack-in-the-Box clown exploded before our eyes. So did public reaction, until the commercials were toned down. Print ads for Club cocktails carried the faces of octogenarians under the headline, "Hit me with a Club"; response was contrary enough to bring the campaign to a stop.

45 Better disguised aggressive appeals are less likely to backfire: Triumph cigarettes has models making a lewd gesture with their uplifted cigarettes, but the individuals are often laughing and usually in the close company of others. When Exxon said, "There's a Tiger in your tank," the implausibility of it concealed the invocation of aggressive feelings.

46 Depicted arguments are a common way for advertisers to tap the audience's needs to aggress. Don Rickles and Lynda Carter trade gibes, and consumers take sides as the name of Seven-Up is stitched on minds. The Parkay tub has a difference of opinion with the user; who can forget it, or who (or what) got the last word in?

47 6. *Need to achieve.* This is the drive that energizes people, causing them to strive in their lives and careers. According to Murray, the need for achievement is signalled by the desires "to accomplish something difficult. To overcome obstacles and attain a high standard. To excel one's self. To rival and surpass others." A prominent American trait, it is one that advertisers like to hook on to because it identifies their product with winning and success.

48 The Cutty Sark ad does not disclose that Ted Turner failed at his latest attempt at yachting's America Cup; here he is represented as a champion on the water as well as off in his television enterprises. If we drink this whiskey, we will be victorious alongside Turner. We can also succeed with O. J. Simpson by renting Hertz cars, or with Reggie Jackson by bringing home some Panasonic equipment. Cathy Rigby and Stayfree Maxipads will put people out front.

49 Sports heros are the most convenient means to snare consumers' needs to achieve, but they are not the only one. Role models can be established, ones which invite emulation, as with the profiles put forth by Dewar's scotch. Successful, tweedy individuals relate they have "graduated to the flavor of Myer's rum." Or the advertiser can establish a prize: two neighbors play one-on-one basketball for a Michelob beer in a television commercial, while in a print ad a bottle of Johnnie Walker Black Label has been gilded like a trophy.

50 Any product that advertises itself in superlatives—the best, the first, the finest—is trying to make contact with our needs to succeed. For many consumers, sales and bargains belong in this category of appeals, too; the

person who manages to buy something at fifty percent off is seizing an opportunity and coming out ahead of others.

51 7. *Need to dominate.* This fundamental need is the craving to be powerful—perhaps omnipotent, as in the Xerox ad where Brother Dominic exhibits heavenly powers and creates miraculous copies. Most of us will settle for being just a regular potentate, though. We drink Budweiser because it is the King of Beers, and here come the powerful Clydesdales to prove it. A taste of Wolfschmidt vodka and "The spirit of the Czar lives on."

52 The need to dominate and control one's environment is often thought of as being masculine, but as close students of human nature, advertisers know it is not so circumscribed. Women's aspirations for control is suggested in the campaign theme, "I like my men in English Leather, or nothing at all." The females in the Chanel No. 19 ads are "outspoken" and wrestle their men around.

53 Male and female, what we long for is clout; what we get in its place is Mastercard.

54 8. *Need for prominence.* Here comes the need to be admired and respected, to enjoy prestige and high social status. These times, it appears, are not so egalitarian after all. Many ads picture the trappings of high position; the Oldsmobile stands before a manorial doorway, the Volvo is parked beside a steeplechase. A book-lined study is the setting for Dewar's 12, and Lenox China is displayed in a dining room chock full of antiques.

55 Beefeater gin represents itself as "The Crown Jewel of England" and uses no illustrations of jewels or things British, for the words are sufficient indicators of distinction. Buy that gin and you will rise up the prestige hierarchy, or achieve the same effect on yourself with Seagram's 7 Crown, which unambiguously describes itself as "classy."

56 Being respected does not have to entail the usual accoutrements of wealth: "Do you know who I am?" the commercials ask, and we learn that the prominent person is not so prominent without his American Express card.

57 9. *Need for attention.* The previous need involved being *looked up to,* while this is the need to be *looked at.* The desire to exhibit ourselves in such a way as to make others look at us is a primitive, insuppressible instinct. The clothing and cosmetic industries exist just to serve this need, and this is the way they pitch their wares. Some of this effort is aimed at males, as the ads for Hathaway shirts and Jockey underclothes. But the greater bulk of such appeals is targeted singlemindedly at women.

58 To come back to Brooke Shields: this is where she fits into American marketing. If I buy Calvin Klein jeans, consumers infer, I'll be the object of fascination. The desire for exhibition has been most strikingly played to in a print campaign of many years duration, that of Maidenform lingerie. The woman exposes herself, and sales surge. "Gentlemen prefer Hanes" the ads dissemble, and women who want eyes upon them know

what they should do. Peggy Fleming flutters her legs for L'eggs, encouraging females who want to be the star in their own lives to purchase this product.

59 The same appeal works for cosmetics and lotions. For years, the little girl with the exposed backside sold gobs of Coppertone, but now the company has picked up the pace a little: as a female, you are supposed to "Flash 'em a Coppertone tan." Food can be sold the same way, especially to the diet-conscious; Angie Dickinson poses for California avocadoes and says, "Would this body lie to you?" Our eyes are too fixed on her for us to think to ask if she got that way by eating mounds of guacamole.

60 10. *Need for autonomy.* There are several ways to sell credit card services, as has been noted: Mastercard appeals to the need to dominate, and American Express to the need for prominence. When Visa claims, "You can have it the way you want it," yet another primary motive is being beckoned forward—the need to endorse the self. The focus here is upon the independence and integrity of the individual; this need is the antithesis of the need for guidance and is unlike any of the social needs. "If running with the herd isn't your style, try ours," says Rotan-Mosle, and many Americans feel they have finally found the right brokerage firm.

61 The photo is of a red-coated Mountie on his horse, posed on a snow-covered ledge; the copy reads, "Windsor—One Canadian stands alone." This epitome of the solitary and proud individual may work best with male customers, as may Winston's man in the red cap. But one-figure advertisements also strike the strong need for autonomy among American women. As Shelly Hack strides for Charlie perfume, females respond to her obvious pride and flair; she is her own person. The Virginia Slims' tale is of people who have come a long way from subservience to independence. Cachet perfume feels it does not need a solo figure to work this appeal, and uses three different faces in its ads; it insists, though, "it's different on every woman who wears it."

62 Like many psychological needs, this one can also be appealed to in a negative fashion, by invoking the loss of independence or self-regard. Guilt and regrets can be stimulated: "Gee, I could have had a V-8." Next time, get one and be good to yourself.

63 11. *Need to escape.* An appeal to the need for autonomy often co-occurs with one for the need to escape, since the desire to duck out of our social obligations, to seek rest or adventure, frequently takes the form of one-person flight. The dashing image of a pilot, in fact, is a standard way of quickening this need to get away from it all.

64 Freedom is the pitch here, the freedom that every individual yearns for whenever life becomes too oppressive. Many advertisers like appealing to the need for escape because the sensation of pleasure often accompanies escape, and what nicer emotional nimbus could there be for a product? "You deserve a break today," says McDonalds, and Stouffer's frozen foods chime in, "Set yourself free."

65 For decades men have imaginatively bonded themselves to the Marl-

boro cowboy who dwells untarnished and unencumbered in Marlboro Country some distance from modern life; smokers' aching needs for autonomy and escape are personified by that cowpoke. Many women can identify with the lady ambling through the woods behind the words, "Benson and Hedges and mornings and me."

66 But escape does not have to be solitary. Other Benson and Hedges ads, part of the same campaign, contain two strolling figures. In Salem cigarette advertisements, it can be several people who escape together into the mountaintops. A commercial for Levi's pictured a cloudbank above a city through which ran a whole chain of young people.

67 There are varieties of escape, some wistful like the Boeing "Someday" campaign of dream vacations, some kinetic like the play and parties in soft drink ads. But in every instance, the consumer exposed to the advertisement is invited to momentarily depart his everyday life for a more carefree experience, preferably with the product in hand.

68 12. *Need to feel safe.* Nobody in their right mind wants to be intimidated, menaced, battered, poisoned. We naturally want to do whatever it takes to stave off threats to our well-being, and to our families'. It is the instinct for self-preservation that makes us responsive to the ad of the St. Bernard with the keg of Chivas Regal. We pay attention to the stern talk of Karl Malden and the plight of the vacationing couples who have lost all their funds in the American Express travelers cheques commercials. We want the omnipresent stag from Hartford Insurance to watch over us too.

69 In the interest of keeping failure and calamity from our lives, we like to see the durability of products demonstrated. Can we ever forget that Timex takes a licking and keeps on ticking? When the American Tourister suitcase bounces all over the highway and the egg inside doesn't break, the need to feel safe has been adroitly plucked.

70 We take precautions to diminish future threats. We buy Volkswagen Rabbits for the extraordinary mileage, and MONY insurance policies to avoid the tragedies depicted in their black-and-white ads of widows and orphans.

71 We are careful about our health. We consume Mazola margarine because it has "corn goodness" backed by the natural food traditions of the American Indians. In the medicine cabinet is Alka-Seltzer, the "home remedy"; having it, we are snug in our little cottage.

72 We want to be safe and secure; buy these products, advertisers are saying, and you'll be safer than you are without them.

73 13. *Need for aesthetic sensations.* There is an undeniable aesthetic component to virtually every ad run in the national media: the photography or filming or drawing is near-perfect, the type style is well chosen, the layout could scarcely be improved upon. Advertisers know there is little chance of good communication occurring if an ad is not visually pleasing. Consumers may not be aware of the extent of their own sensitivity to artwork, but it is undeniably large.

74 Sometimes the aesthetic element is expanded and made into an ad's

primary appeal. Charles Jordan shoes may or may not appear in the accompanying avant-garde photographs; Kohler plumbing fixtures catch attention through the high style of their desert settings. Beneath the slightly out of focus photograph, languid and sensuous in tone, General Electric feels called upon to explain, "This is an ad for the hair dryer."

75 This appeal is not limited to female consumers: J and B scotch says "It whispers" and shows a bucolic scene of lake and castle.

76 14. *Need to satisfy curiosity.* It may seem odd to list a need for information among basic motives, but this need can be as primal and compelling as any of the others. Human beings are curious by nature, interested in the world around them, and intrigued by tidbits of knowledge and new developments. Trivia, percentages, observations counter to conventional wisdom—these items all help sell products. Any advertisement in a question-and-answer format is strumming this need.

77 A dog groomer has a question about long distance rates, and Bell Telephone has a chart with all the figures. An ad for Porsche 911 is replete with diagrams and schematics, numbers and arrows. Lo and behold, Anacin pills have 150 more milligrams than its competitors; should we wonder if this is better or worse for us?

78 15. *Physiological needs.* To the extent that sex is solely a biological need, we are now coming around full circle, back towards the start of the list. In this final category are clustered appeals to sleeping, eating, drinking. The art of photographing food and drink is so advanced, sometimes these temptations are wondrously caught in the camera's lens: the crab meat in the Red Lobster restaurant ads can start us salivating, the Quarterpounder can almost be smelled, the liquor in the glass glows invitingly. Imbibe, these ads scream.

STYLES

79 Some common ingredients of advertisements were not singled out for separate mention in the list of fifteen because they are not appeals in and of themselves. They are stylistic features, influencing the way a basic appeal is presented. The use of humor is one, and the use of celebrities is another. A third is time imagery, past and future, which goes to several purposes.

80 For all of its employment in advertising, humor can be treacherous, because it can get out of hand and smother the product information. Supposedly, this is what Alka-Seltzer discovered with its comic commercials of the late sixties; "I can't believe I ate the whole thing," the sad-faced husband lamented, and the audience cackled so much it forgot the antacid. Or, did not take it seriously.

81 But used carefully, humor can punctuate some of the softer appeals and soften some of the harsher ones. When Emma says to the Fruit-of-the-Loom fruits, "Hi, cuties. Whatcha doing in my laundry basket?" we smile as our curiosity is assuaged along with hers. Bill Cosby gets con-

sumers tickled about the children in his Jello commercials, and strokes the need to nurture.

82 An insurance company wants to invoke the need to feel safe, but does not want to leave readers with an unpleasant aftertaste; cartoonist Rowland Wilson creates an avalanche about to crush a gentleman who is saying to another, "My insurance company? New England Life, of course. Why?" The same tactic of humor undercutting threat is used on the cartoon commercials for Safeco when the Pink Panther wanders from one disaster to another. Often humor masks aggression: comedian Bob Hope in the outfit of a boxer promises to knock out the knock-knocks with Texaco; Rodney Dangerfield, who "can't get no respect," invites aggression as the comic relief in Miller Lite commercials.

83 Roughly fifteen percent of all advertisements incorporate a celebrity, almost always from the fields of entertainment or sports. This approach can also prove troublesome for advertisers, for celebrities are human beings too, and fully capable of the most remarkable behavior; if anything distasteful about them emerges, it is likely to reflect on the product. The advertisers making use of Anita Bryant and Billy Jean King suffered several anxious moments. An untimely death can also reflect poorly on a product. But advertisers are willing to take these risks because celebrities can be such a good link between producers and consumers, performing the social role of introducer.

84 There are several psychological needs these middlemen can play upon. Let's take the product class of cameras and see how different celebrities can hit different needs. The need for guidance can be invoked by Michael Landon, who plays such a wonderful dad on "Little House on the Prairie"; when he says to buy Kodak equipment, many people listen. James Garner for Polaroid cameras is put in a similar authoritative role, so defined by a mocking spouse. The need to achieve is summoned up by Tracy Austin and other tennis stars for Canon AE-1; the advertiser first makes sure we see these athletes playing to win. When Cheryl Tiegs speaks up for Olympus cameras, it is the need for attention that is being targeted.

85 The past and future, being outside our grasp, are exploited by advertisers as locales for the projection of needs. History can offer up heroes (and call up the need to achieve) or traditions (need for guidance) as well as art objects (need for aesthetic sensations). Nostalgia is a kindly version of personal history and is deployed by advertisers to rouse needs for affiliation and for guidance; the need to escape can come in here, too. The same need to escape is sometimes the point of futuristic appeals, but picturing the avant-garde can also be a way to get at the need to achieve.

ANALYZING ADVERTISEMENTS

86 When analyzing ads yourself for their emotional appeals, it takes a bit of practice to learn to ignore the product information (as well as one's own experience and feelings about the product). But that skill comes soon

enough, as does the ability to quickly sort out from all the non-product aspects of an ad the chief element which is the most striking, the most likely to snag attention first and penetrate brains furthest. The key to the appeal, this element usually presents itself centrally and forwardly to the reader or viewer.

87 Another clue: the viewing angle which the audience has on the ad's subjects is informative. If the subjects are photographed or filmed from below and thus are looking down at you much as the Green Giant does, then the need to be guided is a good candidate for the ad's emotional appeal. If, on the other hand, the subjects are shot from above and appear deferential, as is often the case with children or female models, then other needs are being appealed to.

88 To figure out an ad's emotional appeal, it is wise to know (or have a good hunch about) who the targeted consumers are; this can often be inferred from the magazine or television show it appears in. This piece of information is a great help in determining the appeal and in deciding between two different interpretations. For example, if an ad features a partially undressed female, this would typically signal one appeal for readers of *Penthouse* (need for sex) and another for readers of *Cosmopolitan* (need for attention).

89 It would be convenient if every ad made just one appeal, were aimed at just one need. Unfortunately, things are often not that simple. A cigarette ad with a couple at the edge of a polo field is trying to hit both the need for affiliation and the need for prominence; depending on the attitude of the male, dominance could also be an ingredient in this. An ad for Chimere perfume incorporates two photos: in the top one the lady is being commanding at a business luncheon (need to dominate), but in the lower one she is being bussed (need for affiliation). Better ads, however, seem to avoid being too diffused; in the study of post-World War II advertising described earlier, appeals grew more focused as the decades passed. As a rule of thumb, about sixty percent of ads make one paramount appeal; roughly twenty percent have two conspicuous appeals; the last twenty percent have three or more. Rather than looking for the greatest number of appeals, decoding ads is most productive when the loudest one or two appeals are discerned, since those are the appeals with the best chance of grabbing people's attention.

90 Finally, analyzing ads does not have to be a solo activity and probably should not be. The greater number of people there are involved, the better chance there is of transcending individual biases and discovering the essential emotional lure built into an advertisement.

DO THEY OR DON'T THEY?

91 Do the emotional appeals made in advertisements add up to the sinister manipulation of consumers?

92 It is clear that these ads work. Attention is caught, communication

occurs between producers and consumers, and sales result. It turns out to be difficult to detail the exact relationship between a specific ad and a specific purchase, or even between a campaign and subsequent sales figures, because advertising is only one of a host of influences upon consumption. Yet no one is fooled by this lack of perfect proof; everyone knows that advertising sells. If this were not the case, then tight-fisted American businesses would not spend a total of fifty billion dollars annually on these messages.

93 But before anyone despairs that advertisers have our number to the extent that they can marshal us at will and march us like automatons to the check-out counters, we should recall the resiliency and obduracy of the American consumer. Advertisers may have uncovered the softest spots in minds, but that does not mean they have found truly gaping apertures. There is no evidence that advertising can get people to do things contrary to their self-interests. Despite all the finesse of advertisements, and all the subtle emotional tugs, the public resists the vast majority of the petitions. According to the marketing division of the A. C. Nielsen Company, a whopping seventy-five percent of all new products die within a year in the marketplace, the victims of consumer disinterest which no amount of advertising could overcome. The appeals in advertising may be the most captivating there are to be had, but they are not enough to entrap the wiley consumer.

94 The key to understanding the discrepancy between, on the one hand, the fact that advertising truly works, and, on the other, the fact that it hardly works, is to take into account the enormous numbers of people exposed to an ad. Modern-day communications permit an ad to be displayed to millions upon millions of individuals; if the smallest fraction of that audience can be moved to buy the product, then the ad has been successful. When one percent of the people exposed to a television advertising campaign reach for their wallets, that could be one million sales, which may be enough to keep the product in production and the advertisements coming.

95 In arriving at an evenhanded judgment about advertisements and their emotional appeals, it is good to keep in mind that many of the purchases which might be credited to these ads are experienced as genuinely gratifying to the consumer. We sincerely like the good or service we have bought, and we may even like some of the emotional drapery that an ad suggests comes with it. It has sometimes been noted that the most avid students of advertisements are the people who have just bought the product; they want to steep themselves in the associated imagery. This may be the reason that Americans, when polled, are not negative about advertising and do not disclose any sense of being misused. The volume of advertising may be an irritant, but the product information as well as the imaginative material in ads are partial compensation.

96 A productive understanding is that advertising messages involve

costs and benefits at both ends of the communications channel. For those few ads which do make contact, the consumer surrenders a moment of time, has the lower brain curried, and receives notice of a product; the advertiser has given up money and has increased the chance of sales. In this sort of communications activity, neither party can be said to be the loser.

Word Study List

abhorrent	3	reciprocity	32
circumvent	5	instructable	35
psyche	6	salient	37
entree	6	emulation	49
supine	7	potentate	51
importuned	7	accoutrements	56
demographics	10	nimbus	64
psychographics	10	omnipresent	68
aesthetic	11	schematics	77
taxonomy	13	assuaged	81
parsimonious	16	deferential	87
quiescent	16	resiliency	93
inveigle	18	obduracy	93
obliterate	20	apertures	93
satiated	25	curried	96
emblazoned	27		

Questions

1. Why, apparently, must advertisers use emotional appeals to sell products? According to the Harvard study, how many ads are we exposed to daily?

2. Explain how Fowles obtained the final, specific list of fifteen basic appeals to which ads are directed. Why do you suppose Fowles devotes five paragraphs to explaining this process? What contribution do these paragraphs make to the essay?

3. Briefly outline Fowles's organization. What techniques does he use to make his organization clear?

4. How effective are Fowles's explanations of each appeal? What helps to make his analysis convincing?

5. Which appeals must be addressed with great caution? Why?

6. What is the difference between an ad's appeal and its style? What are some stylistic features used by ads? What problems can they create?

7. What is Fowles's final position on advertising? Is it a necessary evil, abusive, helpful to consumers, or something else? How does the tone of the essay help to convey Fowles's attitude toward his subject?

8. Do you agree with Fowles's attitude toward advertising? Why or why not?

Exercise

Analyze the ads in this chapter to determine which one (or two) of the fifteen basic appeals dominates each ad. Be prepared to discuss your analysis with classmates and to debate any disagreements.

It's Natural! It's Organic! Or Is It?

Consumer's Union

Consumer's Union is a nonprofit organization whose chief purpose is to "provide consumers with information and counsel on consumer goods and services." It gains income and makes consumer information available through the publication of *Consumer Reports* magazine. This article appeared in the July 1980 issue of *Consumer Reports.*

Consumer's Union examines the power of a particular word—*natural*—and the ideas and values we associate with it. Why are we so sure that what is natural—be it food or beer or shampoo—is always better, Consumer's Union asks.

1 "No artificial flavors or colors!" reads the Nabisco advertisement in *Progressive Grocer,* a grocery trade magazine. "And research shows that's exactly what consumers are eager to buy."

2 The ad, promoting Nabisco's *Sesame Wheats* as "a natural whole wheat cracker," might raise a few eyebrows among thoughtful consumers of Nabisco's *Wheat Thins* and *Cheese Nips,* which contain artificial colors, or of its *Ginger Snaps* and *Oreo Cookies,* which have artificial flavors. But Nabisco has not suddenly become a champion of "natural" foods. Like other giants of the food industry, the company is merely keeping its eye on what will produce a profit.

3 Nabisco's trade ad, which was headlined "A Natural for Profits," is simply a routine effort by a food processor to capitalize on the concerns that consumers have about the safety of the food they buy.

4 Supermarket shelves are being flooded with "natural" products, some of them containing a long list of chemical additives. And some products that never did contain additives have suddenly sprouted "natural" or "no preservative" labels. Along with the new formulations and labels have come higher prices, since the food industry has realized that consumers are willing to pay more for products they think are especially healthful.

5 The mass merchandising of "natural" foods is a spillover onto supermarket shelves of a phenomenon once confined to health-food stores, as major food manufacturers enter what was once the exclusive territory of small entrepreneurs. Health-food stores were the first to foster and capitalize on the growing consumer interest in nutrition and are still thriving. Along with honey-sweetened snacks, "natural" vitamins, and other "natural" food products, the health-food stores frequently feature "organic" produce and other "organic" foods.

6 Like the new merchandise in supermarkets, the products sold at health-food stores carry the implication that they're somehow better for you—safer or more nutritious. In this report, we'll examine that premise, looking at both "natural" foods, which are widely sold, and "organic" foods, which are sold primarily at health-food stores. While the terms "natural" and "organic" are often used loosely, "organic" generally refers to the way food is grown (without pesticides or chemical fertilizers) and "natural" to the character of the ingredients (no preservatives or artificial additives) and to the fact that the food product has undergone minimal processing.

7 *Langendorf Natural Lemon Flavored Creme Pie* contains no cream. It does contain sodium propionate, certified food colors, sodium benzoate, and vegetable gum.

8 That's natural?

9 Yes indeed, says L. A. Cushman Jr., chairman of American Bakeries Co., the Chicago firm that owns Langendorf. The word "natural," he explains, modifies "lemon flavored," and the pie contains oil from lemon rinds. "The lemon flavor," Cushman states, "comes from natural lemon flavor as opposed to artificial lemon flavor, assuming there is such a thing as artificial lemon flavor."

10 Welcome to the world of natural foods.

11 You can eat your "natural" way from one end of the supermarket to the other. Make yourself a sandwich of *Kraft Cracker Barrel Natural Cheddar Cheese* on *Better Way Natural Whole Grain Wheat Nugget Bread* spread with *Autumn Natural Margarine.* Wash it down with *Anheuser-Busch Natural Light Beer* or *Rich-Life Natural Orange NutriPop.* Snack on any number of brands of "natural" potato chips and "natural" candy bars. And don't exclude your pet: Feed your dog *Gravy Train Dog Food With Natural Beef Flavor* or, if it's a puppy, try *Blue Mountain Natural Style Puppy Food.*

12 The "natural" bandwagon doesn't end at the kitchen. You can bathe in *Batherapy Natural Mineral Bath* (Sodium sesquicarbonate, isopropyl

myristate, fragrance, D & C Green No. 5, D & C Yellow No. 10 among its ingredients), using *Queen Helene "All-Natural" Amino Peptide Shampoo* (propylene glycol, hydroxyethyl cellulose, methylparaben, D & C Red No. 3, D & C Brown No. 1) and *Organic Aid Natural Clear Soaps.* Then, if you're so inclined, you can apply *Naturade Conditioning Mascara with Natural Protein* (stearic acid, PVP, butylene glycol, sorbitan sesquioleate, triethanolamine, imidazolidinyl urea, methylparaben, propylparaben).

13 At its ridiculous extreme, the "natural" ploy extends to furniture, cigarettes, denture adhesives, and shoes.

THE SELLING OF A WORD

14 The word "natural" does not have to be synonymous with "ripoff." Over the years, the safety of many food additives has been questioned. And a consumer who reads labels carefully can in fact find some foods in supermarkets that have been processed without additives.

15 But the word "natural" does not guarantee that. All too often, as the above examples indicate, the word is used more as a key to higher profits. Often, it implies a health benefit that does not really exist.

16 Co-op News, the publication of the Berkeley Co-op, the nation's largest consumer-cooperative store chain, reported on "two 15-ounce cans of tomato sauce, available side-by-side" at one of its stores. One sauce, called *Health Valley,* claimed on its label to have "no citric acid, no sugars, no preservatives, no artificial colors or flavors." There were none of those ingredients in the Co-op's house brand, either, but their absence was hardly worth noting on the label, since canned tomato sauce almost never contains artificial colors or flavors and doesn't need preservatives after being heated in the canning process. The visible difference between the two products was price, not ingredients. The *Health Valley* tomato sauce was selling for 85 cents; the Co-op house brand, for only 29 cents.

17 One supermarket industry consultant estimates that 7 percent of all processed food products now sold are touted as "natural." And that could be just the beginning. A Federal Trade Commission report noted that 63 percent of people polled in a survey agreed with the statement, "Natural foods are more nutritious than other foods." Thirty-nine percent said they regularly buy food because it is "natural," and 47 percent said they are willing to pay 10 percent more for a food that is "natural."

18 According to those who have studied the trend, the consumer's desire for "natural" foods goes beyond the fear of specific chemicals. "There is a mistrust of technology," says Howard Moskowitz, a taste researcher and consultant to the food industry. "There is a movement afoot to return to simplicity in all aspects of life." A spokeswoman for Lever Bros., one of the nation's major food merchandisers, adds: "'Natural' is a psychological thing of everyone wanting to get out of the industrial world."

19 Because consumers are acting out of such vague, undefined feelings, they aren't sure what they should be getting when they buy a product labeled "natural." William Wittenberg, president of Grandma's Food Inc., comments: "Manufacturers and marketers are making an attempt to appeal to a consumer who feels he should be eating something natural, but doesn't know why. I think the marketers of the country in effect mirror back to the people what they want to hear. People have to look to themselves for their own protection." Grandma's makes a *Whole Grain Date Filled Fruit 'n Oatmeal Bar* labeled "naturally Good Flavor." The ingredients include "artificial flavor."

IS 'NATURAL' BETTER?

20 "Natural" foods are not necessarily preferable nor, as we have seen, necessarily natural.

21 Consider "natural" potato chips. They are often cut thick from unpeeled potatoes, packaged without preservatives in heavy foil bags with fancy lettering, and sold at a premium price. Sometimes, such chips include "sea salt," a product whose advantage over conventional "land" salt has not been demonstrated. The packaging is intended to give the impression that "natural" potato chips are less of a junk food than regular chips. But nutritionally there is no difference. Both are made from the same food, the potato, and both have been processed so that they are high in salt and in calories.

22 Sometimes the "natural" products may have ingredients you'd prefer to avoid. *Quaker 100% Natural* cereal, for example, contains 24 percent sugars, a high percentage, considering it's not promoted as a sugared cereal. (*Kellogg's Corn Flakes* has 7.8 percent sugar.) Many similar "natural" granola-type-cereals have oil added, giving them a much higher fat content than conventional cereals.

23 Taste researcher Moskowitz notes that food processors are "trying to signal to the consumer a sensory impact that can be called natural." Two of the most popular signals, says Moskowitz, are honey and coconut. But honey is just another sugar, with no significant nutrients other than calories (see the discussion of honey on page 130), and coconut is especially high in saturated fats.

24 While many processed foods are less nutritious than their fresh counterparts, processing can sometimes help foods: Freezing preserves nutrients that can be lost if fresh foods are not consumed quickly; pasteurization kills potentially dangerous bacteria in milk. Some additives are also both safe and useful. Sorbic acid, for instance, prevents the growth of potentially harmful molds in cheese and other products, and sodium benzoate has been used for more than 70 years to prevent the growth of microorganisms in acidic foods.

25 "Preservative" has become a dirty word, to judge from the number

of "no preservative" labels on food products. Calcium propionate might sound terrible on a bread label, but this mildew-retarding substance occurs naturally in both raisins and Swiss cheese. "Bread without preservatives could well cost you more than bread with them," says Vernal S. Packard Jr., a University of Minnesota nutrition professor. "Without preservatives, the bread gets stale faster; it may go moldy with the production of hazardous aflatoxin. And already we in the United States return [to producers] 100 million pounds of bread each year—this in a world nagged by hunger and malnutrition."

26 Nor are all "natural" substances safe. Sassafras tea was banned by the U.S. Food and Drug Administration several years ago because it contains safrole, which has produced liver cancer in laboratory animals. Kelp, a seaweed that is becoming increasingly fashionable as a dietary supplement, can have a high arsenic content. Aflatoxin, produced by a mold that can grow on improperly stored peanuts, corn, and grains, is a known carcinogen.

27 To complicate matters, our palates have become attuned to many unnatural tastes. "We don't have receptors on our tongues that signal 'natural'," says taste researcher Moskowitz. He points out, for instance, that a panel of consumers would almost certainly reject a natural lemonade "in favor of a lemonade scientifically designed to taste natural. If you put real lemon, sugar, and water together, people would reject it as harsh. They are used to flavors developed by flavor houses." Similarly, Moskowitz points out, many consumers say that for health reasons they prefer less salty food—but the results of various taste tests have contradicted this, too.

THE TACTICS OF DECEPTION

28 In the midst of all this confusion, it's not surprising that the food industry is having a promotional field day. Companies are using various tactics to convince the consumer that a food product is "natural"—and hence preferable. Here are some of the most common:

29 *The inderterminate modifier.* Use a string of adjectives and claim that "natural" modifies only the next adjective in line, not the product itself. Take *Pillsbury Natural Chocolate Flavored Chocolate Chip Cookies.* Many a buyer might be surprised to learn from the fine print that these cookies contain artificial flavor, as well as the chemical antioxidant BHA. But Pillsbury doesn't bat an eyelash at this. "We're not trying to mislead anybody," says a company representative, explaining that the word "natural" modifies only "chocolate flavored," while the artificial flavoring is vanilla. Then why not call the product "Chocolate Chip Cookies with Natural Chocolate Flavoring"? "From a labeling point of view, we're trying to use a limited amount of space" was the answer.

30 *Innocence by association.* Put nature on your side. *Life Cinnamon Flavor*

High Protein Cereal, a Quaker Oats Co. product, contains BHA and artificial color, among other things. How could the company imply the cereal was "natural" and still be truthful? One series of *Life* boxes solves the problem neatly. The back panel has an instructional lesson for children entitled "Nature." The box uses the word "Nature" four times and "natural" once—but never actually to describe the cereal inside. Other products surround themselves with a "natural" aura by picturing outdoor or farm scenes on their packages.

31 *The "printer's error."* From time to time, readers send us food wrappers making a "natural" claim directly contradicted by the ingredients list. We have, for example, received a batch of individually wrapped *Devonsheer* crackers with a big red label saying: "A Natural Product, no preservatives." The ingredients list includes "calcium propionate (to retard spoilage)."

32 How could a manufacturer defend that? "At a given printing, the printer was instructed to remove 'no preservatives, natural product' when we changed ingredients, but he didn't do it," says Curtis Marshall, vice president for operations at Devonsheer Melba Corp.

33 *The best defense.* Don't defend yourself; attack the competition. Sometimes the use of the word "natural" is, well, just plain unnatural. Take the battle that has been brewing between the nation's two largest beer makers, Miller Brewing Co. and Anheuser-Busch. The latter's product, *Anheuser-Busch Natural Light Beer,* has been the object of considerable derision by Miller.

34 Miller wants the word "natural" dropped from Anheuser-Busch's advertisements because beers are "highly processed, complex products, made with chemical additives and other components not in their natural form."

35 Anheuser-Busch has responded only with some digs at Miller, charging Miller with using artificial foam stabilizer and adding an industrial enzyme instead of natural malt to reduce the caloric content of its *Miller Lite* beer.

36 No victor has yet emerged from the great beer war, but the industry is obviously getting edgy.

37 "Other brewers say it's time for the two companies to shut up," the Wall Street Journal reported. "One thing they [the other brewers] are worried about, says William T. Elliot, president of C. Schmidt & Sons, a Philadelphia brewery, is all the fuss over ingredients. Publicity about that issue is disclosing to beer drinkers that their suds may include sulfuric acid, calcium sulfate, alginic acid, or amyloglucosidase."

38 *The negative pitch.* Point out in big letters on the label that the product doesn't contain something it wouldn't contain anyway. The "no artificial preservatives" label stuck on a jar of jam or jelly is true and always has been—since sugar is all the preservative jams and jellies need. Canned goods, likewise, are preserved in their manufacture—by the heat of the

canning process. Then there is the "no cholesterol" claim of vegetable oils, margarines, and even (in a radio commercial) canned pineapple. Those are also true, but beside the point, since cholesterol is found only in animal products.

AN APPROACH TO REGULATION

39 What can be done about such all-but-deceptive practices? One might suggest that the word "natural" is so vague as to be inherently deceptive, and therefore should not be available for promotional use. Indeed, the FTC staff suggested precisely that a few years ago but later backed away from the idea. The California legislature last year passed a weak bill defining the word "organic," but decided that political realities argued against tackling the word "natural."

40 "If we had included the word 'natural' in the bill, it most likely would not have gotten out of the legislature," says one legislative staff member. "When you've got large economic interests in certain areas, the tendency is to guard those interests very carefully."

41 Under the revised FTC staff proposal, which had not been acted on by the full commission as we went to press, the word "natural" can be used if the product has undergone only minimal processing and doesn't have artificial ingredients. That would eliminate the outright frauds, as well as the labeling of such products as Lever Bros.' *Autumn Natural Margarine,* which obviously has been highly processed from its original vegetable-oil state. But the FTC proposal might run into difficulty in defining exactly what "minimal processing" means. And it would also allow some deceptive implications. For instance, a product containing honey might be called "natural," while a food with refined sugar might not, thus implying that honey is superior to other sugars, which it is not.

42 A law incorporating similar regulations went into effect in Maine at the beginning of this year. If a product is to be labeled "natural" and sold in Maine, it must have undergone only minimal processing and have no additives, preservatives, or refined additions such as white flour and sugar.

43 So far, according to John Michael, the state legislator who sponsored the bill, food companies have largely ignored the law, but he expects the state to start issuing warnings this summer.

Word Study List

entrepreneurs	6	carcinogen	26
pesticides	6	derision	33
nutrients	23.24	enzyme	35
microorganisms	24	cholesterol	38
acidic	24	inherently	39

Questions

1. Consumer's Union asserts that rather than being a useful or even accurate description of a product, the term *natural* is used in product names and advertising to increase profits. Were you aware of the extensive use of *natural* as a selling technique?

2. What reason do consumers give for buying natural products, even at higher prices? What other reasons might explain the current popularity of "natural" products?

3. Why should we be wary of the ad writer's use of *natural?* Are natural foods always better? Always safer? Is the term always used honestly?

4. List the specific tactics of deception used to make what is natural seem better.

5. Given the strong positive connotations of the word *natural,* is the word inherently deceptive? Should it be banned from advertising?

Exercise

Find either ads or labels of products in your home or a store to illustrate each tactic of deception.

The Parable of the Ring Around the Collar: and Other Irreverent Observations on the Religious Nature of Commercials

Neil Postman

Neil Postman (b. 1931) is a professor of media ecology at New York University and author of books and articles on teaching and language, including *Crazy Talk, Stupid Talk* (1977) and *Teaching as a Conserving Activity* (1979). "The Parable" was published in the March 1980 issue of *Panorama,* a monthly magazine devoted to television.

In his article Postman provides a clever analysis of the ad writer's use of the parable form to make us see the light and buy the product. Postman's humorous touches do not hide his concern over the values expressed through the effective "parable" ads.

1 Television commercials are a form of religious literature. Thus, to comment on them in a serious vein is to practice hermeneutics, which is the branch of theology concerned with interpreting and explaining the Scriptures. This is what I propose to do here. The heathens, heretics and unbelievers may move on to something else.

2 I do not claim, for a start, that every television commercial has religious content. Just as in church the pastor will sometimes call the congregation's attention to nonecclesiastical matters, so there are TV commercials that are entirely secular in nature. Someone has something to sell; you are told what it is, where it can be obtained, and what it costs. Though these may be shrill and offensive, no doctrine is advanced and no theology invoked.

3 But the majority of important TV commercials—those worthy of the name literature—take the form of religious parables organized around a coherent theology. Like all religious parables, they put forward a concept of sin, intimations of the way to redemption, and a vision of Heaven. They also suggest what are the roots of evil and what are the obligations of the holy.

4 Consider, for example, the Parable of the Ring Around the Collar. This is to TV scripture what The Parable of the Prodigal Son is to the Bible, which is to say it is an archetype containing most of the elements of form and content that recur in its own genre. To begin with, The Parable of the Ring Around the Collar is short, occupying only about 30 seconds of one's time and attention. There are three reasons for this, all obvious. First, it is expensive to preach on television. Second, the attention span of the congregation is not long and is easily susceptible to distraction. And third, a parable does not need to be long; tradition dictates that its narrative structure be tight, its symbols unambiguous, its explication terse.

5 The narrative structure of The Parable of the Ring Around the Collar is, indeed, comfortably traditional. The story has a beginning, a middle and an end. For those unfamiliar with it, a brief description is in order.

6 A married couple is depicted in some relaxed setting—say, a restaurant—in which they are enjoying each other's company and generally having a wonderful time. A waitress approaches their table, notices that the man has a dirty ring around his collar, stares at it boldly, sneers with cold contempt and announces to all within hearing the nature of his transgression. The man is humiliated and glares at his wife with scorn (for she is the instant source of his shame). She, in turn, assumes an expression of self-loathing mixed with a touch of self-pity. This is the parable's beginning: the emergence of a problem.

7 The parable continues by showing the wife at home using a detergent that never fails to eliminate dirt around the collars of men's shirts. She proudly shows her husband what she is doing, and he forgives her with an adoring smile. This is the parable's middle: the solution of the problem. Finally, we are shown the couple in a restaurant once again, but this time they are free of the waitress's probing eyes and bitter social chastisement. This is the parable's end: the moral, the explication, the exegesis. From this, we shall draw the proper conclusion.

8 As in all parables, behind the apparent simplicity there are some profound ideas to ponder. Among the most subtle and important is the notion of where and how problems originate. Embedded in every belief system there is an assumption about the root cause of evil from which the varieties of sinning take form. In science, for example, evil is represented in superstition. In psychoanalysis, we find it in early, neurotic transactions with our parents. In Christianity, it is located in the concept of Original Sin.

9 In TV-commercial parables, the root cause of evil is Technological Innocence, a failure to know the particulars of the beneficent accomplishments of industrial progress. This is the primary source of unhappiness, humiliation and discord in life. And, as forcefully depicted in The Parable of the Ring, the consequences of technological innocence may strike at any time, without warning, and with the full force of their disintegrating action.

10 The sudden striking power of technological innocence is a particularly important feature of TV-commercial theology, for it is a constant reminder of the congregation's vulnerability. One must never be complacent or, worse, self-congratulatory. To attempt to live without technological sophistication is at all times dangerous, since the evidence of one's naivete is painfully visible to the vigilant. The vigilant may be a waitress, a friend, a neighbor or even a spectral figure—a holy ghost, as it were—who materializes in your kitchen, from nowhere, to give witness to your sluggish ignorance.

11 It must be understood, of course, that technological innocence is to be interpreted broadly, referring not only to ignorance of detergents, drugs, sanitary napkins, cars, salves and foodstuffs, but also to ignorance of technical machinery such as savings banks and transportation systems. One may, for example, come upon one's neighbors while on vacation (in TV-commercial parables, this is always a sign of danger) and discover that they have invested their money in a certain bank of whose special interest rates you have been unaware. This is, of course, a moral disaster, and both you and your vacation are doomed.

12 But, as demonstrated in The Ring Parable, there is a road to redemption. The road, however, has two obstacles. The first requires that you be open to advice or social criticism from those who are more enlightened. In The Ring Parable, the waitress serves the function of counselor,

although she is, to be sure, exacting and very close to unforgiving. In some parables, the adviser is rather more sarcastic than severe. But in most parables, as for example in all sanitary-napkin, mouthwash, shampoo and aspirin commercials, the advisers are amiable and sympathetic, perhaps all too aware of their own vulnerability on other matters.

13 The Innocent are only required to accept instruction in the spirit in which it is offered. The importance of this cannot be stressed enough, for it instructs the congregation in two lessons simultaneously: not only must one be eager to accept advice, but one must be just as eager to give it. Giving advice is, so to speak, the principal obligation of the holy. In fact, the ideal religious community may be depicted in images of dozens of people, each in his or her turn, giving and taking advice on technological advances.

14 The second obstacle on the road to redemption involves one's willingness to act on the advice that is given. As in traditional Christian theology, it is not sufficient to hear the gospel or even preach it. One's understanding must be expressed in good works, i.e., action. In The Ring Parable, the once-pitiable wife acts almost immediately, and the parable concludes by showing the congregation the effects of her action.

15 In The Parable of the Person with Rotten Breath, of which there are several versions, we are shown a woman who, ignorant of the technological solution to her unattractiveness, is enlightened by a supportive roommate. The woman takes the advice without delay, with results we are shown in the last 5 seconds: a honeymoon in Hawaii. In The Parable of the Stupid Investor, we are shown a man who knows not how to make his money make money. Upon enlightenment, he acts swiftly and, at the parable's end, he is rewarded with a car, a trip to Hawaii, or something approximating peace of mind.

16 Because of the compactness of commercial parables, the ending—that is, the last 5 seconds—must serve a dual purpose. It is, of course, the moral of the story: if one will act in such a way, this will be the reward. But in being shown the result, we are also shown an image of Heaven. Occasionally, as in The Parable of the Lost Traveler's Cheques, we are given a glimpse of Hell: Technical Innocents lost and condemned to eternal wandering far from their native land. But mostly we are given images of a Heaven both accessible and delicious: that is, a Heaven that is here, now, on Earth, in America, and quite often in Hawaii.

17 But Hawaii is only a convenient recurring symbol. Heaven can, in fact, materialize and envelop you anywhere. In The Parable of the Man Who Runs Through Airports, Heaven is found at a car-rental counter to which the confounded Runner is shepherded by an angelic messenger. The expression of ecstasy on the Runner's face tells clearly that this moment is as close to a sense of transcendence as he can ever hope for.

18 "Ecstasy" is the key idea here, for commercial parables depict the varieties of ecstasy in as much detail as you will find in any body of reli-

gious literature. At the conclusion of The Parable of the Spotted Glassware, a husband and wife assume such ecstatic countenances as can only be described by the word "beatification." Even in The Ring Parable, which at first glance would not seem to pose as serious a moral crisis as spotted glassware, we are shown ecstasy, pure and serene. And where ecstasy is, so is Heaven. Heaven, in brief, is any place where you have joined your soul with the Deity—the Deity, of course, being Technology.

19 Just when, as a religious people, we replaced our faith in traditional ideas of God with a belief in the ennobling force of Technology is not easy to say. While it should be stressed that TV commercials played no role in bringing about this transformation, it is clear that they reflect the change, document it, amplify it. They constitute the most abundant literature we possess of our new spiritual commitment: American youth, for example, will see approximately 400,000 commercials in the first 20 years of their lives. For this reason alone, we have a solemn obligation to keep TV commercials under the continuous scrutiny of hermeneutics.

Word Study List

nonecclesiastical	2	explication	7
secular	2	exegesis	7
coherent	3	psychoanalysis	8
intimations	3	neurotic	8
archetype	4	beneficent	9
genre	4	vulnerability	10, 12
symbols	4	naivete	10
unambiguous	4	transcendence	17
transgression	6	beatification	18
chastisement	7		

Questions

1. What is Postman's thesis? Where is it stated?

2. What are the characteristics of a parable? What kind of ad does not use the parable form?

3. Much of Postman's essay is the detailed analysis of one ad, an ad containing the essential characteristics of the parable-ad form. What are the main elements of the parable-ad? What is the source of evil? What are the two steps to redemption? What do we see at the end of the parable-ad?

4. Postman gives titles to the several ads he mentions; how many of the ads can you identify from his titles? Can you think of other ads that would fit Postman's description of a parable-ad?

5. What is Postman's attitude toward advertising? What characteristics of word choice and style help you to detect tone?

6. What is Postman's purpose in writing? To explain parable-ads? To ridicule parable-ads? To expose and attack faith in technology? To demonstrate the dangerous effects of advertising?

7. Which ads at the end of the chapter best demonstrate an adaptation of the parable form to print advertising?

Exercises

1. Ad writer David Bernstein, in *Creative Advertising* (1974), asserts that all of advertising's promises appeal to one or more of the following basic drives: self-preservation, love for others, self-expression, envy, sloth, lechery, gluttony, pride, covetousness. Make a list of Postman's parable-ads and other ads you can identify as the same type and then consider: to which of the basic human drives listed by Bernstein does each ad appeal? Do parable-ads appeal to some drives or needs more often than others?

2. Take one parable-ad from your list, one that Postman does not discuss in detail, and analyze its structure, explaining how each part of the ad corresponds, in form and content, to the traditional form and content of a parable.

The Rhetoric of Cow and the Rhetoric of Bull

D. G. Kehl and Donald Heidt

Professor of English at Arizona State University, D. G. Kehl (b. 1936) has written three books, including *Poetry and the Visual Arts,* and many articles on literature, rhetoric, and popular culture. He is an active participant in the National Council of Teachers of English Committee on Public Doublespeak. Donald Heidt (b. 1936) teaches courses in English and philosophy at the College of the Canyons and has published articles on writing and the teaching of writing. While a graduate student at ASU, Heidt worked with Kehl on the following article, which was delivered at the 1984 Convention on College Composition and Communication.

Illustrating their points with examples from ads, Kehl and Heidt analyze two popular styles of persuasive writing, styles found in both political rhetoric and advertising.

1 A useful way of classifying rhetoric, particularly the rhetoric of propaganda, is according to the rhetoric of "cow" and the rhetoric of "bull," terms introduced by William G. Perry, Jr., in an essay on examsmanship at Harvard. To "cow," according to Perry is "to list data . . . without awareness of, or comment upon, the contexts, frames of reference, or points of observation which determine the origin, nature, and meaning of the data." It is based on the assumption that a fact (or a pseudo-fact) is a fact. To "bull," on the other hand, is "to discourse upon the contexts, frames of reference, and points of observation which would determine the origin, nature, and meaning of data if one had any." "Pure cow" consists of "data, however relevant, without relevance," whereas "pure bull" consists of "relevancies, however relevant, without data."[1]

2 The purpose of "cow" is to intimidate, to daunt, to overawe, sometimes to cover up through cowing. Interestingly, a synonym is to "buffalo," that is, to take advantage of another by confusion. As Bernard Avishai has correctly noted, "If the reader must be intimidated, then something is wrong."[2] The purpose of "bull" is to exaggerate, to inflate, to impress. A synonym, the counterpoint of "buffalo," is to "bulldog," that is, to attempt to increase the demand for a product or service by blatantly exaggerating its merits. It should be noted that "bull" is not necessarily B. S. In some cases it can be verified; whether it can or not determines whether the "bull" is true or false.

3 This classification of rhetoric stresses the two ways of perceiving: (1) detailing ("cow"), giving the particulars, and (2) generalizing ("bull"), asserting through repetitive labels or what Richard Eastman calls "label language" rather than contents. "Cow" is objective or quasi-objective, whereas "bull" is subjective, though sometimes feigning objectivity. "Cow" tends to be concrete, "bull" abstract.

4 As for methodology, the rhetoric of "cow" often relies on a barrage of scientific or pseudo-scientific, technical jargon, making a fetish of facts. Not surprisingly, the statistic is a favorite device. The rhetoric of "bull," on the other hand, relies on generalization, overstatement, and repetition of labels. Its favorite form is the superlative, its common devices the testimonial and connotative bluster and blather.

5 Examples of both "cow" and "bull" can be found in advertisement—commercial, cultural, and what Hitler, referring in *Mein Kampf* to propaganda, called "political advertising." Despite the fact that *1984*[3] and

---

[1]"Examsmanship and the Liberal Arts: A Study in Educational Epistemology," in *Examining in Harvard College: A Collection of Essays by Members of the Harvard Faculty* (Cambridge, Mass., n.d.), pp. 129–130.

[2]"Orwell and the English Language," in *1984 Revisited: Totalitarianism in Our Century,* ed. Irving Howe (N.Y.: Harper, 1983), p. 66.

[3]Novel by George Orwell. Other allusions to *1984* include references to Winston Smith, the novel's main character, to Newspeak, the politically controlled language in the world of the novel, and to Big Brother, the government "watchdog" who destroys human freedom in the novel.—Ed.

its apocalypse have become something of a cliché, its lessons are more significant and timely than ever. In this connection Anthony Burgess has said, "There's a huge fissure in language. On the one hand, you have the rigidities of science and technology, where terms or words or symbols mean precisely what they say. . . ."[4] Clearly this is the rhetoric of "cow." "On the other hand," Burgess continues, "you have increasing vagueness, an oscillation between total inarticulacy and polysyllabic high-sounding gibberish"—a version of "bull."

6 There is abundant evidence of what Burgess calls "a tendency toward pure verbalization, especially in public utterances, which we expect to be lying or evasive," a tendency toward a Language of Professional Evasion. For example, "a newsman asks a president . . . if there's going to be a war, and the reply is something like, 'There are various parameters of feasibility, all of which merit serious examination in the context of the implications of your question, Joe. The overall pattern of strike capability on both sides of the hypothetical global dichotomy is in the process of detailed scrutiny, and the temporal element involved cannot, of course, be yet quantified with any certainty. Does that answer your question, Joe?'"[5] Rather than meekly replying, "Thank you, Mr. President," Joe should say, "No, that does *not* answer the question. What you've just said is evasive bull, and neither I nor the American people will tolerate being bulled any longer!"

7 By contrast the problem with "cow," despite its putative impression of earnestness, diligent thoroughness, and meticulous evidence, is naive at best and downright pernicious at worst, for it operates on the assumption that a fact is a fact is a fact; it assumes that a piling up of isolated facts constitutes truth. The cowster fails to acknowledge that facts have meaning only in context. Winston Smith, having been cowed, is transformed into a cowster as shown by his acceptance of the formula 2 + 2 = 5. Truth in isolation can become falsehood. "When one is making out one's weekly budget, two and two invariably make four," Orwell wrote in his essay "In Front of Your Nose," but "politics, on the other hand, is a sort of subatomic or non-Euclidean world where it is quite easy for the part to be greater than the whole or for two objects to be in the same place simultaneously. Hence the contradictions and absurdities. . . . , all finally traceable to a secret belief that one's political opinions, unlike the weekly budget, will not have to be tested against solid reality."[6]

8 Is it any wonder that Americans, who have been brought up to bow down to the Golden Calf of Scientism, are impressed by such examples of "cow" as these: "advanced, new improved breakthrough," "ultra, double-

---

[4] *1985* (London: Arrow Books, 1980), p. 235.

[5] *1985*, pp. 235–236.

[6] *In Front of Your Nose*, 1945–1950, *The Collected Essays, Journalism and Letters of George Orwell*, Vol. IV, ed. Sonia Orwell and Ian Angus (N.Y.: Harcourt, 1968), p. 125.

protection formula," and such unpronounceable (and therefore all the more impressive) "active ingredients" as "sodium monofluorophosphate" and "monosodium glutamate," "nonoxynal nine," and "superorb 7"?

9 Automobile ads also offer an array of "cow." For example, Ford Tempo offers a "2300 HSC (High Swirl Combustion) engine," Mazda a "thinking carburetor" and rear suspension with "patented Twin Trapezoidal Link lower arms," Pontiac's Grand Prix a "Y99 Rally Suspension," Toyota Celica "a drag coefficient of a mere .34," "MacPherson struts," and "an Electronically Fuel Injected 2.4 liter single overhead cam engine," and Mitsubishi's Tredia Turbo, the world's smallest "turbine impeller."

10 Note the "cow" in this ad for Dewar's Scotch:

> Sharon Miller
> Home: Salmon, Idaho
> Age: 36
> Profession: White-water guide
> Hobbies: skiing, kayaking, horseback riding, yoga
> Most Memorable Book: *Thomas Wolfe's Letters to his Mother*
> Scotch: Dewar's White Label

Here we have a form of indirect testimonial with eleven specific facts about Sharon Miller, only one of which—her scotch is Dewar's White Label—have any clear connection with the subject of the ad. The details are intended to convince us, by association, that because such a wholesome, all-American, clean-cut, adventuresome girl like Sharon prefers White Label, we should also.

11 Cowsters have recently adopted new strategies using "health fears," misinformation, and innuendoes to confuse and cower the public by claiming that one product is "safer" than another. For example, one popular soft drink is advertised as being caffeine-free, with the strong suggestion that the substance is unhealthful, a conclusion which has not been borne out by scientific studies, according to the American Council on science and health. Similar fear tactics intended to "cow" us are used in advertising decaffeinated coffee despite the fact that it has been proven that such coffees contain only a little less caffeine than do regular coffees. Other "cowing" tactics concern the use of artificial sweeteners despite the fact that new research has shown that normal use of the sweeteners does not cause cancer as previously reported. Further, advertisers for one brand of mayonnaise warn prospective purchasers not to buy any products "with ingredients you can't pronounce" but fail to mention that their own brand of mayonnaise contains "phosphatidyl cholines and glycerol esters of lineleic acid."

12 Ordinarily the testimonial, because of its subjectivity, is used by the bullster, as in a recent add for Smirnoff Vodka which features violinist Pinchas Zukerman saying: "The quality of Smirnoff is classical. Its value

merits a standing ovation. When I play, I strive for the highest quality in my performance. I look for the same standards in my vodka. . . . When it comes to vodka, Smirnoff plays second fiddle to none." This is pure "bull," generalizations with no specific data. If the details about Sharon Miller in the Dewar ad ("cow") lack connection and context, the subjective judgments of Zukerman ("bull") lack particulars, as well as any logical relation to choosing vodka.

13 One of the greatest bullsters in the Southwest is "Tex" Earnhardt, "Arizona's Largest Ford Dealer," whose print ads announce "No bull since 1951" and whose TV commercials, featuring "Tex" astraddle a Brahma bull, conclude with the claim, "And that ain't no bull." Bullsters, it seems, typically feel the need to insist that they are not bulling us. In a sense, most advertisers—commercial, cultural, political—sit on a bull, giving us bull, while insisting "that ain't no bull." This is the essence of Orwellian doublethink, which necessitates doublespeak and leads to the doubledeal. As Orwell said in his essay "In Front of Your Nose," "the point is that we are all capable of believing things which we know to be untrue, and then, when we are finally proved wrong, impudently twisting the facts so as to show that we were right."[7] But with "pure bull" there often *are* no facts, for the bullster's normal response, as Orwell observed in his essay "Writers and Leviathan," is "to push the question of contradictions unanswered, into a corner of one's mind, and then continue repeating contradictory catchwords."[8] Both "cow" and "bull" serve to promote disconnectedness.

14 Accordingly, the major ploy of the bullster is doublespeak in its various forms: gobbledygook, euphemism, jargon, ambiguity, equivocation, circumlocution[9]—anything to serve the purpose of impressing rather than expressing, of making the worse course of action appear the better, the product identical in quality seem the best. Cigarette ads, for example, consisting almost entirely of "bull," blatantly doublespeak with the Surgeon General, on one hand, warning us that smoking is dangerous to our health while the copywriter tells us how wonderful, glamorous, and pleasureful it is to smoke Brand X.

15 It is the skillful use of "bull" which enables the adman or the politician to present honorifically what is so clearly pejorative. Winston cigarettes: "America's best." Vantage: "The taste of success." Viceroy: "Pleasure is where you find it. Discover Viceroy satisfaction." More: "It's More You. It's long. It's slim. It's elegant." (This ad also features an elegantly dressed woman with conspicuous cleavage, which advertising executives reportedly refer to as "eye-candy"—a suitable new entry for the eleventh edition of the Newspeak dictionary.)

---

[7] *In Front of Your Nose,* p. 124.
[8] *In Front of Your Nose,* p. 412.
[9] See the glossary and chapter 5 for explanations of these terms.—ED.

16 A recent ad for True cigarettes attempts to combine "cow" and "bull." In three-inch letters at the top we are given "bull": "It tastes too good to be True!" (Never greatly concerned about what is or is not "true," the adman here seems to have lost control of his pun, which could be read as follows: "A cigarette that tastes this good couldn't possibly be a True cigarette.") Then comes the "cow": "New True Laser-Cut 'Flavor Chamber'" with a scientific-looking diagram showing the "flavor chamber," "filter fiber," "mouthpiece," and "laser shots." Although this ad includes both "cow" and "bull," it does not show how the masculine context embraces the feminine particulars nor how the particulars support the generalizations. This bringing together of "cow" and "bull"—showing how and why the "cow" validates the "bull," how the facts relate to the generalizations, might be called "steer." It is not enough merely to *say* that details verify the generalizations. Any time writing deals with facts and interpretation, there must be "steer" to show how the former lead to the latter.

17 "Bull" also frequently takes the form of fantastic claims—unverified or unverifiable. For example, Lowry's Seasoned Salt claims in a recent ad: "Lowry's makes steaks" ("bull" in more ways than one) and Pontiac claims to "build excitement." Most readers simply smile at such hyperbolic, metonymic "bull," but what about this claim on a poster: "Clean air is a product of the Environmental Protection Agency"? Are we really going to be "bulled" into believing that the best things in life come from the federal government?

18 "Bull" is not limited to commercial or political propaganda, for it appears in cultural advertisement as well. Recently the Secretary of Commerce and Resources ordered that the word "plantation" be no longer used in tourism literature and that "grand manor house" be adopted so as to avoid evoking reminders of slavery. Both "plantation" owners and Civil Rights groups have objected. "What are they trying to do—change history?" This is 1984. Doubleplusungood! Presto-chango: down the memory hole!

19 Cow-talk and bull-talk are pervasive. And if those of us in academia are honest with ourselves, we will admit that we, who should know better and who should model lucid prose, have contributed our share. Psychologist Philip Bobrove of Jefferson Medical College noted recently that academics use inflated language because it gives the impression that they are "professionals." "If you talk or write simply, then maybe it's not worthwhile talking or writing about it. Maybe it's so simple that everybody already knows it. [Inflated language] is bullying. We use language as hoodlums use clubs—to beat people over the head."[10] The abuse of language for the purpose of manipulating people is a disturbing form of psychological violence. It is instructive to note that the words *violence* and *violate*

---

[10]Darrell Sifford, "Academic 'Bullies' Wield Jargon," *The Arizona Republic,* Friday, October 29, 1982.

are cognates; violence involves a violation of something. We are subjected to psychological violence when our basic human rights to honesty, sincerity, comprehensibility, and free choice are violated by unscrupulous cowsters and bullsters. It's time for the violated proles to rise up and say to Big Brother and Big Nurse,[11] to every administrative official from the President and his Cabinet to political candidates, from Pentagon brass to members of Congress, down to governors and state officials, to mayors and city councils, to school boards, school administrators, university presidents and deans, to admen and clergymen: "We will not be *cowed!* We will not be *bullied!* We know your ploys, and we won't be duped." The question we should ask is not simply, "Where's the beef?" but, when they give us "cow," "Where's the bull?" and, when they give us "bull," "Where's the cow?"

Word Study List

discourse	1	pernicious	7
feigning	3	subatomic	7
jargon	4	non-Euclidean	7
connotative	4	pejorative	15
apocalypse	5	hyperbolic	17
fissure	5	metonymic	17
oscillation	5	cognates	19
polysyllabic	5	proles	19
putative	7		

Questions

1. Explain, in your own words, the characteristics of the language of "cow" and the language of "bull."

2. What is the chief problem with cow-talk? What does the cowster fail to understand? Why, according to the authors, are Americans suckers for "cow" ads?

3. What advertising techniques are most used by the bullster?

4. The authors use food and car ads to illustrate cow-talk, cigarette ads and one liquor ad to illustrate bull-talk. Can you think of other products that are generally advertised by cow-talk? By bull-talk? Do you see any pattern?

5. The authors assert that good writing—honest writing—is not achieved just by combining "cow" and "bull," facts and generalizations. What else is needed?

[11]The controlling administrator in Ken Kesey's novel *One Flew over the Cuckoo's Nest.*—Ed.

6. How do the authors want us to respond to "cow" and "bull"? How good are you at recognizing these techniques in ads? In political speeches? In bureaucratic jargon?

Exercise

Which of the ads at the end of this chapter contain mostly cow-talk? Which are primarily "bull"? Do any contain both? Analyze the ads, making a list of all the cow-talk and bull-talk you find. Be prepared to discuss your analysis in class.

Made in Heaven

Leigh Montville

Winner of a Headliner award for his columns, Leigh Montville (b. 1943) has a dual existence at the Boston *Globe:* he writes a sports column during the week and a general column in the Sunday *Globe Magazine* section. Montville has also published in magazines, including *Sports Illustrated.* "Made in Heaven," one of his Sunday columns, was printed May 15, 1983.

In an entertaining parable, Montville comments on the current rage for signature sportswear.

1 And in the spring of one year in the sixth millennium of Creation, the Lord became bored. He watched the long line of human beings heading toward the world and knew He had to make some changes. Just to stay awake.

2 He had an idea.

3 "Put a tiny alligator on the left breast of every human who leaves the shop for the next week," He bellowed to his angels. "And make it snappy."

4 "An alligator?" the angels asked.

5 "An alligator," the Lord said. "Now."

6 The angels hurried to work. A change like this hadn't happened in a long time, not since the Lord requested redheads and peroxide blondes. An alligator . . . an alligator. One of the angels drew a stencil and the others began to work.

7 "Do you think He wants the alligator above or below the nipple?" one angel asked.

8 "We'll try a few spots," a second angel replied. "We'll see what works best."

9 The final choice was slightly above the left nipple. Thousands, then millions of people were sent to the world with the little alligators upon

their breasts. The angels watched with horror. The Lord watched with renewed interest. He found that He was pleased.

10 "Look at that, will you?" He said. "Man seems to like having a little alligator above his left breast. Look how proud he is. He parades around with confidence he never had before."

11 Sure enough, race and creed and ethnic origin made no difference. The people who wore the alligator were the most confident on the planet. They admired each other's alligators. They pitied the poor folk who did not have alligators.

12 "Let us try this," the Lord said. "Let us keep making alligators, but on Tuesdays and Thursdays, perhaps, let's produce people with a little polo player on the left breast."

13 "A polo player, Lord?" the angels asked.

14 "Just do what I ask," the Lord said.

15 The appearance of people with polo players above their left breasts seemed to be as exciting as the appearance of the people with alligators. The Lord laughed as He watched everyone admiring everyone else. He wanted to see more.

16 "Let us make people with little penguins above their left breasts," He told the angels. "Let us make some people with a fox in that spot. A tiger. A hand making a signal with the index finger and thumb. Every now and then, too, make some people with the word 'Rugger' across the right biceps."

17 The new diversity soon dominated the world. Virtually everyone under age 58 bore an insignia or name above the left breast. Humankind viewed these changes as blessings supplied by a Benevolent Being.

18 "You are a genius, Lord," the angels said.

19 "I have only begun," the Lord replied.

20 He turned his attention now to the right buttock. He thought and thought, searching for the right expression. He decided upon names.

21 "Names, Lord?" the angels asked.

22 "Take these down," the Lord said in a flash of inspiration. "Calvin Klein. Gloria Vanderbilt. Sasson. Sergio Valenti. Lee. And . . . let me think . . . yes, Jordache."

23 The names on the right buttock were at least as successful as the animals above the left breast. Some names were printed. Some were written in script. People looked each other over, fore and aft, and cooed at the different markings.

24 "Love your alligator," one of them would say to a complete stranger. "And love your Sergio Valenti, too."

25 "Wonderful, Lord," the angels said. "Man has not been so interested in his surroundings for a long time."

26 "Take out your pads," the Lord said. "There is more work to do."

27 He now turned his attention to feet. He ordered some feet to be made with three stripes down the sides. He ordered other feet made with two stripes. With stars. He ordered feet made with little green tabs with

the word "Bass" or "Dexter" written on the tabs. He ordered feet made with metal plates on the side that read "Candie's."

28 "Feet may be the ultimate," the Lord said. "I have a hunch we haven't seen anything, compared to what will happen with feet."

29 He was right again, of course. The designs on the feet were the best of all. People boasted about their feet. People admired each other's feet. To walk down the street with an animal on the left breast, a name on the right buttock, and swirls on the feet was to be as close to heaven as possible.

30 "I am pleased," the Lord said as he sat upon a cloud and watched the activity. "I am very, very pleased."

31 The angels were pleased because He was pleased. They stood in a line and awaited orders. There was nary a waver when the Lord decreed that some people should now be made with little plugs in their ears that played Top 40 music all day long.

32 Everyone simply went to work.

Word Study List

millennium	1	biceps	16

Questions

1. At what point in your reading did you realize that this is a humorous piece? What, exactly, is Montville making fun of?

2. Rather than writing a satiric essay, Montville makes his point indirectly through a story. What kind of story does this remind you of?

3. What details in the story contribute to its humor?

4. Montville mentions the brand names of one shirt, of the jeans, and of three kinds of shoes. How many of the other brands can you name from their logos or designs? Clearly, Montville expects his readers to be able to recognize most of the brands. How does your knowledge of the brands help to reinforce the point of Montville's story?

5. Examine Murray's list of basic human needs in Fowles's "Advertising's Fifteen Basic Appeals" (pp. 180–181). To which needs do the designer-labeled clothes seem intended to appeal?

6. Do you like to buy clothes with recognizable logos or brand names on them? Why or why not? Do you think people who buy designer-labeled clothes have been primarily suckered by advertising, or influenced by peer groups, or influenced by a desire for quality clothes?

Exercise

Writing fables or parables to make a point about human character or morality can be fun. Try writing yours to make some point about advertising or about what motivates humans to purchase particular products. (You might think, for example, about the many different car models available today and about the types—or stereotypes—of people drawn to each model. And surely the array of sports equipment, even running shoes alone, can spark some clever, fun-poking tales.) Here are some guidelines to help you along:

1. Keep your story short, no more than two or three pages.
2. Make it a story, not an essay, with characters and dialogue and a sequence of events.
3. Remember that "characters" do not have to be human.
4. Make it concrete, filled with specific details (e.g., the designer labels on jeans are placed on the *right buttock*).
5. Avoid any direct statement of your story's point.

Student Essay: Primary Research and Analysis

A Man's Drink?

One would think that manufacturers are eager for every conceivable user to purchase their products, but this does not seem to be the case with liquor companies. After studying the techniques of magazine advertising by liquor companies, I have conluded that distillers do not consider women a potential market for liquor, nor do they attempt to influence them to become one. Rather, liquor advertisements are directed principally at men while only a minority even acknowledge the existence of drinking females save upon romantic occasions.

Attention-getting opening

Thesis

After pulling sixty-four liquor ads from thirteen issues of men's, ladies', and general readership magazines, I observed four types of ads. Listed in their descending order of frequency of appearance, the four categories are: romantic or sexually themed, tradition or age oriented, taste or drinkability concerned, and testimonials. After

Methods of conducting study and categories of ads

narrowing the scope of the study to the twenty-seven ads employing the most blatant and least overlapping of these techniques, my categories broke down as follows: ten romance; six age; seven taste, four "smooth" and three "unique"; and four testimonials.

Methods of conducting study and categories of ads

Gathering ads for this study forced me to realize the degree to which liquor is considered a male product. The men's magazines averaged seven ads per issue while ladies' magazines averaged only two. General readership periodicals ranged from four to six. The magazines used in the study were *Glamour, Ladies' Home Journal, Cosmopolitan,* and *Vogue* (for women); *Playboy, Penthouse,* and *Esquire* (for men); and *Omni, Science Digest, Time,* and *Newsweek* as representative of general readership sources.

The gender difference became more pronounced when I examined the content of liquor ads directed at women. With the exception of one, all the women's ads studied had romantic themes. Three are selling Amaretto, a drink homonymic of "amour," while two place a rose in front of the bottle with drinks for two. Johnnie Walker Red (in *Cosmopolitan*) looks more like an ad for a florist, as an arrangement of flowers occupies 70 percent of the page. Glasses for two are barely visible in the lower left corner of the page. Two other ads suggest the woman gives her product to a loved one, which I assume is a male, in hopes that he may share some with her. Most explicit on the romantic theme is the Grand Marnier ad which depicts a couple floating through the heavens as they toast each other with snifters of drink. At this point it also becomes notable that the ads directed to women are predominantly pitches for creamed drinks or liqueurs rather than mixers. The message seems clear. Women do not drink alone, buy liquor for themselves, or drink much more than a liqueur in a romantic setting.

Analysis of ads using romance

Variety in techniques employed to sell booze seems reserved for the male market. The largest category, romance, takes a turn toward sex in male magazines as "Tony Roberts talks about his first time." His subject, after some careful reading, is revealed to be his indoctrination to Campari, not his sexual awakening. Boodles gin takes a slightly more subtle approach with its presentation of a handsome couple happily occupying the same seat, drinks in hand, with the man asking, "Is it proper to Boodle before the guests arrive?" Looks as if he'd like to make it a private party, and she of course is pleasantly amused.

Drink and man are a combination that appear to lead to sex.

Analysis of ads using romance

In the remaining categories the men's and general readership magazines display a proportional number of examples of each. In two stunningly similar ads for Old Charter Bourbon and Canadian Mist, both emphasize the smoothness of their drink as they display their bottles in the foreground of scenes of great mountain lakes at sunset with barely a ripple on their surfaces. Others present their product before images of the great outdoors of the snowy North. The message is that these drinks go down like ice water in July. None have the audacity to take it the step further and label their booze a natural high—yet.

Analysis of ads using appeal to taste

In the tradition and age department we find the drinks with age already a part of the label and image. Old Bushmills, Old Grandad, and Grand Old Parr's—"Older is better" speak for all of them. Age is further marketed by drinks that present the endorsements of leaders past. Drink Courvoisier, the "cognac of Napoleon." Or why not try Wolfschmidt, "The spirit of his majesty the Czar." While they wish us to associate their drink with greatness, I have difficulty swallowing the idea that the Czar of Russia ever tasted a vodka made in Baltimore. The Myers's Rum people seem obsessed with age as they rely on associations with it to sell four of their products. Old sailing ships and antique watches are the props of their liquor ads. We are encouraged to taste the old world flavor of a drink quite possibly concocted last year.

Analysis of ads using age or tradition

Finally we come to testimonials. If there aren't enough great dead ones to go around, we'll have to use contemporary notables. F. Lee Bailey (in *Esquire*) and Diahann Carroll (in *Newsweek*) will do nicely for Smirnoffs. Or if you are selling vodka, get a Russian to endorse it, even if it is from Japan. Suntory bought Nureyev's praises. And for you fellas out there with the "Right Stuff," Chuck Yeager wants you to drink Cuttysark with him.

Analysis of ads using testimonials

Lest we forget Tony Roberts and Campari too soon, it appears that drinking is to be associated with sex, men, and the successful, and if you possess any of these three qualities while holding a drink in your hand, the other two should not be far from your grasp. And as for the majority of you women, the industry seems to be saying, if you cannot handle success like Diahann Carroll it would be better if you stuck with liqueurs, flowers, romance, and those pretty, low tar cigarettes.

Amusing conclusion that restates thesis

0-50 in 5.7 seconds. Plymouth Turismo 2.2. Match it! Or move over to the slow lane.

0-50 in 5.7 seconds:* Catch it, Camaro Z28!
Turismo 2.2's advanced technology helps separate it from the mob. Its 2.2-liter engine is a powerhouse of advanced technology. It's teamed with a 5-speed manual transaxle with performance gear ratios. It has front-wheel drive (Fiero and Camaro have rear-wheel) and rack and pinion steering for controlled cornering, secure going over wet spots. Match it, Z28! Match it, Fiero!

5-speed, sports suspension, full instrumentation. Standard. $7280. Match it, Firebird!**
With all its fast-lane mechanicals, you'd expect a high price to go with it. But Turismo 2.2 is more than just sports car performance. It's also a terrific value. For 1984, there are graphics, 2-tone paint, a spoiler, 14-inch rallye road wheels, Goodyear Eagle GT radials and more. Standard. To match it, Firebird could cost over a thousand more.

A five-year or 50,000-mile Protection Plan:† Match it, anyone!
The 1984 Turismo 2.2: Match it! No other sports car can match the protection you get with Turismo 2.2: 5-year or 50,000-mile protection on engine, powertrain and against outer body rust-through at no extra cost. With its New Chrysler Technology, Turismo 2.2 has the quality and durability you demand and we back it!

43 est. hwy. [27] EPA est. mpg:‡ Match it, Mustang!
With gas mileage so great many domestic and import sports cars can't beat it, Turismo 2.2 is one exciting sports car you can afford to enjoy; especially when you know it's backed with a 5-year or 50,000-mile Protection Plan. For excitement, for affordability, for protection, it's Turismo 2.2. Match it! (If you can.)
Buckle up for safety.

The 5/50 Plymouth. The best built, best backed American cars.°

*Based on acceleration tests performed by NHRA. Comparison only applies to cars with standard engines and transmissions. **Sticker price excluding title, taxes and destination charges. Comparison based on sticker prices of comparably equipped vehicles. †5 years or 50,000 miles, whichever comes first. Limited warranty. Deductible applies. Excludes leases. See dealer for details. ‡Use EPA est. mpg for comparison. Your mileage may vary depending on speed, trip length and weather. Actual highway lower.
°Lowest percentage of recalls based on National Highway Traffic Safety Administration data for '82 and '83 models designed and built in North America.

We dream of excellence. She shows us what it looks like. Now, after years of struggle and dedication, her moment is here. Win or lose, she has done something remarkable. And when she flies our hearts and our dreams and pride go with her.

That's the Spirit of the Games. adidas.

Courtesy of Adidas®.

Fresh Start advertisement furnished courtesy Colgate Palmolive Co.

Mother Nature is lucky her products don't need labels.

All foods, even natural ones, are made up of chemicals. But natural foods don't have to list their ingredients. So it's often assumed they're chemical-free. In fact, the ordinary orange is a miniature chemical factory. And the good old potato contains arsenic among its more than 150 ingredients.

This doesn't mean natural foods are dangerous. If they were, they wouldn't be on the market. The same is true of man-made foods.

All man-made foods are tested for safety. And they often provide more nutrition, at a lower cost, than natural foods. They even use many of the same chemical ingredients.

So you see, there really isn't much difference between foods made by Mother Nature and those made by man. What's artificial is the line drawn between them.

© Monsanto Company 1980

For a free booklet explaining the risks and benefits of chemicals, mail to:
Monsanto, 800 Lindbergh Blvd., St. Louis, Mo. 63166. Dept. A3NA-SR3

Name ______________________

Address ______________________

City & state ______________________ Zip ________

Monsanto

Without chemicals, life itself would be impossible.

Courtesy of Monsanto Corporation.

THE SOLES OF YOUR FEET ARE BURNING. IT'S MATCH POINT, FIFTH SET.

YOU CHARGE THE NET, SLAM A BACKHAND VOLLEY DOWN THE LINE TO BREAK SERVE AND WIN.

MAYBE IT WASN'T POLITE. OR EASY. OR PARTICULARLY SAFE.

BUT THEN NO ONE'S EVER CALLED YOUR GAME TIMID. OR HAD TO ASK WHAT RACQUET IS IN YOUR HAND.

BECAUSE ONLY ONE RACQUET HAS THE UNIQUE OVAL SHAPE SPECIFICALLY DESIGNED TO BRING CONTROL TO OVER-SIZED POWER.

ONLY ONE RACQUET DELIVERS THE MANEUVERABILITY AND PRECISION THAT AN AGGRESSIVE SERVE AND VOLLEY GAME DEMANDS.

AND ONLY ONE RACQUET WAS RATED BEST OVERALL IN THE TENNIS INDUSTRY PLAYTEST OF 24 GRAPHITE RACQUETS.*
THE OVER-SIZED DIRECTOR FROM HEAD.

YOU CAN PLAY WITH IT OR AGAINST IT... THE CHOICE IS YOURS.

NO ONE'S EVER CALLED YOUR GAME TIMID.

THE OVER-SIZED DIRECTOR
HEAD
WE WANT YOU TO WIN

*Test conducted by Tennis Industry magazine and published in their November, 1983 issue.

BUS
STOP

ROCSPORTS: THE FEELING IS PURE MAGIC. THE EXPLANATION IS PURE SCIENCE.

The world's leading lightweight shoes are so comfortable, they're magical.

RocSports make your feet lighter. They make the streets softer. They add a bounce to your step that puts you far above the ordinary.

But there's a very rational explanation for the way RocSports make you feel. It's the way RocSports are made. With the Rockport Walk Support System™—the unique synthesis of running shoe technology, space-age materials, and innovative design that gives RocSports the light weight, firm support, and effective shock absorption that makes them more comfortable than any shoes you've ever worn.

It took us years of research and development to get RocSports off the ground. You can do it in one step: try on a pair. See what you've been missing.

And feel how truly magical modern science can be.

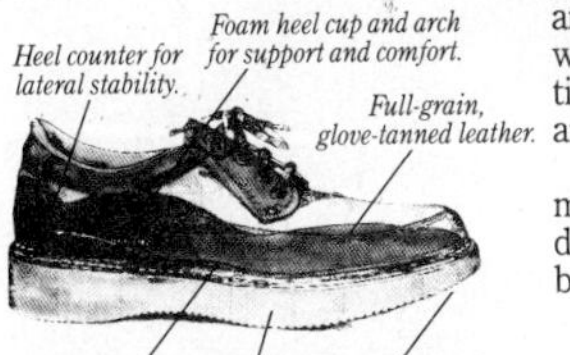
Foam heel cup and arch for support and comfort.
Heel counter for lateral stability.
Full-grain, glove-tanned leather.
Resilient foam insole.
Rocker profile aids natural walking motion.
Morflex™ sole by Vibram.™ Super light, great shock absorption.

Rockport®

INNOVATIONS IN COMFORT

The Rockport Company, 72 Howe Street,
Marlboro, Massachusetts 01752

Copyright © The Rockport Company. Agency: Gearon Hoffman Goransson, Inc. Art: Bob Wilcox. Copy: Doug Goransson. Photographer: Fred Collins.

Reproduced courtesy of Prince Matchabelli, Inc.

Reproduced courtesy of General Foods Corp. owner of the trademark GAINES COMPLETE

California Raisins.
Nature's Candy.
May we present the guy who makes our snack so good for kids.
He's a familiar sight. An old friend. And makes a snack kids love without using preservatives, additives, or the artificial this-or-that you find in most manufactured snacks.
Because the sun dries raisins naturally, he doesn't need artificial help to make them chewy or sweet.
Next time your kids want snacks, give them raisins.
Raisins
Why not give your kids a bit of the sun.
Raisins from California.
© 1979 California Raisin Advisory Board

Courtesy of California Raisin Advisory Board.

Exercises

1. Many product names are highly connotative or suggestive. Explain how each of the following product names helps to sell the product.

   Princess cruises
   Belair cigarettes
   Cuisinart food processor
   Clinique beauty products
   Thunderbird car
   Sea Breeze skin cleanser
   Footworks shoes
   Lestoil cleaner
   Daisy 2 home pregnancy test
   Light 'n Lively cottage cheese
   Equitable Life Insurance
   Clairesse hair color
   Ivory Snow detergent
   Brut toilet articles
   Seagram's *Crown Royal* whiskey
   Canon *Sure Shot* camera

2. If you have read the want ads recently in search of a job, you may have observed that many of the techniques of advertising discussed in this chapter can be found in the newspaper's classified section. Analyze the style of the following ads, paying particular attention to connotative language and to vague or abstract words. What image of the company does the ad present? What sort of person does the company expect to hire? Do you know any such person?

   ADMIN. ASST./SECY.
   GLAMOUR
   Celebrity president of international media/PR association is looking for the best secretary in town! Demanding position in luxurious offices requires top communication and diplomatic skills for contact with the internationally famous. In-depth knowledge of professional office procedures is a primary requirement as well as a professional demeanor. Superb typing & shorthand are a must. $16,000 to start with substantial raises & excellent benefits. Call . . .

   SALES
   CAN YOU MAKE THIS TEAM?
   Pat Ryan & Associates is seeking District Sales Managers for our nationwide network of 48 district offices. As the leader in automobile finance and insurance management, we have grown from $100,000 in sales in 1964 to over $200 million in 1980!

   Position responsibilities include ability to effectively sell to top management, recruit quality key personnel for our dealer clients, do key performance analysis to identify and creatively solve problems, and direct internal operating procedures with a high level of energy and commitment.

   Our sales managers are self-motivated individuals, most of whom are college graduates, all of whom assume tremendous responsibility. Sales, management, and people skills are essential. If you are of excellent character with an outstanding track record in professional marketing, send your resume and salary history to: . . .

3. Have you ever been annoyed by a product's failure to perform to your expectations? Did the product also fail to perform to expectations established by the description on the container or by advertising? Write a letter of complaint to the manufacturer of a product that did not live up either to the advertising claim or to the claims stated on the container. Share the company's response with the class, after analyzing its style and tone. Questions to consider: Is the company's letter apologetic? Defensive? Sweet Talking? Does the letter respond specifically to the complaint you made? Does the letter contain vague, abstract, or technical words? Does it contain jargon? (See Chapter 5.)
4. With an increasing number of ads providing more "facts" and less image, we need to become as skilled in evaluating the validity of an ad's statements as we are in recognizing the appeal of the picture. In the following two ads, both make the same claim: ours is the best-tasting low tar cigarette. Examine the copy of each ad, answering the following questions, to see if you accept either ad's claim.

TRIUMPH BEATS MERIT!

Triumph, at less than half the tar, preferred over Merit.

In rating overall product preference, more smokers independently chose Triumph over Merit. In fact, an amazing 60% said 3 mg. Triumph tastes as good or better than 8 mg. Merit. Results showed that Triumph was *also* preferred over •14 mg. Winston Lights •12 mg. Marlboro Lights •11 mg. Vantage. Now, test for yourself. Compare Triumph with any other so-called "low tar" or "light" cigarette. You'll taste why we named it triumph. Also available in Menthol.

MERIT CUTS THROUGH LOW TAR CLUTTER!

"Best-tasting low tar I've tried," say 96% of MERIT smokers in latest survey.

There is a difference between other low tar cigarettes and MERIT. A proven difference. MERIT Solid Winner. Test after test with thousands of smokers continues to provide evidence—not mere claims—that low tar MERIT delivers the flavor of high tar brands, and continues to satisfy *long term. Blind Taste Tests:* In tests where brand identity was concealed, a significant majority of smokers rated the taste of low tar MERIT as good as—or better than—leading high tar brands. Even cigarettes having twice the tar! *Smoker Preference:* Among the 95% of smokers stating a preference, the MERIT low tar/good taste combination was favored 3 to 1 over high tar leaders when tar levels were revealed! . . .

Questions:

a. How does Triumph emphasize the difference between its tar content and Merit's? Has it chosen the most emphatic way to state the difference? How else could a comparison of tar content have been made?
b. What does the Triumph ad fail to tell you about its survey? Is 60 percent an "amazing" figure? What information not given might make the 60 percent figure even less amazing?
c. Are you surprised that Merit claims to be a low tar cigarette?
d. What does the statement "96% of MERIT smokers in latest survey" actually say? What does the statement fail to tell you?
e. How much is "a significant majority"? What important information is not given about Merit's Blind Taste Tests?
f. How does the phrase "Among the 95% of smokers stating a preference" hedge or qualify the rest of the sentence?
g. Should you be convinced by either cigarette's survey results?

5. Some ads do not seem to be selling a product at all. For example, what is being sold in the following ad? What attitude is being advocated? What techniques are being used to sell the attitude? How explicit is the ad's message?

Writing Assignments

1. Like *natural,* the words *new* and *old* appear in many ads helping to promote different kinds of products. Choose either *new* or *old*; then collect and examine ads containing the word you chose to determine the different meanings or connotations the word has when used in advertising. Write an essay in which you explain and illustrate the different uses in advertising of either *new* or *old.*
2. Examine advertisements for one type of product (cigarettes, liquor, cars, shampoo, perfumes) to determine the main techniques used to sell it. Examine many ads, but in your essay limit your analysis to those that best illustrate your conclusions and make general reference to others that contributed to your conclusions.
3. Some companies tailor the techniques they use to sell a product to fit the anticipated audience. Select one type of product and examine ads for that product from two different kinds of magazines to determine how the selling techniques change with a change in audience. You could compare, for example, car ads in women's magazines with those in men's magazines. Examine many ads but limit the detailed analysis in your essay to representative ads that illustrate your conclusions.

A Fable For Now:

The Emperor's New Clause

Once upon a time there lived an Emperor who believed in only what he could tell through his senses, especially his sight. Perhaps this was because once upon a slightly earlier time he had disregarded his senses and so appeared completely unsuited to be a dandy leader.

In redress, he banned the abstract and immaterial. Truth and Beauty he ordered cloistered, Fair Play he locked up in the tower, and the Spirit of Brotherly Love he exiled to Philadelphia. Only Revenge he spared, stashed under his bed in case those swindling weavers should return.

Soon, every criminal was presumed guilty. "Behold my innocence," the accused would cry. "Nope, just can't see it," the Emperor would reply, nodding so his crown slid over his eyes onto his nose. "Out of sight!" his courtiers would cry.

None in the Empire really grieved, for though the Emperor banished Happiness, he also did away with Misery, and Hunger, and other such Evils. The Empire thus continued to thrive, until the day the Emperor banned Profits.

"Knave, what is this?" he thundered to the Royal Haberdasher. "In this new robe I see flax and weaving...yes, wonderfully opaque...and embroidery and tailoring, but what is this extra 'thirteen per centum' you would receive?"

"Just a bit of Profit, oh Potentate."

"Profit? Why?" demanded the Emperor. "You are keeping me warm, and thereby serving all that's good. A Profit on goodness is obscene."

"Out of sight," his retinue parroted in glee.

"Out of his mind," the Haberdasher thought, "calling it 'obscene' to earn a lousy thirteen per centum on everything I've put into the business. Is there to be no reward for my investment and labor?" He fled to a saner land.

The Emperor, however, was pleased at his latest coup, and added a No-Profit clause to all contracts. The news swept quickly through the Trades and Guilds. "Oh dear," the Royal Provisioner fretted, "if I am restricted just to my costs, where will I get the extra money to expand?" The Merchant of Venison thus realized he wouldn't be able to pay for a global voyage he had planned to seek more deer. "I'm afraid there'll be no herd shot 'round the world," he told the Explorer, who thereupon advised the Tinker to give up trying to build a better crossbow.

So it went. The Tinker reconciled himself to using his old, worn tools longer and canceled his order for new ones. The Blacksmith, in turn, shelved plans to rebuild his smithy to make it more efficient and productive, and sat down to brood beneath a chestnut tree (but that's another story). That eliminated work for the Builder, and thus for the Woodsman. And so the Emperor's nephew had no summer job chopping trees.

"What's that?" muttered His Highness on hearing the nephew would be idle. "Well, I'll just nationalize the woods, and have the Army cut the trees. I'll make my nephew a major."

"Wait!" said the Royal Vizier. "You cannot seize the forest for the trees. The Army has deserted. Some soldiers ran away when you ordered them to drain that fen of stagnant waters after there was no longer private money for the cleanup. Others fled when you took over that bankrupt colliery and made the soldiers scrub the coal by hand so it would burn clean. The rest left when they weren't paid."

"Not paid?" the mogul asked. "Why?"

"Because the Treasury is empty," said the adviser. "Money it lent to spur industrial development never came back because the borrowers could make no Profits to permit repayment. Less money came in because of no Profits to tax."

"No taxes?" said the ruler. "That's obscene."

"Worse yet," said the Vizier, "the whole economy is falling apart. Your ban on Profits crippled investment and invention, expansion and exploration. It precludes new jobs, and keeps old ones from being made more productive. In fact, you indirectly banned Prosperity itself!"

Well, of course the Emperor saw the error of his ways (else this would be a grim fairy tale) and retracted the ban. This time, at least, the bare facts meant a happy ending.

Moral: A profit is not without honor—something to remember at a time when America's economy needs more strength, more jobs, more investment, more productivity...and less inflation. Stronger corporate profits can help the U.S. reach all those goals. And that's no fable.

CHAPTER 5

"My life was as nothing, Ann, until you impacted on it."

The Baffling World of Jargon

GETTING STARTED: Measuring Your Jargon Quotient

Test your jargon quotient by decoding the elaborate language of the following course description from the Freshman Registration issue of *Harvard Lampoon* (Fall 1973). Can you figure out what the course covers?

APPLIED MATHEMATICS 121. PERMUTATIONS IN A NINE-CELL MATRIX

> An exhaustive study of the nine-cell rectilinear grid with particular emphasis on its function as the frame of reference of a circle/cross system sequentially deployed so as to achieve unique tri-collinearity. Techniques such as controlling the middle square, forking in the corners, and tactical diversion with simultaneous erasure will be considered.

Examine the course descriptions in your college catalogue. Compare the wording of the descriptions with the *Harvard Lampoon* version. What similarities do you see? Can you account for the type of wording that characterizes course descriptions?

The Highfalutin and the Mighty

James K. Kilpatrick

James J. Kilpatrick (b. 1920) has been an outspoken political conservative through his syndicated column "A Conservative View," in his role as news commentator on "Agronsky and Company," and as a contributing editor to *National Review* since 1968. This article appeared in *Nation's Business,* July 1974.

Kilpatrick's article takes a humorous look at the jargon used by educators and contends that jargon is a mumbo-jumbo used to impress others outside the field and to conceal the fact that these educators have nothing new or important to say.

1 There once was a great statesman of Virginia, John Taylor of Caroline. He was a farmer, soldier, scholar, lawyer, philosopher, and three times a United States Senator. He is today altogether forgotten. Taylor's problem was this. He thought richly, but he wrote poorly. His clearest ideas were etched in mud. Taylor's notion of a fine title for a book was, "Construction Construed, and Constitutions Vindicated." John Randolph of Roanoke plowed through the work, and put the volume aside

with an acid remark: It would be better, he thought, if Col. Taylor's work had only been translated into English.

2 A Washington correspondent, condemned to read government prose, is likely to think at least 10 times a week of Taylor's ailment and Randolph's cure. It is one of the curious aspects of our Washington Wonderland that here words are used not to convey thought, but to muffle thought. We stumble about through forests of jargon, trying in vain to find our way. Often we are lost, for jargon is a parasitic growth: It gathers on the limbs of thought like Spanish moss on Charleston oaks; it does not altogether conceal, but it softens, disguises and blurs.

3 John Taylor's trouble is endemic here these days. The Supreme Court, sad to say, seems to be hopelessly mired in the murky goo of legalese; not since the deaths of Justices Harlan and Black has the Court produced consistently cogent and lucid opinions. The Congress is as bad; its bills grow longer, and the explanations of the bills grow longer still. The White House has its own peculiar difficulties, translating what the President said into what he meant.

4 I am prompted toward these observations especially by what is going on in the world of education. It is hard to tell what is going on in the world of education. It is becoming the world of Humpty-Dumpty, where words mean what a speaker chooses them to mean, and neither more nor less. The condition is characterized by what might be termed the Highfalutin Syndrome. The most ordinary ideas are decked out in party clothes. It is like putting bootees on a dachshund.

5 By way of example, consider a recent item from the *Ford Foundation Letter.* It would appear that the University of California is offering a Confluent Education program. There is even a program of Development and Research in Confluent Education. This is the name, we are told, that is given "to an approach to learning and teaching that integrates the emotional concerns of both teacher and student—the 'affective' dimension of education—with cognitive aspects of classroom objectives."

6 Now, for the record, I have been reading and writing the English language for 50 years. I have written, rewritten or edited some 30 million words for publication. The foregoing description appears to be written in my mother tongue—through the Spanish moss the limbs can be seen dimly—but I would be hard put to translate it into English. What does it *mean*? I suspect it means nothing. I suspect the "confluent" approach to learning and teaching is nothing more than the familiar interaction of pupil and master—an interaction as old as teaching itself. But I may be wrong. The editors of the Council for Basic Education *Bulletin* asked a graduate student of education to explain what is meant by "confluent education." He guessed it to mean "the touchies and feelies movement."

7 Let me try another example. The CBE *Bulletin* for May, 1974, carries a passionate little essay by Harry E. Foster on "The Debasement of School Libraries." Mr. Foster is librarian at the Anne Arundel Commu-

nity College in Arnold, Md. He notes with dismay the changes that have hit libraries in the past 15 years. These changes are manifestations, in part at least, of the Highfalutin Syndrome.

8 Thus it appears that libraries no longer are known as libraries. They have donned a new nomenclature—bootees on the dachshund—and now appear as instructional materials centers, or learning resources centers, or media centers, or even as multimedia centers. Such impressive institutions are not to be run by mere librarians; they are run by multimedia specialists, aided by resource consultants. Mr. Foster quotes from the 1969 edition of *Standards for School Media Programs:*

9 "Media convey information, affect the message, control what is learned, and establish the learning environment. They will help to determine what the pupil sees and what his attitude will be toward the world in which he lives. Therefore it is important that every media specialist participate actively in shaping the learning environment and the design of instruction, and that every media facility, piece of equipment, book or material be selected, produced and used so that the students in our schools are challenged to a dynamic participation in a free, exciting and enriched life."

10 What does all that *mean*? What in the hell is "dynamic participation?" Do we translate this into English as "active participation"? Is there some significance in the distinction between students, who are to participate dynamically, and those media specialists, who are to participate actively? Who are these attitude shapers? And what are they molding with their plastic syntax?

11 Words are like pollen: They trigger allergic reactions. Such words as "facility," "enriched" and "dynamic" strike upon sensitive membranes; they produce intellectual hives. I walk into this goldenrod prose and emerge with a rash. "Utilize" causes positive pain. The director of the National Right to Read Program, a gentlewoman of distinguished reputation, turned up some months ago before a Senate subcommittee. This is how she began her testimony:

12 "Mr. Chairman and Senators, the Right to Read Office utilizes in the demonstration program standardized tests as well as criterion reference instruments—that is, tests that measure the specific objectives of a program as opposed to any test that is standardized on a national norm."

13 The reading director went on to discuss an "anchor study test which gives us a national interpretive table." She testified that in terms of adults, her office "utilizes criterion tests." She spoke of a seed money program in Minnesota "to utilize some of the Rights to Read resources and materials we developed, like needs assessment instruments and what-have-you." Her office, she said, stresses "the retraining of the staff development of existing personnel, rather than adding new people." She spoke of summer reading programs that would include "a lot of enrichment type activities as well." Said Sen. Eagleton: "Let me see if I understand."

14 The trouble with these words, these phrases and circumlocutions, is not that the words themselves are so bad. English is a tolerant and accommodating language; it can find room for "facility," "enriched" and "dynamic," and perhaps—I am doubtful about this—there is some construction in which "to utilize" would be better than "to use." (If you wanted to swat flies, ordinarily you would use a fly swatter but you could utilize *The New York Times.*) If these weedy nouns, adjectives and verbs are kept at a distance, nobody sneezes. The trouble is rather with the purpose to which the jargon is put.

15 In the case of the librarians, perhaps the fancy-shmancy terminology makes a certain rough sense: The skinflint City Council that may resist funds for a library may be more willing to support a learning resources center. Mostly, as in the case of Confluent Education, the usages are sham. They are pretentious, devious and fake. The idea is to impress city councilmen, Senators and ordinary citizens with the erudition of the educator. This is the hocus-pocus of the medicine man, whose skills embrace the art of mumbo jumbo: Let us evaluate the instructional system component! What that means, Col. Taylor, is let us look at the classroom.

16 It should be needless to add, but I add it anyway, that jargon is one thing and precise usage is something else entirely. The arts, sciences, learned professions and workaday trades all have their own special vocabularies. The lawyer is comfortably at home with his mandamus, and the podiatrist with his metatarsals. The reading specialist who says a child has dyslexia may be imagining a brain disorder (true dyslexia is pretty rare), but the word is legitimate. I am not complaining, heaven knows, against exactness; I am complaining against flummery—against the flummery that converts "textbooks" and "blackboards" and "chalk" into the "configuration of instructional resources."

17 It is rank discrimination, of course, to single out the educators. If they are conspicuously afflicted with the Highfalutin Syndrome, they surely are not alone. The process of semantic promotion has been going on at least since trashmen became sanitation engineers. City planners, urban sociologists and consultants-on-practically-anything are masters of the arts of opacity. Impelled by a sense of duty, I once read 400 pages of testimony on child development centers: half the witnesses had Ph.D.'s, and all of them spoke in alien tongues.

18 Why is the elementary business of human communication thus hung about with Spanish moss? Two explanations come to mind. The first is that persons who use jargon are doing only what comes naturally. They do not intend to obfuscate; they are merely incapable of speaking or writing clearly. The second is that the obfuscators obfuscate on purpose. Their purpose is to conceal the miserable truth, otherwise plainly evident, that they have nothing worth saying or writing. Or perhaps they see some advantage in deliberately befuddling their auditors or readers.

19 Nothing can be done for the second group; they will go on utilizing

their manipulative facilities unto the end of time. The first group can be helped (if they want help) by teaching them that it it not so difficult, honest to goodness, to translate jargon into English. Such offenders can be led to the Strunk-White "Elements of Style," or to Rudolph Flesch's books on plain talk and readable writing.

20 Overblown businessmen can be persuaded that they do not sound impressive, but merely sound silly, when they "finalize an upward corrective adjustment in product lines." They have raised their prices. The remedies lie in deflating the windbag rhetoric—in letting the air out—or, if you please, in excising the adipose tissue. In translation, that means trimming away the fat. The goal, believe me, is worth pursuing.

Word Study List

Spanish moss	2	criterion	12, 13
endemic	3	circumlocutions	14
bootees	4	skinflint	15
confluent	5, 6, 15	erudition	15
debasement	7	flummery	16
dismay	7	opacity	17
manifestations	7	alien	17
nomenclature	8	obfuscate	18
media	8	manipulative	19

Questions

1. What is effective about Kilpatrick's opening his article by discussing a man his readers are not likely to know? Also consider why he begins with remarks about government jargon, since his article is primarily about the "highfalutin" jargon of education.

2. Kilpatrick compares jargon to Spanish moss. What physical characteristics does Spanish moss have that make it an apt description of jargon? What other similes or metaphors does Kilpatrick use to describe jargon?

3. How would you describe the tone of Kilpatrick's article: stuffy, sophisticated, cynical, witty, flippant, serious, erudite? Defend your choice by explaining what (words, metaphors, sentence patterns, etc.) in his writing helps to shape his tone.

4. In paragraph 10, Kilpatrick uses the phrase "plastic syntax" to describe jargon. What meaning of *plastic* is he using here? Explain why the phrase should be called a metaphor. (Review Sale, "Metaphors: Live, Dead, and Silly," pp. 115–121.)

5. Does Kilpatrick see any valid reasons for the use of jargon by educators?

6. What is the difference between the jargon Kilpatrick dislikes and the special language of various professions and jobs? What jobs or courses have you had where a special vocabulary was used? Did the words have specific meanings? Why was it helpful to learn the vocabulary for the course or job?

7. Do we need to distinguish between legitimate uses of jargon and the misuse of language? If so, in what situations is jargon wrongly used?

Exercise

Check the jargon level at your college. Is your library called a library, or is it a learning resource center, a media center, or instructional materials center? By what names are the science and foreign language labs known? The cafeteria and the coffee shop? The counseling office? The placement office?

The Language of Bureaucracy

Henry A. Barnes

Henry A. Barnes (1906–1968) was Commissioner of Traffic in New York City and a contributor to professional journals and magazines. He wrote the following essay for the anthology *Language in America* (1969).

Barnes takes a humorous poke at the puffy but stale and often clumsy language that characterizes bureaucratic communication. Like Kilpatrick in his look at educational jargon in "The Highfalutin and the Mighty," Barnes observes that jargon is used by those in business and government to cover up inadequacies while impressing outsiders.

1 The word *bureau* has grown in significance for me over the past half century. Its earliest meaning was a chest of drawers for the bedroom, intended for the storage of personal gear unsuited to hanging in a closet or hiding under a bed.

2 Family ground rules demanded that the lower drawers of a bureau be maintained in reasonably orderly array, but tradition permitted the top drawer to be reserved for clutter. The top drawer was a catchall for baseball cards, pencil stubs, watch fobs, unmated shoestrings, 23-skiddoo buttons, and similar miscellany.

3 Unaware as I was of any other kind of bureau, I was, nevertheless, learning many useful facts for my later years spent among the bureaus of public life. Early experience taught me that a bureau requires constant

supervision lest it become a mare's-nest of disorder. Another lesson fixed in memory is the knowledge that the periodic reorganizing of a bureau can become a refuge from reality, a dawdler's delight which provides the aimless with endless hours of seemingly productive endeavor.

4 An early organizing technique was to divide the bureau into divisions. This might be accomplished in the lower drawers, but never in the top drawer. The attempt was usually made with the aid of partitions consisting of discarded cigar and candy boxes. The boxes were seldom suitable for the job, being selected to fit the space rather than the purpose. The result resembled the printed forms of modern bureaucracy—small boxes for long items and big boxes for short items.

5 *Bureaucrat* and *bureaucracy* were words I had never heard. I probably would have associated them with *aristocrat* and *aristocracy,* and concluded that a bureaucrat was a boy who didn't have to share a bureau with his brother. A bureaucracy would, no doubt, have been a fanciful state in which such affluent isolation prevailed.

6 Since those days of innocence, I have learned that many words have more than one meaning—*bureau* among them. Many such words have been directed my way—*bureaucrat* among them. These confrontations lose their jolt with time, but I am still dismayed when anyone, in evident compliment, refers to me as a "top-drawer bureaucrat."

7 Bureaucracy generally carries the connotation of an impersonal governmental agency insulated alike from reality and responsibility by layers of red tape. It is in this context that I intend to pursue the subject of the language of bureaucracy. It would be unrealistic, however, to ignore the fact that bureaucracy arises also in private enterprise, and its language is spoken wherever an organization becomes so large and complex and detached that it loses the common urge to communicate in the common tongue with others.

8 The grating voice of bureaucracy's jargon may be heard in any organization, public or private, which feels itself free of the need to share a bureau with its brothers.

9 When the profits of industry go down, the towers of bureaucratic babel go up. I have read corporation reports which were based on the assumption that the stockholder has at his disposal as many lawyers, accountants, and word-splitters as the firm itself. I have heard executives from the "private sector of the economy" spatter audiences with such eloquent nonsense as: "This is a novel innovation of such dimension, scope, and proportion that, without a certain doubt, it is a boon and benefit not only to all mankind but to every customer, employee, and stockholder of this enterprise."

10 While much of the language of bureaucracy defies precise decipherment, it will be found that about 50 percent of the spoken language, including the foregoing example, consists of variations of a single sentence—"Keep your eye on the girl with the pretty legs while I prepare to pull another rabbit out of the hat."

11 At this point it may be to my advantage to state that the examples of the language of bureaucracy presented here have been subjected to considerable paraphrasing to protect the guilty.

12 One very useful method of translating the spoken language of bureaucracy is to commit it to print. In the following example, truth crushed to earth in a bureaucrat's dictation rose again, inadvertently, in his secretary's typing.

Example:
This little-publicized program has been endorsed by a hundred-odd officials.
Translation:
This little, publicized program has been endorsed by a hundred odd officials.

13 It will be noted that the hidden meaning of the dictated version was revealed in the typing by simple revision of punctuation. One who has worked for an appreciable time in areas where the jargon of bureaucracy prevails learns other simple translation devices. For instance, all expressions of confidence should be interpreted as evidences of doubt. A simple way to remember this rule is to bear in mind the true significance of *confidence man.*

14 As indicated below, a little practice with simple words and phrases of assurance and conviction will enable the student to move quickly to more complex sentences.

Example:
Doubtless
Translation:
Unverified

Example:
Interesting fact
Translation:
Drivel

Example:
Universally recognized principle
Translation:
A risky proposition

Example:
We are assigning major priority to the early completion of the preliminary stages of the program.
Translation:
With any luck we can forget the matter completely.

15 It must not, however, be assumed that translations may always be accomplished so readily. Since the technique of the bureaucrat is to pour more words than light on his subject, all surplus words must be deleted before any translation can be attempted. To fully understand this principle, one must remember that an important rule of the language of bureaucracy requires, wherever possible, the use of two or more difficult words selected by sound, rather than one simple word chosen for meaning.

Example:

The respondent correspondent gave expression to the unqualified opinion that the subject missive was anterior to his facile comprehension.

Translation:

He replied that he didn't understand our letter.

16 The thought presents itself here that English grammarians can be rather bureaucratic in their insistence on conformity. Some of the most interesting addresses I have heard have been among the least grammatical. But this is a subject of a different discussion.

17 The language of bureaucracy is essentially a professional jargon. Like other professional jargons it lends itself to exclusiveness, defensiveness, and laziness. A thorough study of this or any other private language would require psychological and sociological analyses of the structure, functions, conditions, and mentality which created the desire for a special lingo. Two difficulties to this approach present themselves—the space limitations of this article, and the author's inability to understand the professional jargons of the psychologists and sociologists. So without extensive examination of the motivational aspects, let us consider a few of the factors bearing on the formation of the private bureaucratic jargon.

18 Bureaucracy is often called "The System." This is, perhaps, some small recognition of the fact that a bureaucracy has its origin in the good intention of achieving systematic operation. All "inside" languages begin with a group's desire to foster efficiency. It is only when the group loses or discards its initial motivation to serve the general public that the "outside" language falls into discard. The "inside" tongue now develops in direct proportion to the group's new inclination to isolate itself and deceive or confuse outsiders.

19 Contrary to popular belief, the language of bureaucracy is not essential to success in public life. The names of Adlai Stevenson and Robert Moses come readily to mind as examples of public figures who have used the common English language with grace, skill, and effectiveness.

20 Such men have no need for the protective cover of an "inside" language. The jargon of bureaucracy developed from the needs of lesser men to make their lives easier, shield their shortcomings, or cover the drabness of their operations with some tawdry gloss.

21 The desire to make life easier fosters the growth of routine phrasing to fit routine situations. Clichés replace original thought. Perfunctory phrases chill response. Dullness is mistaken for dignity. Ready-made replies are stockpiled to handle recurring questions.

22 The form letter is, perhaps, the most exasperating evidence of this tendency. From the standpoint of the bureaucrat, the form letter is a survival kit on the barren mountain of correspondence. To the citizen with a unique problem, the form letter is an abomination.

23 Originating as bureaucracy's fence against avalanches of official correspondence, the form letter becomes in time a despotic protector against work and worry. The periodic attempts of committees to revise form letters or to make them applicable to new types of correspondence often succeed only in spreading the same old ineffective unction more thinly over additional wounds. The time-saving device now becomes a time-wasting irritant as bureaucracy vainly attempts to channel the warm pulsings of civic life into cold classifications like so many columns of want ads.

24 Heavy reliance on ready-made replies eventually reduces bureaucracy's ability to express itself clearly when a tailormade reply is required. New constructions are introduced into its language to mask its deficiencies. Emphasis is sought by stacking superlative on superlative. Unpleasant facts are hidden behind screens of flamboyant words. Tautology impedes meaning. The plague of *-ants*—pursu*ant*, cogniz*ant*, convers*ant*, resul*tant*,— is turned loose. Ideas are lost in the maze of complex sentences. A shortage of meaning develops in direct proportion to the surplus of words.

25 Just as bureaucracy feeds on carbon copies, its language fattens on the repetition of words. Adjectives must always be accompanied by their identical twins and all known relatives. To a bureaucrat, the United States is not merely a big country, it is a huge, vast, and spacious nation. Certain words in the bureaucrat's vocabulary may not decently appear in public without their chaperons. The story is told of an agency which could not prepare a notice for an employees' social because it was impossible to separate *social* from *political* and *economic* in an official document.

26 Some of the long and legalistic phrasing in the language of bureaucracy results from the public servant's duty to protect the public interest. If any fault attaches to it, the special jargon of the law should be held accountable. Contracts are prime examples. In a contract which I signed for my department recently was a sentence composed of 279 words. This lengthy sentence merely stated that the contractor could lose his contracts and be barred from further bidding if he refused to testify in any legal proceedings. Although the thought can be stated here in a couple of dozen words, this simple version would be powerless to withstand the attacks of an astute attorney. Loophole-stuffing of this kind accounts for a considerable amount of the padding in official correspondence.

27 In my years in public service, I have noted a gradual improvement

in the language of bureauracy as used externally. Internally, however, where committee reports rise like magnificent tombstones over the remains of the English language, improvements have been scarce.

28 Much of the fault lies in bureaucracy's passion for prepackaged decisions—advance planning to remove all possibility of personal judgment and initiative. Although as an individual man is seldom gifted with prophetic vision, as a member of a committee he feels himself equal to any future emergency. With his co-oracles, he finds no difficulty in producing such dogma as this.

PROCEDURES, EMERGENCY

Instruction #20973 A-3 (1964)

Section 794—Attack, Atomic

In the possible event of an atomic attack, the senior administrative officer in effective attendance (see Personnel Order 000.06) shall proceed in strict compliance and accordance with applicable provisions of General Circular #87 (1951), paragraphs 843 to 976 as amended by General Circular #103 (1952), paragraphs 237 to 743 and 821 to 934.

Due care must be exercised to comply completely and fully with Office Procedure Manual #1 (1901) Section F-103 (Catastrophes, major) Section V-19 (Absence, excused) and Section W-47 (Routines, time-cards).

Reference may profitably be made to Emergency Procedures—Instruction #45678 R-7 (1964) under the subsequently following headings:

Cave-in, roof (Section 279)
Pipes, steam, broken (Section 293)
Pipes, water, broken, hot (Section 483-A)
Pipes, water, broken, cold (Section 483-J)
Elevators, service, none (Section 791)
Stairways, use of (Section 904)

Reports will be made in quadruplicate to the executive office on Forms #3290R (1904), #5280 (1907) and 7654321-G (1960). Separate forms will be completed for each employee concerned. Filing of reports is mandatory and required during the work day on which emergeny occurs.

NOTE: The above enumeration of forms is not to be construed or interpreted to excuse the senior administrative officer from using all other appropriate forms applicable to the circumstance obtaining.

IMPORTANT: No disbursements of agency funds will be permitted nor may agency vehicles be used by other than assigned personnel without prior approval in writing from the bureau head or his duly appointed representative on written request to be filed at least two (2) weeks in advance of the date upon which permission shall become operative.

29 Assuming that the documents, pertinent, have not been consumed in a holocaust, fiery, the officer, adminstrative, senior, need spend only an hour or two decoding the instructions and another few hours in preparing reports to emerge as the hero, unquestioned, of the situation.

30 A word might be said for the public servant who struggles daily

through this jungle of bureaucratic entanglements. His pretentious phrasings are often the reflection of a dull and repetitious existence rather than a pompous personality. Frequent flowery redundancies in the language of bureaucracy are comparable to the sports writer's thesaurus-like reports. A person doomed to tell the same story daily deserves some commendation for his efforts to tell it in a new way.

31 All the elements for continual growth persist, but one small peril to the language of bureaucracy has begun to develop. This is a problem of bureaucracy's own making—the long evasive answer. For years this technique permitted a bureaucrat the advantage of a revolving door of words from which he could emerge on either side at his own convenience. A classic instance of its use is in the final moments of a radio or TV interview to prevent the moderator from asking the question he was saving for the final discomfiture of the bureaucrat. Moderators are now learning to counter this tactic with the long evasive question which leaves the bureaucrat only seconds to answer a query he probably doesn't understand. Thus a medium of communications with major influence on the development of language patterns begins to veer toward the language of bureaucracy. If the trend continues, bureaucracy may be forced for self-protection to return to the use of the English language.

Word Study List

miscellany	2	abomination	22
dawdler	3	unction	23
babel	9	tautology	24
decipherment	10	oracle	28
lingo	17	pertinent	29
tawdry	20	holocaust	29
clichés	21	redundancies	30
perfunctory	21		

Questions

1. Barnes discusses bureaus or chests of drawers in the first six paragraphs of his article. What has a bureau to do with bureaucracy? What connection does the analogy have with his thesis?

2. What is Barnes's attitude toward bureaucratic language? Give examples of words or phrases, sentence structure, or types of development to support your answer.

3. Why does Barnes compare bureaucratic jargon to a magician's trick (paragraph 10)?

4. What needs brought about the use of bureaucratic jargon? Are you sympathetic to these needs? Why or why not?

5. What is humorous about the example of bureaucratic jargon that he gives in paragraph 28?

6. Do you pour out more words than needed or use "expressions of confidence" when you are unsure of what you want to say or have little to say? Or do you keep your words to a minimum in such situations? What is the advantage of one tactic over the other?

7. Why do people use bureaucratic jargon if it does not insure success or fame?

Exercise

Study the examples of bureaucratic language that Barnes includes in this article and then write at least three rules for producing this jargon.

Doctor Talk

Diane Johnson

Diane Johnson (b. 1934) has been a professor of English at the University of California (Davis) and is the author of several novels, including *Burning* (1971), *Lying Low* (1978), and *The Shadow Knows* (1982). This article, adapted from a paper written for *The State of the Language* (1980), appeared in the *New Republic* on August 18, 1979.

Our third article examining jargon looks at the special languages that doctors have devised—to use with their patients and with each other—now that they have lost the magic language of Latin that for so long gave them power because it mystified and impressed those who came to them for cure.

1 In Africa or the Amazon, the witch doctor on your case has a magic language to say his spells in. You listen, trembling, full of hope and dread and mystification; and presently you feel better or die, depending on how things come out. In England and America too, until recent times, doctors talked a magic language, usually Latin, and its mystery was part of your cure. But modern doctors are rather in the situation of modern priests; having lost their magic languages, they run the risk of losing the magic powers too.

2 For us, this means that the doctor may lose his ability to heal us by

our faith; and doctors, sensing powerlessness, have been casting about for new languages in which to conceal the nature of our afflictions and the ingredients of cures. They have devised two main dialects, but neither seems quite to serve for every purpose—this is a time of transition and trial for them, marked by various strategies, of which the well-known illegible handwriting on your prescription is but one. For doctors themselves seem to have lost faith too, in themselves and in the old mysteries and arts. They have been taught to think of themselves as scientists, and so it is first of all to the language of science that they turn, to control and confuse us.

3 Most of the time scientific language can do this perfectly. We are terrified, of course, to learn that we have "prolapse of the mitral valve"—we promise to take our medicine and stay on our diet, even though these words describe a usually innocuous finding in the investigation of an innocent heart murmur. Or we can be lulled into a false sense of security when the doctor avoids a scientific term: "you have a little spot on your lung"—even when what he puts on the chart is "probable bronchogenic carcinoma."

4 With patients, doctors can use either scientific or vernacular speech but with each other they speak Science, a strange argot of Latin terms, new words, and acronyms, that yearly becomes further removed from everyday speech and is sometimes comprised almost entirely of numbers and letters: "His PO2 is 45; PCO2, 40; and pH, 7.4." Sometimes it is made up of peculiar verbs or main dialects, but neither seems quite to serve for every purpose—"Well, we've bronched him, tubed him, bagged him, cathed him, and PEEPed him," the intern tells the attending physician. ("We have explored his airways with a bronchoscope, inserted an endotrachial tube, provided assisted ventilation with a resuscitation bag, positioned a catheter in his bladder to monitor his urinary output, and used positive end-expiratory pressure to improve oxygenation.") Even when discussing things that can be expressed in ordinary words, doctors will prefer to say "he had a pneumonectomy" to saying "he had a lung removed."

5 One physician remembers being systematically instructed, during the 1950s, in scientific-sounding euphemisms to be used in the presence of patients. If a party of interns were examining an alcoholic patient, the wondering victim might hear them say that he was "suffering from hyperingestation of ethynol." In front of a cancer victim they would discuss his "mitosis." But in recent years such discussions are not conducted in front of the patient at all, because, since Sputnik,[1] lay understanding of scien-

[1]Name of Russian earth-circling satellites, first launched in late 1957 only two months before the first U.S. satellites. The Sputniks started a decade-long space race between the United States and Russia.—ED.

tific language has itself increased so greatly that widespread ignorance cannot be assumed.

6 Space exploration has had its influence, especially on the *sound* of medical language. A CAT-scanner (computerized automated tomography), de rigeur in an up-to-date diagnostic unit, might be something to look at the surface of Mars with. The resonance of physical, rather than biological, science has doubtless been fostered by doctors themselves, who, mindful of the extent to which their science is really luck and art, would like to sound astronomically precise, calculable, and exact, even if they cannot be so.

7 Acronyms and abbreviations play the same part in medical language that they do in other walks of modern life: we might be irritated to read on our chart that "this SOB patient complained of DOE five days PTA." (It means "this Short of Breath patient complained of Dyspnea On Exertion five days Prior To Admission.") To translate certain syllables, the doctor must have yet more esoteric knowledge. Doctor A, reading Dr. B's note that a patient has TTP, must know whether Doctor B is a hemotologist or a chest specialist in order to know whether the patient has thrombotic thrombocytopoenic puerpura, or traumatic tension pneumothorax. That pert little word *ID* means identification to us, but Intradermal to the dermatologist, Inside Diameter to the physiologist, Infective Dose to the bacteriologist; it can stand for our inner self, it can mean *idem* (the same), or it can signify a kind of rash.

8 But sometimes doctors must speak vernacular English, and this is apparently difficult for them. People are always being told to discuss their problems with their doctors, which, considering the general inability of doctors to reply except in a given number of reliable phrases, must be some of the worst advice ever given. Most people, trying to talk to the doctor—trying to pry or to wrest meaning from his evasive remarks ("I'd say you're coming along just fine")—have been maddened by the vague and slightly inconsequential nature of statements which, meaning everything to you, ought in themselves to have meaning but do not, are noncommittal or unengaged, have a slightly rote or rehearsed quality, or sometimes a slight inappropriateness in the context ("It's nothing to worry about really"). This is the doctor's alternative dialect, phrases so general and bland as to communicate virtually nothing.

9 This dialect originates from the emotional situation of the doctor. In the way passers-by avert their eyes from the drunk in the gutter or the village idiot, so the doctor must avoid the personality, the individuality, any involvement with the destiny, of his patients. He must not let himself think and feel with them. This shows in the habit doctors have of calling patients by the names of their diseases: "put the pancreatitis in the other ward and bring the chronic lunger in here." In order to retain objective professional judgment, the doctor has long since learned to withdraw his

emotions from the plight of the patient and has replaced his own ability to imagine them and empathize with them with a formula language—the social lie and the understatement—usually delivered with the odd jocularity common to all gloomy professions.

10 "Well, Mrs. Jones, Henry is pretty sick. We're going to run a couple of tests, have a look at that pump of his." ("Henry is in shock. We're taking him to the Radiology Department to put a catheter in his aorta and inject contrast material. If he has what I think he has, he has a forty-two percent chance of surviving.") We might note an apparent difference of style in English and American doctors, with the English inclined to drollery in such situations. One woman I know reported that her London gynecologist said to her, of her hysterectomy, "We're taking out the cradle, but we're leaving in the playpen!" Americans on the other hand often affect tough talk: "Henry is sick as hell."

11 The doctor's *we,* by the way, is of special interest. Medical pronouns are used in special ways that ensure that the doctor is never out alone on any limb. The referents are cleverly vague. The statement "we see a lot of that" designates him as a member of a knowledgeable elite, "we doctors"; while "how are we today?" means you, or him and you, if he is trying to pass himself off as a sympathetic alter ego. Rarely does he stand up as an *I.* Rarely does he even permit his name to stand alone as Smith, but affixes syllables before and after—the powerful abbrevation *Dr.* itself, which can be found even on his golf bags or skis; or the letters *M.D.* after, or on rare occasions the two buttressing his name from both sides like bookends: "Dr. Smart Smith, M.D."; in England a little train of other letters may trail behind: *F.R.C.P.* In America another fashionable suffix has been observed recently: *Inc.* Dr. Smart Smith, M.D., Inc. This stands for Incorporated, and indicates that the doctor has made himself into a corporation, to minimize his income taxes. A matrix of economic terms already evident in the vocabulary of some doctors is expected to become more pervasive as time goes on.

12 We may complain of how the doctor talks to us; doctors will say, on the other hand, that it is we who do not listen. Very likely this is true. Our ears thunder with hope and dread. We cannot hear the doctor. He says "bone marrow test," we think he says "bow and arrow test." We have all been struck with disbelief, listening to an account by a friend or family member of his trip to the doctor; the doctor cannot possibly have said it was okay to go on smoking, that she doesn't need to lose weight, that he must never eat carrots. This is the case. According to doctors, patients hear themselves. The patient says, "I can't even look at a carrot," and then imagines the doctor has interdicted them. Doctors' sense of our inability to understand things may increase their tendency to talk in simple terms to us, or not to speak at all. Nonetheless, we all hear them talking, saying things they say they never say.

Word Study List

mystification	1	inconsequential	8
dialects	2, 8, 9	noncommittal	8
strategies	2	rote	8
innocuous	3	empathize	9
carcinoma	3	jocularity	9
vernacular	4, 8	drollery	10
argot	4	elite	11
acronyms	4, 6	buttressing	11
euphemisms	5	matrix	11
de rigueur	6	pervasive	11
resonance	6	interdicted	12
esoteric	7		

Questions

1. How does the author's reference to witch doctors in the opening paragraph lead the reader into her thesis? What is her thesis?

2. What languages or dialects are doctors using now to communicate with their patients? What does the author see as the weaknesses of each type?

3. Does the scientific language that doctors use mean that they have a more precise understanding of human illnesses?

4. Why does the author think that doctors are not the ones we should talk over our health problems with?

5. Why does Johnson disapprove of doctors' cheerful or witty conversation?

6. Why is it difficult for doctors to communicate with patients, whatever language or dialects the doctors use?

7. How should doctors talk to their patients? Would we be better off if we, as patients, had less education in science? Would we be better off if we had more?

Exercise

The author gives many examples to illustrate her discussion of doctors' talk. What examples can you add to hers from your own experience? Which type of doctor talk do you remember hearing most often? Write a paragraph explaining which type of "talk" you prefer and why. Be sure to include some of your examples.

Lawyers and Their Language Loopholes

Ronald Goldfarb

A Washington lawyer, Ronald Goldfarb (b. 1933) has written extensively on legal issues and on writing both for other lawyers and the general public. One recent work, written with James Raymond, is *Clear Understandings: A Guide to Legal Writing* (1983). The following article appeared in the *Washington Post* on October 28, 1976.

Lawyers, even more than bureaucrats, are known for their special jargon, characterized by redundancy and awkward phrasing. This article provides many entertaining examples of bad writing that have led to confusion and even to litigation.

1 Most lawyers must plead guilty to killing the English language. Since lawyers speak the words and write the documents that define and govern our lives, there should be a keen public interest in their skillfulness. Yet, legal language is little examined, and rarely challenged. It is a paradox that a group that is so well educated and that relies so crucially on communication uses such bad language.

2 In law schools, poorly trained students who do not write well get no help, and those who do not write well are indoctrinated to write "legalese." The models of legal writing that guide neophyte lawyers are bad prototypes. Law journals, judicial opinions and legal textbooks are all loaded with jargon, pomp, Latinisms—what Yale law professor Fred Rodell once called "high-class mumbo-jumbo." Rodell claimed decades ago in his book, "Woe Unto You Lawyers," that though it deals with ordinary facts and occurrences of everyday business and government and life,"the law is carried on in a foreign language."

3 Lawyers commit unnatural acts on language. Who would ever say to his wife, one Southern judge asked, "Dear, my car keys are on the kitchen counter. Would you please throw me said keys?" Who would write, "I was telling my secretary, hereinafter referred to as Cuddles . . ."? All specialized groups use linguistic shorthand, but it is more of a public problem when lawyers do it.

4 Consider this excerpt from a divorce decree, composed by a lawyer and signed by a judge:

> There should be a finality to litigation; all types of evils can arise from a situation where a party seeks a divorce, such party obtains their own independent counsel, such counsel prepares agreements and documents to consummate a divorce, such counsel presents the documents to the Court and the same are approved by the Court and made a part of the final decree and thereafter the party who initiated such divorce action and sought such counsel and had the same presented to the Court challenged such agreement of the parties that became part of the divorce decree, no matter what the grounds of challenge might be.

5 In reviewing a book about crime and punishment written by a group of prominent lawyers and law professors, I came across this sentence:

> It may be possible to delineate the limits on magnitude better than we have done, but the foregoing should suffice to illustrate the basic idea; in deciding the magnitude of the scale, deterrence may be considered within whatever leeway remains after the outer bounds set by a scale of a certain magnitude has been chosen, however, the internal composition of the scale should be determined by the principle of commensurate deserts.

6 Judged by standards of aesthetics, efficiency or accuracy, legal language is indictable. According to UCLA law professor David Mellinkoff, the problem arises because legal language comes from an archaic melting pot. Its etymological sources are Celtic, Saxon, Jute, Danish, German, French and Latin. We still use Old English (manslaughter, ward), Latin (de minimus, arguendo), Gallic (descent, fee tail, cy pres), and such combinations as breaking and entering, free and clear (Old English and French), peace and quiet, will and testament (Latin and Old English).

7 This archaic language leads to awkward jargon. Such phrases as "assume arguendo" and "ipso facto" pepper lawyers' conversation and briefs. For members of the bar, a case under consideration is a matter "sub judice." Something unique is "sui generis" to the attorney "in the above-mentioned matter." This fluff is habitual, and it is confused with erudition.

8 Lawyers would rather utilize something than use it. They use what Rodell has called "the backhanded passive," encumbering their remarks with such hedges as "it would seem" and "it is suggested." They love polysyllabic prose, preferring "notwithstanding" to "despite" or "however," and loading on all the "alleges," "hereinafters" and "thereupons" that will fit their forms.

9 Lawyers are so careful they become clumsy and repetitive. They alone find the need to "cease" as well as "desist," to "give" as well as "bequeath and devise." An Arkansas judge tells of a contempt order that was reported to have been "reversed, vacated, and held null and void." He suggested: "and stomped on."

10 A legitimate reason for using such language exists in the area of developing constitutional law where flexibility is necessary. The words "reasonable," "freedom," "equal protection" and "due process of law" need constant redefinition in light of changing times and mores. The story is told that after Solon wrote the ancient Greek constitution he left the country for several years so that he would not be asked to say what his words meant. Interpretation of subjective concepts should be left to active decision-makers and to the inspiration of the times.

11 This virtue, however, does not apply to statutory language or the language of documents, judicial opinions or public statements of policy.

12 Courtroom talk is more baffling than it needs to be. "I direct your attention to October 1975 and ask you if there came a time when . . ." takes the place of "What happened in October 1975?" I recall a Kentucky judge's telling a jury that he wished he didn't have to give them long-winded technical instructions. Instead, he said, he would prefer to tell them what Andrew Jackson told a jury when he was on the bench: "Go out and do right by these people."

13 The style of legal writing is bad enough to warrant alarm and reform, for bad substance follows bad form. Poor language, even erroneous punctuation, has caused litigation and brought about unwanted results. Consider these examples:

14 Many lawyers use forms and canned legal lingo. One attorney added a set clause to a will, directing the executor "to pay all my just debts" before distributing the estate's proceeds. A New York court rules that the addition of this clause (not requested by the client) revived a debt that had been barred by the statute of limitations.

15 Faulty punctuation can cause serious problems, too. The Kentucky Court of Appeals was called upon to interpret a clause in a will that gave a large estate to nine different individuals and institutions. The clause enumerated equal shares but did not place a semicolon between the names of two of the recipients as it did between the other seven. The question was whether there were eight or nine shares—whether the two individuals within but not separated by semicolons got one full one-ninth share each or divided a one-eighth share between them. A lot of money rested upon the interpretation of a missing semicolon.

16 An Alabama judge told me about a divorce trial he presided over where the issue was whether the husband had committed adultery. The wife's lawyer asked a woman witness whether she had had sexual relations with the husband. She replied that she had. After her testimony was completed, as she was leaving the courtroom, she stopped and asked the judge: "Did you mean to ask whether I had intercourse with this guy?" When the judge replied that this indeed was the purpose of the question, she turned to the witness stand and testified that she never had "intercourse," only "sexual relations." Loose legal language had almost turned the trial around.

17 It is time for lawyers to shape up their language. Unfortunately, Rodell's dated and hyperbolic charge, that lawyers are "purveyors of pretentious poppycock" whose "writing style is unfit for the consumption of cultured men," still hits uncomfortably close to home.

Word Study List

paradox	1	passive	8
indoctrinated	2	polysyllabic	8
neophyte	2	subjective	10
prototypes	2	statutory	11
Latinisms	2	erroneous	13
linguistic	3	litigation	13
excerpt	4	lingo	14
decree	4	statute of limitations	14
aesthetics	6	enumerated	15
indictable	6	hyperbolic	17
etymological	6	purveyors	17
archaic	7	pretentious	17
erudition	7	poppycock	17

Questions

1. What is Goldfarb's purpose in this article: to show how lawyers misuse the language or to make fun of lawyers for using bad language? Prove your answer by pointing out the thesis, examples used to develop the thesis, and pertinent information about the author.

2. Is this article primarly directed at lawyers, law school professors, or the general public? To support your answer, look at Goldfarb's word choice and examples.

3. Is any defense given for why lawyers write and speak in legal "mumbo-jumbo?" Is any defense possible?

4. Many of us have assumed that lawyers speak and write in long, complex sentences because they must close all loopholes to protect their clients. What specific criticisms does Goldfarb present to show that this complex language is often unnecessary or that as many loopholes are opened as closed?

5. Can you translate the examples in paragraphs 4 and 5 into plain English? Is it necessary to understand these paragraphs of legalese to follow the author's point?

6. Do you think that simplifying legal language would build more trust between lawyers and their clients? Before you answer consider what

Diane Johnson (see "Doctor Talk," page 246) says about the power of doctors' language to cure.

Exercise

Bring to class examples of legalese from contracts, credit terms stated on charge applications or billing slips, or family wills. Circle the jargon words and unnecessary words. Try rewriting one of them to remove the legalese.

Psychobabble

Cyra McFadden

Cyra McFadden (b. 1937) has contributed articles to literary journals and popular magazines and written the best-selling novel *The Serial* (1977), which satirizes the psychobabble culture of her neighbors in Marin County, California. This article was published in *Harpers & Queen,* a British magazine, in February 1978.

In this article, McFadden takes a lively look at the conversational pattern she considers to be the mindless exchanges of those who are "into" the human potential movement, feelings, and consciousness raising.

1 A woman who lives here in the San Francisco Bay Area, where every prospect pleases and only man is vile, is teaching 'inner cooking.' 'I'm out of the closet,' a newspaper interview quotes her as saying. 'All this time I've been interested in people and feelings, but I've been in the disguise of a cooking teacher.'

2 Joyce Goldstein conducts her classes in Kitchen Consciousness in her Berkeley home. Cooking, she believes, is a metaphor for life. It involves 'taking risks,' 'expressing feelings,' 'releasing body energy' and 'sharing space.' That her techniques of guided fantasy and gestalt in the kitchen fill yet another need in the collective Bay Area consciousness is apparent in a student testimonial quoted in the same interview: 'Joyce's classes have changed my whole outlook in the kitchen. I don't feel all those ought-tos and should-haves any more. I am a free woman.'

3 I know, I know. It's also a free country. If, as Goldstein suggests, you find cleaning shrimp 'a meditative experience,' and if you, too, believe that foods have personalities ('the tomato . . . is thin-skinned and bruises easily, but likes to bring things together'), that, as we say in the consciousness-raising capital of the western world, is your own trip. Dig it, relate to it, groove on it, get behind it, even, if you choose. Only spare me your

account of the whole transcendent experience. Living here in beautiful Marin County,[1] between the fern bars and the deep blue sea, I hear all the mindless prattle about feelings, human and vegetable, that I can tolerate without 'acting out' and drowning the users of the Newspeak of the Seventies, like unwanted kittens, in their own hot tubs.

4 'You've really got a thing about language, haven't you?' said a man who sat next to me at a luncheon recently. 'What's your hang-up? I think the whole new language trip is because people are really into being upfront about their feelings these days instead of intellectualising, so we need a whole new way of describing all that stuff . . . the feelings. I mean, ten years ago we didn't even know they were there. And anyway, you can't say it doesn't communicate. Like, right now we're having this discussion, for example, and I say, "I know where you're coming from." Are you going to tell me you don't know what I mean by that?'

5 Arguing with such people, I have learned, is as futile as trying to scrape fresh bubble gum off one's shoe. Still, I insisted that I didn't know what my luncheon partner meant in any concrete sense and that 'I know where you're coming from' was meaningless in the context. Did he mean he knew where I'd grown up, or where I'd been immediately before malevolent fate planted me at the table beside him, or what education and experience had shaped my thinking about the issue between us?

6 Intellectualising, said my companion. Nit-picking. I knew very well that he meant that he could relate, that he knew what space I was in. Where my head was coming from.

7 By this time I wished my head and everything appended to it were elsewhere. 'Are you trying to say you understand why I feel the way I do about empty, rubber-stamp language?' I asked, coming down hard on the consonants.

8 My luncheon partner smiled infuriatingly, 'You see?' he said. 'I *knew* you knew where I was coming from.'

9 Writer Richard Rosen calls such language psychobabble. He defines it as 'monotonous patois . . . psychological patter, whose concern is to faithfully catalogue the ego's condition.'

10 I define it as semantic spinach, and I say the hell with it. Conversations like the above, if one can call such an exchange a conversation, have all but supplanted anything resembling intelligent human discourse here, where the human-potential movement takes the place of other light industry and where the redwood-shingled offices of the healer/masseurs, the gurus and the 'life-goals consultants' line the main approach to Mill Valley along with the hamburger stands. They make any real exchange of ideas impossible; block any attempt at true communication; substitute what Orwell called 'prefabricated words and phrases' for thought.

---

[1]County north of San Francisco across the Golden Gate Bridge.—Ed.

11 Just as surely as the Styrofoam boxes one sees everywhere are evidence of the popularity of McDonald's, such conversations, too, are the fallout from the fast-food outlet approach to therapy of the Seventies. With the self the only subject worth examining, one's purely intuitive 'off-the-wall' response the only reference point, all verbal exchange is soon reduced to a kind of mechanical chatter in the infield. Speakers of psychobabble, I believe, are not so much concerned with describing feelings 'we didn't even know were there' ten years ago as with avoiding any mental exertion whatsoever; any effort at precision of expression, or even thought itself, falls under the pejorative label 'intellectualising.' Thus the number of words and phrases in the Bay Area vocabulary that describe mental inertia: 'mellowing out,' 'kicking back,' 'going with the flow,' being 'laid back.' All suggest that the laid-back, mellowed-out speaker achieves a perfect relation with the universe while in a state of passivity just short of that produced by full anesthetic.

12 How much easier it is, after all, to 'verbalise' in platitudes rather than to think. Trite, cliché-ridden language is always a sign of inattention at best, intellectual laziness at worst. One either speaks or writes the occasional cliché because his mind, for some reason or other, has momentarily switched over to automatic pilot, or he uses prefabricated words and phrases routinely because as far as he's concerned, it's six of one, half a dozen of the other.

13 Psychobabble is no more difficult to use than drawing the girl on the matchbook cover, and it has another attraction as well: speakers associate its platitudes with profundity and mouth its Words to Live By in the apparent conviction that having said nothing, they have said it all.

14 'I can't get behind school right now,' said a student in a college composition class of mine, when I warned him that if he continued to show no vital signs, he would fail the course. 'But I'm not into Fs,' he added, 'and, anyway, I don't think you ought to lay that authority trip on me. I mean, failing someone . . . wow, that's a value judgment.'

15 'I can't relate to the dude,' said another, in a contemporary literature class, pressed for his opinion of a short story by Ray Bradbury.[2]

16 'How about being more specific?' I said. 'Do you mean you weren't interested in his ideas, or that you didn't find them sympathetic? Were you bored? Did you have trouble following the action of the story?'

17 'Actually I didn't exactly read it,' said the student.

18 'For God's sake, how do you know you "can't relate" then?' I asked, knowing better.

19 My student turned his serene blue gaze upon me. 'I just flashed on it,' he explained.

20 A *value judgment.* Give me the trench-coat type flasher any time over

---

[2]Ray Bradbury (b. 1920) is a popular science fiction writer.—ED.

the one who whips open an empty mind to display his poor excuse for an insight.

21 What is most alarming about psychobabble, however, is not its appalling smugness but that it spreads like Dutch elm disease. Unlike most cult language—private vocabularies small groups use to distinguish themselves from the larger language community—the fatuous fallout from the human potential movement seems to have jumped all the usual fences. And while elsewhere in the country one hears psychobabble spoken by the members of the 'counterculture,' here the counterculture has come out from under the counter and become the dominant culture itself, its dialect the language of polite society that one must speak in order to belong. Rock-band roadies, stockbrokers, academics, teeny-boppers, butchers—sometimes it appears that everyone one meets has taken the same course in Deep Feelerese at Berlitz.[3]

22 'Your arms are crossed. Do you realise that's a very defensive posture?' says the friend I meet in the supermarket. 'You're afraid of me. I can tell from your body language.'

23 I'm not afraid, I assure her. My arms are crossed because I couldn't find a cart, and if I adopt a less defensive posture, I will drop a dozen catfood cans on her foot.

24 My friend smiles wisely, bemused by my transparent self-deception. Some of the people can fool themselves all of the time, she is thinking. 'Look,' she says, 'it's OK. *You're* OK. I just think maybe some time when the vibes are right, we ought to get clear . . .'

25 At a dinner party, a new acquaintance tells me about her intimate life. Although she is still 'processing' her ex-husband (not, I hope, in the Waring blender her language brings to mind), she just spent a weekend with another man from whom she gets 'a lot of ego reinforcement. My therapist keeps telling me to go where the energies are,' she says, 'so that's what I'm doing, because that's what went wrong last time. I didn't just kick back and go with the energies.'

26 Suddenly I realise why Marin's own George Lucas is getting rich from *Star Wars,* a film in which people go where the energies are, at speeds faster than 'hyperspace,' and deliver themselves of simple-minded philosophy in one-syllable words.

27 Why has psychobabble saturated Bay Area conversation so? One hears it nearly everywhere else to some extent, it is true, but only in San Francisco, Los Angeles and environs has it all but replaced English. (Los Angeles has its own bizarre variation, incidentally, incorporating film and television industry money talk. Example: 'I'm gonna be totally upfront with you, sweetheart. The bottom line is 50 thou and points.')

---

[3]School that teaches foreign language by immersing the student in the language immediately on starting the course.—ED.

28 In part, the appeal is the gravitational pull urban California has always felt toward the new, the Now, the trendy, no matter how ludicrous its current manifestation. In an area where opening night at the opera featured at least one socialite in an elegant designer gown and a punk-rock safety-pin in her hair, one shouldn't be too surprised when a butcher asks you, 'Could you relate to a pork loin roast?'

29 Partly responsible, too, is the legacy of the Haight-Ashbury and the Summer of Love. Former flower children whose own vocabulary of peace and love focused on the primacy of feelings, who found concrete reality largely irrelevant, now abound in the hills and canyons of Marin, driving car pool to Montessori school on alternate Thursdays or working as claims adjusters at Fireman's Fund.

30 Fallen victim to cellulite and revolving credit, wistful for the days of LSD and roses, they naturally embrace a language pattern that declares they have not repudiated their Sixties selves.

31 'Listen,' one of them told a friend of mine recently, as they exchanged driver's licenses and phone numbers after a minor traffic accident, 'I just want you to know that you've been so beautiful about all this, it's really been a beautiful experience.'

32 My friend said he didn't agree and that most of the traffic accidents he had known couldn't really be described as beautiful, though some were pretty and others compensated for their plainness with lots of charm.

33 Finally, in these pleasant, prosperous suburbs, enough people have enough money to spend on weekend after weekend at psychological boot camps for civilians like *est* and Silva mind control; consulting holistic healers and doing dream or body work; being Rolfed, getting centered, or—in Marin County—taking their horses to be treated for anxiety by a veterianarian who specialises in equine acupuncture.

34 What Tom Wolfe[4] calls 'the Me decade' can burgeon here under ideal conditions: affluence, leisure and what has been traditionally a high level of tolerance for fads and human foibles. Joyce Goldstein, the Berkeley teacher of inner cooking, might have a little trouble collecting disciples in, say, the Middle West, but she is doing nicely, thank you, in balmy Berkeley. 'Joyce is nifty and a half,' says another of her students, a woman assistant-vice president at Wells Fargo Bank. 'I was a cooking cripple until I met her. Now I can't cook, but Joyce has showed me that it's OK.'

35 Los Angeles, too, has the money, the leisure and the fondness for fakery that nurture the rapid growth of the new subculture, and in greater abundance. There, Maseratis and chauffeured limousines double park in front of the mystical bookstores, the offices of the Astrological Guidance counsellors and the Kirlian 'aura photo' workshops. Understandably.

36 After all, when you've built the palatial house in Beverly Hills,

---

[4]Tom Wolfe (b. 1931) writes about popular culture with a sharp wit and vivid style.—Ed.

bought cocaine as if it were baby powder, had cosmetic surgery on everything and still have money left, you've got to spend it somewhere.

37 One could argue that such preoccupations and diversions are essentially harmless in that they keep people off the streets, or what are called in Los Angeles (to distinguish them from the freeways) the surface roads. In this era of do your own thing, however, my thing, as my luncheon partner some weeks past either understood or didn't, is despair at the effects of Seventies egocentrism on the language.

38 I have read too many essays by and held too many conferences with college students whose written and spoken English had the clarity of Quaker Oats.

39 I have listened to too many *est* graduates, living walkie-talkies, tell me, unsolicited, what they were 'getting.' (Clear, creative divorces, double messages, in touch with themselves, not necessarily in that order.)

40 I have argued too many times about things that matter to me passionately with people who dismissed both arguments and me with 'How come you're so uptight?' or 'Your head's really in a funny place, you know?'

41 Crack-brained California, you say complacently; it's always been Cloud Cuckooland[5] out there. True, but California foolishness has a historic tendency to seep through the water tables and across state lines. What if one day soon it is impossible to carry on a reasonably coherent conversation north of Yucatan and south of the Bering Sea?

42 Meanwhile I stand on the roof of my Mill Valley house, watching the flood of psychobabble rising, ever rising, and wishing I knew how to turn the situation around. It won't be easy. The psychobabblers not only outnumber the rest of us, but, what is worse, they have The Force on their side.

Word Study List

metaphor	2	cliché	12
gestalt	2	profundity	13
transcendent	3	fatuous	21
malevolent	5	manifestation	28
consonants	7	cellulite	30
patois	9	repudiated	30
semantic	10	burgeon	34
pejorative	11	foibles	34
platitudes	12, 13	egocentrism	37

[5]The name of the utopoian city in the sky that an Athenian youth persuades birds to build in the play *The Birds* by Aristophanes, a fifth century B.C. comic dramatist.—ED.

Questions

1. What does the author see as the principal weakness of psychobabble?

2. What is McFadden's attitude toward those who use psychobabble? Which examples do you think best convey her attitude? Explain why.

3. What are the reasons for the popularity of psychobabble? Why is it more prevalent in California than in other areas of the country? What social or economic class does she implicitly connect its use to? Why would it be more popular with that group?

4. McFadden compares psychobabble to "semantic spinach" (paragraph 10) and "Quaker Oats" (paragraph 38). What picture of language do these phrases create? What quality of psychobabble do they make visual?

5. If you have seen the film *Star Wars* or its sequel *The Empire Strikes Back,* defend or refute McFadden's charge that the characters reflect what is popular in the psychobabble culture.

Exercises

1. Were you familiar with any of the psychobabble language included in this article before reading it? Where did you hear it? Do you use it? If so, write a short paragraph explaining why you use it.

2. What is the connotation of the word *psychobabble*? Is it a compliment to say that someone "babbles"? How do the "babble" jargons, such as psychobabble and urbababble (the new term for the jargon used by bureaucrats in urban development that includes such words as *impact on, viability* and *gentrification*), differ from other jargons such as legalese or journalese? Write a paragraph in which you assert and illustrate, with some appropriate examples, one major difference between the "babble" jargons and the "-ese" jargons.

3. Review Sale's analysis of the use of words as a metaphor in "Metaphors: Live, Dead, and Silly." Then explain the meaning of the following examples of metaphoric expressions that are popular in the world of psychobabble.
   a. Why is she so uptight?
   b. I can't figure out what space you're in.
   c. I know where you're coming from.
   d. Hang in there and things will get better.
   e. I have to get my head together.

Journalese as a Second Tongue

John Leo

Formerly an editor of *Commonweal* and a reporter for the *New York Times*, John Leo (b. 1935) is an associate editor of *Time* magazine and editor of its Behavior/Sexes section. The following article appeared in *Time* on January 6, 1984.

Using journalese effectively to make his point, Leo pokes fun at the jargon of the news industry.

1 As a cub reporter, Columnist Richard Cohen of the Washington *Post* rushed out one day to interview a lawyer described in many newspaper reports as "ruddy-faced." The man was woozily abusive and lurched about with such abandon that young Cohen instantly realized that the real meaning of ruddy-faced is drunk. This was his introduction to journalese, the fascinating second tongue acquired by most reporters as effortlessly as an Iranian toddler learns Farsi or a Marin County child learns psychobabble.[1]

2 Fluency in journalese means knowing all about "the right stuff," "gender gap," "life in the fast lane" and the vexing dilemma of being caught "between a rock and a hard place," the current Scylla-Charybdis[2] image. The Middle East is "strife-torn," except during those inexplicable moments when peace breaks out. Then it is always "much troubled." Kuwait is located just east of the adjective "oil-rich," and the Irish Republican Army always lurks right behind the word "outlawed." The hyphenated modifier is the meat and potatoes of journalese. Who can forget "the break-away province of Biafra," "the mop-top quartet" (the mandatory second reference to the Beatles) and the "ill-fated Korean jetliner," not to be confused with the "ill-fitting red wig" of Watergate fame. Murderers on death row are often saved by "eleventh-hour" reprieves, which would be somewhere between 10 and 11 p.m. in English but shortly before midnight in journalese.

3 Much of the difficulty in mastering journalese comes from its slight overlap with English. "Imposing," for instance, when used to describe a male, retains it customary English meaning, but when used in reference to a female, it always means battle-ax. "Feisty" refers to a person whom the journalist deems too short and too easily enraged, though many in the journalese-speaking fraternity believe it is simply the adjective of choice for any male under 5 ft. 6 in. who is not legally dead. This usage reflects

[1]See Cyra McFadden, "Psychobabble," pp. 255–260.—ED.

[2]In Greek mythology, Odysseus and others had to sail between the dangerous rock of Scylla and the whirlpool of Charybdis.—ED.

the continual surprise among tall journalists that short people have any energy at all. Women are not often feisty, though they are usually short enough to qualify. No journalist in America has ever referred to a 6-ft. male as feisty. At that height, men are simply "outspoken" (*i.e.,* abusive).

4 In general, adjectives in journalese are as misleading as olive sizes. Most news consumers know enough to translate "developing nations" and "disadvantaged nations" back into English, but far smaller numbers know that "militant" means fanatic, and "steadfast" means pigheaded. "Controversial" introduces someone or something the writer finds appalling, as in "the controversial Miss Fonda," and "prestigious" heralds the imminent arrival of a noun nobody cares about, as in "the prestigious Jean Hersholt Humanitarian Award."

5 Television anchorpersons add interest to their monologues by accenting a few syllables chosen at random. Since print journalists cannot do this, except when reading aloud to spouse and children, they strive for a similar effect by using words like crisis and revolution. Crisis means any kind of trouble at all, and revolution means any kind of change at all, as in "the revolution in meat packing." "Street value" lends excitement to any drug-bust story, without bearing any financial relationship to the actual value of drugs being busted. Many meaningless adjectives, preferably hyphenated for proper rhythm, are permanently welded to certain nouns: blue-ribbon panel, fact-finding mission, devout Catholic, and rock-ribbed Republican. In journalese there are no devout Protestants or Jews, and no Democrats with strong or stony ribs.

6 Historians of journalese will agree that the first flowering of the language occurred in the sexist descriptions of women by splashy tabloids during the '30s and '40s. In contrast to Pentagonese, which favors oxymorons (Peacekeeper missiles, build-down), the tabloids relied on synecdoche (leggy brunette, bosomy blonde, full-figured redhead). Full-figured, of course, meant fat, and "well-endowed" did not refer to Ford Foundation funding. "Statuesque" (too large, mooselike) and "petite" (too small, mouselike) were adjectives of last resort, meaning that the woman under discussion had no bodily parts that interested the writer. A plain, short woman was invariably "pert." For years, masters of this prose cast about for a nonlibelous euphemism for "mistress." The winning entry, "great and good friend," used to describe Marion Davies' relationship to William Randolph Hearst, was pioneered, as it happens, by a non-Hearst publication, TIME magazine. "Constant companion" evolved later, and gave way to such clunking modernisms as "roommate" and "live-in lover." Nowadays, the only sexuality about which journalese is coy tends to be homosexuality, and that is adequately covered by "he has no close female friends" or "he is not about to settle down."

7 In political campaigns, underdogs fight uphill battles and hope for shifts of momentum and coattail effects, all leading to rising tides that will enable the favorite to snatch defeat from the jaws of victory. A politician

who has no idea about what is going on can be described as one who prefers "to leave details to subordinates." A gangster who runs a foreign country will be referred to as "strongman" until his death, and dictator thereafter. Strongman, like many terms in journalese, has no true correlative. "Nicaraguan Strongman Somoza" is not balanced with "Cambodian Weakman Prince Sihanouk."

8 What to say about a public figure who is clearly bonkers? Since it is unsporting and possibly libelous to write: "Representative Forbush, the well-known raving psychopath," journalese has evolved the code words difficult, intense and driven. If an article says, "Like many of us, Forbush has his ups and downs," the writer is wigwagging a manic-depressive.

9 Political journalese, of course, requires a knowledge of sources. An unnamed analyst or observer can often be presumed to be the writer of the article. The popular plural "observers," or "analysts," refers to the writer and his cronies. Insiders, unlike observer-analysts, sometimes exist in the real world outside the newsroom. This, however, is never true of quotable chestnut vendors in Paris, Greenwich Village bartenders and other colorful folk conjured up on deadline to lend dash to a story.

10 Almost all sources, like most trial balloonists, live in or around Washington. In order of ascending rectitude, they are: informants, usually reliable sources, informed sources, authoritative sources, sources in high places and unimpeachable sources. Informants are low-level operatives, whose beans are normally spilled to police rather than to reporters. Informed sources, because of their informed nature, are consulted most often by savvy journalists. An unimpeachable source is almost always the President, with the obvious exception of Richard Nixon, who was not unimpeachable.

11 Journalese is controversial but prestigious, and observers are steadfast in averring that it has the right stuff.

Word Study List

reprieves	2	psychopath	8
tabloids	6	wigwagging	8
oxymorons	6	manic-depressive	8
synecdoche	6	rectitude	10
nonlibelous	6	unimpeachable	10
correlative	7	savvy	10
bonkers	8	averring	11

Questions

1. Although Leo establishes that journalese is the special jargon of journalists, he never defines the term. After studying Leo's many examples, particularly noting how he has grouped them by paragraph, describe the specific types of words and phrases that make up journalese.

2. Leo says that journalese began with sexist descriptions of women, with such euphemisms as *statuesque* for fat and *petite* for mousy. What other euphemisms does Leo include in his article? Can you add still others we use to describe both men and women?

3. According to Leo, Pentagonese uses oxymorons while journalese favors synecdocho. Study Leo's examples of each term and then try to define the two terms. Compare your definitions with those in a desk dictionary.

4. Leo suggests that reporters may turn to journalese for emphasis and rhythm. When you write, do you consciously seek words and phrases (perhaps clichés) to add punch to your sentences? Do you change sentences that don't "sound" right? Are your sentences usually better when you concentrate on their rhythms?

5. Would you characterize Leo's tone as serious, lighthearted, humorous, witty, cynical, flippant? Defend your choice.

6. What is Leo's attitude toward journalese? How do you know? Some writers in this chapter state or imply solutions to language misuse; Leo does not. Does that mean he doesn't care what happens to journalism or that he doesn't think change is possible?

Exercise

Select three articles from the front page of a newspaper or from the first two sections of a newsmagazine. Analyze them carefully, listing all words and phrases that Leo would characterize as journalese. Determine the "journalese quotient" of each article by calculating the percentage of journalese words in each one. How serious is the disease in the newspaper or newsmagazine you studied? Present your findings in a paragraph.

Videospeak

Tom Shales

Recipient of the Distinguished Alumnus Award of the American University in 1973, Tom Shales is the *Washington Post*'s TV editor and reviewer. He also writes the syndicated column "On the Air"; a collection of his columns was published in book form in 1982. "Videospeak" appeared in the *Washington Post Magazine* on January 23, 1983.

In an amusing style, Shales examines both the special jargon of TV broadcasting and the words added to our language from the TV shows.

1 Television don't talk good. One could say it massacres the language, but one could also say, just as justifiably, that it establishes the language. What we say is greatly affected by what we watch, and hear, on television, and that's not incredible, that's inevitable.

2 TV invents words, changes words and, most of all, soaks up words and phrases from regions and subcultures and introduces them into the mainstream. So that born-again adjectives like "heavy" and "into" were plucked out of the hippie culture of the '60s and, through their use on television, have passed into everyday vocabulary, just as the new meanings given words like "closet" are no longer the property of homosexual subculture because television has absorbed and homogenized them.

3 Now giddy contestants on game shows regularly identify themselves as closet gardeners or closet poets or closet nuclear physicists (well, that's a rare one), and nobody wonders what they're talking about. Nobody wonders because everybody watches television, and videospeak is the national language. Television is America's dictionary, as well as its mirror.

4 Aside from enterprising politicians who occasionally come up with a beaut like "South Succotash," nothing introduces buzzwords into the culture with more efficiency than TV commercials, which are designed to be instantly memorable and conditioned-responsive. For years grammarians and English teachers have railed against the debasement of language by commercials that tell viewers it's all right to say "Winston tastes good like a cigarette should" and "Raid hunts bugs down and kills them dead," but to no avail.

5 Yes, a classroom full of toddlers in some American town (sufferin' South Succotash, perchance?) really did once tell a teacher that they spelled "relief" r-o-l-a-i-d-s. You can rail against this sort of thing, but you can't fight it. Children are bound to respond to appeals on behalf of candy that tastes more "chocolatey" and catsup that is sworn to be "thickerer" and cheese snackies that have "more ummm-ummmmm in every crunch." Their baloney has a first name; it's O-s-c-a-r.

6 A 3-year-old in the back seat of his parents' car in Georiga reminded them of his dependence on television commercials recently when he pointed to a fast-food restaurant and said, "Look—a participating Hardee's!"

7 The language doesn't have to be mangled, just catchy—"Hey, I could have had a V-8!" Set to music equally catchy, it can infect millions of minds and amend millions of vocabularies at once. Thus the father of three daughters in Arlington, Va., having purchased a video game for the family, has grown accustomed to the girls' asking the musical question, always to the tune of the jingle they hear in a commerical, "Can we play Atari today?"

8 Writers of weekly TV series try to introduce similar ring-around-the-collarisms into their shows; it's free world-of-mouth advertising if they can get kids to imitate a Fonzie[1] or a Gary Coleman[2] in a few simple words. At a family Christmas gathering in Garden City, N.Y., a 10-year-old boy offered his impression of Johnny Slash on "Square Pegs"; he put on a

---

[1]A main character in the sitcom "Happy Days"—Ed.

[2]A young comedian who plays a character in the sitcom "Diff'rent Strokes."—Ed.

pair of sunglasses and said, "Totally different head." The writers of the show and the CBS Television Network would have been pleased.

9 "Totally different head" is an expression by way of Valley talk. The Valley is the San Fernando Valley, just over the hills from Hollywood, and most entertainment television is produced there. That fact, and a Frank Zappa[3] song, are what made Valley talk a national phenomenon.

10 In the '50s, television emanated from New York, and New York expressions and references permeated the language. No more. We are now all being taught the language according to Southern California, much of it as translated in the Midwest by Phil Donahue,[4] who has made buzzwords out of "caring" and "supportive," "mainstream" and "parent" as verbs, and the expressions "speaks to the issue" (or "speaks to the whole question of . . .") and "The record should show."

11 We try to be "straight" and "open" now because these clichés are passed along daily and nightly in television dramas and comedies, as well as sensitivity talk shows, along with what has in recent years become the most common adjective in the American lexicon, "special." Special has become a not very specialized word. It's like "um-gawah" in the Tarzan movies; it can mean anything. It can mean physically handicapped or physically dexterous. When you reach out, reach out and touch someone, you tell them, "You're very special to me." Pity the girlfriend who's not been told by her boyfriend by now, "You're a very special lady." How special could she be?

12 Television has its own internal language, but much of it becomes external and seeps into everyday usage. Everyone knows what a "sitcom" is now (a word coined in trade papers—"the trades"—and just about everyone knows what they are, too), and that programs "air" tonight or "aired" last night. "Prime time" has caught on, though "day parts" hasn't—yet. The public knows what "ratings" and "Nielsens" are, what an "anchor" is and, although Johnny Carson[5] still can't pronounce "puberty" (he says "pooh-berty"), he has helped educate America on what "sweep weeks" and "overnights" mean to the TV industry—roughly, everything and a half.

13 "Freeze-frame" is so common now it became a hit song, and kids on every backlot ball diamond in the country call playfully for "replays." In fact, replay is old-hat. More common now is the household phrase attributable to trailblazing sportscaster Warner Wolf, "Let's go to the videotape," along with the ever-popular, "Let's see that again."

14 Because there is so much chitchat about show business on the Carson show and other talk shows, many people who don't need to be are probably now familiar with terms like "rim shot" (comic punctuation from a drummer), "shtick," and "segue" (pronounced "seg-way," dating back

---

[3]A rock musician who recorded a song entitled "Valley Girl."—Ed.

[4]Host of a popular morning talk show.—Ed.

[5]Long-time host of the late-evening talk show "Tonight."—Ed.

to radio and meaning a change from one thing to another); know when a comedian is "on a roll" or doing "a bit" or "a piece of material"; and certainly realize what a singer means when he refers to a "gig." Television tells us more about detergents, cat foods and show business than any mortal could ever want or desire to know.

15 Of all the words corrupted by misuse on television—from "infer," which is invaribly confused with "imply," to squandered hyperboles like "unbelievable," "revolutionary," and "fantastic," to the perverse appropriation of once-meaningful words like "natural"—none is currently more maligned than the word "live." Live television used to mean that what you were watching was happening as you saw it. But at this season's "Kennedy Center Honors," Walter Cronkite[6] told the crowd in the Opera House that the program was "live-on-tape" and added,"I've never quite understood what that means." It's similar to phrases like "recorded live" that are helping to kill the word live dead. It's been reduced to such meaninglessness that local stations now boast that their newscasts are "Live at 5:30" or "Live at 11." This is news, that the news is live?

16 This just in: the news is live. Still ahead: "Coming up next." Don't go away; we'll be right back.

17 Now this: to air is human; to survive television, divine.

Word Study List

homogenized	2	permeated	10
conditioned-responsive	4	dexterous	11
debasement	4	attributable	13
emanated	10		

Questions

1. What is Shales's main point or thesis? Where does he state it?

2. Explain the two metaphors in Shales's statement that "television is America's dictionary, as well as its mirror."

3. Where do the words and phrases come from that become videospeak? What regions and subcultures seem to contribute the most to videospeak today?

---

[6]For many years the anchorman of the CBS Evening News, now a special correspondent with CBS.—ED.

4. Videospeak comes through the tube into our own vocabularies primarily through what TV sources in addition to ads?

5. What types of shows (sitcoms, news, sports, series) do you generally watch? Try to list five to ten words or phrases now part of your vocabulary that you have picked up from watching TV shows, not from ads.

6. Now list ten lines or slogans from commercials, such as "Can we play Atari today?" or "ring around the collar." Which list was easiest to produce—the one you were asked to do in question 5 or this one? If the ad slogans were easiest, why do you think they were? If not, why not?

Exercise

To test Shales's thesis of the widespread knowledge of videospeak, make a list of all his examples just from the TV industry (e.g., sitcom, instant replay, etc.) and ask five people to define each word or phrase for you. Keep an accurate record of how many times each example is accurately defined. Based on your tabulated results, judge whether or not Shales's examples were good ones, or if some were better than others. (You might also analyze the relationship between correct answers and the age/education/interests of each person interviewed.)

Exercises

1. A word frequently used for "highfalutin" language is *gobbledygook,* coined by U.S. Representative Maury Maverick (1895–1954) of Texas. Revise the following examples of gobbledygook to read as briefly and clearly as you can make them. Keep in mind the audience that each is directed to.

   a. Sign posted behind cosmetic counter of a large drugstore:

   > Before end of your shift, see that all cases of merchandise containing high unit dollar value are removed from sales area and placed in the area designated by your manager.

   b. Directions on application for check cashing card at a local liquor store:

   > Application for a check cashing card, valid for the amount of my purchase is made. It is also understood that this authorization card, if approved and issued, will be null and void if any of the information given changes before expiration date shown on check cashing authorization card, unless the change has been recorded hereon. Signatures as will be signed on checks. (If joint account, both signatures must be affixed hereto.)

   c. School board statement on budget plans to elementary schools:

   > The purchase of printed and bound instructional materials is inconsistent with the allocation of funds at this time because such materials are prioritized below other urgent needs.

   d. The conclusion reached by the National Marine Fisheries Service after tallying 500 responses to a questionnaire on changing the names of certain fish to make them more appealing:

   > A need exists for clarification and refinement of policies and procedures that govern the nomenclature of fish and fishery products for purposes of marketing and labeling of these products.

   e. Opening paragraph from a pamphlet advertising *est* training (even the editors are at a loss with this one):

   > The *est* training is a 60-hour educational experience which creates an opportunity for people to realize their potential to transform the quality of their lives. It is about an expansion of that area of life called aliveness—an expansion of the experience of happiness, love, health, and full self-expression.

2. We see the sign "Credit Terms Available" prominently displayed in stores, but have you ever tried to read *and* understand those terms? Below is an example of a credit-card agreement in gobbledygook followed by a revision in plain English.

> The Purchases Finance Charge Balance is an average daily balance determined by adding the outstanding principal balance of "Purchases Subject to Finance Charge" on each day of the Billing Cycle (after applying Debits and Credits posted that day), and dividing the total by the Number of Days in Billing Cycle. "Purchases Subject to Finance Charge" are all Purchases, from the date they are posted to the account, with the exception of any New Purchases posted during a Billing Cycle when either (i) the Previous Balance for the Billing Cycle is zero, or (ii) the total Payments or other Credits posted during that Billing Cycle are equal to or greater than the Previous Balance for that Billing Cycle. The FINANCE CHARGE at periodic rate for Purchases is computed by (i) multiplying each portion of the Purchases Finance Charge Balance shown on the face of the statement by the Number of Days In Billing Cycle, (ii) applying to the resulting products the applicable daily periodic rate of .04109%, (iii) adding these products together. The ANNUAL PERCENTAGE RATE is 15% (Minimum Finance Charge $.50).
>
> —*Northeastern Bank Master Charge Agreement*

> The "purchases finance charge balance" is an average daily balance. It is determined by dividing the total balance by the number of days in the billing cycle. All purchases are subject to finance charge, unless the previous bill was paid in full. The finance charge is computed by multiplying the average daily balance by the number of days in the billing cycle, then multiplying that number by .04109%. The annual percentage rate is 15% (Minimum Finance Charge 50 cents).
>
> —*Translation, approved by assistant vice president Donald Vermilya*

List the most obvious differences between the original and the revision. List the missing information. Is the revision missing essential information? Does the revision contain any ambiguities? Which version would you prefer to sign?

Look at the credit-card agreements issued by the companies that you have credit with. Are they written in gobbledygook? Bring an example of one to class.

3. When writers combine polite phrases (euphemisms), specialized terms (jargon), and inflated wordiness (gobbledygook), the result is *doublespeak.* While euphemisms and jargon have appropriate uses, doublespeak is a term invariably used judgmentally. Since 1971 the National Council of Teachers of English has presented an annual doublespeak award for a public statement considered offensive because it obscures in unacceptable ways. Three of the award-winning statements are listed below. What is offensive about the statements? Is the public likely to be deceived by them? Are these dangerous deceptions?

1975
Yasir Arafat's reply to an Israeli charge that the Palestinian Liberation Organization wants to destroy Israel: "They are wrong. We do not want to destroy my people. It is precisely because we have been advocating coexistence that we have already shed so much blood."

1976
Announcement from the State Department that said a certain coordinator would "review existing mechanisms of consumer input, thruput, and output and seek ways of improving these linkages via the consumer consumption channel."

1977
Pentagon's description of the neutron bomb (which kills every living creature within its reach but leaves physical structures unharmed) as "a radiation enhancement weapon."

4. The "Guess What" Game
   a. Write a paragraph that describes a familiar place or landmark on your campus using "highfalutin" language. Do not include the name of the spot in your paragraph.
      Rules for "highfalutin" language:
      1. Use "shun" words (words ending in *tion*) whenever possible. Example: *explanation of* for *explain*
      2. Use passive verbs instead of active ones.
         Example: I gave my name to the operator. (active)
         My name was given to the operator by me. (passive)
      3. Use many meaningless qualifiers. Example: He *rather* likes baseball. The weather is *somewhat* cool.
      4. Use vague nouns and abstract phrases. See the excerpt from the *est* pamphlet in 1e above for an example.
      5. Use euphemisms or words with a positive connotation in place of plain words. Exchange your description with a classmate's and guess what is being described.
   b. Revise your paragraph to eliminate the jargon.
5. The following paragraph is one college instructor's parody of jargon that relates a situation in "highfalutin" language. Underline the jargon and then translate it into plain English. Rewrite the paragraph using your simpler, more familiar terms.

Upon arrival at the local two-year institution of higher learning, I positioned my previously-owned Datsun in the vehicular stasis accommodator. Once inside the building, I took notice of two educators standing near the maintenance supply enclosure discussing their minimal remunerative increments. I entered the participative recitation station, opened my portable document container and removed my educational materials. The educator then entered the station and indicated that we were to be administered a brief evaluative instrument. "Oh no!" I indicated to myself; I had neglected to complete the assigned module. To make matters worse, my pen lacked a sufficient quantity of liquid graphic medium! My cognitive faculties in a state of disruption, I exited the aforementioned station. The interior pedestrian transit complex seemed deserted. After momentary utilization of the thirst abatement station and the male purification facility, I negotiated the sidewalk and located my vehicle. How was I going to indicate to my primary influential factors that my grade on the aforementioned brief evaluative instrument was, no doubt, going to be an ultimate negative academic evaluation symbol?

Compare the number of words in your revision with the number in the original paragraph. Were you able to reduce it by half?

Writing Assignments

1. Choose a service profession or job that requires effective communication with the public and write a paper that explains why the language people in this profession use makes working with them difficult or upsetting. You might consider the trouble you have had discussing problems with automobile mechanics, doctors, teachers, or lawyers.
2. Write a paper describing a particular jargon that you are familiar with, such as the language of CB radios, sports (or one sport), or fast food restaurants, and defend its usefulness. Include as many examples of the jargon as you can.
3. In our democratic society education is considered the great leveler of social and economic classes. Make a study of the language used by educators in their efforts to ignore or camouflage individual differences among students. Consider such words as *exceptional* (in reference to both the superior and the weak student), *self-paced* (in reference to course design), and *special* (in reference to all types of educational programs, especially those for the emotionally or physically disabled). Write a paper that
   a. analyzes the possible or real effects on society of educational jargon that minimizes differences among students;
   b. discusses the reasons why this particular jargon came into use in the mid to late 1960s.

CHAPTER 6

"Your Honor, after the trial will it be possible to purchase items from the exhibit table?"

Subtle—and Not So Subtle—Stereotyping and Prejudice

GETTING STARTED: Testing Your Human-Rights Quotient

Examine the following list of human rights. How many can you honestly say you grant yourself? How many do you grant all other human beings? If there are any you think you don't deserve, ask yourself why. If there are any you deny to particular groups—males or females, ethnic or racial minorities, young or old, employers or employees—try to specify the reasons for your prejudices.

1. The right to the same fair treatment as any other human being
2. The right to be listened to, taken seriously, and treated courteously, even by experts
3. The right to seek information from professionals or people in authority
4. The right to set your own goals and decide how to spend your time
5. The right to ask for what you want while accepting the right of others to refuse
6. The right to be independent or "different," as defined by others
7. The right to be assertive sometimes and conciliatory or supportive other times without having to justify your choices to yourself or to any person, group, or standard
8. The right to be honest with yourself, to change your mind, to reverse your position, and to say no without feeling guilty
9. The right to be talkative without being considered gossipy, quiet without being considered dumb, angry without being considered hysterical, strong without being considered tough, assertive without being considered pushy

The Language of Prejudice

Stephen Steinberg

A professor in the Department of Urban Studies at Queens College, Stephen Steinberg (b. 1940) is a research sociologist and author of books on prejudice and ethnic issues, including *The Ethnic Myth: Race, Ethnicity and Class in America* (1981). This essay appeared in February 1971 in *Today's Education,* a journal of the National Education Association.

Steinberg explores the process of acquiring the language of prejudice and the power of abusive language. He also demonstrates the effect of education on prejudice.

1 Prejudice in some ways resembles language. *Kike, dago, nigger,* and *wetback* are all part of the graceless vocabulary of prejudice. They differ from *Jew, Italian, Black,* and *Mexican* in that they convey meanings and images that disparage these groups and imply contempt. When blacks repudiate the use of the word *Negro,* they are attempting to leave behind the connotations of submissiveness and dependency this word can imply.

2 Like language, prejudice has a syntax—a system of rules—that designates which adjectives can properly be attached to which social groups. *Primitive, lazy,* and *immoral* are typically applied to blacks, not to Jews. Instead, Jews are identified as *rich, unethical, clannish;* Italians as *greasy* or *impulsive;* Poles as *dumb;* Mexicans as *shiftless;* Japanese as *sneaky;* Catholics as *priest-ridden* and *superstitious;* women as *passive, emotional,* and *incompetent.*

3 One of the lesser inequities of prejudice is that the dominant group is rarely subjected to the same abusive characterization. It is not difficult to understand why this is so. The dominant group is able to set the standards of what is worthy and respectable in physical appearance, cultural values, and social behavior. Unsurprisingly, it chooses the styles of its own group, so defined that they can only be imperfectly approximated by members of other groups. The clearest example is the high value that has been placed on white skin, which automatically diminishes the prestige and life chances of large groups and entire cultures.

4 It is perhaps a feature of cultural domination that the stereotypes minorities create of the dominant group typically make reference to their own victimization. Thus whites or white Christians (depending on who is making the judgment) are seen as *insensitive, bigoted, exploitative,* and *cruel.* In a society such as ours, where prejudice has deep roots in history and culture, hardly any group escapes negative stereotyping, and few individuals are unburdened by prejudiced attitudes toward groups other than their own.

5 The old refrain that "sticks and stones can break my bones, but names can never hurt me" is true only in part. There are few people whose psychological armor is so sturdy that they do not feel wounded by unkind words, let alone a steady flow of derogatory language. However, prejudice is not just a social grammar, a way of talking about cultural minorities. The behavioral expressions of prejudice, and the many forms of discrimination practiced against minority groups, are even more damaging.

6 The consequences of prejudice and discrimination are all too evident. Most of our nation's minorities live in distressing social conditions,

while the majority enjoys relative security and affluence. Others, like Jews, who have managed to bypass or overcome many of the discriminatory barriers once confronting them, are still excluded from major areas of economic activity and are still stigmatized as socially undesirable. For members of victimized groups, the result is diminished self-esteem and a defensive withdrawal within one's self or one's own group. For society as a whole, the result is intense social conflict and loss of civic unity. Like other kinds of verbal abuse, the language of prejudice carries a heavy price.

7 The most important similarity between prejudice and language is that prejudice is typically acquired as easily, and in much the same way, as language itself. From an early age, children hear the adjective *lazy* attached to blacks, *shady* to Jews, *emotional* to women—just as they learn that men are *strong,* flowers are *beautiful,* and a particular laundry soap leaves clothes *dazzling.*

8 Once these images are adopted, they operate as filters on the individual's perception and understanding of the world around him. Should he encounter a black who appears lazy, he interprets this as confirming the stereotype. At the same time, he filters out all those cases that contradict the stereotype. Since our society has no image of whites as lazy, the unambitious white, like the industrious black, receives little notice. This self-confirming mechanism is part of the reason people cling to their prejudices with so much conviction.

9 Another reason is that prejudiced beliefs sometimes succeed in producing the very social conditions assumed by those beliefs. Every teacher knows that high expectations and encouragement can bring out the best in children and spur them on to higher levels of performance.

10 Low expectations and unsupportive attitudes generally have the opposite result. For example, as an experiment, teachers were assigned a group of minority children with average IQ scores but were told that the children were underachievers with high aptitude. These children subsequently showed far greater improvement on objective tests than did those in a control group where teachers were not given an overgenerous estimate of the students' capacities.

11 In the same way, when a society fosters the image of women as incompetent (outside the home, of course), and if women have little opportunity to develop and exercise their talents, it is hardly surprising that in many cases the stereotype will be fulfilled. Every instance of incompetence is then used as evidence of the original stereotype. In this way, the language of prejudice becomes self-fulfilling and self-justifying.

12 Despite the intense racial conflict of the past decade, in some respects an improved climate of tolerance has developed in the nation, at least in comparison to the first half of the century. This is most clearly the case in the official sphere of our society. Governing agencies, courts, the

mass media, and many public officials have gone on record, in word if not in deed, against racism and prejudice. Partly as a result, there has been a decline in some of the more blatant forms of discrimination prevailing in earlier decades.

13 A well-established proposition in sociology states that such changes in the official society will inevitably produce changes in popular attitudes, though there is apt to be a lag between the two. This was the rationale of the population survey that Gertrude Selznick and I conducted in late 1964.[1] Based on a nationally representative sample, the study sought to assess the extent and sources of contemporary anti-Semitism. We also examined other forms of intolerance that are part and parcel of anti-Jewish prejudice.

14 A few of our findings are presented in the accompanying table (see page 281). The column on the extreme right shows the proportion of the national sample that gave intolerant responses to various questions. The center of the table shows the breakdown by amount of education. For example, 12 percent of the sample said that Jews have too much power in the United States, and this figure varied from 18 percent among those with only a grade school education to 5 percent among college graduates.

15 This question on Jewish power again illustrates the similarity between prejudice and language. The late 1930's and early 1940's saw an upsurge of anti-Semitic propaganda, and the connection between *power* and *Jew* was a regular occurrence. Public acceptance of this characterization in this country reached alarming proportions.

16 A 1938 national poll reported that 41 percent thought Jews had too much power in the United States. This figure steadily increased during the war years to a peak of 58 percent in 1945. The present figure of 12 percent thus indicates great improvement. However, the lesson of the past is that even such politically dangerous beliefs are subject to precipitous change in a crisis situation.

17 Unlike the belief in Jewish power, certain economic beliefs that have always been at the heart of anti-Semitism have hardly declined. For example, 42 percent of our sample accepted the characterization of Jews as prone to shady practices, and 28 percent disagreed that "Jews are just as honest as other businessmen." These figures are not very different from those reported in polls during the 1950's. Even the old canard about Jewish control of international banking is still held by a fourth of the population.

[1]The findings are reported in *The Tenacity of Prejudice: Anti-Semitism in Contemporary America* by Gertrude J. Selznick and Stephen Steinberg. (Harper, 1969.) Much of the substance of this paper derives from the larger study, which was conducted under a grant from the Anti-Defamation League.

18 A major conclusion of our study was that at least a third of the adult population show definite signs of anti-Semitic prejudice. Many others, while not themselves prejudiced, are willing to acquiesce in or condone the prejudice of others.

19 The basic finding concerning anti-Negro prejudice is much the same. Comparisons with past surveys indicate a rather steady decline in certain beliefs, but there still remains a sizable amount of prejudice.

20 As the table shows, in the nation as a whole, 19 percent believe that blacks have lower intellectual capabilities than whites; 38 percent favor separate schools for blacks and whites; and 40 percent agree that Negroes are lazy and don't like to work hard. In both the North and South, these figures represent improvement over times past. But past levels of prejudice were so high that, despite steady improvement for over two decades, there is still a very long way to go before either anti-Semitism or anti-Negro prejudice can be said to be vanishing.

21 As with blacks and Jews, our society has a stereotype of teachers, with the important exception that it is favorable in most respects and leads to respectful rather than unequal and exploitative relationships. Teachers are *dedicated, conscientious, correct* in appearance, and *devout* in spirit. Nonconformity to this image arouses intolerant attitudes. When our 1964 sample was asked whether persons with beards should be allowed to teach in the schools, one in every four answered "no." When the same question was asked about persons who did not believe in God, 60 percent said they would bar such people from the classroom.

22 The last two items in the table deal with foreigners. Despite the legendary image of America as a "nation of immigrants," about one quarter of our sample denied that "America owes a great deal to the immigrants who came here." And 70 percent went along with the statement that "nothing in other countries can beat the American way of life." Xenophobia, provincialism, intolerance of nonconformity, antiintellectualism—these are the cousins of the kinds of prejudices directed against specific groups.

23 Each of the items listed in the table measures the extent to which people tolerate one or another kind of social diversity: Jews, blacks, atheists, foreigners, people with beards. All but one is strongly and systematically related to education. No matter what the specific content of the item, the more educated tend to be tolerant in their attitudes; the less educated, to be intolerant.

24 This leads to two conclusions: First, prejudice tends to come in bundles. Few people are prejudiced against just one group. For example, those who are prejudiced against blacks also tend to be prejudiced against Jews, and those who are prejudiced against Jews tend to discriminate against bearded teachers.

PERCENT AT EACH EDUCATIONAL LEVEL WHO GIVE INTOLERANT ANSWERS TO QUESTIONS DEALING WITH SOCIAL AND CULTURAL DIVERSITY

(Based on a 1964 National Sample of Adults)

Amount of Education	*Grade School*	*High School*	*Some College*	*College Graduates*	*Total*
Do you think Jews have too much power in the United States? (yes)	18%	10%	4%	5%	12%
Jews are just as honest as other businessmen (disagree)	34%	28%	24%	14%	28%
Jews are more willing than others to use shady practices to get what they want (agree)	54%	42%	36%	21%	42%
In general, do you think that Negroes are as intelligent as white people—that is, can they learn things just as well if they are given the same education and training? (no)	21%	18%	22%	16%	19%
Do you think white children and Negro children should go to the same schools or to separate but equal schools? (separate)	55%	38%	24%	17%	38%
Generally speaking, Negroes are lazy and don't like to work hard (agree)	49%	41%	31%	23%	40%
Persons who insist on wearing beards should not be allowed to teach in public schools (agree)	39%	23%	16%	12%	25%
Suppose a man admitted in public that he did not believe in God. Should he be allowed to teach in a public high school? (no)	78%	58%	46%	38%	60%
America owes a great deal to the immigrants who came here (disagree)	30%	26%	16%	12%	24%
Nothing in other countries can beat the American way of life (agree)	86%	71%	54%	41%	70%

25 The bigot always pleads he is not prejudiced, but is responding to actual traits of the groups in question. This defense is rendered suspect when he exhibits a pattern of intolerance against virtually everything outside a narrow range of acceptability.

26 A second conclusion is that the tendency to tolerate differences is acquired with greater education. This finding challenges the theory that

the capacity for tolerance or intolerance is primarily a matter of personality, inalterably laid down in early childhood. As teachers know firsthand, the educational process can modify and counteract social influences and personality factors conducive to prejudice. Education does so by providing people with moral and intellectual criteria for evaluating and rejecting the beliefs in their environment.

27 Some of these criteria are scientific; many prejudiced beliefs can be shown to be overgeneralized, inaccurate, or untrue. Until very recently, racial theories that explained social differences between groups in terms of biological or genetic factors were almost universally accepted. Today they are regarded as the folklore of a prescientific age. Social science, through its improved understanding of social and psychological processes, has also debunked many racial theories.

28 Other criteria for rejecting prejudice involve democratic principles. People are better equipped to reject prejudice if they understand that in a democracy certain rights are guaranteed to all, and that inequality of wealth and power, while not itself incompatible with democracy, cannot be so great as to result in the subordination of some groups to others. Indeed, our study showed that persons with greater knowledge and understanding of the Constitution were less prejudiced as a result.

29 Finally, there are humanitarian reasons for rejecting prejudice—especially when its consequences are considered. The net effect of prejudice is to diminish the humanity of the prejudiced and their victims alike.

Scientific, democratic, and humanitarian principles are unfortunately not part of man's natural endowment, but rather the products of advanced civilization. They are subtle and complex principles, and, if only for this reason, the task of transmitting them falls largely on educational institutions.

30 The figures in the table testify to both the success and failure of these institutions. To the extent that open-mindedness, tolerance, and respect for civil liberties increase with greater education, the schools are succeeding in their educational functions. To the extent that students leave schools with prejudiced attitudes toward the nation's minorities, with little patience for social and intellectual diversity, and with little understanding or respect for the democratic process, the schools are failing.

31 Other studies show that the schools are rife with the same intolerant and provincial attitudes which exist in society as a whole. Of course, it is not the fault of the schools that students mirror the prejudices found elsewhere in society. But it *is* the schools' responsibility to alter that situation by seeing that their graduates have the intellectual and moral sophistication to reject vulgar prejudices and other such retrograde belief systems. The nation's legal and political institutions can do a great deal to combat discrimination and remedy some of the tragic social conditions that result. But the schools are practically the only institutions in our society equipped to counteract prejudices in our culture.

32 To avoid this responsibility would indicate not just a moral failure, but an educational failure as well.

Word Study List

connotations	1	xenophobia	22
syntax	2	provincialism	22
stereotypes	4, 8, 11, 21	bigot	25
derogatory	5	genetic	27
stigmatized	6	debunked	27
canard	17	humanitarian	29
conscientious	21	retrograde	31

Questions

1. Who is Steinberg's audience? (Look at the introductory note.) If you did not know that the article was printed in a journal for teachers, at what point in your reading might you guess that Steinberg is writing to teachers? For what other audience might this article be appropriate?

2. How, according to Steinberg, are prejudice and language similar?

3. How do our perceptions help to maintain and reinforce prejudice? What role does stereotyping play in shaping and maintaining prejudice?

4. Steinberg's article is clearly organized, dividing into several subsections. List the main points, or subtopics, in the order in which they are discussed. What are the connections between subtopics? Do you see a logical progression developing as Steinberg moves from the language of prejudice to results of surveys of prejudice to the role of education?

5. Were you aware that "prejudice tends to come in bundles"? Think of people you know who are intolerant. How many groups are they intolerant of? To what degree does your experience coincide with the survey results?

6. What three kinds of reasons for rejecting prejudice does Steinberg give? Are better-educated people less prejudiced because they know these reasons or criteria for rejecting prejudice?

7. Think about your education to date. To what degree have schools given you scientific, democratic, and humanitarian principles for rejecting prejudice? Would you conclude that a high school education prepares one for tolerance? Or do most people need a college education to reject prejudice?

Exercise

Consider: Are there new prejudices that some college-educated people might develop even though they reject the more widespread prejudices against minority groups and women? Make a list of groups or personality types that college-educated people might develop prejudices against. Compare your list with those of classmates. Take a poll in class to see which of the prejudices listed are already held by college students.

You Are What You Say

Robin Lakoff

A Harvard Ph.D. and professor of English at Berkeley, Robin Lakoff (b. 1942) has turned her interest from formal linguistics to the study of how language is used in practical situations. Lakoff has written *Language and Women's Place* (1975), a fuller treatment of the following article that appeared in the July 1974 issue of *Ms.* magazine.

In this article Lakoff illustrates characteristics of women's talk, examines derogatory ways of referring to women, and calls for change.

1 "Women's language" is that pleasant (dainty?), euphemistic, never-aggressive way of talking we learned as little girls. Cultural bias was built into the language we were allowed to speak, the subjects we were allowed to speak about, and the ways we were spoken of. Having learned our linguistic lesson well, we go out in the world, only to discover that we are communicative cripples—damned if we do, and damned if we don't.

2 If we refuse to talk "like a lady," we are ridiculed and criticized for being unfeminine. ("She thinks like a man" is, at best, a left-handed compliment.) If we do learn all the fuzzy-headed, unassertive language of our sex, we are ridiculed for being unable to think clearly, unable to take part in a serious discussion, and therefore unfit to hold a position of power.

3 It doesn't take much of this for a woman to begin feeling she deserves such treatment because of inadequacies in her own intelligence and education.

4 "Women's language" shows up in all levels of English. For example, women are encouraged and allowed to make far more precise discriminations in naming colors than men do. Words like *mauve, beige, ecru, aquamarine, lavender,* and so on, are unremarkable in a woman's active vocabulary, but largely absent from that of most men. I know of no evidence suggesting that women actually *see* a wider range of colors than men do. It is simply that fine discriminations of this sort are relevant to women's

vocabularies, but not to men's; to men, who control most of the interesting affairs of the world, such distinctions are trivial—irrelevant.

5 In the area of syntax, we find similar gender-related peculiarities of speech. There is one construction, in particular, that women use conversationally far more than men: the tag-question. A tag is midway between an outright statement and a yes-no question; it is less assertive than the former, but more confident than the latter.

6 A *flat statement* indicates confidence in the speaker's knowledge and is fairly certain to be believed; a *question* indicates a lack of knowledge on some point and implies that the gap in the speaker's knowledge can and will be remedied by an answer. For example, if, at a Little League game, I have had my glasses off, I can legitimately ask someone else: "Was the player out at third?" A *tag question,* being intermediate between statement and question, is used when the speaker is stating a claim, but lacks full confidence in the truth of that claim. So if I say, "Is Joan here?" I will probably not be surprised if my respondent answers "no"; but if I say, "Joan is here, isn't she?" instead, chances are I am already biased in favor of a positive answer, wanting only confirmation. I still want a response, but I have enough knowledge (or think I have) to predict that response. A tag question, then, might be thought of as a statement that doesn't demand to be believed by anyone but the speaker, a way of giving leeway, of not forcing the addressee to go along with the views of the speaker.

7 Another common use of the tag-question is in small talk when the speaker is trying to elicit conversation: "Sure is hot here, isn't it?"

8 But in discussing personal feelings or opinions, only the speaker normally has any way of knowing the correct answer. Sentences such as "I have a headache, don't I?" are clearly ridiculous. But there are other examples where it is the speaker's opinions, rather than perceptions, for which corroboration is sought, as in "The situation in Southeast Asia is terrible, isn't it?"

9 While there are, of course, other possible interpretations of a sentence like this, one possibility is that the speaker has a particular answer in mind—"yes" or "no"—but is reluctant to state it baldly. This sort of tag question is much more apt to be used by women than by men in conversation. Why is this the case?

10 The tag question allows a speaker to avoid commitment, and thereby avoid conflict with the addressee. The problem is that, by so doing, speakers may also give the impression of not really being sure of themselves, or looking to the addressee for confirmation of their views. This uncertainty is reinforced in more subliminal ways, too. There is a peculiar sentence intonation-pattern, used almost exclusively by women, as far as I know, which changes a declarative answer into a question. The effect of using the rising inflection typical of a yes-no question is to imply that the speaker is seeking confirmation, even though the speaker is clearly the

only one who has the requisite information, which is why the question was put to her in the first place:

(Q) When will dinner be ready?

(A) Oh . . . around six o'clock . . . ?

It is as though the second speaker were saying, "Six o'clock—if that's okay with you, if you agree." The person being addressed is put in the position of having to provide confirmation. One likely consequence of this sort of speech-pattern in a woman is that, often unbeknownst to herself, the speaker builds a reputation of tentativeness, and others will refrain from taking her seriously or trusting her with any real responsibilities, since she "can't make up her mind," and "isn't sure of herself."

11 Such idiosyncrasies may explain why women's language sounds much more "polite" than men's. It is polite to leave a decision open, not impose your mind, or views, or claims, on anyone else. So a tag-question is a kind of polite statement, in that it does not force agreement or belief on the addressee. In the same way a request is a polite command, in that it does not force obedience on the addressee, but rather suggests something be done as a favor to the speaker. A clearly stated order implies a threat of certain consequences if it is not followed, and—even more impolite—implies that the speaker is in a superior position and able to enforce the order. By couching wishes in the form of a request, on the other hand, a speaker implies that if the request is not carried out, only the speaker will suffer; noncompliance cannot harm the addressee. So the decision is really left up to the addressee. The distinction becomes clear in these examples:

Close the door.
Please close the door.
Will you close the door?
Will you please close the door?
Won't you close the door?

12 In the same ways as words and speech patterns used *by* women undermine her image, those used *to describe* women make matters even worse. Often a word may be used of both men and women (and perhaps of things as well); but when it is applied to women, it assumes a special meaning that, by implication rather than outright assertion, is derogatory to women as a group.

13 The use of euphemisms has this effect. A euphemism is a substitute for a word that has acquired a bad connotation by association with something unpleasant or embarrassing. But almost as soon as the new word

comes into common usage, it takes on the same old bad connotations, since feelings about the things or people referred to are not altered by a change of name; thus new euphemisms must be constantly found.

14 There is one euphemism for *woman* still very much alive. The word, of course is *lady*. *Lady* has a masculine counterpart, namely *gentleman,* occasionally shortened to *gent*. But for some reason *lady* is very much commoner than *gent(leman)*.

15 The decision to use *lady* rather than *woman,* or vice versa, may considerably alter the sense of a sentence, as the following examples show:

(a) A woman (lady) I know is a dean at Berkeley.
(b) A woman (lady) I know makes amazing things out of shoelaces and old boxes.

16 The use of *lady* in (a) imparts a frivolous, or nonserious, tone to the sentence: the matter under discussion is not one of great moment. Similarly, in (b), using *lady* here would suggest that the speaker considered the "amazing things" not to be serious art, but merely a hobby or an aberration. If *woman* is used, she might be a serious sculptor. To say *lady doctor* is very condescending, since no one ever says *gentleman doctor* or even *man doctor*. For example, mention in the San Francisco *Chronicle* of January 31, 1972, of Madalyn Murray O'Hair as the *lady atheist* reduces her position to that of scatterbrained eccentric. Even *woman atheist* is scarcely defensible: sex is irrelevant to her philosophical position.

17 Many women argue that, on the other hand, *lady* carries with it overtones recalling the age of chivalry: conferring exalted stature on the person so referred to. This makes the term seem polite at first, but we must also remember that these implications are perilous: they suggest that a "lady" is helpless, and cannot do things by herself.

18 *Lady* can also be used to infer frivolousness, as in titles of organizations. Those that have a serious purpose (not merely that of enabling "the ladies" to spend time with one another) cannot use the word *lady* in their titles, but less serious ones may. Compare the *Ladies' Auxiliary* of a men's group, or the *Thursday Evening Ladies' Browning and Garden Society* with *Ladies' Liberation* or *Ladies' Strike for Peace*.

19 What is curious about this split is that *lady* is in origin a euphemism—a substitute that puts a better face on something people find uncomfortable—for *woman*. What kind of euphemism is it that subtly denigrates the people to whom it refers? Perhaps *lady* functions as a euphemism for *woman* because it does not contain the sexual implications present in *woman;* it is not "embarrassing" in that way. If this is so, we may expect that, in the future, *lady* will replace woman as the primary word for the human female, since *woman* will have become too blatantly sexual. That this distinction is already made in some contexts at least is

shown in the following examples, where you can try replacing *woman* with *lady:*

(a) She's only twelve, but she's already a woman.
(b) After ten years in jail, Harry wanted to find a woman.
(c) She's my woman, see, so don't mess around with her.

20 Another common substitute for *woman* is *girl.* One seldom hears a man past the age of adolescence referred to as a boy, save in expressions like "going out with the boys," which are meant to suggest an air of adolescent frivolity and irresponsibility. But women of all ages are "girls": one can have a man—not a boy—Friday, but only a girl—never a woman or even a lady—Friday; women have girlfriends, but men do not—in a nonsexual sense—have boyfriends. It may be that this use of *girl* is euphemistic in the same way the use of *lady* is: in stressing the idea of immaturity, it removes the sexual connotations lurking in *woman. Girl* brings to mind irresponsibility: you don't send a girl to do a woman's errand (or even, for that matter, a boy's errand). She is a person who is both too immature and too far from real life to be entrusted with responsibilities or with decisions of any serious or important nature.

21 Now let's take a pair of words which, in terms of the possible relationships in an earlier society, were simple male-female equivalents, analogous to *bull:cow.* Suppose we find that, for independent reasons, society has changed in such a way that the original meanings now are irrelevant. Yet the words have not been discarded, but have acquired new meanings, metaphorically related to their original senses. But suppose these new metaphorical uses are no longer parallel to each other. By seeing where the parallelism breaks down, we discover something about the different roles played by men and women in this culture. One good example of such a divergence through time is found in the pair, *master:mistress.* Once used with reference to one's power over servants, these words have become unusable today in their original master-servant sense as the relationship has become less prevalent in our society. But the words are still common.

22 Unless used with reference to animals, *master* now generally refers to a man who has acquired consummate ability in some field, normally nonsexual. But its feminine counterpart cannot be used this way. It is practically restricted to its sexual sense of "paramour." We start out with two terms, both roughly paraphrasable as "one who has power over another." But the masculine form, once one person is no longer able to have absolute power over another, becomes usable metaphorically in the sense of "having power over *something.*" *Master* requires as its object only the name of some activity, something inanimate and abstract. But *mistress* requires a masculine noun in the possessive to precede it. One cannot say: "Rhonda is a mistress." One must be *someone's* mistress. A man is defined

by what he does, a woman by her sexuality, that is, in terms of one particular aspect of her relationship to men. It is one thing to be an *old master* like Hans Holbein, and another to be an *old mistress*.

23 The same is true of the words *spinster* and *bachelor*—gender words for "one who is not married." The resemblance ends with the definition. While *bachelor* is a neuter term, often used as a compliment, *spinster* normally is used pejoratively, with connotations of prissiness, fussiness, and so on. To be a bachelor implies that one has the choice of marrying or not, and this is what makes the idea of a bachelor existence attractive, in the popular literature. He has been pursued and has successfully eluded his pursuers. But a spinster is one who has not been pursued, or at least not seriously. She is old, unwanted goods. The metaphorical connotations of *bachelor* generally suggest sexual freedom; of *spinster*, puritanism or celibacy.

24 These examples could be multiplied. It is generally considered a *faux pas*, in society, to congratulate a woman on her engagement, while it is correct to congratulate her fiancé. Why is this? The reason seems to be that it is impolite to remind people of things that may be uncomfortable to them. To congratulate a woman on her engagement is really to say, "Thank goodness! You had a close call!" For the man, on the other hand, there was no such danger. His choosing to marry is viewed as a good thing, but not something essential.

25 The linguistic double standard holds throughout the life of the relationship. After marriage, bachelor and spinster become man and wife, not man and woman. The woman whose husband dies remains "John's widow"; John, however, is never "Mary's widower."

26 Finally, why is it that salesclerks and others are so quick to call women customers "dear," "honey," and other terms of endearment they really have no business using? A male customer would never put up with it. But women, like children, are supposed to enjoy these endearments, rather than being offended by them.

27 In more ways than one, it's time to speak up.

Word Study List

euphemistic	1	aberration	16
linguistic	1, 25	perilous	17
syntax	5	denigrates	19
corroboration	8	blatantly	19
subliminal	10	analogous	21
requisite	10	divergence	21
unbeknownst	10	pejoratively	23
idiosyncrasies	11	puritanism	23
derogatory	12	*faux pas*	24

Questions

1. Lakoff begins by asserting that women are in a linguistic no-win situation. Explain their problem in your own words.

2. List the words and speech patterns typically used by women that hurt a woman's image.

3. List the words and speech patterns that are derogatory to women.

4. To generalize from Lakoff's examples, what traits and characteristics of women are implied by the ways they speak? By the ways they are spoken of?

5. What is Lakoff's attitude toward sexist language? How do you know?

6. If you are a woman, how accurately has Lakoff described the way you speak? (How many of you are surprised to be addressed as a *woman* rather than *girl?*) Do you—man or woman—use sexist language to refer to women? Many people today are careful to avoid sexist language. Are you more aware of your speech habits now than, say, five years ago?

Exercise

Make a conscious effort, for a few days, to listen to the language of women and then list examples of women's speech to add to Lakoff's. Include both words and speech patterns or intonations (e.g., "The baby's *so* (special emphasis) cute!"). Compare your list with classmates.

The Desexing of English

Sol Steinmetz

Born in Czechoslovakia and now a United States citizen, Sol Steinmetz (b. 1930) has been a lexicographer since 1957. He has edited several dictionaries, including the *World Book Dictionary* and the *Barnhart Dictionary of New English.* His most recent work is *Yiddish and English: A Century of Yiddish in America* (1985). This article appeared in the *New York Times Magazine* on April 1, 1982.

Documenting his point with examples, Steinmetz argues that the campaign against sexist language has been successful.

1 After a dozen years of aggressive campaigning by the women's-rights movement to purge the English language of sexism, the time has surely come to ask whether its crusade has been successful. From the start, resistance to the campaign was surprisingly mild, confined mainly to facetious comments in the press on the proliferation of "person" compounds (chairperson, spokesperson) and the elimination of "man" in occupational titles (camera operator, mail carrier). But despite frequent references to these developments in the popular press, one vainly looks in recent books on language for a serious discussion of the subject. (A book that specifically addresses this subject is "Words and Women" by Casey Miller and Kate Swift, which was published in 1977.)

2 To take one example, in Jim Quinn's "American Tongue and Cheek: A Populist Guide to Our Language" (1981), a provocative book that lays to rest many a myth about English grammar, a full chapter is devoted to "Language Changers," people such as ghetto blacks, teen-agers and influential intellectuals whose speech and writings leave their stamp on the language. Yet in this chapter, and for that matter in the entire book, no mention is made of the influence on language of the antisexist movement. I could list at least six other recent books on language whose authors are guilty of the same omission. The authors, incidentally, are all males and I leave it to the reader to draw his or her own conclusions.

3 Note that I have just used "his or her." My choice of this phrase to avoid using the so-called generic pronoun "his" is directly due to the influence of the antisexist campaign. My study of new usages during the past 10 years has convinced me that a good many similar changes have made their way into the writing and speech of many Americans. The changes have been wide-ranging, affecting not only our stock of common words but such diverse areas of language as forms of address, proper names, phrases and idioms, word endings and grammatical constructions.

4 Writers, editors and educators in particular have become acutely self-conscious about using words and phrases implying sexual bias. Their consciousness, to use a phrase introduced by the feminists, has been raised. In the introduction to a 1979 book on words and their misuse, the writer William Woolfolk laments that there is no appropriate formal salutation in English for a letter addressed to both a man and a woman. He toys with "Dear Gentlepeople" and "Dear Gentlepersons," but cannot get himself to use either. Then he recalls that we also don't have a word for "his or her" or for "brothers and sisters together" (he considers "siblings" inadequate). For him and many others, there are suddenly pitfalls everywhere: Should one use "housewife" or the less natural "homemaker"? Will "actor" do the service of "actress," and "hero" that of "heroine"? Is it all right to use the awkward "humankind" in place of "mankind"?

5 Guidelines issued by various groups to promote nonsexist usage

make the going tougher by proposing alternatives like "of human origin" or "synthetic" to replace "man-made," and urging the abolition of certain emotionally loaded words such as "womanish," effeminate," "manly" and "man-size." For the benefit of people like Mr. Woolfolk, Webster's Secretarial Handbook (1976) lists "Dear People" and "Dear Sir, Madam, or Ms." as possible nonsexist letter salutations for groups that include men and women.

6 But there is more. The Government's Dictionary of Occupational Titles (1977) has purged itself of all "sex and age-referent language and job titles considered to be potentially discriminatory." You won't find in it such homely old words as "shoeshine boy" (now "shoeshiner"), "bellboy" (now only "bellhop"), "cleaning woman" (now "cleaner"), "washerwoman" or "laundress" (now "laundry worker"), to mention a few. Not to be outdone, the General Accounting Office Thesaurus (1978) has replaced "manned undersea research" with "oceanographic research" and "manpower management" with "personnel management," among others.

7 While in the 1970's cyclones were still designated by female names (Hurricane Edith, Typhoon Hester), by 1980 alternating male and female names became the standard (Hurricane Frederic, Typhoon Judy). And in 1980, in an editorial entitled "Gender Justice," The New York Times congratulated the members of the Supreme Court for dropping the title "Mr. Justice" from their orders and opinions and adopting the unadorned title "Justice So-and-So." Of course, they will no longer be called "the Brethren."

8 Opponents of such deliberate tampering with the language—liberals and conservatives alike—might well argue that by allowing this to happen we are in effect exchanging one set of taboos for another. For even as books, periodicals and dictionaries (not all, to be sure) are liberally opening their pages to obscenities and vulgarisms, they are unliberally leaning over backward to ostracize all usage deemed offensive to the sexes. Some might call this blatant hypocrisy. Others might view it as the expression of a new morality. Yet, strangely, nary a voice is raised anywhere in either protest or praise. And this great silence seems to me to imply that the matter has been settled already in the minds of most people, and that the feminist campaign against sexism has made a triumphant breakthrough in the area of language.

9 If this is so, we are confronting for the first time since the 18th century the success of a small but vocal group of activists bent on reforming the English language. While attempts to reform English go back to the Middle Ages, no previous or subsequent reforms have matched those of the 18th century grammarians and lexicographers, who promulgated most of the rules and prescriptions that have come down to us enshrined as laws in innumerable English grammars and textbooks.

10 After this successful "fixing" of the language, further attempts at

reformation met with invariable failure. The public, resentful of extreme innovations in what it now regarded as an immutable language, rejected the simplified spelling systems widely advocated in the 19th century, just as it rejected artificial languages for international use, and even a simplified form of the English language such as Basic English.

11 How to account, then, for the success of the antisexist reforms? Part of the answer is that these reforms have been long in the making and that present social conditions merely helped to bring them to fruition. As long ago as 1858 the composer Charles Converse coined the word "thon" (a contraction of "that one") as a neuter pronoun to replace the generic "he," and this coinage was actually entered in two unabridged dictionaries: in Funk & Wagnalls in 1913; in Webster's Second Edition, 1934.

12 There have been many similar proposals since then, the latest being the orthographic "he/she," which is more widely used than is generally realized. It is also not generally known that the recently defeated equal rights amendment was first introduced in Congress in 1923, and that the title "Ms." was in use in the 1940's.

13 But the real answer might simply be that the feminist movement's interest in language is ultimately not linguistic but moral. Its concern is not with changing the language itself, but with modifying that part of it that is discriminatory and morally offensive. The feminists' crusade appeals particularly to those who deplore and wish to eliminate other "wrong" uses of language, such as racial epithets and opprobrious terms.

14 The feminist cause also touches a responsive chord in individuals who believe, along with the American linguists Edward Sapir and Benjamin Lee Whorf, that the structure of a language influences and often shapes a person's view of reality. For them, a language that is structurally biased against one of the sexes can inflict serious psychic damage to members of that sex. This argument is as hard to prove as it is to disprove, but to many people it makes profound psychological sense.

15 Twelve years is a short time. It is too early to predict the future course of the feminist movement and its reforms. Suffice it to recognize that the antisexist movement has made remarkable inroads in the language. But even from the worm's-eye view we now possess, it seems fairly clear that the "King's English" will no longer be his exclusive domain.

Word Study List

purge	1	lexicographers	9
facetious	1	promulgated	9
proliferation	1	immutable	10
taboos	8	orthographic	12
ostracize	8	opprobrious	13
blatant	8	psychic	14

Questions

1. What is Steinmetz's subject? What changes in language use has he observed?

2. Steinmetz devotes two paragraphs to his introduction before stating his thesis in paragraph 3. You have probably learned various techniques for getting an essay started; what type of introductory technique does this writer use?

3. What groups of people, according to Steinmetz, have been most conscious of avoiding sexist language? Can you think of another group that probably should be added to Steinmetz's list, a group aware of the power of language and anxious not to offend?

4. Steinmetz, writing in 1982, describes "homemaker" as less natural than "housewife." Does "homemaker" seem less natural to you? Which do you hear more often today, "man-made" or "synthetic"? "Airline stewardess" or "flight attendant"?

5. What evidence does Steinmetz offer to demonstrate the "triumphant breakthrough" of the "campaign against sexism"?

6. How does Steinmetz account for the campaign's success in reforming English? What are the three reasons he gives? (Notice the number of writers and teachers represented in this text who believe that language shapes our perceptions of reality. Have you joined the group yet?)

Exercise

Read Robin Lakoff's "You Are What You Say" (pp. 284–289) and then, in a paragraph, explain how both Lakoff and Steinmetz can be right—that is, reconcile their positions by showing that they are not discussing exactly the same problems with sexist language.

Give Up Six Words and Change Your Life

Marian S. Burtt and George Burtt

Marian S. Burtt (b. 1930) and George Burtt (b. 1914) are counselors and freelance writers. Educated in clinical psychology, Marian Burtt is the director of counselor training at the Vector Counseling Institute in Mount Vernon, Washington. George Burtt is a minister, lecturer, founder of the Vector Counseling

Institute, and author of books and articles. This article appeared in *Glamour* in July 1979.

Providing new insights into the oppressive language of stereotyping, Burtt and Burtt examine such words as *try, always,* and *should,* words that we use to control others and limit ourselves.

1 Alfred Korzybski, the father of general semantics, observed that how we talk affects how we handle problems and how we behave. He found that scientists, trained to be specific, handled both personal and laboratory problems better than non-scientists. Non-scientists, then as now, used words loaded with feeling and prejudgment and got into trouble.

2 Changing the way we use certain everyday words can actually shift the way we see the world and other people, helps change the emotion-laden attitudes behind the words and makes us less apt to make inappropriate demands on ourselves and others.

3 There is also a change in the effect on others. Teachers, told that certain students have hidden talents, will help them develop, even if the students were selected blindly by researchers. People act as they think they have been defined, and like it or not, our words play a large part in expressing that definition.

4 In our work, we have found six words that are often used in damaging ways: *try, always, is, can't, should* and *everybody.* These words are really "families" of words. *Always* can be expanded to *never, every time. Should* is also *ought to, must, have to.* We use *nobody, no one, all,* the way we use *everybody.*

5 Each of these words is linked to the concept of *time.* "Everybody does it" implies *every person always* does it. *Should* reflects a standard adopted in the past, governing how we must always behave. *Is* implies a permanent characteristic of something or someone, as "she is impossible to deal with." Alfred Korzybski called humans "time binders": Facts, opinions and behaviors are learned, repeated and passed on, even though they may not necessarily have been true in the first place. Both Korzybski and S. I. Hayakawa, who is a respected semanticist (though better known as a senator from California), caution us against using such "allness" terms.

6 Yet we do use them, as though by doing so we could somehow manage the present and future. "With words," says Hayakawa in *Language in Thought and Action,* "we influence and to an enormous extent control." "I'll meet you at three Thursday" is an attempt to make another person—and ourselves—be at a certain place at a certain time. Hayakawa writes, "The future is a specifically human dimension. To a dog, 'hamburger tomorrow' is meaningless. With words . . . we (humans) impose a certain predictability upon future events."

7 Similarly, we attempt to control people's actions and even characteristics with *can't, should, everybody* and related words. We try thus to create "reliable" data, however unrelated it is to the facts.

8 According to Freud, to schizophrenic patients certain words become magical, symbols of whole trains of thought condensed. Seriously ill neurotics maintain some of that magic: "Everybody's against me" or "I have to do this." And nearly all of us have the same bad habit to a less intense degree.

9 When and where do we begin this pattern of restrictive words and beliefs?

10 According to the late speech pathologist Wendell Johnson, as adults we are still "using information, attitudes, beliefs, procedures, practices . . . adapted to an earlier time." Our beliefs, and the words we use to support them and to protect ourselves from change, come from early in our lives. Willis Harman, Ph.D., a futurist at SRI (formerly Stanford Research Institute), maintains that we are all in a way hypnotized from infancy. "We do not perceive ourselves and the world about us as they are, but as we have been persuaded to perceive them," says Dr. Harman. Research shows that objects and people with *some* familiar characteristics tend to be perceived by the infant as identical. The newborn cannot distinguish between self and surrounding. When the baby is hungry, everybody is hungry. Later, any man becomes "Daddy" and every animal "doggie."

11 We use such early biases to make life easy, as well as comfortable and familiar. If I adopt the belief as a child that "I am dumb," it is easier to act it out continually than to resist it—thus I unconsciously make sure it stays true.

12 Taking each family of words separately, here is what they represent and how to stop using them destructively.

13 *Try* Benjamin Keller, head of the Los Angeles branch of the Vector Counseling Institute, tells of one desperate young woman: "Her marriage wasn't going well. As she put it, 'no matter how hard I try, I just can't clean, cook and work at the same time.' She was *trying* so hard she was constantly tense and exhausted." She agreed to stop *trying* and just *do* those things the best she could. Without the inner struggle, she found that she could schedule some things, let others go, and accomplish more.

14 When we switch from *try,* which anticipates failure, to "do the best I can," we do exactly that. We could *not* have done better, or we would have. Check it out: Consciously delete *try* from your vocabulary for a month.

15 *Always* *Always* and *never* are our creations. Much more accurate are words that represent gradation, that cover a spectrum, such as *almost always, many times, frequently, not often, hardly ever.*

16 When we believe a person is *always* faithful, and he proves otherwise, we are devastated. When we believe we will *never* lose a particular friend, or our money, or a job, and we do, we respond with grief and resentment. Popular songs, expressing cultural truths, reflect this. "Always and Forever," we say. "You Belong to Me" or "I Can't Smile Without You" we sing.

17 *Is* Our use of *is, are,* I *am* in English is virtually unique. In Spanish,

separate verbs distinguish temporary from permanent: *estar, to be* in a temporary sense, and *ser, to be* in a permanent sense. So with French and many other languages. But in English, we can only describe a permanent, unalterable condition.

18 A youngster who repeatedly hears how lazy he is tends to agree: "I am lazy." Adopted as his own reality, "the way I am," it can become a fact of his life. If I call him lazy ("the way he is"), I will see his actions colored by that judgment. Anger, resentment and rigidity may develop in both of us as a result.

19 *Can't* *Can't* carries the same burden of permanence, expressed this time in a negative way. "You can't do anything right," say our parents. When we try our hand at algebra or cooking or calligraphy, and don't do well, if we conclude, "I can't do it," we are apt not to attempt it again. Thus language has done our thinking for us. If we accept our first-round failure for what it really is—doing the best we can at that moment—we are much freer to try again. Or by learning to be more precise: "perhaps I can't . . . with the education, experience, or information I now have," we free ourselves to seek out the necessary information, experience or education.

20 *Should* Notice how you feel when you say, "I should call her," or "I must get this done." *Shoulds* are a mainline to guilt. If the guilt is appropriate, fine. But it's a waste to trigger it by using language that reflects other people's standards or precepts of our own that we've outgrown.

21 *Everybody* Perhaps we use *everybody, nobody, no one* to make things seem better known than they are, or to have our opinions supported. If "*everybody* does it" we're safe. *Everybody* includes too much, and *nobody* excludes too much. These terms prevent seeing differences between individuals. When we use them, we're inaccurate most of the time; we also miss a lot.

22 What can we expect when we change our use of *try, always, is, can't, should* and *everybody*? You will notice no "overnight" changes but you will definitely be easing yourself into a less dogmatic frame of mind, more open, less demanding—in some ways scarier. Did you mean *every*body? Or could it be *some people,* or *many people* I know? *Is* he really that way, or does he *seem* that way to *you, now*? *Should* you really be more (or less) ambitious, or are you judging yourself by someone else's standard? Are *all* your dates broken, or just the last two?

23 It takes time, and it takes honesty. Try it.

24 No, *do* it.

Word Study List

prejudgment	1	calligraphy	19
semanticist	5	precepts	20
schizophrenic	8		

Questions

1. The only person the authors refer to but do not identify by profession is Freud. Thus we can conclude that they expect the *Glamour* audience to know who Freud is. If you do not know, consult a biographical dictionary or encyclopedia.

2. What is the authors' thesis? Where is it stated? How many changes can take place when we change our language? List the changes.

3. What general characteristics do the six damaging words have in common?

4. How often have you caused yourself pain and unhappiness by using the words *try, can't,* and *should*? What people who influence our lives seem to love to use these three words? Is it any wonder these words have such power?

5. How are the words *always, never, everybody,* and others in their families used to reinforce stereotyping? Why do they produce illogical or unsupportable statements most of the time? What is the best response to arguments based on overstatements or faulty generalizations?

Exercises

1. Were you surprised to be told that with language we try to control time? To manage the future? Compose five sentences that are statements that attempt to control the present or the future.

2. Compose five sentences using the verb to be (am, is, are) to describe a condition that is not permanent (e.g., My hair is wet). Do your sentences seem to assert an unalterable truth even though you know that the conditions described are temporary?

Talking New York: It's Not What You Say, It's the Way That You Say It

Deborah Tannen

Deborah Tannen (b. 1945), an associate professor of linguistics at Georgetown University, is interested in problems of cross-cultural communication. She is one of the authors of *Conversational Style* (1983) and editor of the text *Coherence in Spoken & Written Discourse* (1983). The following article appeared on March 30, 1981, in *New York* magazine.

Providing examples from taped conversations, Tannen contrasts the conversational style of New Yorkers with westerners—anyone west of the Hudson.

1 One of the nice things about the United States is that, wherever you go, people speak the same language. So native New Yorkers can move to San Francisco, Houston, or Milwaukee and still understand and be understood by everyone they meet. Right? Well, not exactly. Or, as a native New Yorker might put it, "Wrong!" Even though people all over the country speak English, the ways they let others know how they mean what they say—whether they're being friendly, ironic, or rude—can be very different.

2 Now, I'm not referring to the two aspects of language that everyone notices and a lot of people talk about: accent and vocabulary. Plenty has been said about the New York accent—pronunciation of vowels (*caw*fee), consonants (*t*ree for *th*ree), leaving out some r's (*toidy-toi*d street) and putting others in (Lind*er* Ronstadt). And much has been said about vocabulary—if you say "dungarees" instead of "jeans"; if you stand "in" line or, as only a New Yorker can do, stand "on" line.

3 But there are other aspects of language that people tend not to notice because they seem so natural—when you start and stop talking; how fast you talk; how you use pitch, loudness, tone of voice, rhythm; what your "point" is likely to be and how you get to it; what you talk about, when, and to whom. If people do notice these aspects of speech, they don't attribute them to language habits but to the speaker's personality—thinking of New Yorkers, for instance, as loud and pushy.

4 As a sociolinguist, I want to know how cultural differences affect the ways people talk and listen. My research method, inspired by the work of Robin Lakoff and John Gumperz of the University of California at Berkeley, is sociolinguistic microanalysis. I tape-record and transcribe naturally occurring conversations. Then I identify "rough spots" (segments in which there is evidence that communication broke down) and compare these with segments in which communication worked. I focus on such usually overlooked features as what (of all possible) information is said or left unsaid, how it is strung together, and how it is said—pitch, tone of voice, and so on. To check my interpretations, I play back taped conversations with the participants. Finally, I play the tape for others, to see if there are cultural patterns in the way they interpret what they hear.

5 I'm from New York City and of East European Jewish background, and I used to live in Berkeley, California, so a lot of the conversations I have taped and analyzed involve native New Yorkers talking to Californians. I found out that New York Jews have ways of talking that often have one effect (a good one) when used with one another and another effect (not so good) when used with others. Of course, some New Yorkers who

are not of East European Jewish background talk this way, and so do people who are neither from New York nor Jewish. But there are many who do—enough to account for the negative stereotype, and enough for many people, when I talk about these phenomena, to react with a very loud "*Aha!*" and a sigh of relief, saying this explains something that's been giving them trouble for a long time.

6 New Yorkers seem to think the best thing two people can do is talk. Silence is okay when you're watching a movie (though it might be better punctuated by clever asides), or when you're asleep (collecting dreams to tell when you awake), but when two or more people find themselves together, it's better to talk. That's how we show we're being friendly. And that's why we like to talk to strangers—especially if we won't be with them long, such as in an elevator or on a bank line. This often makes non–New Yorkers think we're trying to start something more than a conversation.

7 Once, when I was visiting San Francisco, my friend and I stopped in the street to look something up in her guidebook, and she complained that the book wasn't very clear. A man who was walking by turned to us and said, "Oh, that book's no good. The one you should get is this," pulling a guidebook out of his bag to show us. I couldn't resist checking out my hypothesis, so I asked him where he was from. He had just flown in from New York.

8 After we talked about New York–California differences for a few minutes, the visiting New Yorker suggested that we exchange our guidebook for the one he recommended, so we all went back to the store where my friend had bought her book a few hours before. In the bookstore, our new friend called over his shoulder, "Have you read *Garp*?" I answered, "No, should I?" "Yes," he said, animatedly. "It's great!" Then I heard a voice behind us saying, "Oh, is it? I've been thinking of reading that." I looked around and saw a woman no longer paying attention to us. I asked her where she was from: another New Yorker.

9 Most non–New Yorkers, finding themselves within hearing range of strangers' conversation, think it's nice to pretend they didn't hear. But many New Yorkers think it's nice to toss in a relevant comment. Californians are shocked to have strangers butt into their conversations, but if they accept the intrusion, they are shocked again if the stranger bows out as suddenly as he butted in.

10 There was something else about our conversation that made it tempting for a New Yorker to chime in: the fact that my friend was complaining. A Californian who visited New York once told me he'd found New Yorkers unfriendly when he'd tried to make casual conversation. I asked what he made conversation about. Well, for example, how nice the weather was. Of course! No New Yorker would start talking to a stranger about the weather—unless it was really bad. We find it most appropriate to make comments to strangers when there's something to complain about—"Why don't they do something about this garbage!" "Ever since

they changed the schedules, you can't get a bus!" Complaining gives us a sense of togetherness in adversity. The angry edge is aimed at the impersonal "they" who are always doing things wrong. The person is thus welcomed into a warm little group. Since Californians don't pick up this distinction between "us" and "them," they are put off by the hostility, which they feel could be turned on them at any moment.

11 New Yorkers have lots of ways of being friendly that put non New Yorkers off, such as the way we ask questions. When we meet someone, we think it's nice to show interest by asking questions. Often we ask "machine-gun questions": fast, with an unusually high or low pitch, in a clipped form, and often thrown in right at the end of someone else's sentence, or even in the middle of it.

12 One conversation I taped, between a woman from New York (Diane) and a man from Los Angeles (Chad) who had just met, will show what I mean:

Diane: You live in L.A.?

Chad: Yeah.

Diane: Y'visiting here?

Chad: Yeah.

Diane: Whaddya do there?

Chad: I work for Disney Press—Walt Disney.

Diane: You an artist?

Chad: No, no.

Diane: Writer?

Chad: Yeah.

Now, anyone can see that something is wrong. Diane is doing all the asking, and Chad is giving minimal, even monosyllabic answers. He's uncomfortable enough to stumble over the name of his own company. When I played the tape for Chad, he said that he felt under interrogation. But Diane didn't want to ask all the questions. She was trying to show interest and get Chad talking. She couldn't understand why he was so unfriendly. But, being a nice person, she kept trying—by doing more of what was putting him off.

13 The intonation, high pitch, and clipped form of Diane's questions would have tipped off fellow New Yorkers: "This is a casual question. Answer if you feel like it; otherwise, say something else." But Chad wasn't used to questions like that. When someone asks him a question, he feels he has to answer. So all that attention on him seemed pushy and nosy. He was also put off by the speed with which Diane's questions came at him. People who are not from New York often complain that New Yorkers interrupt them, don't listen, and don't give them a chance to talk. Typically, the New Yorker starts talking before the Californian is finished, so the Californian, piqued, stops talking. So who's interrupting? The New Yorker? Not necessarily. Who said only one person can talk at a time?

14 In a really good New York conversation, more than one person is talking a lot of the time. Throughout the conversations I have taped and analyzed, New York listeners punctuate a speaker's talk with comments, reactions, questions (often asking for the very information that is obviously about to come). None of this makes the New York speaker stop. On the contrary, he talks even more—louder, faster—and has even more fun, because he doesn't feel he's in the conversation alone. When a non–New Yorker stops talking at the first sign of participation from the New Yorker, *he's* the one who's creating the interruption, making a conversational bully out of a perfectly well-intentioned cooperative overlapper.

15 On the tape of two and a half hours of conversation from which the Diane/Chad example comes, I had hoped to analyze the styles of all six people present, but there was no time when non–New Yorkers talked to one another without the New Yorkers saying anything. This happened mainly because the non–New Yorkers expected a certain amount of pause before they started talking, but before that much pause came about, a New Yorker started to think there was an uncomfortable silence, and kindly set about filling it up with talk.

16 A short segment from that conversation—a discussion of the neighborhood around the Coliseum—will show this principle in action.

Kurt: Remember where WINS used to be?

Diane: No.

Kurt: Then they built a big huge skyscraper there?

Diane: No. Where was that?

Kurt: Right where Central Park met Broadway. That building . . .

Diane: By Columbus Circuit? . . .

Kurt: . . . shaped like that *(makes a pyramid of his hands)* . . .

Diane: . . . that—Columbus Circle?

Kurt: . . . right on Columbus Circle. Here's Columbus Circle. . . .

Diane: Now it's the . . .

Kurt: . . . here's Central Park West. . . .

Diane: . . . Huntington Hartford museum.

Peter: That's the Huntington Hartford, right?

Kurt: Nuhnuhno

17 For much of the above conversation, two or three people are often talking at the same time. But how do I know that they thought it was a good idea? When Diane suggests, "Now it's the Huntington Hartford museum," Peter says almost the same thing. But Kurt tells Peter and Diane they are both wrong. How could they have made the same mistake? Listening to the tape later, Peter admitted he really had no idea what Kurt was talking about; he hadn't lived in New York since high school, and he felt very much out of his element in this conversation. So, figuring that Diane ought to know, he just said the same thing she said, beginning a split second later so he could hear what she was saying and echo it. The wonderful thing is that it worked: Everyone had the impression that Peter knew the area. So knowing what you're talking about is not necessary in order to take part in this kind of conversation; knowing what kind of comment to make, when, and how fast is not only necessary but sufficient.

18 A New York listener does a lot of talking. And if you like a story, or if you think someone has made a good point, you don't appreciate it in silence. You show your reaction fast and loud. This creates trouble when New Yorkers talk to non–New Yorkers. In conversations I taped, again and again the Californians and Midwesterners stopped dead in their vocal tracks when a New Yorker tried to encourage them by exclaiming, "What!," "Wow!," or "Oh, God!" What was intended as a show of interest and appreciation sounded to the speaker like rude disbelief, or scared him into speechlessness. My sister, who grew up in New York City but hasn't lived here in seventeen years, has this problem with her children. When they tell her something and she gives them an enthusiastic response, they jump and jerk around to see what scared her.

19 New Yorkers also think it's nice to let others in on their thoughts and tell about their personal experiences; the expectation is that others will do the same. Often, however, the others do not understand this unspoken arrangement. A friend of mine from the Midwest had a date with a Jewish man who regaled her with stories of his personal life. In exasperation, she asked, "Why are you telling me all this?" and was utterly bewildered when he explained, "I want to get to know you."

20 Few forms of entertainment are as well loved by New Yorkers as telling stories. New Yorkers will often use dramatic gestures and facial expressions, change the pitch of their voices, or imitate the people they are quoting. A Midwesterner who worked for a few years in New York had a native friend who liked to tell him stories while they were walking down the street. When the New Yorker got to the climax of the story, he'd stop walking, nudge his friend to stop too, and deliver the punch line face to face. The Midwesterner found this a public embarrassment. But a New Yorker can't walk and tell a good story at the same time. He needs to gesture and to watch his audience watching him.

21 After observing many hours of conversation and analyzing tape recordings of many more, I am convinced that the style of New York conversation grows out of the desire to show involvement with other people, and they seem to New Yorkers like self-evident ways of being a good person. But conversational habits are not universal. People from different ethnic and social backgrounds have different conversational habits that seem self-evident to *them.* Some people wait longer than others before they feel it's appropriate to start talking. Some think it's polite to talk more softly, keep their intonation flatter, keep their faces and gestures in check, and talk about different topics.

22 What makes misunderstandings resulting from conversational-style differences so hard to clear up is that we don't have a way of talking about them. We don't think of saying, "When my voice has that quality, it means I'm being friendly," or "I'll leave a half-second pause when I'm finished." Such linguistic cues are sent and perceived automatically. All we can say is "I didn't mean it that way," which no one is ever going to believe if he knows that *he* would have meant it that way if he had said it that way. And we don't walk away from conversations thinking, "Gee, you use pitch and intonation differently from me." We think, "He's in a rotten mood," or "She's weird."

23 So what's a New Yorker to do? You can try to change your conversational style, as some New Yorkers have tried to change their accents—and probably with a similarly patched-up effect. You can teach yourself to count to three after you *think* someone else has finished talking. This may work sometimes, although it may give you a belabored look when you're counting. But can you change your sense of irony, of the way to tell a story—even if you sit on your hands?

24 I don't know. But in any case, don't feel guilty when you're accused

of interrupting. In fact, you can complain, "Don't just sit there—interrupt me!"

Word Study List

sociolinguist	4	interrogation	12
microanalysis	4	intonation	13, 21, 22
hypothesis	7	piqued	13
intrusion	9	regaled	19

Questions

1. After a clever opening, Tannen explains what she will and will not examine and how she gathered her evidence. What aspects of language are not a part of her study? What aspects of a New Yorker's conversation will she study? How did she obtain her information?

2. List the specific characteristics of a New Yorker's conversational style.

3. How many of these characteristics were you aware of? Which ones has Tannen brought to your attention for the first time? Do the old and the new seem to fit together, to create a unified conversational style consistent with your image of a New Yorker?

4. Tannen not only illustrates New York conversations, she also explains what the behavior means. Why do New Yorkers butt in? Interrupt? Complain? Gesture and mimic when telling stories and jokes?

5. How do non–New Yorkers generally respond to New York styles? How do they frequently interpret the New Yorker's behavior?

6. If you are not a New Yorker, do you think that you will now be able to respond more positively to New York behavior in conversations? Will you be more conscious of how you behave in conversation? Of how others may be misunderstanding your intentions?

Exercise

See if you can quietly obtain ten to fifteen minutes of taped conversation of three or four people—friends, family, or officemates. Carefully transcribe the conversation, noting in your written version if participants are speaking at the same time. Then analyze the conversation for the kinds of characteristics studied by Tannen, relating traits to the geographical, ethnic, and/or cultural backgrounds of the participants. Report the results of your study in a short paper.

Tune That Name: An Honorable American Tradition

Justin Kaplan

Justin Kaplan (b. 1925) is a professional writer best known for his biographies of Lincoln Steffens and Walt Whitman and for *Mr. Clemens and Mark Twain* (1966), winner of a Pulitzer Prize. "Tune That Name" was printed in *The New Republic* on May 7, 1984.

In response to the disclosure that presidential candidate Gary Hart changed his name, Kaplan explains that name-changing is part of the American tradition.

1 The disclosure, if that's not too strong a word, that Gary Hart used to be Gary Hartpence sent reporters to the court records. They learned that in September 1961, in response to a petition filed by four people—Gary himself, who was then 24 years old; Gary's wife Oletha (who now calls herself Lee); and Gary's parents, Mr. and Mrs. Carl Hartpence—a judge in Franklin County, Kansas, authorized the shorter form. Apparently Gary was already planning a political career and initiated the bobtailing process because he thought "Hart" would look better on a ballot. (He was probably right. Even so, "Hartpence," with its subliminal suggestions of thoughtfulness and budgetary prudence, might not be such a bad name for a Presidential contender in 1984.) It has also been learned that Hart fudges his age, that he changed his signature about ten years ago, that he's deleted from his current biography his stint as George McGovern's campaign manager in 1972, and that the original family name was not "Hart," as the Senator claims, but rather "Pence," as in, "Take care of the pence, for the pounds will take care of themselves," a maxim quoted by the Earl of Chesterfield.

2 The mild furor that ensued suggests that in changing his name—and making concomitant revisions in personal style and history—Hart did something shameful and petty, like kicking the dog. But he's got plenty of precedent and plenty of reason to believe that there was nothing either shameful or petty about it. Popes and kings take new names, and so do revolutionaries (Lenin, Trotsky, and Stalin, for example); nuns, monks, and Black Muslims; "missing persons," fugitives from justice, and social climbers; and married women, at least until recently. At 21 Freud started calling himself "Sigmund" instead of "Sigismund" (the equivalent of "Hymie" in Austrian anti-Semitic jokes). Erik ("Identity Crisis") Erikson used to be Erik Homburger. Karen Christentze Dinesen became Isak

Dinesen and before she was buried as Karen Blixen had at least half a dozen other names, all of them, according to Judith Thurman's biography, with "their own etiquette, logic, and geography."

3 New names have been a particularly American option, more American by far than apple pie, ever since the first adventurers came to the colonies to start from scratch and the colonies decided to change their name to the United States of America. "Before the Civil War," says Daniel Boorstin, "changing the names of towns had become almost as common as changing personal or family names was among immigrants in the later nineteenth century." Swedes, Armenians, Jews, and African slaves arrived without family names. Slaves took their owners' names—when Frederick Bailey escaped from his owner he changed his last name to Douglass. Thousands of newcomers either naturalized their names on arrival or had it done for them by immigration officers who had trouble with spelling and pronunciation. Like the Great Gatsby,[1] new Americans claimed the right to make themselves over into the persons they wished to be. "James Gatz—that was really, or at least legally, his name. . . . Jay Gatsby of West Egg, Long Island, sprang from his Platonic conception of himself."

4 In the same spirit, countless American writers created themselves when they created new names. Samuel L. Clemens, a 27-year-old newspaper reporter, began signing his work "Mark Twain." The drifter Walter Whitman Jr. became the poet Walt Whitman. Nathanael West started out as Nathan Weinstein and Nathanial von Wallenstein Weinstein; he had invented a "new identity," says his biographer Jay Martin, and become "a new man by an act of his own will." David Henry Thoreau preferred to be known as Henry David Thoreau, Hawthorne added the "w" in his name and Faulkner the "u" in his, while, on another level, Pearl Grey of Zanesville, Ohio, was reborn as Zane Grey, the famous horse-opera librettist. The silent movies transformed Theodosia Goodman, daughter of a Cincinnati tailor, into the bedouin femme fatale Theda Bara, a name that, according to the front-office, was an anagram of "Arab Death." Samuel Goldwyn (born Goldfish), William Fox (born Fried), Lewis Selznick (born Zeleznik), and other moguls of this prototypical melting-pot industry were determined to transform their hirelings either into exotics on the Theda Bara model or WASPs with euphonious or at least inoffensive names. If the great dream factory could make Mary Pickford out of Gladys Smith, Rudolph Valentino out of Rodolpho d'Antonguolla, Cary Grant out of Archibald Leach, Judy Garland out of Frances Gumm, and John Garfield out of Julius Garfinkle, why shouldn't ordinary people take new names

---

[1]Main character in F. Scott Fitzgerald's *The Great Gatsby*. The following quotation is from the novel.—ED.

and have a go at fame and riches of their own? With the sole exception of a name, as Saul Bellow says in *Seize the Day,* "There's really very little that a man can change at will." Names are not just nominal. They are integral with what psychologists call self-image, a proposition that can be demonstrated easily by observing the effect of getting someone's name wrong, as Jimmy Carter (formerly James Earl Carter Jr.) did when he eulogized Hubert Humphrey as Hubert Horatio Hornblower.

5 In addition to Carter, Gary Hart can point to the present incumbent, who, at Nancy's urging, changed the pronunciation of Reagan to give it a little more class; to Mondale, whose grandfather was named Mundal; and to Gerald Ford, formerly Leslie Lynch King Jr. (Harry S Truman, on the other hand, insisted that "S" was his middle name and resisted all attempts to insert a period after it.) No one has ever faulted Wilson for doing with his first name, Thomas, what Gary Hart has done with his last. After a nervous breakdown at about age 25 and experiments with "T. W. Wilson" and "T. Woodrow Wilson," he decided to be "Tommy" no longer, as his repressive father called him, but "Woodrow," his mother's maiden name. Grant was just plain lucky—through no doing of his own, his name was his fortune. His parents had him christened Hiram Ulysses Grant, and on the flyleaves of his schoolbooks he signed himself "Hiram U. Grant," not a name (or acronym, HUG) to turn an opposing army's bowels to water. He was "Ulysses Hiram Grant" when he signed the adjutant's record at West Point, but an irreversible clerical error made him over into Ulysses Simpson Grant and eventually the general-in-chief and President whose first two initials stood for Uncle Sam, Unconditional Surrender, and United States.

6 Hart and his critics would do well to look up the chapters about name-changing in Ted Morgan's book, *On Becoming American.* Morgan, formerly Sanche de Gramont, is our leading authority on the subject. When he decided to Americanize himself, he says, he submitted his old name to a whiz at anagrams who, in addition to "Ted Morgan," came up with "Tom Danger," "O. D. Garment," "Mr. de Tango," "Mo Dragnet," and "R. D. Megaton." Morgan's brother argued that the whole business was a sign of arrested development, "identity diffusion," and probable impotence, and told him, "Psychoanalysts' offices are full of name-changers." Morgan stood firm: "They're also full of people who haven't changed their name."

Word Study List

subliminal	1	moguls	4
furor	2	prototypical	4
concomitant	2	hirelings	4
naturalized	3	euphonious	4
librettist	4	nominal	4
bedouin	4	eulogized	4

femme	4	repressive	5
fatale	4	diffusion	6
anagram	4, 6	impotence	6

Questions

1. Essayists frequently write in response to a particular event, seeing a larger issue in that event. What was the occasion for Kaplan's article?

2. What is Kaplan's subject? What is his thesis or attitude toward his subject?

3. Kaplan gives many examples of people who changed their names. He draws his examples from what categories of people?

4. Most of us are aware that names of movie stars have been created in Hollywood. Were you surprised at the number of writers and political figures who have changed their names? Can you add others to Kaplan's list?

5. Kaplan says that name-changing is more American than apple pie. Why can he make this statement?

6. Kaplan concludes by suggesting that a name change can be important to mental health. Why? What *is* in a name?

Exercise

Have you ever thought of changing your name? Fantasize for a moment about the kind of person you would like to be or life you would like to be living. What name would you select to match your fantasy? In a short paper explain why you would select that name to go with your imagined person or life.

The Language of Clothes

Alison Lurie

Professor of English at Cornell University, Alison Lurie (b. 1926) is the author of several novels, including *The War Between the Tates* (1974), a work filmed for TV, and children's books, including *Clever Gretchen and Other Forgotten*

Folktales (1980). What follows is a chapter from her book *The Language of Clothes* (1981).

In this excerpt, Lurie examines some of the nonverbal messages our clothes and appearance convey to others.

1 For thousands of years human beings have communicated with one another first in the language of dress. Long before I am near enough to talk to you on the street, in a meeting, or at a party, you announce your sex, age and class to me through what you are wearing—and very possibly give me important information (or misinformation) as to your occupation, origin, personality, opinions, tastes, sexual desires and current mood. I may not be able to put what I observe into words, but I register the information unconsciously; and you simultaneously do the same for me. By the time we meet and converse we have already spoken to each other in an older and more universal tongue.

2 The statement that clothing is a language, though occasionally made with the air of a man finding a flying saucer in his backyard, is not new. Balzac, in *Daughter of Eve* (1839), observed that for a woman dress is "a continual manifestation of intimate thoughts, a language, a symbol." Today, as semiotics becomes fashionable, sociologists tell us that fashion too is a language of signs, a nonverbal system of communication. The French structuralist Roland Barthes, for instance, in "The Diseases of Costume," speaks of theatrical dress as a kind of writing, of which the basic element is the sign.

3 None of these theorists, however, have gone on to remark what seems obvious: that if clothing is a language, it must have a vocabulary and a grammar like other languages. Of course, as with human speech, there is not a single language of dress, but many: some (like Dutch and German) closely related and others (like Basque) almost unique. And within every language of clothes there are many different dialects and accents, some almost unintelligible to members of the mainstream culture. Moreover, as with speech, each individual has his own stock of words and employs personal variations of tone and meaning.

THE VOCABULARY OF FASHION

4 The vocabulary of dress includes not only items of clothing, but also hair styles, accessories, jewelry, make-up and body decoration. Theoretically at least this vocabulary is as large as or larger than that of any spoken tongue, since it includes every garment, hair style, and type of body decoration ever invented. In practice, of course, the sartorial resources of an individual may be very restricted. Those of a sharecropper, for instance, may be limited to five or ten "words" from which it is possible to create only a few "sentences" almost bare of decoration and expressing only the most basic concepts. A so-called fashion leader, on the other hand, may

have several hundred "words" at his or her disposal, and thus be able to form thousands of different "sentences" that will express a wide range of meanings. Just as the average English-speaking person knows many more words than he or she will ever use in conversation, so all of us are able to understand the meaning of styles we will never wear.

5 To choose clothes, either in a store or at home, is to define and describe ourselves. Occasionally, of course, practical considerations enter into these choices: considerations of comfort, durability, availability and price. Especially in the case of persons of limited wardrobe, an article may be worn because it is warm or rainproof or handy to cover up a wet bathing suit—in the same way that persons of limited vocabulary use the phrase "you know" or adjectives such as "great" or "fantastic." Yet, just as with spoken language, such choices usually give us some information, even if it is only equivalent to the statement "I don't give a damn what I look like today." And there are limits even here. In this culture, like many others, certain garments are taboo for certain persons. Most men, however cold or wet they might be, would not put on a woman's dress, just as they would not use words and phrases such as "simply marvelous," which in this culture are considered specifically feminine.

ARCHAIC WORDS

6 Besides containing "words" that are taboo, the language of clothes, like speech, also includes modern and ancient words, words of native and foreign origin, dialect words, colloquialisms, slang and vulgarities. Genuine articles of clothing from the past (or skillful imitations) are used in the same way a writer or speaker might use archaisms to give an air of culture, erudition or wit. Just as in educated discourse, such "words" are usually employed sparingly, most often one at a time—a single Victorian cameo or a pair of 1940s platform shoes or an Edwardian velvet waistcoat, never a complete costume. A whole outfit composed of archaic items from a single period, rather than projecting elegance and sophistication, will imply that one is on one's way to a masquerade, acting in a play or film or putting oneself on display for advertising purposes. Mixing garments from several different periods of the past, on the other hand, suggests a confused but intriguingly "original" theatrical personality. It is therefore often fashionable in those sections of the art and entertainment industry in which instant celebrities are manufactured and sold.

7 When using archaic words, it is essential to choose ones that are decently old. The sight of a white plastic Courrèges miniraincoat and boots (in 1963 the height of fashion) at a gallery opening or theater today would produce the same shiver of ridicule and revulsion as the use of words such as "groovy," "Negro," or "self-actualizing."

8 *In Taste and Fashion,* one of the best books ever written on costume, the late James Laver proposed a timetable to explain such reactions; this

has come to be known as Laver's Law. According to him, the same costume will be

Indecent	10 years before its time
Shameless	5 years before its time
Daring	1 year before its time
Smart	
Dowdy	1 year after its time
Hideous	10 years after its time
Ridiculous	20 years after its time
Amusing	30 years after its time
Quaint	50 years after its time
Charming	70 years after its time
Romantic	100 years after its time
Beautiful	150 years after its time

Laver possibly overemphasizes the shock value of incoming fashion, which today may be seen merely as weird or ugly. And of course he is speaking of the complete outfit, or "sentence." The speed with which a single "word" passes in and out of fashion can vary, just as in spoken and written languages.

FOREIGN WORDS

9 The appearance of foreign garments in an otherwise indigenous costume is similar in function to the use of foreign words or phrases in standard English speech. This phenomenon, which is common in certain circles, may have several different meanings.

10 First, of course, it can be a deliberate sign of national origin in someone who otherwise, sartorially or linguistically speaking, has no accent. Often this message is expressed through headgear. The Japanese-American lady in Western dress but with an elaborate Oriental hairdo, or the Oxford-educated Arab who tops his Savile Row[1] suit with a turban, are telling us graphically that they have not been psychologically assimilated; that their ideas and opinions remain those of an Asian. As a result we tend to see the non-European in Western dress with native headgear or hairdo as dignified, even formidable; while the reverse outfit—the Oriental lady in a kimono and a plastic rain hat, or the sheik in native robes and a black bowler—appears comic. Such costumes seem to announce that their wearers, though not physically at ease in our country, have their heads full of half-baked Western ideas. It would perhaps be well for Anglo-American tourists to keep this principle in mind when traveling to exotic

[1] Location of fashionable clothing stores in London—Ed.

places. Very possibly the members of a package tour in Mexican sombreros or Russian bearskin hats look equally ridiculous and weak-minded to the natives of the countries they are visiting.

11 More often the wearing of a single foreign garment, like the dropping of a foreign word or phrase in conversation, is meant not to advertise foreign origin or allegiance but to indicate sophistication. It can also be a means of advertising wealth. When we see a fancy Swiss watch, we know that its owner either bought it at home for three times the price of a good English or American watch, or else he or she spent even more money traveling to Switzerland.

SLANG AND VULGAR WORDS

12 Casual dress, like casual speech, tends to be loose, relaxed and colorful. It often contains what might be called "slang words": blue jeans, sneakers, baseball caps, aprons, flowered cotton housedresses and the like. These garments could not be worn on a formal occasion without causing disapproval, but in ordinary circumstances they pass without remark. "Vulgar words" in dress, on the other hand, give emphasis and get immediate attention in almost any circumstances, just as they do in speech. Only the skillful can employ them without some loss of face, and even then they must be used in the right way. A torn, unbuttoned shirt, or wildly uncombed hair, can signify strong emotions: passion, grief, rage, despair. They are most effective if people already think of you as being neatly dressed, just as the curses of well-spoken persons count for more than those of the customarily foul-mouthed.

13 Items of dress that are the sartorial equivalent of forbidden words have more impact when they appear seldom and as if by accident. The Edwardian lady, lifting her heavy floor-length skirt to board a tram, appeared unaware that she was revealing a froth of lacy petticoats and embroidered black stockings. Similarly, today's braless executive woman, leaning over her desk at a conference, may affect not to know that her nipples show through her silk blouse. Perhaps she does not know it consciously; we are here in the ambiguous region of intention vs. interpretation which has given so much trouble to linguists.

14 In speech, slang terms and vulgarities may eventually become respectable dictionary words; the same thing is true of colloquial and vulgar fashions. Garments or styles that enter the fashionable vocabulary from a colloquial source usually have a longer life span than those that begin as vulgarities. Thigh-high patent leather boots, first worn by the most obvious variety of rentable female as a sign that she was willing to help act out certain male fantasies, shot with relative speed into and out of high fashion; while blue jeans made their way upward much more gradually from work clothes to casual to business and formal wear, and are still engaged in a slow descent.

ADJECTIVES AND ADVERBS: THE DECORATED STYLE OF DRESS

15 Though the idea is attractive, it does not seem possible to equate different articles of clothing with the different parts of speech. A case can be made, however, for considering trimmings and accessories as adjectives or adverbs—modifiers in the sentence that is the total outfit—but it must be remembered that one era's trimmings and accessories are another's essential parts of the costume. At one time shoes were actually fastened with buckles, and the buttons on the sleeves of a suit jacket were used to secure turned-up cuffs. Today such buttons, or the linked brass rods on a pair of Gucci[2] shoes, are purely vestigial and have no useful function. If they are missing, however, the jacket or the shoes are felt to be damaged and unfit for wear.

16 Accessories, too, may be considered essential to an outfit. In the 1940s and 1950s, for instance, a woman was not properly dressed unless she wore gloves. Emily Post, among many others, made this clear:

> Always wear gloves, of course, in church, and also on the street. A really smart woman wears them outdoors always, even in the country. Always wear gloves in a restaurant, in a theatre, when you go to lunch, or to a formal dinner, or to a dance. . . . A lady never takes off her gloves to shake hands, no matter when or where. . . . On formal occasions she should *put gloves on* to shake hands with a hostess or with her own guests.

17 If we consider only those accessories and trimmings that are currently optional, however, we may reasonably speak of them as modifiers. It then becomes possible to distinguish an elaborately decorated style of dress from a simple and plain one, whatever the period. As in speech, it is harder to communicate well in a highly decorated style, though when this is done successfully the result may be very impressive. A costume loaded with accessories and trimmings can easily appear cluttered, pretentious or confusing. Very rarely the whole becomes greater than its many parts, and the total effect is luxurious, elegant and often highly sensual.

THE CHANGING VOCABULARY OF FASHION

18 As writers on costume have often pointed out, the average individual above the poverty line has many more clothes than he needs to cover his body, even allowing for washing and changes of weather. Moreover, we often discard garments that show little or no wear and purchase new ones. What is the reason for this? Some have claimed that it is all the result of brainwashing by commercial interests. But the conspiracy theory of fashion change—the idea that the adoption of new styles is simply the result of a plot by greedy designers and manufacturers and fashion editors—has, I think, less foundation than is generally believed. Certainly the fash-

[2]Italian manufacturer of expensive clothes, shoes.—ED.

ion industry might like us to throw away all our clothes each year and buy a whole new wardrobe, but it has never been able to achieve this goal. For one thing, it is not true that the public will wear anything suggested to it, nor has it ever been true. Ever since fashion became big business, designers have proposed a bewildering array of styles every season. A few of these have been selected or adapted by manufacturers for mass production, but only a certain proportion of them have caught on.

19 As James Laver has remarked, modes are but the reflection of the manners of the time; they are the mirror, not the original. Within the limits imposed by economics, clothes are acquired, used and discarded just as words are, because they meet our needs and express our ideas and emotions. All the exhortations of experts on language cannot save outmoded terms of speech or persuade people to use new ones "correctly." In the same way, those garments that reflect what we are or want to be at the moment will be purchased and worn, and those that do not will not, however frantically they may be ballyhooed.

20 In the past, gifted artists of fashion from Worth to Mary Quant have been able to make inspired guesses about what people will want their clothes to say each year. Today a few designers seem to have retained this ability, but many others have proved to be as hopelessly out of touch as designers in the American auto industry. The classic case is that of the maxiskirt, a style which made women look older and heavier and impeded their movements at a time (1969) when youth, slimness and energy were at the height of their vogue. The maxiskirt was introduced with tremendous fanfare and not a little deception. Magazines and newspapers printed (sometimes perhaps unknowingly) photos of New York and London street scenes populated with hired models in long skirts disguised as passers-by, to give readers in Podunk and Lesser Puddleton the impression that the capitals had capitulated. But these strenuous efforts were in vain: the maxiskirt failed miserably, producing well-deserved financial disaster for its backers.

21 The fashion industry is no more able to preserve a style that men and women have decided to abandon than to introduce one they do not choose to accept. In America, for instance, huge advertising budgets and the wholehearted cooperation of magazines such as *Vogue* and *Esquire* have not been able to save the hat, which for centuries was an essential part of everyone's outdoor (and often of their indoor) costume. It survives now mainly as a utilitarian protection against weather, as part of ritual dress (at formal weddings, for example) or as a sign of age or individual eccentricity.

PERSONAL FASHION: SITUATION AND SELF

22 As with speech, the meaning of any costume depends on circumstances. It is not "spoken" in a vacuum, but at a specific place and time, any change in which may alter its meaning. Like the remark "Let's get on with this damn business," the two-piece tan business suit and boldly

striped shirt and tie that signify energy and determination in the office will have quite another resonance at a funeral or picnic.

23 According to Irving Goffman,[3] the concept of "proper dress" is totally dependent on situation. To wear the costume considered "proper" for a situation acts as a sign of involvement in it, and the person whose clothes do not conform to these standards is likely to be more or less subtly excluded from participation. When other signs of deep involvement are present, rules about proper dress may be waived. Persons who have just escaped from a fire or flood are not censured for wearing pajamas or having uncombed hair; someone bursting into a formal social occasion to announce important news is excused for being in jeans and T-shirt.

24 In language we distinguish between someone who speaks a sentence well—clearly, and with confidence and dignity—and someone who speaks it badly. In dress too, manner is as important as matter, and in judging the meaning of any garment we will automatically consider whether it fits well or is too large or too small; whether it is old or new; and especially whether it is in good condition, slightly rumpled and soiled or crushed and filthy. Cleanliness may not always be next to godliness, but it is usually regarded as a sign of respectability or at least of self-respect. It is also a sign of status, since to be clean and neat always involves the expense of time and money.

25 In a few circles, of course, disregard for cleanliness has been considered a virtue. Saint Jerome's[4] remark that "the purity of the body and its garments means the impurity of the soul" inspired generations of unwashed and smelly hermits. In the sixties some hippies and mystics scorned overly clean and tidy dress as a sign of compromise with the Establishment and too great an attachment to the things of this world. There is also a more widespread rural and small-town dislike of the person whose clothes are too clean, slick and smooth. He—or, less often, she—is suspected of being untrustworthy, a smoothie or a city slicker.

26 In general, however, to wear dirty, rumpled or torn clothing is to invite scorn and condescension. This reaction is ancient; indeed it goes back beyond the dawn of humanity. In most species, a strange animal in poor condition—mangy, or with matted and muddy fur—is more likely to be attacked by other animals. In the same way, shabbily dressed people are more apt to be treated shabbily. A man in a clean, well-pressed suit who falls down in a central London or Manhattan street is likely to be helped up sooner than one in filthy tatters.

27 At certain times and places—a dark night, a deserted alley—dirt and rags, like mumbled or growled speech, may be alarming. In Dickens's *Great Expectations* they are part of the terror the boy Pip feels when he first sees the convict Magwitch in the graveyard: "A fearful man, all in

---

[3]University of Pennsylvania sociologist, author of *Behavior in Public Places* (1963) and *Interaction Ritual* (1982)—Ed.

[4]Early Biblical scholar and ascetic (340?–420).—Ed.

coarse grey, with a great iron on his leg. A man with no hat, and with broken shoes, and with an old rag tied round his head."

28 A costume not only appears at a specific place and time, it must be "spoken"—that is, worn—by a specific person. Even a simple statement like "I want a drink," or a simple costume—shorts and T-shirt, for example—will have a very different aspect in association with a sixty-year-old man, a sixteen-year-old girl and a six-year-old child. But age and sex are not the only variables to be considered. In judging a costume we will also take into account the physical attributes of the person who is wearing it, assessing him or her in terms of height, weight, posture, racial or ethnic type and facial features and expression. The same outfit will look different on a person whose face and body we consider attractive and on one whom we think ugly. Of course, the idea of "attractiveness" itself is not only subjective, but subject to the historical and geographical vagaries of fashion, as Sir Kenneth Clark[5] has demonstrated in *The Nude.* In twentieth-century Britain and America, for instance, weight above the norm has been considered unattractive and felt to detract from dignity and status; as Emily Post put it in 1922, "The tendency of fat is to take away from one's gentility; therefore, any one inclined to be fat must be ultra conservative—in order to counteract the effect." The overweight person who does not follow this rule is in danger of appearing vulgar or even revolting. In Conrad's *Lord Jim* the shame of the corrupt Dutch captain is underlined by the fact that, though grossly fat, he wears orange-and-green-striped pajamas in public.

ECCENTRIC AND CONVENTIONAL SPEECH

29 In dress as in language there is a possible range of expression from the most eccentric statement to the most conventional. At one end of the spectrum is the outfit of which the individual parts or "words" are highly incongruent, marking its wearer (if not on stage or involved in some natural disaster) as very peculiar or possibly deranged. Imagine for instance a transparent sequined evening blouse over a dirty Victorian cotton petticoat and black rubber galoshes. (I have observed this getup in real life; it was worn to a lunch party at a famous Irish country house.) If the same costume were worn by a man, or if the usual grammatical order of the sentence were altered—one of the galoshes placed upside down on the head, for example—the effect of insanity would be even greater.

30 At the opposite end of the spectrum is the costume that is the equivalent of a cliché; it follows some established style in every particular and instantly establishes its wearer as a doctor, a debutante, a hippie or a whore. Such outfits are not uncommon, for as two British sociologists have remarked, "Identification with and active participation in a social

[5]Art historian (1903–1983) best known for having written *Civilisation* and narrated the public television series.—ED.

group always involves the human body and its adornment and clothing." The more significant any social role is for an individual, the more likely he or she is to dress for it. When two roles conflict, the costume will either reflect the more important one or it will combine them, sometimes with incongruous effects, as in the case of the secretary whose sober, efficient-looking dark suit only partly conceals a tight, bright, low-cut blouse.

31 The cliché outfit may in some cases become so standardized that it is spoken of as a "uniform": the pin-striped suit, bowler and black umbrella of the London City man, for instance, or the blue jeans and T-shirts of high-school students. Usually, however, these costumes only look like uniforms to outsiders; peers will be aware of significant differences. The London businessman's tie will tell his associates where he went to school; the cut and fabric of his suit will allow them to guess at his income. High-school students, in a single glance, can distinguish new jeans from those that are fashionably worn, functionally or decoratively patched or carelessly ragged; they grasp the fine distinctions of meaning conveyed by straight-leg, flared, boot-cut and peg-top. When two pairs of jeans are identical to the naked eye a label handily affixed to the back pocket gives useful information, identifying the garment as expensive (so-called designer jeans) or discount-department-store. And even within the latter category there are distinctions: in our local junior high school, according to a native informant, "freaks always wear Lees, greasers wear Wranglers, and everyone else wears Levis."

32 Of course, to the careful observer all these students are only identical below the waist; above it they may wear anything from a lumberjack shirt to a lace blouse. Grammatically, this costume seems to be a sign that in their lower or physical natures these persons are alike, however dissimilar they may be socially, intellectually or aesthetically. If this is so, the opposite statement can be imagined—and was actually made by my own college classmates thirty years ago. During the daytime we wore identical baggy sweaters over a wide variety of slacks, plaid kilts, full cotton or straight tweed or slinky jersey skirts, ski pants and Bermuda shorts. "We're all nice coeds from the waist up; we think and talk alike," this costume proclaimed, "but as women we are infinitely various."

Word Study List

semiotics	2	sombreros	10
structuralist	2	vestigial	15
sartorial(ly)	4, 10, 13	pretentious	17
taboo	5, 6	exhortations	19
colloquialisms	6	ballyhooed	19
vulgarities	6	capitulated	20
archaisms	6	resonance	22
erudition	6	censured	23
indigenous	9	vagaries	28
linguistically	10	incongruent	29

Questions

1. Why is an article on clothing in this book? What, in other words, is Lurie's central point about clothing?

2. Lurie develops her point and organizes her piece (note the subheadings) by comparing clothing to what? Lurie develops her metaphor by first asserting that some people have a larger "vocabulary" than others. What is her point with regard to clothing?

3. According to Lurie, adding a garment from another era can be stunning, but only if the garment is "decently" old. What terms does Laver provide in his chart to describe clothes from one to twenty years out of fashion? Who seems to benefit the most from these attitudes? What evidence does Lurie provide to suggest that the fashion industry does not completely control our selection of styles?

4. What messages are typically sent by the mixing of foreign with native clothing?

5. When accessories, the modifiers of fashion, are appropriately selected, what can be gained? When worn to excess, what happens?

6. Lurie says that clothes, like words, are chosen for a specific context. Explain what is inappropriate about a tan business suit and striped shirt at a funeral and at a picnic. What would others at these gatherings think about a person so dressed? What can happen to a person inappropriately dressed for a particular occasion?

7. How carefully do you choose your clothes for each occasion? Do you dress more carefully for some situations than others? Does the amount of care reflect the situation's importance to you or to others?

Exercise

It is of course the cliché outfit or "uniform" of groups that helps to reinforce stereotypes. Make a list of the various groups in our society that you associate with a particular type of dress and describe the clothes you associate with each group. Examine your list to see for which groups you can be the most detailed regarding their dress. (Lurie points out, for example, that high-school students dress differently even though they all wear jeans.) Compare your list with classmates and discuss whether or not there is a connection between the degree of detail in your clothes descriptions and the degree to which a group is stereotyped.

Exercises

Most writers represented in this chapter are concerned about the abuse and oppression experienced by individuals and groups whom society discriminates against; they are also well aware of the power of language to reinforce and perpetuate control by some over others. The solution: increased understanding of the stereotypes we hold and a willingness to change language to coincide with and reinforce changed attitudes.

I. EXAMINING POPULAR STEREOTYPES

To examine job stereotypes, complete the following statement for each of the workers listed below: When I think of a ____, I think of ____. Fill in a brief description or list of traits you associate with people in each field:

1. scientist
2. nurse
3. college professor
4. marine
5. flight attendant
6. librarian
7. truck driver
8. football player
9. used car salesman
10. tennis instructor

Compare your lists of characteristics with classmates. For each group, what traits were most frequently recorded? Which groups produced the greatest agreement? Now, to counter possible stereotyping, think of all the people you know in each category. What characteristics do these people have that make them different from the composite description? Based on the class study, which job groups seem to have the greatest diversity? Which seem to come closest to fitting the stereotypes? Why do you suppose that the experience of class members upholds some job stereotypes? Is it a lack of experience within the class? Do employers recruit certain types for certain jobs, thus reducing diversity within the field?

II. IDENTIFYING AND CORRECTING LOGICAL FALLACIES

Errors in logical thinking (logical fallacies) result either from ignoring the issue under discussion or from oversimplifying the issue in some way. Many times fallacious arguments result from stereotyping, prejudice, and the desire to control ourselves or others with words such as *always* and *should.* Here are some examples.

IGNORING THE ISSUE

Ad hominem (argument to the man): He should not be senator; he's divorced and his daughter's a dancer. (A writer tries to appeal to our emotions by attacking the private life of the candidate. The writer assumes that we hold certain negative attitudes about divorced people and professional dancers.)

Testimonial or Bandwagon. Look at all the sports figures who drink 7-Up. It must be a great drink. (Neither the number of people nor the fame of people endorsing a product can guarantee the product's quality.)

Straw Man: Those who favor the right to abortion just hate children. (Attributing a position to one's opponents that they do not hold is to stray from the issue and, usually, to interject emotion as well.)

SIMPLIFYING THE ISSUE

Stereotyping: We can't admit her to this school; you know fat people are lazy. (To attribute similar traits to all members of a group is to oversimplify reality.)

Hasty or Faulty Generalization: Of course New York will vote Democratic; think of all the poor people, blacks, and Jews who live there. (Often faulty generalizations are the result of stereotyping. Not all poor people, or all blacks, or all Jews think or act the same way.)

Overstatement: Nobody from the South can possibly become successful. (A sweeping generalization, obviously illogical since famous writers, political leaders, educators, and others have been or are Southerners. The statement is designed to have an emotional impact on people who are still fighting the Civil War.)

False Dilemma: A student will either get good grades or be a good athlete. (To assume only two possibilities when more exist is illogical. Some students will do both; some neither. Notice that falsely grouping students into types—stereotyping—underlies the illogical statement.)

1. For each of the statements below, explain what is illogical and then name the fallacy or fallacies that the statement best illustrates.
    a. We had to put Indians on reservations, or American civilization would not have advanced.
    b. Let's have plenty of beer to serve; Bob's bringing Polish friends to the party.
    c. Kodak film must be the best; handsome Michael Landon endorses it.
    d. We can't elect her to the County Board; she used to live with her boyfriend.
    e. To do well in school, a student must study all of the time or cheat.
    f. People who favor gun legislation probably work for the Mafia.
    g. Sally's friend won a tennis scholarship to Brighten University. I'll bet she's ugly as a cow.
    h. Aggressive women who want managerial jobs obviously grew up hating their fathers.
2. Write two of your own examples for each of the seven fallacies identified above. Exchange papers with a classmate and identify the fallacies illustrated by your classmate.

Writing Assignments

1. Write an essay that refutes (or disproves) the fallacious reasoning, weak evidence, or incorrect facts of an article, editorial, or letter to the editor of a newspaper or magazine. Support for your refutation should come from one written source (newspapers, magazines, reference books), personal experience, and your own logical reasoning. Your essay should follow this organization: a statement of the thesis, logic, or evidence to be refuted; your position or thesis; your logic, experience, and knowledge.
2. In an essay, develop, by examples, the thesis that within the group we call young people (teen-agers and those in their early twenties) a variety of stereotypes exist that class young people into distinct groups and set barriers between the groups, making friendship across group boundaries difficult. Examine the words used to designate the various groups, discussing the power of these names to set barriers.
3. Working with the same groups of young people established for assignment 2, describe as precisely as you can the clothes, accessories, hair styles, and general appearance of each group. Consider that your audience is composed of adults in whose eyes all teen-agers look alike. You are going to explain the subtle differences in attire among young people, differences that send nonverbal messages to other teen-agers indicating the group that a young person wants to be identified with. (Note: This topic calls for great detail. If you are the kind of person who does not pay much attention to dress, you probably should select a different topic.)

CHAPTER 7

"Splendid, Williams! One can't tell where style ends and substance begins."

The Politics of Language

GETTING STARTED: "next to of course god america i"

The powerful uses of language are nowhere more evident than when politicians speak on war, for the language is stretched and strained for words to make it seem the glorious, heroic event that it isn't. Through an observer, we hear in the following poem by E. E. Cummings the hollow rhetoric of a chauvinist proclaiming the glories of war.

"next to of course god america i
love you land of the pilgrims' and so forth oh
say can you see by the dawn's early my
country 'tis of centuries come and go 4
and are no more what of it we should worry
in every language even deafanddumb
thy sons acclaim your glorious name by gorry
by jingo by gee by gosh by gum 8
why talk of beauty what could be more beautiful than these heroic happy dead
who rushed like lions to the roaring slaughter
they did not stop to think they died instead 12
then shall the voice of liberty be mute?"

He spoke. And drank rapidly a glass of water

1. What is the effect of the absence of punctuation and capitalization from the poem?
2. Are any phrases or lines of the poem familiar? If so, where have you seen or heard them? What does the use of these phrases tell you about the person speaking in lines 1–13?
3. What do you learn about the situation portrayed in the poem in line 14? What is the listener's attitude toward what has been said in the first thirteen lines? Point out words or phrases or omissions of words or punctuation that convey this attitude. Can you summarize in one sentence what the listener has heard?

Politics and the English Language

George Orwell

George Orwell (1903–1950), the pseudonym of Eric Arthur Blair, was a British essayist and novelist best known for his political satires *Animal Farm* (1945) and *1984* (1949). The following essay was first published at the end of World War II in the collection *Shooting an Elephant and Other Essays* (1945).

As the opening essay of this chapter, "Politics and the English Language" establishes the link between the decline of a language and the political abuse of language to defend the indefensible. In the thirty-five years since its publication, many articles on politics, language, and power—including two others in this chapter—have opened with a reference to Orwell's essay.

1 Most people who bother with the matter at all would admit that the English language is in a bad way, but it is generally assumed that we cannot by conscious action do anything about it. Our civilisation is decadent, and our language—so the argument runs—must inevitably share in the general collapse. It follows that any struggle against the abuse of language is a sentimental archaism, like preferring candles to electric light or hansom cabs to aeroplanes. Underneath this lies the half-conscious belief that language is a natural growth and not an instrument which we shape for our own purposes.

2 Now, it is clear that the decline of a language must ultimately have political and economic causes: it is not due simply to the bad influence of this or that individual writer. But an effect can become a cause, reinforcing the original cause and producing the same effect in an intensified form, and so on indefinitely. A man may take to drink because he feels himself to be a failure, and then fail all the more completely because he drinks. It is rather the same thing that is happening to the English language. It becomes ugly and inaccurate because our thoughts are foolish, but the slovenliness of our language makes it easier for us to have foolish thoughts. The point is that the process is reversible. Modern English, especially written English, is full of bad habits which spread by imitation and which can be avoided if one is willing to take the necessary trouble. If one gets rid of these habits one can think more clearly, and to think clearly is a necessary first step towards political regeneration: so that the fight against bad English is not frivolous and is not the exclusive concern of professional writers. I will come back to this presently, and I hope that by that time the meaning of what I have said here will have become clearer. Meanwhile, here are five specimens of the English language as it is now habitually written.

3 These five passages have not been picked out because they are especially bad—I could have quoted far worse if I had chosen—but because they illustrate various of the mental vices from which we now suffer. They are a little below the average, but are fairly representative samples. I number them so that I can refer back to them when necessary:

> 1. I am not, indeed, sure whether it is not true to say that the Milton who once seemed not unlike a seventeenth-century Shelley had not become, out of an experience ever more bitter in each year, more alien (sic) to the founder of that Jesuit sect which nothing could induce him to tolerate.
>
> *Professor Harold Laski* (*Essay in* Freedom of Expression).

2. Above all, we cannot play ducks and drakes with a native battery of idioms which prescribes such egregious collocations of vocables as the Basic *put up with* for *tolerate* or *put at a loss* for *bewilder.*

Professor Lancelot Hogben (Interglossa).

3. On the one side we have the free personality: by definition it is not neurotic, for it has neither conflict nor dream. Its desires, such as they are, are transparent, for they are just what institutional approval keeps in the forefront of consciousness; another institutional pattern would alter their number and intensity; there is little in them that is natural, irreducible, or culturally dangerous. But *on the other side,* the social bond itself is nothing but the mutual reflection of these self-secure integrities. Recall the definition of love. Is not this the very picture of a small academic? Where is there a place in this hall of mirrors for either personality or fraternity?

Essay on psychology in Politics *(New York).*

4. All the "best people" from the gentlemen's clubs, and all the frantic Fascist captains, united in common hatred of Socialism and bestial horror of the rising tide of the mass revolutionary movement, have turned to acts of provocation, to foul incendiarism, to medieval legends of poisoned wells, to legalise their own destruction to proletarian organisations, and rouse the agitated petty-bourgeoisie to chauvinistic fervour on behalf of the fight against the revolutionary way out of the crisis.

Communist pamphlet.

5. If a new spirit *is* to be infused into this old country, there is one thorny and contentious reform which must be tackled, and that is the humanisation and galvanisation of the BBC. Timidity here will bespeak canker and atrophy of the soul. The heart of Britain may be sound and of strong beat, for instance, but the British lion's roar at present is like that of Bottom in Shakespeare's *Midsummer Night's Dream*—as gentle as any sucking dove. A virile new Britain cannot continue indefinitely to be traduced in the eyes, or rather ears, of the world by the effete languors of Langham Place, brazenly masquerading as "standard English". When the Voice of Britain is heard at nine o'clock, better far and infinitely less ludicrous to hear aitches honestly dropped than the present priggish, inflated, inhibited, schoolma'amish arch braying of blameless bashful mewing maidens!

Letter in Tribune.

4 Each of these passages has faults of its own, but, quite apart from avoidable ugliness, two qualities are common to all of them. The first is staleness of imagery: the other is lack of precision. The writer either has a meaning and cannot express it, or he inadvertently says something else, or he is almost indifferent as to whether his words mean anything or not. This mixture of vagueness and sheer incompetence is the most marked characteristic of modern English prose, and especially of any kind of political writing. As soon as certain topics are raised, the concrete melts into the abstract and no one seems able to think of turns of speech that are not hackneyed: prose consists less and less of *words* chosen for the sake of their meaning, and more of *phrases* tacked together like the sections of a

prefabricated hen-house. I list below, with notes and examples, various of the tricks by means of which the work of prose construction is habitually dodged:

5 *Dying Metaphors.* A newly invented metaphor assists thought by evoking a visual image, while on the other hand a metaphor which is technically "dead" (e.g. *iron resolution*) has in effect reverted to being an ordinary word and can generally be used without loss of vividness. But in between these two classes there is a huge dump of worn-out metaphors which have lost all evocative power and are merely used because they save people the trouble of inventing phrases for themselves. Examples are: *Ring the changes on, take up the cudgels for, toe the line, ride roughshod over, stand shoulder to shoulder with, play into the hands of, no axe to grind, grist to the mill, fishing in troubled waters, rift within the lute, on the order of the day, Achilles' heel, swan song, hotbed.* Many of these are used without knowledge of their meaning (what is a "rift," for instance?), and incompatible metaphors are frequently mixed, a sure sign that the writer is not interested in what he is saying. Some metaphors now current have been twisted out of their original meaning without those who use them even being aware of the fact. For example, *toe the line* is sometimes written *tow the line.* Another example is *the hammer and the anvil,* now always used with the implication that the anvil gets the worst of it. In real life it is always the anvil that breaks the hammer, never the other way about: a writer who stopped to think what he was saying would be aware of this, and would avoid perverting the original phrase.

6 *Operators,* or *Verbal False Limbs.* These save the trouble of picking out appropriate verbs and nouns, and at the same time pad each sentence with extra syllables which give it an appearance of symmetry. Characteristic phrases are: *render inoperative, militate against, prove unacceptable, make contact with, be subjected to, give rise to, give grounds for, have the effect of, play a leading part (rôle) in, make itself felt, take effect, exhibit a tendency to, serve the purpose of,* etc etc. The keynote is the elimination of simple verbs. Instead of being a single word, such as *break, stop, spoil, mend, kill,* a verb becomes a *phrase,* made up of a noun or adjective tacked on to some general-purposes verb such as *prove, serve, form, play, render.* In addition, the passive voice is wherever possible used in preference to the active, and noun constructions are used instead of gerunds (*by examination of* instead of *by examining*). The range of verbs is further cut down by means of the *-ise* and *de-* formations, and banal statements are given an appearance of profundity by means of the *not un-* formation. Simple conjunctions and prepositions are replaced by such phrases as *with respect to, having regard to, the fact that, by dint of, in view of, in the interests of, on the hypothesis that;* and the ends of sentences are saved from anticlimax by such resounding commonplaces as *greatly to be desired, cannot be left out of account, a development to be expected in the near future, deserving of serious consideration, brought to a satisfactory conclusion,* and so on and so forth.

7 *Pretentious Diction.* Words like *phenomenon, element, individual* (as

noun), *objective, categorical, effective, virtual, basic, primary, promote, constitute, exhibit, exploit, utilise, eliminate, liquidate,* are used to dress up simple statements and give an air of scientific impartiality to biassed judgements. Adjectives like *epoch-making, epic, historic, unforgettable, triumphant, age-old, inevitable, inexorable, veritable,* are used to dignify the sordid processes of international politics, while writing that aims at glorifying war usually takes on an archaic colour, its characteristic words being: *realm, throne, chariot, mailed fist, trident, sword, shield, buckler, banner, jackboot, clarion.* Foreign words and expressions such as *cul de sac, ancien régime, deus ex machina, mutatis mutandis, status quo, Gleichschaltung, Weltanschauung,* are used to give an air of culture and elegance. Except for the useful abbreviations *i.e., e.g.,* and *etc.,* there is no real need for any of the hundreds of foreign phrases now current in English. Bad writers, and especially scientific, political and sociological writers, are nearly always haunted by the notion that Latin or Greek words are grander than Saxon ones, and unnecessary words like *expedite, ameliorate, predict, extraneous, deracinated, clandestine, sub-aqueous* and hundreds of others constantly gain ground from their Anglo-Saxon opposite numbers.[1] The jargon peculiar to Marxist writing (*hyena, hangman, cannibal, petty bourgeois, these gentry, lacquey, flunkey, mad dog, White Guard,* etc) consists largely of words and phrases translated from Russian, German or French; but the normal way of coining a new word is to use a Latin or Greek root with the appropriate affix and, where necessary, the *-ise* formation. It is often easier to make up words of this kind (*deregionalise, impermissible, extramarital, non-fragmentatory* and so forth) than to think up the English words that will cover one's meaning. The result, in general, is an increase in slovenliness and vagueness.

8 *Meaningless words.* In certain kinds of writing, particularly in art criticism and literary criticism, it is normal to come across long passages which are almost completely lacking in meaning.[2] Words like *romantic, plastic, values, human, dead, sentimental, natural, vitality,* as used in art criticism, are strictly meaningless, in the sense that they not only do not point to any discoverable object, but are hardly even expected to do so by the reader. When one critic writes, "The outstanding features of Mr X's work is its living quality", while another writes, "The immediately striking thing

[1]An interesting illustration of this is the way in which the English flower names which were in use till very recently are being ousted by Greek ones, *snapdragon* becoming *antirrhinum, forget-me-not* becoming *myosotis,* etc. It is hard to see any practical reason for this change of fashion: it is probably due to an instinctive turning-away from the more homely word and a vague feeling that the Greek word is scientific.

[2]Example: "Comfort's catholicity of perception and image, strangely Whitmanesque in range, almost the exact opposite in aesthetic compulsion, continues to evoke that trembling atmospheric accumulative hinting at a cruel, an inexorably serene timelessness . . . Wrey Gardinèr scores by aiming at simple bullseyes with precision. Only they were not so simple, and through this contented sadness runs more than the surface bitter-sweet of resignation." *(Poetry Quarterly.)*

about Mr X's work is its peculiar deadness", the reader accepts this as a simple difference of opinion. If words like *black* and *white* were involved, instead of the jargon words *dead* and *living,* he would see at once that language was being used in an improper way. Many political words are similarly abused. The word *Fascism* has now no meaning except in so far as it signifies "something not desirable". The words *democracy, socialism, freedom, patriotic, realistic, justice,* have each of them several different meanings which cannot be reconciled with one another. In the case of a word like *democracy,* not only is there no agreed definition, but the attempt to make one is resisted from all sides. It is almost universally felt that when we call a country democratic we are praising it: consequently the defenders of every kind of régime claim that it is a democracy, and fear that they might have to stop using the word if it were tied down to any one meaning. Words of this kind are often used in a consciously dishonest way. That is, the person who uses them has his own private definition, but allows his hearer to think he means something quite different. Statements like *Marshal Pétain was a true patriot, The soviet press is the freest in the world, The Catholic Church is opposed to persecution,* are almost always made with intent to deceive. Other words used in variable meanings, in most cases more or less dishonestly, are: *class, totalitarian, science, progressive, reactionary, bourgeois, equality.*

9 Now that I have made this catalogue of swindles and perversions, let me give another example of the kind of writing that they lead to. This time it must of its nature be an imaginary one. I am going to translate a passage of good English into modern English of the worst sort. Here is a well-known verse from *Ecclesiastes:*

> I returned, and saw under the sun, that the race is not to the swift, nor the battle to the strong, neither yet bread to the wise, nor yet riches to men of understanding, nor yet favour to men of skill; but time and chance happeneth to them all.

10 Here it is in modern English:

> Objective consideration of contemporary phenomena compels the conclusion that success or failure in competitive activities exhibits no tendency to be commensurate with innate capacity, but that a considerable element of the unpredictable must invariably be taken into account.

11 This is a parody, but not a very gross one. Exhibit 3, above, for instance, contains several patches of the same kind of English. It will be seen that I have not made a full translation. The beginning and ending of the sentence follow the original meaning fairly closely, but in the middle the concrete illustrations—race, battle, bread—dissolve into the vague phrase "success or failure in competitive activities". This had to be so, because no modern writer of the kind I am discussing—no one capable

of using phrases like "objective consideration of contemporary phenomena"—would ever tabulate his thoughts in that precise and detailed way. The whole tendency of modern prose is away from concreteness. Now analyse these two sentences a little more closely. The first contains 49 words but only 60 syllables, and all its words are those of everyday life. The second contains 38 words of 90 syllables: 18 of its words are from Latin roots, and one from Greek. The first sentence contains six vivid images, and only one phrase ("time and chance") that could be called vague. The second contains not a single fresh, arresting phrase, and in spite of its 90 syllables it gives only a shortened version of the meaning contained in the first. Yet without a doubt it is the second kind of sentence that is gaining ground in modern English. I do not want to exaggerate. This kind of writing is not yet universal, and outcrops of simplicity will occur here and there in the worst-written page. Still, if you or I were told to write a few lines on the uncertainty of human fortunes, we should probably come much nearer to my imaginary sentence than to the one from *Ecclesiastes.*

12 As I have tried to show, modern writing at its worst does not consist in picking out words for the sake of their meaning and inventing images in order to make the meaning clearer. It consists in gumming together long strips of words which have already been set in order by someone else, and making the results presentable by sheer humbug. The attraction of this way of writing is that it is easy. It is easier—even quicker, once you have the habit—to say *In my opinion it is a not unjustifiable assumption that* than to say *I think.* If you use ready-made phrases, you not only don't have to hunt about for words; you also don't have to bother with the rhythms of your sentences, since these phrases are generally so arranged as to be more or less euphonious. When you are composing in a hurry—when you are dictating to a stenographer, for instance, or making a public speech—it is natural to fall into a pretentious, latinised style. Tags like *a consideration which we should do well to bear in mind* or *a conclusion to which all of us would readily assent* will save many a sentence from coming down with a bump. By using stale metaphors, similes and idioms, you save much mental effort, at the cost of leaving your meaning vague, not only for your reader but for yourself. This is the significance of mixed metaphors. The sole aim of a metaphor is to call up a visual image. When these images clash—as in *The Fascist octopus has sung its swan song, the jackboot is thrown into the melting pot*—it can be taken as certain that the writer is not seeing a mental image of the objects he is naming; in other words he is not really thinking. Look again at the examples I gave at the beginning of this essay. Professor Laski (1) uses five negatives in 53 words. One of these is superfluous, making nonsense of the whole passage, and in addition there is the slip *alien* for akin, making further nonsense, and several avoidable pieces of clumsiness which increase the general vagueness. Professor Hogben (2) plays ducks and drakes with a battery which is able to write prescriptions,

and, while disapproving of the everyday phrase *put up with,* is unwilling to look *egregious* up in the dictionary and see what it means. (3) if one takes an uncharitable attitude towards it, is simply meaningless: probably one could work out its intended meaning by reading the whole of the article in which it occurs. In (4) the writer knows more or less what he wants to say, but an accumulation of stale phrases chokes him like tea-leaves blocking a sink. In (5) words and meaning have almost parted company. People who write in this manner usually have a general emotional meaning—they dislike one thing and want to express solidarity with another—but they are not interested in the detail of what they are saying. A scrupulous writer, in every sentence that he writes, will ask himself at least four questions, thus: What am I trying to say? What words will express it? What image or idiom will make it clearer? Is this image fresh enough to have an effect? And he will probably ask himself two more: Could I put it more shortly? Have I said anything that is avoidably ugly? But you are not obliged to go to all this trouble. You can shirk it by simply throwing your mind open and letting the ready-made phrases come crowding in. They will construct your sentences for you—even think your thoughts for you, to a certain extent—and at need they will perform the important service of partially concealing your meaning even from yourself. It is at this point that the special connection between politics and the debasement of language becomes clear.

13 In our time it is broadly true that political writing is bad writing. Where it is not true, it will generally be found that the writer is some kind of rebel, expressing his private opinions, and not a "party line". Orthodoxy, of whatever colour, seems to demand a lifeless, imitative style. The political dialects to be found in pamphlets, leading articles, manifestos, White Papers and the speeches of Under-Secretaries do, of course, vary from party to party, but they are all alike in that one almost never finds in them a fresh, vivid, homemade turn of speech. When one watches some tired hack on the platform mechanically repeating the familiar phrases—*bestial atrocities, iron heel, blood-stained tyranny, free peoples of the world, stand shoulder to shoulder*—one often has a curious feeling that one is not watching a live human being but some kind of dummy: a feeling which suddenly becomes stronger at moments when the light catches the speaker's spectacles and turns them into blank discs which seem to have no eyes behind them. And this is not altogether fanciful. A speaker who uses that kind of phraseology has gone some distance towards turning himself into a machine. The appropriate noises are coming out of his larnyx, but his brain is not involved as it would be if he were choosing his words for himself. If the speech he is making is one that he is accustomed to make over and over again, he may be almost unconscious of what he is saying, as one is when one utters the responses in church. And this reduced state of consciousness, if not indispensable, is at any rate favourable to political conformity.

14 In our time, political speech and writing are largely the defence of the indefensible. Things like the continuance of British rule in India, the Russian purges and deportations, the dropping of the atom bombs on Japan, can indeed be defended, but only by arguments which are too brutal for most people to face, and which do not square with the professed aims of political parties. Thus political language has to consist largely of euphemism, question-begging and sheer cloudly vagueness. Defenceless villages are bombarded from the air, the inhabitants driven out into the countryside, the cattle machine-gunned, the huts set on fire with incendiary bullets: this is called *pacification.* Millions of peasants are robbed of their farms and sent trudging along the roads with no more than they can carry: this is called *transfer of population* or *rectification of frontiers.* People are imprisoned for years without trial, or shot in the back of the neck or sent to die of scurvy in Arctic lumber camps: this is called *elimination of unreliable elements.* Such phraseology is needed if one wants to name things without calling up mental pictures of them. Consider for instance some comfortable English professor defending Russian totalitarianism. He cannot say outright, "I believe in killing off your opponents when you can get good results by doing so". Probably, therefore, he will say something like this:

> While freely conceding that the Soviet regime exhibits certain features which the humanitarian may be inclined to deplore, we must, I think, agree that a certain curtailment of the right to political opposition is an unavoidable concomitant of transitional periods, and that the rigours which the Russian people have been called upon to undergo have been amply justified in the sphere of concrete achievement.

15 The inflated style is itself a kind of euphemism. A mass of Latin words falls upon the facts like soft snow, blurring the outlines and covering up all the details. The great enemy of clear language is insincerity. When there is a gap between one's real and one's declared aims, one turns as it were instinctively to long words and exhausted idioms, like a cuttlefish squirting out ink. In our age there is no such thing as "keeping out of politics". All issues are political issues, and politics itself is a mass of lies, evasions, folly, hatred and schizophrenia. When the general atmosphere is bad, language must suffer. I should expect to find—this is a guess which I have not sufficient knowledge to verify—that the German, Russian and Italian languages have all deteriorated in the last ten or fifteen years, as a result of dictatorship.

16 But if thought corrupts language, language can also corrupt thought. A bad usage can spread by tradition and imitiation, even among people who should and do know better. The debased language that I have been discussing is in some ways very convenient. Phrases like *a not unjustifiable assumption, leaves much to be desired, would serve no good purpose, a consideration which we should do well to bear in mind,* are a continuous temp-

tation, a packet of aspirins always at one's elbow. Look back through this essay, and for certain you will find that I have again and again committed the very faults I am protesting against. By this morning's post I have received a pamphlet dealing with conditions in Germany. The author tells me that he "felt impelled" to write it. I open it at random, and here is almost the first sentence that I see: "(The Allies) have an opportunity not only of achieving a radical transformation of Germany's social and political structure in such a way as to avoid a nationalistic reaction in Germany itself, but at the same time of laying the foundations of a co-operative and unified Europe." You see, he "feels impelled" to write—feels, presumably, that he has something new to say—and yet his words, like cavalry horses answering the bugle, group themselves automatically into the familiar dreary pattern. This invasion of one's mind by ready-made phrases *(lay the foundations, achieve a radical transformation)* can only be prevented if one is constantly on guard against them, and every such phrase anaesthetises a portion of one's brain.

17 I said earlier that the decadence of our language is probably curable. Those who deny this would argue, if they produced an argument at all, that language merely reflects existing social conditions, and that we cannot influence its development by any direct tinkering with words and constructions. So far as the general tone or spirit of a language goes, this may be true, but it is not true in detail. Silly words and expressions have often disappeared, not through any evolutionary process but owing to the conscious action of a minority. Two recent examples were *explore every avenue* and *leave no stone unturned,* which were killed by the jeers of a few journalists. There is a long list of fly-blown metaphors which could similarly be got rid of if enough people would interest themselves in the job; and it should also be possible to laugh the *not un-* formation out of existence,[3] to reduce the amount of Latin and Greek in the average sentence, to drive out foreign phrases and strayed scientific words, and, in general, to make pretentiousness unfashionable. But all these are minor points. The defence of the English language implies more than this, and perhaps it is best to start by saying what it does *not* imply.

18 To begin with, it has nothing to do with archaism, with the salvaging of obsolete words and turns of speech, or with the setting-up of a "standard English" which must never be departed from. On the contrary, it is especially concerned with the scrapping of every word or idiom which has outworn its usefulness. It has nothing to do with correct grammar and syntax, which are of no importance so long as one makes one's meaning clear, or with the avoidance of Americanisms, or with having what is called a "good prose style". On the other hand it is not concerned with fake simplicity and the attempt to make written English colloquial. Nor does it

---

[3]One can cure oneself of the *not un-* formation by memorising this sentence: *A not unblack dog was chasing a not unsmall rabbit across a not ungreen field.*

even imply in every case preferring the Saxon word to the Latin one, though it does imply using the fewest and shortest words that will cover one's meaning. What is above all needed is to let the meaning choose the word, and not the other way about. In prose, the worst thing one can do with words is to surrender to them. When you think of a concrete object, you think wordlessly, and then, if you want to describe the thing you have been visualising, you probably hunt about till you find the exact words that seem to fit it. When you think of something abstract you are more inclined to use words from the start, and unless you make a conscious effort to prevent it, the existing dialect will come rushing in and do the job for you, at the expense of blurring or even changing your meaning. Probably it is better to put off using words as long as possible and get one's meaning as clear as one can through pictures or sensations. Afterwards one can choose—not simply *accept*—the phrases that will best cover the meaning, and then switch round and decide what impression one's words are likely to make on another person. This last effort of the mind cuts out all stale or mixed images, all prefabricated phrases, needless repetitions, and humbug and vagueness generally. But one can often be in doubt about the effect of a word or a phrase, and one needs rules that one can rely on when instinct fails. I think the following rules will cover most cases:

i. Never use a metaphor, simile or other figure of speech which you are used to seeing in print.
ii. Never use a long word where a short one will do.
iii. If it is possible to cut a word out, always cut it out.
iv. Never use the passive where you can use the active.
v. Never use a foreign phrase, a scientific word or a jargon word if you can think of an everyday English equivalent.
vi. Break any of these rules sooner than say anything outright barbarous.

These rules sound elementary, and so they are, but they demand a deep change of attitude in anyone who has grown used to writing in thc style now fashionable. One could keep all of them and still write bad English, but one could not write the kind of stuff that I quoted in those five specimens at the beginning of this article.

19 I have not here been considering the literary use of language, but merely language as an instrument for expressing and not for concealing or preventing thought. Stuart Chase and others have come near to claiming that all abstract words are meaningless, and have used this as a pretext for advocating a kind of political quietism. Since you don't know what Fascism is, how can you struggle against Fascism? One need not swallow such absurdities as this, but one ought to recognise that the present political chaos is connected with the decay of language, and that one can prob-

ably bring about some improvement by starting at the verbal end. If you simplify your English, you are freed from the worst follies of orthodoxy. You cannot speak any of the necessary dialects, and when you make a stupid remark its stupidity will be obvious, even to yourself. Political language—and with variations this is true of all political parties, from Conservatives to Anarchists—is designed to make lies sound truthful and murder respectable, and to give an appearance of solidity to pure wind. One cannot change this all in a moment, but one can at least change one's own habits, and from time to time one can even, if one jeers loudly enough, send some worn-out and useless phrase—some *jackboot, Achilles' heel, hotbed, melting pot, acid test, veritable inferno* or other lump of verbal refuse—into the dustbin where it belongs.

Word Study List

decadent	1	parody	11
archaism	1, 21	euphonious	12
regeneration	2	simile	12
hackneyed	4	idiom	12
metaphor	5, 14, 20	egregious	12
evocative	5	scrupulous	12
gerund	6	orthodoxy	13, 19
banal	6	dialect	13, 18, 19
profundity	6	euphemism	14, 15
affix	7	schizophrenia	15
Fascism	8, 12, 19		

Questions

1. How does Orwell link the decline of the English language to politics?

2. What political climate had Orwell lived through that provoked his observations on politics and language?

3. In Chapter 3, the article "Metaphors: Live, Dead, and Silly" discusses the use of metaphors to liven up writing. Review Sale's article in Chapter 3 and Orwell's remarks on metaphors; then explain the difference between a dying or dead metaphor and a live one. Why are live ones recommended over the familiar but dead ones?

4. In Chapter 1, the article "The Power of Words" claims many advantages for enlarging your vocabulary, yet Orwell is highly critical of what he calls "pretentious diction." How can you expand your vocabulary without becoming a pretentious writer?

5. Does Orwell contradict in paragraph 18 what you thought were the minimum requirements of good writing—i.e., use of "standard English," "cor-

rect grammar and syntax," or "good prose style"? if these guides cannot be relied on to produce good writing, why are they a part of composition courses? What, for Orwell, is the key to good writing?

6. Why, according to Orwell, are political rebels more likely to produce good writing than more conservative party members or bureaucrats?

Exercise

In 1945 Orwell complained about the meaningless language of vagueness and stale metaphors. To see if such writing is still in use, look through textbooks, journals, or newspapers for articles analyzing art or literature. If you cannot find any bad writing, report these findings in a paragraph. If you find a piece of bad writing, explain in a paragraph, using examples from the piece, that the language Orwell describes is still with us.

The Language of War

Haig Bosmajian

Haig Bosmajian (b. 1928) has been writing on the connection between language and oppression since the late 1950s when he began studying the techniques of Nazi persuasion. Currently a professor of parliamentary procedure, rhetoric, and freedom of speech of the University of Washington, he has edited and written articles and books on language and sexism, racism, and civil rights. "The Language of War" is from a collection of his articles entitled *The Language of Oppression* (1974).

This article examines the way language was twisted during one particular war—the Vietnam War—"to justify the unjustifiable."

1 Resources control . . . regrettable by-products . . . impact area . . . hardware . . . hornets' nests . . . protective reaction . . . pacification . . . strategic hamlet . . . New Life Hamlet . . . incursion . . . Operation Ranch Hand . . . Operation Independence . . . Operation Sunrise . . . defoliation . . . advisers.

2 If one did not know better one would never suspect a war was going on, that human beings were being mutilated, tortured, forcibly removed from their villages, wounded, and killed. This was the language of a war in which 60,000 United States soldiers and "advisers" were killed, in which over one million Vietnamese soldiers were killed. The words and terms used by governmental officials to report what was occurring in Vietnam and Southeast Asia between 1962 and 1972 constitute an excellent

case study in how language is corrupted to mask the cruelty and inhumanity of war, to attempt to justify the unjustifiable.

3 Linguistically legitimatizing the killing of "the enemy" during wartime has long been a preoccupation of military and civilian officials bent on waging war. Language is the tool to be used to make acceptable what civilized people would ordinarily not see as acceptable.

4 "War," according to Aldous Huxley,[1] "is enormously discreditable to those who order it to be waged and even to those who merely tolerate its existence. Furthermore, to developed sensibilities the facts of war are revolting and horrifying. . . . By suppressing and distorting the truth, we protect our sensibilities and preserve our self-esteem. Now, language is, among other things, a device men use for suppressing and distorting the truth. Finding the reality of war too unpleasant to contemplate, we create a verbal alternative to that reality, parallel with it, but in quality quite different from it. That which we contemplate thenceforth is not that to which we react emotionally and upon which we pass our moral judgments, is not war as it is in fact, but the fiction of war as it exists in our pleasantly falsifying verbiage."

5 In his now famous essay "Politics and the English Language," George Orwell pointed out that "political speech and writing are largely the defense of the indefensible. . . . Defenseless villages are bombarded from the air, the inhabitants driven out into the country-side, the cattle machine-gunned, the huts set on fire with incendiary bullets: this is called *pacification*."

6 Huxley's and Orwell's observations were especially relevant during the decade of United States military involvement in Southeast Asia. In 1972 Representative Robert F. Drinan of Massachusetts told an audience of English professors: "It is my duty to report to you that the objects of Orwell's observation are at this moment comfortably ensconced in the State and Defense Departments and, ironically or predictably, they are the very individuals who in so many other respects are bringing us closer to the Orwellian version of a sterile 1984." Regarding the deceptive use of language in describing the Vietnam War Peter Farb observed: "The predominant strategy was the ornate euphemism—an effort to divert attention from the true horrors of death and destruction by labeling something the opposite of what it truly was. An aggressive attack by an armada of airplanes, which most speakers of English call simply an *air raid,* was instead spoken of as a momentary defensive strategy, a *routine limited duration protective reaction.* Defoliation of an entire forest, with the result that it may not sprout another green leaf for decades or even hundreds of years, was labeled a *resources control program.*"

---

[1]A British essayist and novelist (1894–1963) whose interests ranged from language and culture to politics and science.—ED.

7 During the war in Indochina the American military took words which carried connotations of peace, nonviolence, and conciliation and used them to hide cruelty and inhumanity inflicted on the Vietnamese people. A "pacification" program was established and month after month, year after year, government officials declared, as in some primitive incantation, that the United States was making "progress in pacification."

8 Writing of the situation in 1962, David Halberstam reported in his *The Making of a Quagmire:* "Some general or official would arrive in Vietnam, would spend one day in Saigon being briefed and meeting the Ngo family, and another day or two in the field inspecting selected strategic hamlets and units. Then he would hold an airport press conference in which he would say that the war was being won, that the people were rallying to the government, that he had been impressed by the determination of President Diem, who was a great leader." All through 1963 officials in Saigon and Washington, D.C., recited the words, "We are winning in Vietnam." When in May, 1964, South Vietnamese General Khanh took the offensive and South Vietnamese casualties began to rise, the Pentagon reported that the General was "on the right track." In August, 1965, officials in Saigon and Washington expressed exuberant optimism over the course of the war. And in July, 1966, Vice-President Hubert Humphrey declared: "We are gaining on all four major fronts—the economic front, the political front, the diplomatic front and the military front."

9 Late in the 1960's the American people were told again and again, "We now have the initiative in Vietnam." During the early 1970's high civilian and military leaders announced that the end was in sight, that "the light at the end of the tunnel could be seen."

10 Official recitations and incantations about the war in Vietnam would have done justice to any primitive medicinemen attempting to cast a spell over members of their tribes or over tribal enemies.

11 The "pacification" which officials described as progressing so well turned out to be the "pacification" described by Orwell. One journalist disclosed how this "pacifying" of Vietnamese villages was carried out: "The Vietnamese woman ignored the crying baby in her arms. She stared in hatred as the American infantrymen with shotguns blasted away at chickens and ducks. Others shot a water buffalo and a pet dog. While her husband, father, and young son were led away, the torch was put to the hut that contained the family belongings. The flames consumed everything—including the shrine to the family ancestors."

12 "Pacification" was used as a label for actions which involved entering a village with bayonets at the ready, "persuading" the people to evacuate their huts, rounding up all the males and shooting those who resisted, prodding the elderly, the women and the children into camps set up by the United States military, slaughtering the domesticated animals and burning the pitiful dwellings to the ground. A news source reported that "one village so persistently resisted pacification that finally it had to be destroyed." See Webster: Pacify: to make peaceful, calm; to tranquilize.

13 The forcible migration of Vietnamese civilians from their villages to "strategic hamlets" was described in a variety of terms to minimize the inhumanity of it all. Paul Dickson observed in 1972 that "the forced transfer of civilians was invariably given a nice 'operation' or 'program' title like 'Operation Independence,' or 'Operation Sunrise.' Such transfers were officially termed 'compulsory relocation' and the civilians involved were either moved to 'strategic hamlets' or 'resettlement centers'—locales that were often no more than what were called 'refugee camps' in other wars. As a *New York Times* reporter observed . . . 'A few people were driven together, a roll of barbed wire was thrown over their heads, and the strategic hamlet was finished.'"

14 "Pacification" in Vietnam, wrote Edward and Onora Nell in 1967, "has included at various times the construction of 'New Life Hamlets,' and of 'Prosperity Zones' containing 'strategic hamlets.' More recently a 'Rural Construction Program' came on the scene, followed by a 'Revolutionary Development Program' which in turn gave way to a 'Rural Development Program.'"

15 What occurs when a perfectly good word like "pacification" is used as a euphemism for acts of cruelty and inhumanity is that the word loses its former meaning and cannot be uttered later without connoting some of what it attempted to hide in Vietnam. This "destruction" of words occurred in Germany under the Nazis; perfectly good words were misused and distorted with the result that after the war these same words could not be used without carrying with them the distorted meanings attributed to them by the Nazis.

16 Steiner[2] has pointed out that the bestialities of Nazism infected the German language. It was used "to enforce innumerable falsehoods, to persuade the Germans that the war was just and everything victorious. As defeat began closing in on the thousand-year Reich, the lies thickened to a constant snowdrift. The language was turned upside down to say 'light' where there was blackness and 'victory' where there was 'disaster.'" This distorted use of language eventually has its negative effects on the language itself and as Steiner says, "there comes a breaking point. Use a language to conceive, organize, and justify Belsen; use it to make out specifications for gas ovens; use it to dehumanize man during twelve years of calculated bestiality. Something will happen to it. Make words that Hitler and Goebbels[3] and a hundred thousand *Unterstrumführer* made: conveyors of terror and falsehood. Something will happen to the words. Something of the lies and sadism will settle in the marrow of the language."

17 Words such as "restraint" and "protective" were debased when Richard Nixon used the former to describe United States military activities in Vietnam and when the Air Force used the latter in the term "pro-

[2]George Steiner (b. 1929), British professor of English at Cambridge and author of many books including *Language and Silence,* from which the following quotations are taken.—ED.

[3]German Nazi propaganda leader (1897–1945).—ED.

tective reaction" to minimize large scale bombings. "Throughout the war . . .," Nixon declared on May 8, 1972, "the United States has exercised a degree of restraint unprecedented in the annals of war." But as Ronald Kriss commented in the *Saturday Review: "Restraint?* We have grown discouragingly accustomed to the abuse, misuse, and even nonuse of words. But this was a rather blatant example, even coming from a politican. I assume the President meant that because we never supported an invasion of North Vietnam, because we never breached the Red River dikes, because we never resorted to nuclear weapons, because, in short, we never totally laid waste the country, we can congratulate ourselves for our unprecedently civilized behavior."

18 "Still," Kriss added, "it requires an extraordinary insensitivity to the language to talk of 'restraint,' when we have dumped twice as many tons of explosives on South Vietnam alone as we did in all combat zones during all of World War II, when we have contributed to the killing or maiming of hundreds of thousands—if not millions—of civilians, when we have turned countless acres of once-lush forests and farmlands into hideous moonscapes, barren and brown-hued . . . Nor does the word ring true when we consider that the Vietnam War is the longest in our history and, in terms of battle deaths, the fourth-costliest (after World War II, the Civil War, and World War I, in that order)."

19 The extensive "protective reaction" air raids over North Vietnam were part of this "restraint." In an item titled "Terminology in Air War," the *New York Times* said on June 16, 1972: "Under 'protective reaction,' American commanders were authorized to seek out and attack enemy troops or planes or missiles that threatened them. The use of the phrase by Mr. Laird [Secretary of Defense] at the 1969 news conference marked a shift from previous American military orders in which United States ground forces were to put 'maximum pressure' on the enemy."

20 The *New York Times* reported that "three former members of a photo-intelligence team assigned to Pacific Air Force headquarters in Hawaii said in an interview today that at least 20 to 25 planned bombing raids later decribed as 'protective reaction' strikes were flown each month by Air Force planes over North Vietnam throughout 1970 and 1971. . . . All three airmen interviewed today agreed that the concept of 'protective reaction' was widely considered throughout the Pacific Air Force command as simply another way of describing bombing raids." One of the airmen stated: 'We were constantly hitting truck depots and storage areas and describing them as P. R. strikes." Another airman, who had seen all of the pilot reports for Seventh Air Force missions flown in Laos, Cambodia and North Vietnam, said that "invariably, after such missions . . . the pilots would enter 'protective reaction' on their reports." Finally, on April 4, 1972, "the policy of 'protective reaction' was suspended with the resumption of full-scale bombing of North Vietnam after the start of the North Vietnamese offensive."

21 The depersonalization of the Vietnamese people reached its height in the B-52 bombers which flew from Anderson Air Force Base in Guam, six hours flying time away from their targets in Vietnam, to drop their high explosive bombs on the people and land below. To the crew aboard the B-52, it had become an "impersonal war." Joseph Treaster reports that "for the crewmen, sitting in their air-conditioned compartments more than five miles above the steamy jungle of South Vietnam, the bomb run had been merely another familiar technical exercise. The crew knew virtually nothing about their target and they showed no curiosity. Only the radar-navigator, who in earlier wars would have been called the bombardier, saw the bombs exploding, and those distant flashes gave no hint of the awesome eruption of flames and steel on the ground. No one in the plane, including this correspondent, heard the deafening blast." Treaster describes the effects of the exploding bombs: "On the ground a B-52 strike—or 'arclight' as they are commonly called—is a chillingly spectacular event, sometimes electric with excitement. Tremendous clouds of smoke and dust boil up and a thunder of kettle drums splits the ears. People in the 'impact' areas are killed or sent reeling in shock."

22 None of these devastating effects were ever perceived by the men in the B-52; nothing and nobody that had been destroyed on the ground were ever seen by the airmen. One Air Force captain declared: "Essentially I feel I'm a nonparticipant in the war . . . I'm intelligent and I know I'm in it, but I don't feel it." A pilot "said that he often thought of himself as a long-distance truck driver. A crewman said that bombing South Vietnam from a B-52 was like 'delivering the mail.'" Another captain stated that "if we were killing anybody down there with our bombs I have to think we were bombing the enemy and not civilians. I feel quite sure about our targetting." The killing had become so impersonal that the captain could say: "As far as losing any sleep over what we're doing, how many people we kill . . . we never get to see the damage."

23 Here was a war in which a B-52 pilot could say as he dropped his lethal bombs: "I am a nonparticipant in the war." What higher praise is there for the success of governmental officials and technology than for a military officer to make such a statement?

24 Keeping the killing by ground forces impersonal has always been more difficult and therefore a variety of euphemisms have been created to conceal the reality of war. During the late 1930's, according to Aldous Huxley, militarists were "clamouring for war planes numerous and powerful enough to go and 'destroy the hornets in their nests'—in other words, to go and throw thermite, high explosives and vesicants upon the inhabitants of neighboring countries before they have time to come and do the same to us."

25 Metaphors are used to conceal the fact that human beings are killing human beings. One military officer described the parachuting of his troops into an area occupied by the Vietcong: "Our tigers jumped from

the helicopters into the VC hornets' nest." For those who like their wars less picturesque and more "sanitized" there was the suggestion that a "sanitized belt" be established stretching south of the 17th parallel at the demilitarized zone. This suggestion, made during a March 1967 meeting between Presidents Johnson and Ky meant, in effect, forcibly expelling from their homes and villages all the inhabitants of the area in question, cutting down all the trees, bulldozing the land clear, and erecting "defensive positions" provided with machine guns, mortars, and mines. See Webster: To sanitize: to bring about absence of dirt and agents of infection or disease; to promote health and healthful conditions.

26 The bombs and other means of destruction used in the Vietnam war were given names which concealed the devastation they wreaked upon the land and the people. Sydney Schanberg reported in 1972 that American briefers in Saigon who were supposed to pass on to newsmen the "facts" about the war used a language which had "no connection with everyday English" and was "designed to sanitize the war": "Planes do not drop bombs, they 'deliver ordnance.' Napalm is a forbidden word and when an American information officer is forced under direct questioning to discuss it he calls it 'soft ordnance.' In the press releases and the answers to newsmen's questions, there is never any sense, not even implicit, of people being killed, homes being destroyed, thousands of refugees fleeing."

27 Ordnance, it turned out, meant fragmentation bombs which exploded on impact and killed or mutilated all humans and animals within range of the sharp pieces of flying metal; napalm canisters, jellied gasoline bombs which exploded and sent out showers of fiery jelly, stuck to and burned into the victim's flesh.

28 Even the ordnance used to destroy vegetation during defoliation operations had to be concealed behind euphemisms, "'Operation Ranch Hand,'" Paul Dickson tells us, "was the folksy name created in 1965 for a series of concentrated airborne chemical defoliation missions during which, according to officials at that time, the chemicals being dropped were likened to 'weed killers'—even though they could kill a plant fifteen miles from the point at which they were dropped. Terms like 'Ranch Hand,' 'weed killer' ('the same as you buy in the hardware store at home,' said an American official in 1966), 'routine improvement of visibility in jungle areas,' 'non-toxic,' and 'resources control' conspired to make defoliation and crop destruction sound like a major 4-H Club project."

29 What of the victims of all this "pacification," "sanitizing," "defoliation," and "protective reactions"? While the weapons of war had to be euphemized, the people against whom they were used had to be dehumanized. Anthony Lewis wrote in the *New York Times* on June 12, 1972, that "some of those involved in the policy of heavy bombing and shelling must, unconsciously or otherwise, regard the Vietnamese as *untermenschen,* as creatures somehow not so human as us."

30 In his short essay "The Nonwhite War," Herbert Mitgang recounted

a government official's reference to bombed civilian installations, and presumably the people inside those buildings, as "regrettable by-products." Mitgang, after referring to the withholding of bombing raid information from the American people, wrote:

> But the greatest omission of all concerns the nonwhite people on the receiving end of the terror falling from the skies. Watching Senator Kennedy's subcommittee on refugees attempt to extract the facts from Administration spokesmen is a despairing sight. A few days ago, in the old Senate Office Building, he asked: Why is it easy for you to tell us how many bridges have been destroyed in North Vietnam and the precise number of trucks hit along the Ho Chi Minh Trail but not how many hospitals, schools, churches and other civilian installations have been hit by our bombs? The evasive response by an Assistant Secretary of State was that these were not deliberate military targets but only 'regrettable by-products' of the violence of warfare.

31 If the "regrettable by-product" was the death of a South Vietnamese civilian, the family of the victim was awarded thirty-four dollars, officially referred to as "condolence awards."

32 The "most shocking fact about war, Aldous Huxley reminds us, "is that its victims and its instruments are individual human beings, and that these individual human beings are condemned by the monstrous conventions of politics to murder or be murdered in quarrels not their own, to inflict upon the innocent and, innocent themselves of any crime against their enemies, to suffer cruelties of every kind. The language of strategy and politics is designed, as far as it is possible, to conceal this fact, to make it appear as though wars were not fought by individuals drilled to murder one another in cold blood and without provocation, but either by impersonal and therefore wholly nonmoral and impassible forces, or else by personified abstraction."

33 The language and strategy of which Huxley spoke became an integral part of the Vietnam war in which politicians and military leaders distorted language to conceal and justify their inhumanity.

Word Study List

linguistically	3	initiative	9
verbiage	4	debased	17
incendiary	5	blatant	17
ensconced	6	thermite	24
euphemism	6, 15	vesicants	24
defoliation	6	metaphors	25
incantation	7, 10	ordnance	26, 27
quagmire	8	impassible	32
hamlet	8, 13		

Questions

1. Why are euphemisms and metaphors especially useful to military leaders and politicians who want to wage war?

2. Why does the author choose the language of the Vietnam War to illustrate "how language is corrupted to mask the cruelty and inhumanity of war"? Does our role in this war differ from that in other wars (e.g., Korean War, World Wars I and II, Revolutionary War)? Why do you think the Nazis' use of language in World War II is included in this discussion of the Vietnam War?

3. Explain the effectiveness of the attention-getter Bosmajian uses to open his article.

4. What effect has the technology of warfare and communication had on the use of euphemistic language in waging war?

5. Which was more important in making the war impersonal for the B-52 bombers—technology or language? Which is more critical for depersonalizing the war for the ground forces?

Exercises

1. After World War II, the Department of War was reorganized into the Department of Defense. Write a paragraph in which you explain the significance of this change for policy makers and military leaders seeking increased military budgets for equipment and personnel in times of peace and war.

2. Write a definition of *pacification* and *sanitized* as used by military and political spokespersons during the Vietnam conflict. Compare your definitions to those that the author quotes from Webster's dictionary. How do they differ? How are they similar?

The Words Race

Ellen Goodman

Author of *Close to Home* (1979) and *At Large* (1981), collections of her essays, Ellen Goodman (b. 1941) has been a feature writer for the *Boston Globe* since 1967 and a syndicated columnist since 1976. "The Words Race" appeared in the *Globe* and other newspapers on November 27, 1982.

In her column Goodman satirizes "nukespeak," the jargon of our era that is designed to "help us think about the unthinkable."

1 Boston—Throw away the rest of your entry blanks. Throw away your miserable little attempts to win the big prize. The contest for the 1982 George Orwell War-Is-Peace Sweepstakes is over. Ladies and gentlemen, the winner, hands down, is The Great Communicator himself, Ronald Reagan.

2 It was Ronald Reagan who alone among all of you had the insight, the flash, the sheer unmitigated nerve to rename the MX missile, "The Peacekeeper"!

3 Not once in recent years, not since the Atomic Energy Commission began to measure atomic fallout in "Sunshine Units," not since India dubbed its bomb a "peaceful nuclear device," have we witnessed such a dazzling example of linguistic alchemy. The judges were simply overwhelmed.

4 By the use of euphemism, the wave of a verbal olive branch, the most destabilizing weapon yet suggested for our arsenal of weapons was transformed on network television into a candidate for the Nobel Peace Prize. Who among us can but admire the way in which the president won the title of Master of the Word Game of the War Game.

5 There is a bit of history behind this victory. In the beginning of our nuclear age, there was only the most meager atomic vocabulary. In the '40s, before the Department of War had been renamed the Department of Defense, our government struggled mightily with the big, bad public relations given the poor little atom. Even in the 1950s, the Atomic Energy Commission was unsuccessful in its attempts to promote atomic bomb-watching vacations.

6 But slowly, the nuclear wordgamesmen found ways to help us think about the unthinkable, to regard the bomb as a handmaiden of peace. Now, we are into the post-psychobabble era of nukespeak.

7 "Nukespeak," for all of you who are still unaware, is the word culled from George Orwell's description of "newspeak," and the name of an insightful new book. "Newspeak" was the language developed by the government of Orwell's "1984" to manipulate the way people think. Nukespeak is the language developed by our government.

8 "The key reason for using language like that," says "Nukespeak" co-author Stephen Hilgarten, "is to try and make the public believe this weapon is something we need for our security. The reason for euphemisms is to justify the military position as being morally correct."

9 There is nothing startling in all of this. The government has been cleaning up and cooling down the language of conventional war since Vietnam. But it's reached a fine art in nukespeak. The experts not only talk about "clean bombs" and "devices" and "nuclear exchanges," but they have made terms so obscure that only the Military Experts could talk the same language.

10 Rory O'Connor, another co-author, has been amazed at the rash of new entries into nukespeak. O'Connor, a television producer, says, "I think that there is a 'veritable energetic disassembly,' as they say in nukespeak, a proliferation of nuclear language, simply around MX and Dense Pack."

11 Among the words that he ticks off his list are old ones given nuke meanings, such as "fratricide" and "decapitation."

12 O'Connor is convinced that the public has to learn the vocabulary of nukespeak or be left out of the debate about survival.

13 But the worst insult of nukespeak is the manipulation of war and peace. "It is pure Orwell," says O'Connor. "In newspeak, everything means the opposite. In nukespeak as well. Atoms for peace are really atoms for war. START (the name of Reagan's disarmament initiative) really means stop, as far as I'm concerned. If they adopt the MX, the Department of Defense is really the Department of Offense, because the MX is a first-strike weapon."

14 No one knows yet whether the MX Peacekeeper will be laughed out of the dictionary or added to the current MAD(mutual assured destruction)ness. No one knows whether it will win a role in the "scenarios," carry weight in the "balance of terror," and be responsible for "megadeaths."

15 But the hawks have one consolation. We are beating the Russians in the words race.

Word Study List

unmitigated	2	fratricide	11
linguistic	3	decapitation	11
alchemy	3	scenarios	14
proliferation	10	megadeaths	14
Dense Pack	10		

Questions

1. What term does Goodman focus her attack on by saying it has won the War-Is-Peace Sweepstakes?

2. Goodman describes the term as "linguistic alchemy." Look up these words if necessary and then explain why Goodman's description is clever. Why does she call the term a euphemism?

3. What other words does Goodman introduce that are part of the nuclear wordgames (read wargames) of our time? What general term has been coined to refer to this nuclear-age language?

4. From what source does the term *nukespeak* come? Do you think it's safe

to conclude that Orwell is the father of all who analyze and object to political doublespeak? (If you haven't read *1984,* do you think it's time to do so?)

5. Goodman objects to some nukespeak terms because they are euphemisms. Others, she says, are so obscure only experts can understand them. What label is appropriate for the obscure nukespeak terms? (If you are in doubt, see Chapter 5.)

6. How would you characterize Goodman's tone? How does the essay's tone help to convey Goodman's attitude toward her subject?

Exercise

Goodman's successful journalistic style deserves study. What are the specific elements of her writing style that create tone and help convey attitude? Study her word choice, use of metaphors, sentence patterns, choice of examples. In a short essay, explain and illustrate the dominant characteristics of her writing style.

I Have a Dream

Martin Luther King, Jr.

Martin Luther King, Jr. (1929–1968), was a Baptist minister, writer, and leader of the American civil rights movement for over a decade. He was assassinated on April 4, 1968, in Memphis, Tennessee, where he was organizing striking garbage workers. "I Have a Dream" was delivered by King from the steps of the Lincoln Memorial on the afternoon of August 28, 1963. This speech climaxed on all-day freedom march and demonstration by 200,000 people in Washington, D.C.

King's speech is a fervent plea for blacks to struggle for the equality that was promised a hundred years before by Lincoln. There are echoes of the imagery in Lincoln's "Gettysburg Address" and of the imagery of the Bible. Note how King uses stylistic devices described in Chapter 3.

1 Five score years ago, a great American, in whose symbolic shadow we stand, signed the Emancipation Proclamation. This momentous decree came as a great beacon light of hope to millions of Negro slaves who had been seared in the flames of withering injustice. It came as a joyous daybreak to end the long night of captivity.

2 But one hundred years later, we must face the tragic fact that the Negro is still not free. One hundred years later, the life of the Negro is

still sadly crippled by the manacles of segregation and the chains of discrimination. One hundred years later, the Negro lives on a lonely island of poverty in the midst of a vast ocean of material prosperity. One hundred years later, the Negro is still languished in the corners of American society and finds himself an exile in his own land. So we have come here today to dramatize an appalling condition.

3 In a sense we have come to our nation's Capital to cash a check. When the architects of our republic wrote the magnificent words of the Constitution and the Declaration of Independence, they were signing a promissory note to which every American was to fall heir. This note was a promise that all men would be guaranteed the unalienable rights of life, liberty, and the pursuit of happiness.

4 It is obvious today that America has defaulted on this promissory note insofar as her citizens of color are concerned. Instead of honoring this sacred obligation, America has given the Negro people a bad check; a check which has come back marked "insufficient funds." But we refuse to believe that the bank of justice is bankrupt. We refuse to believe that there are insufficient funds in the great vaults of opportunity of this nation. So we have come to cash this check—a check that will give us upon demand the riches of freedom and the security of justice.

5 We have also come to this hallowed spot to remind America of the fierce urgency of *now*. This is no time to engage in the luxury of cooling off or to take the tranquilizing drug of gradualism.[1] *Now* is the time to make real the promises of democracy. *Now* is the time to rise from the dark and desolate valley of segregation to the sunlit path of racial justice. *Now* is the time to open the doors of opportunity to all of God's children. *Now* is the time to lift our nation from the quicksands of racial injustice to the solid rock of brotherhood.

6 It would be fatal for the nation to overlook the urgency of the moment and to underestimate the determination of the Negro. This sweltering summer of the Negro's legitimate discontent will not pass until there is an invigorating autumn of freedom and equality. Nineteen sixty-three is not an end, but a beginning. Those who hope that the Negro needed to blow off steam and will now be content will have a rude awakening if the nation returns to business as usual. There will be neither rest nor tranquillity in America until the Negro is granted his citizenship rights. The whirlwinds of revolt will continue to shake the foundations of our nation until the bright day of justice emerges.

7 But there is something that I must say to my people who stand on the warm threshold which leads into the palace of justice. In the process of gaining our rightful place we must not be guilty of wrongful deeds. Let us not seek to satisfy our thirst for freedom by drinking from the cup of bitterness and hatred. We must forever conduct our struggle on the high

---

[1]The policy of achieving integration by gradual rather than by drastic change.—Ed.

plane of dignity and discipline. We must not allow our creative protest to degenerate into physical violence. Again and again we must rise to the majestic heights of meeting physical force with soul force.

8 The marvelous new militancy which has engulfed the Negro community must not lead us to a distrust of all white people, for many of our white brothers, as evidenced by their presence here today, have come to realize that their destiny is tied up with our destiny and their freedom is inextricably bound to our freedom. We cannot walk alone.

9 And as we walk, we must make the pledge that we shall march ahead. We cannot turn back. There are those who are asking the devotees of civil rights, "When will you be satisfied?"

10 We can never be satisifed as long as the Negro is the victim of the unspeakable horrors of police brutality.

11 We can never be satisfied as long as our bodies, heavy with the fatigue of travel, cannot gain lodging in the motels of the highways and the hotels of the cities.

12 We cannot be satisfied as long as the Negro's basic mobility is from a smaller ghetto to a larger one.

13 We can never be satisfied as long as a Negro in Mississippi cannot vote and a Negro in New York believes he has nothing for which to vote.

14 No, no, we are not satisfied, and we will not be satisfied until justice rolls down like waters and righteousness like a mighty stream.

15 I am not unmindful that some of you have come here out of great trials and tribulations. Some of you have come fresh from narrow jail cells. Some of you have come from areas where your quest for freedom left you battered by the storms of persecution and staggered by the winds of police brutality. You have been the veterans of creative suffering. Continue to work with the faith that unearned suffering is redemptive.

16 Go back to Mississippi, go back to Alabama, go back to South Carolina, go back to Georgia, go back to Louisiana, go back to the slums and ghettos of our Northern cities, knowing that somehow this situation can and will be changed. Let us not wallow in the valley of despair.

17 I say to you today, my friends, that in spite of the difficulties and frustrations of the moment I still have a dream. It is a dream deeply rooted in the American dream.

18 I have a dream that one day this nation will rise up and live out the true meaning of its creed: "We hold these truths to be self-evident; that all men are created equal."

19 I have a dream that one day on the red hills of Georgia the sons of former slaves and the sons of former slaveowners will be able to sit down together at the table of brotherhood.

20 I have a dream that one day even the state of Mississippi, a desert state sweltering with the heat of injustice and oppression, will be transformed into an oasis of freedom and justice.

21 I have a dream that my four little children will one day live in a

nation where they will not be judged by the color of their skin but by the content of their character.

22 I have a dream today.

23 I have a dream that one day the state of Alabama, whose governor's lips are presently dripping with the words of interposition and nullification, will be transformed into a situation where little black boys and black girls will be able to join hands with little white boys and white girls and walk together as sisters and brothers.

24 I have a dream today.

25 I have a dream that one day every valley shall be exalted, every hill and mountain shall be made low, the rough places will be made plain, and the crooked places will be made straight, and the glory of the Lord shall be revealed, and all flesh shall see it together.

26 This is our hope. This is the faith with which I return to the South. With this faith we will be able to hew out of the mountain of despair a stone of hope. With this faith we will be able to transform the jangling discords of our nation into a beautiful symphony of brotherhood.

27 With this faith we will be able to work together, to pray together, to struggle together, to go to jail together, to stand up for freedom together, knowing that we will be free one day.

28 This will be the day when all of God's children will be able to sing with new meaning, "My country 'tis of thee, sweet land of liberty, of thee I sing. Land where my fathers died, land of the Pilgrims' pride, from every mountainside, let freedom ring."

29 And if America is to be a great nation, this must become true. So let freedom ring from the prodigious hilltops of New Hampshire. Let freedom ring from the mighty mountains of New York. Let freedom ring from the heightening Alleghenies of Pennsylvania!

30 Let freedom ring from the snowcapped Rockies of Colorado! Let freedom ring from the curvaceous peaks of California! But not only that; let freedom ring from Stone Mountain of Georgia! Let freedom ring from Lookout Mountain of Tennessee!

31 Let freedom ring from every hill and molehill of Mississippi. From every mountainside, let freedom ring!

32 When we let freedom ring, when we let it ring from every village and every hamlet, from every state and every city, we will be able to speed up that day when all of God's children, black men and white men, Jews and Gentiles, Protestants and Catholics, will be able to join hands and sing in the words of the old Negro spiritual, "Free at last! Free at last! Thank God Almighty, we are free at last!"

Word Study List

symbolic	1	languished	2
manacles	2	defaulted	4

hallowed	5	hew	26
degenerate	7	prodigious	29
inextricably	8	curvaceous	30
interposition	23	persecution	15
nullification	23	redemptive	15

Questions

1. What is (are) the purpose(s) of King's speech? How does King's style reinforce his subject and purpose?

2. What phrase or slogan does King use to stir his audience? Why is it effective?

3. To whom does King express his indebtedness in the opening of his speech (paragraph 2)? How is that reference significant to the point of his speech?

4. Orwell writes in "Politics and the English Language" (see p. 331) that political writing is bad writing and where that is not true, "it will generally be found that the writer is some kind of rebel, expressing his private opinions, and not a 'party line.'" Does this observation apply to King? To show that his speech is well-written, compare King's metaphors and word choice to Orwell's list of tricks in paragraphs 5–8.

5. What do you see as the most vivid metaphors used to describe the black condition in 1963? Why are they effective?

Exercise

King's speech is about equality, a slippery term that is, therefore, difficult to define. We all assume that we know what it means, but in practice its application has been uneven and unfair, as King reminds us. Below is an excerpt from Lincoln's Springfield Speech interpreting *The Declaration of Independence* (delivered June 26, 1857). After reading it, answer these questions:

1. What is Lincoln's meaning of equality?

2. How does Lincoln make Jefferson's statement on equality, written at a time when slaves were held, apply to his antislavery position?

3. Does King imply the same definition of *equality* in his speech?

I think the authors of that notable instrument intended to include *all* men, but they did not intend to declare all men equal *in all respects.* They did not mean to say all were equal in color, size, intellect, moral developments, or social capacity. They defined with tolerable distinctness in what respects they did consider all men created equal—equal with "certain inalienable rights, among which are life, liberty, and the pursuit of happiness." This they said, and this they meant. They did not mean to assert the obvious untruth that all were then actually enjoying that equality, nor yet that they were about to confer such a boon. They meant simply to declare the right, so that enforcement of it might follow as fast as circumstances should permit.

They meant to set up a standard maxim for free society, which would be familiar to all, and revered by all; constantly labored for, and even though never perfectly attained, constantly approximated, and thereby constantly spreading and deepening its influence and augmenting the happiness and value of life to all people of all colors everywhere. The assertion that "all men are created equal" was of no practical use in effecting our separation from Great Britain; and it was placed in the Declaration not for that, but for future use. Its authors meant it to be—as, thank God, it is now proving itself—a stumbling block to all those who in after times might seek to turn a free people back into the hateful paths of despotism. They knew the proneness of prosperity to breed tyrants, and they meant when such should reappear in this fair land and commence their vocation, they should find left for them at least one hard nut to crack.

White English: The Politics of Language

June Jordan

June Jordan (b. 1936), professor of English at the State University of New York at Stony Brook, has written poems, articles, and reviews that have appeared in such publications as the *New Republic, Esquire, Partisan Review,* and the *American Poetry Review.* Among her fourteen books are a history book and an award-winning teen novel, both of which were written in black English. This article was published in *Black World,* August 1973.

In a biting, hard-hitting style, Jordan mixes black English with standard English to stress her position that blacks should not willy-nilly forsake their language, and thereby their culture, for the language of the more powerful white group, a language that has been used repeatedly to deceive and manipulate.

1 By now, most Blackfolks—even the most stubbornly duped and desperately light-headed nigger behind his walnut, "anti-poverty" desk—has heard The Man talking that talk, and the necessary translation into Black—*on white terms*—has taken place. Yeah. The Man has made his stan-

dard English speech, his second inaugural address, his budget statements, and ain' no body left who don't understand the meaning of them words falling out that mouth: Dick Nixon has described the genocide perpetrated by America in Vietnam as *"one of the most unselfish missions ever undertaken by one nation in the defense of another."*[1]

2 Now, you just go ahead and let any little Black child lead you to the truth behind that particular, monstrous lie: let him tell you about the 12 days of Christmas "carpet bombing," My Lai, day-by-day incineration of human lives, the mining of rivers, the bombing of hospitals, and "defoliation" of the land "over there." They all—all of them whitefolks ruling the country—they all talk that talk, that "standard (white) English." It is the language of the powerful. Language is political. That's why you and me, my Brother and my Sister, that's why we sposed to choke our natural self into the weird, lying, barbarous, unreal, white speech and writing habits that the schools lay down like holy law.

3 Because, in other words, the powerful don't play; they mean to keep that power, and those who are the powerless (you and me) better shape up—mimic/ape/suck—in the very image of the powerful, or the powerful will destroy you—you and our children.

4 Dick Nixon has declared that, since the U.S. of A. has completed its "unselfish mission" in Vietnam, America can turn "more fully to the works of compassion, concern and social progress at home."[2] Sounds pretty good, right? Translation: He means the death of all human-welfare programs to end hunger, hazardous housing, inequity in court, injustice, and the suffering of poor health. Check it out.

5 Standard English use of the word "compassion" actually means the end of milk programs for needy school kids, an 18-month halt to every form of Federal assistance for low-income new housing/rehabilitation, the termination of Community Action Programs across the nation, and the subtraction of Federal aid from elementary and junior high and high school systems especially intended to aid impoverished youngsters. And, since that's what "compassion" means in White English, I most definitely do not see why any child should learn *that* English/prize it/participate in such debasement of this human means to human community: this debasement of language, *per se.*

6 See, the issue of white English is inseparable from the issues of mental health and bodily survival. If we succumb to phrases such as "winding down the war," or if we accept "pacification" to mean the murdering of unarmed villagers, or "self-reliance" to mean bail money for Lockheed Corporation and for the mis-managers of the Pennsylvania Railroad, on the one hand, but on the other, allow "self-reliance" to mean starvation

---

[1]*N.Y. Times,* February 25, 1973.
[2]*N.Y. Times,* February 25, 1973.

and sickness and misery for poor families, for the aged and for the permanently disabled/permanently discriminated against—then our mental health is seriously in peril: we have entered the world of double-speak-bullshit, and our lives may soon be lost behind that entry.

7 In any event, the man has brought the war home, where it's always really been at: sometimes explosive, sometimes smoldering, but currently as stark, inhuman and deliberate as the "perfect grammar" of Nixon's war-cries raised, calm as a killer, against the weak, the wanting and the ones who cannot fight back: How will we survive this new, this—to use a standard English term—"escalated" phase of white war against Black life?

8 Well, first let me run down some of the ways we will *not* survive:

We will not survive by joining the games according to the rules set up by our enemies; we will not survive by imitating the double-speak/bullshit/non-think standard English of the powers that be. Therefore, if the F.B.I. asks you do you know so-and-so, a member of The Black Panther Party, for example, you will *not* respond in this Watergate "wise": "I do seem to recall having had some association with the person in question during, or, rather, *sometime* during the past." You will say, instead, for example: "What's it to you? What do I look like to you? What right do you have to ask me that question?"

9 Second, we will *not* try to pretend that we are The Pennsylvania Railroad or some enormous, profiteering corporation such as Grumman Aerospace, and consider the government pennies to "small businesses" initiated by "minority businessmen" to be anything other than what they are: pennies copping out on the mass situation of increasing disparity between the white Haves and the Black Have-nots.

10 Third, we will not help ourselves into extinction by deluding our Black selves into the belief that we should/can become white, that we can/should sound white, think white because then we will be *like* the powerful and therefore we will *be* powerful. That is just a terrible, sad joke. You cannot obliterate yourself and do anything else, whatever, let alone be powerful: that is a logical impossibility. We must cease this self-loathing delusion and recognize that power and happiness and every good thing that we want and need and deserve must come to us as we truly are: must come to us, a Black people, on our terms, respecting our definitions of our goals, our choice of names, our styles of speech, dress, poetry and jive. Otherwise, clearly, the "victory" is pyrrhic, altogether: you have won a job, you think, because you have "successfully" hidden away your history—your mother and your father and the man or woman that you love and *how* you love them, *how* you dance that love, and sing it. That is victory by obliteration of the self; that is not survival.

11 Fourth, we will not survive unless we realize that we remain jeopardized, as a people, by a fully conscious political system to annihilate whoever/whatever does not emulate its mainstream vocabulary, values,

deceit, arrogance and killer mentality. This is a time when those of us who believe in people first, must become political in every way possible: we must devise and pursue every means for survival as the people we are, as the people we want to become.

12 Therefore, when a magazine like Newsweek has the insolence to ask, on its cover: "WHATEVER HAPPENED TO BLACK AMERICA?", we must be together, ready and strong to answer, on our own terms, on our own *political* terms: "None of your goddamned business. You know, anyway; you did it: you stripped the programs; you ridiculed/humiliated the poor; you laughed when we wept. Don't ask; we gone make you *answer* for this shit."

13 *White power uses white English as a calculated, political display of power to control and eliminate the powerless.* Let us deal with that fact, directly, as a positive beginning toward our self-determined survival. It's about language. Language is the main way we learn and we tell who we are, and what we want, and what we need, believe, or why we tremble, or hide, or kill, or nurture and love. Language is the naming of experience and, thereby, the possession of experience. Language makes possible a social statement of connection that can lead into social reality. For all these reasons, language is political. Power belongs to the ones who have the power to determine the use, abuse, the rejection, definition/re-definition of the words—the messages—we must try and send to each other.

14 In America, that power belongs to white people. School, compulsory public-school education, is the process whereby Black children first encounter the punishing force of this white power. "First grade" equals first contact with the politics of white language and its incalculably destructive consequences for Black lives. This is what I mean, exactly: both Black and white youngsters are compelled to attend school. Once inside this system, the white child is rewarded for his mastery of his standard, white English: the language he learned at his mother's white and standard knee. But the Black child is punished for his mastery of his non-standard, Black English; for the ruling elite of America have decided that *non*-standard is *sub*-standard, and even dangerous, and must be eradicated. Moreover, the white child receives formal instruction in his standard English and endless opportunities for the exercise and creative display of his language. But where is the elementary-school course in Afro-American language, and where are the opportunities for the *accredited* exercise and creative exploration of Black language?

15 The two languages are not interchangeable. They cannot, nor do they attempt to communicate equal or identical thoughts, or feelings. And, since the experience to be conveyed is quite different, Black from white, these linguistic dissimilarities should not surprise or worry anyone. However, both are communication systems with regularities, exceptions and values governing their word designs. Both are equally liable to poor,

good, better and creative use. In short, they are both accessible to critical criteria such as clarity, force, message, tone and imagination. Besides this, standard English is comprehensible to Black children, even as Black language is comprehensible to white teachers—supposing that the teachers are willing to make half the effort they demand of Black students.

16 Then what is the difficulty? The problem is that we are saying *language,* but really dealing with *power.* The word "standard" is just not the same as the word "technical" or "rural" or "straight." *Standard* means the rule, the norm. Anyone deviating from the standard is therefore "wrong." As a result, literally millions of Black children are "wrong" from the moment they begin to absorb and imitate the language of their Black lives. Is that an acceptable idea?

17 As things stand, childhood fluency in Afro-American language leads to reading problems that worsen, course failure in subjects dependent upon reading skill, and a thoroughly wounded self-esteem. Afterwards, an abject school career is eclipsed by an abject life career. "Failing" white English leads straight to "failure" in adult life. This, I submit is a fundamental, nation-wide experience of Black life up against white English used to destroy us. Literally accept the terms of the oppressor, or perish: that is the irreducible, horrifying truth of the politics of language.

18 Well, number one, we grownups—we, the Black mothers and Black fathers, and Black teachers, and Black writers, and grown Blackfolk, in general—we do not have to let this damnable situation continue; we must make it stop. We cannot accept the terms, the language of our enemy and expect to win anything; we cannot accept the coercion of our children into failure and expect to survive, as a people.

19 The legitimacy of our language must be fully acknowledged by all of us. That will mean insisting that white/standard English be presented simply as The Second Language. That will mean presenting the second language, obviously, with perpetual reference to the first language, and to the culture the first language bespeaks. Sincere recognition of Black language as legitimate will mean formal instruction and encouragement in its use, within the regular curriculum. It will mean the respectful approaching of Black children, *in the language of Black children.* Yes: it's true that we need to acquire competence in the language of the currently powerful: Black children in America must acquire competence in white English, for the sake of self-preservation. *But you will never teach a child a new language by scorning and ridiculing and forcibly erasing his first language.*

20 We can and we ought to join together to protect our Black children, our Black language, our terms of reality, and our defining of the future we dream and desire. The public school is one, ready-made battleground. But the war is all around us, and the outcome depends on how we understand, or fail to perceive, the serious, political intention to homogenize us, Blackfolks, out of existence. In our daily business phone calls, in our

"formal" correspondence with whites, in what we publish, let us dedicate ourselves to the revelation of our true selves, on our given terms, and demand respect for us, as we are. Let us study and use our Black language, more and more: it is not A Mistake, or a Verbal Deficiency. It is a communication system subsuming dialect/regional variations that leave intact, nevertheless, a language that is invariable in profound respects. For example:

A. Black language practices minimal inflection of verb forms (*e.g., I go, we go, he go,* and *I be, you be, etc.*) This is *non*-standard and, also, an obviously more logical use of verbs. It is also evidence of a value system that considers the person—the actor—more important than the action.
B. Consistency of syntax: *You going to the store.* (Depending on tone, can be a question, a command, or a simple, declarative statement.)
C. Infrequent, irregular use of the possessive case.
D. Clear, logical use of multiple negatives within a single sentence, to express an unmistakably negative idea *(e.g., You ain gone bother me no way no more, you hear?).*
E. Other logical consistencies, such as: *ours, his, theirs* and, therefore, *mines.*

21 Our Black language is a political fact suffering from political persecution and political malice. Let us understand this and meet the man, politically; let us meet the man *talking the way we talk*; let us not fail to seize this means to our survival, despite white English and its power. Let us condemn white English for what it is: a threat to mental health, integrity of person and survival as a people of our own choosing.

22 And, as for our children: let us make sure that the whole world will welcome and applaud and promote the words they bring into our reality; in the struggle to reach each other, there can be no right or wrong words for our longing and our needs; there can only be the names that we trust and we try.

Word Study List

genocide	1	pyrrhic	10
perpetrated	1	eradicated	14
impoverished	5	coercion	18
debasement	5	homogenize	20
disparity	9	subsuming	20

Questions

1. What type of English does Jordan label as standard English? Do all whites use this type of language? Would "doublespeak" or "doubletalk" be a more accurate label? Why?

2. To what audience is Jordan writing? Does she primarily use standard English or black English? What is the effect of her mixing the two?

3. Based on the words that Jordan uses and the examples of black English grammar that she includes in paragraph 20, describe black English.

4. Do you agree with Jordan's labeling of the characteristics of black English as logical consistencies? Should standard English incorporate some of these consistencies?

5. Why does the author refer to then-President Nixon as Dick Nixon? What is the effect on the reader?

6. How would you describe the tone of this article? What do you think would be the most common reaction of white readers to Jordan's article? The reaction of black readers?

7. Why does Jordan feel it is important for the survival of blacks that they retain their language?

8. How does she suggest that the English of blacks and whites be handled when a black child enters school?

9. Explain why the issue of standard English versus black English is a political one. Given that standard (or white) English is the language of the powerful, are schools that accept black English (or Spanish) being fair to their students?

Exercises

1. Jordan writes that "language is the naming of experience and, thereby, the possession of experience" (paragraph 13). What other articles have you read in this book that give this same view of the power of language? Write a paragraph in which you explain how the renaming of an event or a relationship in your personal life made it real for you.

2. List arguments for and against giving students who speak a minority dialect or language other than English the right to use and be taught in their own language in school.

Is This a Dagger Which I See Before Me? No, Congressman, It's Korea

Barney Frank

Barney Frank (b. 1940) has been a member of the House of Representatives since 1972. He is a Democrat from Massachusetts and has been active in Americans for Democratic Action. His article was printed in the *Washington Post* on July 27, 1983.

In an amusing style Frank objects to several popular metaphors that reinforce distorted perceptions of social realities and relations among nations.

1 Sometimes the First Amendment can be aggravating. Ten years of legislating dissuades me from allowing legislators to tell adults what to write or say. But then I read about our soft Middle Eastern underbelly being menaced by a radical Shiite dagger. Or I am threatened by the spectacle of Central American dominoes hurtling through our window of vulnerability. And I fantasize about how pleasant it would be to ban all metaphors from political discussions.

2 Metaphors can be fun. My favorite budget debate on the House floor was the one in 1982 when an anguished Republican insisted that the Democrats "stop milking this dead horse." (In a spirit of conciliation, one Democrat advised him in return "not to carry all his spilt milk in one basket.") But few metaphor users can meet this standard.

3 People claim they use metaphors to advance understanding, by explaining complex or obscure phenomena in terms of simple and familiar ones. They don't. What they usually do is to become so enamored of a simplistic figure of speech that they substitute it for reality, and consequently discuss issues in a distorted and mechanistic fashion.

4 Foreign policy is especially vulnerable to this displacement of complex reality by metaphoric simple-mindedness. Physical shapes of countries lead otherwise sensible people to discuss international events in the terms 10-year-olds use when assembling geographic jigsaw puzzles.

5 Take soft underbellies. People who worry about being attacked from the south, or who would like to attack other people from their south, tend to be "underbelly" fetishists. Winston Churchill drove Allied war planners to distraction 40 years ago by opposing a cross-channel invasion in favor of a Mediterranean attack on the "Axis" soft underbelly. Finally, someone seems to have gotten across the point that southern France is, in fact, no softer than northern France. Crocodiles and turtles have hard backs and

soft underbellies. Countries do not. They have northern and southern borders, neither of which is necessarily more vulnerable than the other.

6 But the fact that it is distinctly unhelpful does not prevent this metaphor from remaining in use. A recent Post story quoted an Indonesian general as justifying an attack on Timor as necessary to stave off "a Marxist threat to our soft underbelly." I understand why Indonesians shudder at the thought of a bristly-bearded Karl Marx approaching their underbellies. But this has nothing to do with oppressing East Timor.

7 Another physical metaphor popular in foreign affairs is the country-as-weapon. I have grown up being told that Korea is essential to our security because it is pointed like a dagger at the back of Japan. First of all, I doubt very much that countries have fronts or backs. And if Japan does have a back, it seems unduly ethnocentric for us to decide that it is the part nearest Asia. But metaphor-mongers understand the value of making them graphic. Underbellies must always be soft, and threats always aimed at one's rear, except of course when they are aimed at one's heart (see box).

8 The popular current variant of the "they're coming up behind us" metaphor is the one which warns of the Marxist danger in our Central American back yard. Confirming the suspicion of Central Americans that we regard them as not just an appendage, but as a rear appendage, hardly seems the best way to inspire their confidence in our intentions. But it apparently sounds more ominous to conjure up Castroites and Sandinistas capturing our back yard than it would be to warn of them infesting our lawn, or infiltrating our side porch.

9 To return to Korea, it is relevant that Korea is near Japan. It is wholly irrelevant that it is roughly dagger shaped. Unless levitation is far more advanced in the East than I realize, the danger of Korea's being stuck into Japan seems negligible.

10 This does not mean that we should ignore Korea, nor cease our effort to protect it from any invasion from its north. It does not mean that because of its shape, people have greatly overrated its threat to Japan. Historically of course, the threat has been the other way—from Japan to Korea. And as to Korea's use as a communist weapon against Japan, given communist control of all of China, the extra threat Korea presents would not have been seen as significant if that country were round or flat instead of lumpily pointed.

11 Speaking of lumpiness, recently there has been division in the metaphor camp about how best to describe Korea. William Manchester's biography of MacArthur refers to it as a "lumpy phallus." In the Victorian era, deciding whether Korea was a dagger or a phallus would have meant determining whether Japan preferred death to dishonor. In our time, it probably means we will soon be told about the prophylactic role assigned to the Seventh Fleet.

'TO BORROW A PHRASE'

Daggers can be at your front as well as your back. A sampling from reports in this newspaper over the past few years shows the dagger aimed at the heart may be anything from a nation-state to a hamburger stand:

- Aug. 23, 1977: A report in The Post says Israelis see a fully independent state controlled by Palestinians as a "dagger pointed at the heart of Israel."
- Dec. 12, 1977: A broadcast by Saudi Arabia's official radio says there is little hope for peace in the Mideast "as long as Israeli occupation of Arab territory and Jerusalem continues. . . . This occupation is a dagger stuck in the heart of the Arab nation. . . . "
- April 9, 1979: A Post story on the "sagebrush rebellion" says some federal officials consider the movement "a dagger aimed at the heart of the Bureau of Land Management."
- Sept. 9, 1979: The Soviets say in an English-language broadcast beamed to the United States that the American naval base at Guantanamo is "a dagger pointed at the heart of the young republic" of Cuba.
- Sept. 12, 1979: An Annapolis resident, testifying before the city council on a proposal to put a hamburger dispensary in his neighborhood, says, "Put a McDonald's here and you will place a dagger in the heart of Hillsmere."
- Oct. 2, 1979: Sen. Edward Zorinsky (D-Neb.) says, "Let's face it, 2,000 to 3,000 Soviet combat troops in Cuba is, to borrow a phrase, a thorn in our side, not a dagger in our hearts."
- Sept. 18, 1980: The Ethiopian government, in a letter to President Carter, describes a recent agreement between the United States and Somalia on U.S. military access as "a dagger poised at the heart of Ethiopia."
- Nov. 2, 1981: Israeli Foreign Minister Yitzhak Shamir, discussing a list of Saudi peace proposals, says each is a "poisoned dagger thrust into the heart of Israel's existence."
- March 23, 1983: President Reagan describes a Democratic budget proposal as "a dagger aimed straight at the heart of America's rebuilding program."

12 And then of course we have the dominoes. It is undeniable that events in one country can have a profound effect on its neighbors. It is

demonstrably untrue that the "fall" of any one nation automatically or even probably means the "fall" of all of its neighbors. (Apparently, countries, unlike dominoes, can fall in several directions at once.) Either the automaticity of the domino theory is wrong, or Thailand and Malaysia have been secretly communist since the late '70s. Incidentally, the domino theory is at its most impressive when it describes the impact of an island nation on its neighbors across the water. Presumably this variant is the domino wave effect.

13 Domestic policy also suffers from metaphor distortion by people who tire of complexity. A popular argument against the need for concern about the distribution of our national income is the argument that a rising tide lifts all boats. This means that an increase in the overall GNP will make everyone better off, so that government need not concern itself with how particular segments fare.

14 As many Republicans like to point out, one of the first to use this metaphor was John Kennedy, who said a number of profound and useful things. This was not one of them. People are not boats. The economy is not a tide. And an increase in GNP may occur in a way that leaves some people no better off than they were, while others find their condition worsening. It would be possible to combat this metaphor on its own terms by pointing out that a rising tide is not great news to people who are on tiptoes in the water. It would be better to stop using it, and to recognize that concern for economic equity requires a good deal more than simply pumping up the GNP.

15 Then we have the comforting metaphor that suggests that government can be made efficient as easily as a sponge is made drier. This one assumes that government spending consists of two elements of different consistencies: socially useful, or hard spending; and socially wasteful, or soft spending. Thus you can make government efficient by simply compressing the whole, so that the softer substance—fat, water or something less pleasant—is squeezed out, leaving a mass of hard stuff—bone, muscle, etc., behind.

16 This is often the justification for across-the-board cuts in government programs. Unfortunately, the metaphor is dead wrong. There is little correlation between the social usefulness of programs and their ability to survive massive cutbacks. To meet the metaphor on its own terms, what is socially soft is often politically hard, and vice versa. Squeeze the budget like a sponge and you may well victimize poor children while wealthy farmers remain unscathed. The hard way to cut out wasteful spending is to identify it, and work to get the political support necessary to remove it. It's much easier to pretend by use of a convenient metaphor that simply reducing the total will automatically leave a more efficient mass behind.

17 Fortunately, for all my discomfort, the First Amendment endures. I am resigned to continuing to live my life among camels putting their noses

into tents; lawyers sliding down slippery slopes; and cancers spreading in unlikely ways across the landscape or on what is known as the body politic. But the next time I hear a colleague on the Foreign Affairs Committee ask "Is this a dagger which I see before me?", I think I will say, "No, Congressman, it's Korea."

Word Study List

dissuades	1	levitation	9
phenomena	3	prophylactic	11
enamored	3	automaticity	12
fetishists	5	equity	14
appendage	8	correlation	16
ominous	8	unscathed	16

Questions

1. In paragraph 2, Frank says that "metaphors can be fun." Why, since this is not his main point or thesis, does he make this assertion? How does it connect to his thesis?

2. What is Frank's thesis? Where is it stated?

3. Why are foreign-policy discussions especially vulnerable to metaphors that simplify and distort reality?

4. List the foreign-policy metaphors that Frank discusses. Which ones have you heard? Which are new to you?

5. What do these metaphors have in common? Taken together, what view of relations among nations do they encourage?

6. Explain the two domestic-policy metaphors Frank analyzes. What are Frank's objections to each? Why are these inaccurate metaphors comforting to people?

Exercise

Search your newspaper or weekly newsmagazine for a metaphor, used in a discussion of foreign policy, that you think distorts reality. In a paragraph explain first what image of reality the metaphor conveys and then why the metaphor distorts the social or political issue it is supposed to clarify.

Behind the War Metaphor: The Vocabulary of Crime

Stephen Gillers

Professor of law at New York University, Stephen Gillers (b. 1943) is the author or editor of six books and many articles on law and law-related subjects, among them *Looking at Law School: A Student Guide* (2d ed., 1984). The following article appeared in the *Nation* on March 27, 1982.

Objecting, like Orwell, to metaphors that distort political realities, Gillers focuses specifically on metaphors used in discussions of crime fighting.

1 This article is not about crime. It is about how government talks about crime, about the vocabulary of crime. I recently testified for the American Civil Liberties Union in opposition to a Senate bill (S. 653) that would severely limit the ability of a state prisoner to challenge in Federal court the constitutional fairness of his trial. Such a challenge is made by filing what the legal trade calls "a petition for a writ of *habeas corpus,*" which is nothing more than a prisoner asking a Federal judge to decide whether a state court honored his constitutional rights.

2 In preparing my testimony, I read much of what President Reagan and the Justice Department have been saying about crime, and I became intrigued with the language and images used. These are instructive in themselves, but I also found it illuminating to test the imagery against statistics, which was possible in the case of *habeas corpus.*

3 Consider Attorney General William French Smith's statement last October 23 [1981] to the Senate Subcommittee on Criminal Law. Crime is four times called a "menace." It is described as something we must "fight against." It is said to have reached "alarming proportions" and to confront us with "crises" requiring "action" or even "vigorous action." We are told we need a "coordinated national strategy" and "to remove inefficiencies that plague the criminal justice system." In the areas of organized crime and drug trafficking, we are said to need even more. We need "a truly powerful weapon." To protect ourselves form "criminal attacks," we must recognize that we have "become timid and reluctant to assert vigorously our rights." We must "take action immediately." Only then can we "restore the balance between the forces of law and the forces of lawlessness."

4 The Reagan Administration is not the first to use the war metaphor to defend what it would like its law enforcers to be empowered to do about crime. While one may bemoan a lack of imagination, the imagery does serve the government's purpose. As with war, there is an enemy to fight. As with war, defeat means the end of America as we know it. As with war, we must not quibble about whether the army (the police) is too

aggressive, given the consequences should the enemy (the "forces of lawlessness") prevail. This imagery enables the government to make quick, dramatic arguments for the implementation of its programs. Because the vocabulary is strong, it necessarily denies the presence of nuances or subtlety. It is intended to deny their presence.

5 The war metaphor permits an additional manipulation of a kind George Orwell surely would have appreciated. By depicting only two sides—"the forces of law and the forces of lawlessness"—it implies that contrary views necessarily assist the other side. Since this is war, the other side must be the enemy, and the word for those who aid the enemy in time of war is "traitor." Am I pushing the analogy too far?

6 Sadly, no. White House counselor Edwin Meese 3d came near to this characterization last May when he called the A.C.L.U. part of a "criminals' lobby" that made law enforcement difficult. And William Wilson, a University of California Regent who is a friend of the President's, charged in the same week that it was logical to conclude that the A.C.L.U. was "supported by . . . organized crime." Given the war analogy, we can understand how logic may lead to that conclusion.

7 A war metaphor for crime can be criticized linguistically or philosophically, but it cannot be disproved empirically. With regard to *habeas corpus,* however, the imagery was different, and my research in preparing my testimony gave me an opportunity to assess its accuracy. State prisoner petitions for Federal *habeas corpus* relief, the Attorney General told the Senate Subcommittee on Criminal Law, "continue to flood the courts." This "unending" flood was "undermining" the "greatest single deterrent to crime, swift and sure punishment," as state prisoners engage in a "ceaseless effort to set aside the convictions." The legislation the Attorney General envisions would close the floodgates or, in the real world, the Federal courthouse door.

8 The Attorney General's remarks create the incidental misapprehension that state convicts escape "punishment" through the tactic of filing "ceaseless" *habeas* petitions. In fact, in virtually every case, the state defendants are litigating from their prison cells. But never mind that. Let us look instead behind the image the Attorney General used.

9 Is there a flood? That we can test. The statistics show that at most there is a trickle, perhaps merely a drip. Only 3.5 percent of the cases filed in Federal courts in the year ending June 1980 were brought by state prisoners seeking release. About 1 percent of all Federal trials involved *habeas corpus* pleas (199 out of 19,585). Since most such cases take a day or less to try, not even one quarter of 1 percent of all trial days were devoted to *habeas* cases in this period. The Attorney General did not mention these numbers in his statement to the Senate subcommittee. "I will not burden you with the statistics," he said. No wonder. How much more persuasive it is to speak of "floods" than fractions of a percent.

10 None of this is to deny that crime is a serious problem in need of

government attention or that *habeas* petitions do create work for the judiciary. But the real battle, if there is one, is not between the forces of law and the forces of lawlessness. Nor is it among those whose differing views lead them to different solutions. It is rather a battle to stop the use of language to distort what it pretends to describe. Thirty-five years ago, George Orwell wrote that the "great enemy of clear language is insincerity." He concluded that political language is "designed to give an appearance of solidity to pure wind." He accepted that "one cannot change this all in a moment," but thought the situation "probably curable." I doubt he still would.

Word Study List

intrigued	2	philosophically	7
bemoan	4	empirically	7
nuances	4	misapprehension	8
linguistically	7	litigating	8

Questions

1. What metaphor has the Reagan administration used when talking about crime? In your own words, explain the points of comparison between crime and war.

2. What does the war metaphor eliminate from a discussion of crime? What manipulation does the metaphor create?

3. Gillers says that the war metaphor can be objected to philosophically but not disproved with evidence. But the flood metaphor used to object to *habeas corpus* petitions can be disproved. How does Gillers challenge the flood metaphor?

4. Is Gillers opposed to reducing crime or in favor of a busier court schedule? What does he want to do battle with?

5. Why, for Gillers, is the battle against language an important one? In his battle Gillers associates himself with whom? Are you no longer surprised at the invoking of this famous name?

Exercise

Frank objects to some foreign- and domestic-policy metaphors, and Gillers shows the flaws in metaphors about crime. Are there currently some interesting—perhaps objectionable—metaphors in discussions of education? Examine some recent issues of an educational journal or study the statements of educational policy in your college's catalog for two or three metaphors about education. Be prepared to explain and judge the appropriateness of one of your metaphors. Prepare a class list of all discovered metaphors to serve as a basis for a discussion of how we talk about education today.

Exercises

1. Not all political language is pretentious or meaningless, as King's famous speech in this chapter shows. Some of the more memorable phrases of recent administrations are listed below. Explain what makes each phrase so vivid that it has become a part of our vocabulary. How many of these can you define? With what administration do you associate each of these terms?

silent majority	New Frontier
Establishment	Third World
New Deal	war on poverty
domino theory	trickle-down economics

2. a. In "Politics and the English Language" Orwell wrote that words such as *democracy* and *freedom* are meaningless (pp. 328–329). During World War II, E. B. White, a noted essayist and author of children's books, wrote the following definition of *democracy* for the *New Yorker* magazine. Has White given the vague word a clear meaning? If so, what makes the definition clear? What techniques of style discussed in Chapter 3 has White used?

July 3, 1944

> We received a letter from the Writers' War Board the other day asking for a statement on 'The Meaning of Democracy.' It presumably is our duty to comply with such a request, and it is certainly our pleasure.
>
> Surely the Board knows what democracy is. It is the line that forms on the right. It is the don't in Don't Shove. It is the hole in the stuffed shirt through which the sawdust slowly trickles; it is the dent in the high hat. Democracy is the recurrent suspicion that more than half of the people are right more than half of the time. It is the feeling of privacy in the voting booths, the feeling of communion in the libraries, the feeling of vitality everywhere. Democracy is the score at the beginning of the ninth. It is an idea which hasn't been disproved yet, a song the words of which have not gone bad. It's the mustard on the hot dog and the cream in the rationed coffee. Democracy is a request from a War Board, in the middle of a morning in the middle of a war, wanting to know what democracy is.

   b. Choose one of the following words and write a definition of it in White's style.

patriotism	freedom
justice	peace

3. The abortion issue is one of many moral and political issues whose outcome depends on the careful choice of positive words by those who are for and against it. How would you react to the Supreme Court's

1973 legalization of abortion-on-demand if the word *murder* or *fetus killing* were substituted for *abortion*? What is the difference in meaning between *abortion* and *murder*? Why have those opposed to abortion labeled their cause as *pro-life* rather than *anti-abortion*? Why do those who support the Supreme Court's decision call their position *pro-choice* rather than *pro-abortion*?

4. Below are the public statements of world leaders in response to the death in 1980 of Muhammad Riza Pahlavi, the deposed Shah of Iran. Which of these responses are like the examples of abstract, meaningless prose that Orwell objects to? Which are genuine expressions of sympathy? Which indicate support for the deposed Shah? Which hedge? Which support the new leadership in Iran?

    a. Tehran radio:
    The bloodsucker of the world has died.

    b. Pars New Agency of Iran:
    Behold how history repeats itself: the treacherous Shah dies next to the tomb of ancient Egyptian Pharaohs and in the asylum of Sadat in disgrace, misery and vagrancy, in the same state of despair in which the Pharaoh and his army were drowned in the sea. How admonitory is history.

    c. The Independent Republican Party of President Valéry Giscard d'Estaing of France:
    The Shah had wanted by every means, even the most brutal, to force his people to imitate the West . . . and failed. The world has not finished paying for the Shah's miscalculation.

    d. United States Department of State:
    We have been informed that the former Shah has died in Cairo. The President and Mrs. Carter are sending their personal condolences to the Shah's family.

    At this time of great personal grief for the members of the Shah's family, they deserve sympathy and an atmosphere of tranquillity.

    Ambassador Atherton has been asked to deliver the Carters' condolences.

    The Shah was the leader of Iran for an exceptionally long period of time—38 years. History will record that he led his country at a time when profound changes were taking place.

    His death marks the end of an era in Iran, which all hope will be followed by peace and stability.

    e. Former President Richard Nixon:
    For over 30 years the Shah was a loyal friend and ally of the United States and a personal friend as well. Tragically, he died a man without a country. Now that his personal ordeal is over, the government of

Iran has no excuse whatever for continuing to hold innocent American hostages.

f. President Anwar el-Sadat of Egypt:
Let history judge the reign of the Shah as a ruler, but we, in Islamic Egypt, will remain loyal to ethics and faithful to [humane] values. The Shah stood with Egypt as it faced an ordeal and, therefore, it was our duty to stand by him during the hard times.

5. In "Politics and the English Language" Orwell asserts that "in certain kinds of writing, particularly in art criticism and literary criticism, it is normal to come across long passages which are almost completely lacking in meaning" (paragraph 8). Examine each of the following examples of criticism for meaningless words or phrases. If you were an experienced judge of wine or music, what terms would you be likely to know?

From *Wines and Spirits,* a Time/Life Book:
Both of these regions [Bordeaux and Burgundy] produce red and white wine—and in each the best is generally conceded to rank with the best in the world. Bordeaux comes in tall, slender bottles and has been called the queen of red wines. It is subtle, inclined to be on the light, dry side, with an aftertaste that is indescribable. Its appeal is discreet and aristocratic. By contrast, Burgundy is the king. Its bottle is stouter in shape, with sloping shoulders, and the wine is stouter too. It is heavier, "chewier"; it hurls its imperial brilliance at you with a shout.

From "Chamber Music: Happy Surprises," a column on new classical recordings in *The Washington Post:*
I cannot readily recall a happier little surprise package in the realm of lightweight chamber music. The freshness, color and uncomplicated charm of these four works make them handsome companions for each other, and these qualities do not seem to fade with repeated exposures. All in all, an enchanting release, alike for the music itself, the superb performances and the incredibly lifelike recording.

Write a paragraph in which you describe a favorite record or food. What difficulties do you encounter?

6. The following excerpt is from the *Handbook of Policy* of the Arizona Department of Education:

Textbook content shall not interfere with the school's legal responsibility to teach citizenship and patriotism. Textbooks adopted shall not include selections or works which contribute to civil disorder.

Does this policy seem unreasonably restrictive to you? Why or why not? What definition of citizenship and patriotism do you think the state officials who wrote this had in mind? Is there a direct relationship between what people read and what they do? In other words, is there evidence that books can incite riot? Under this policy would a textbook containing *The Declaration of Independence* or Thoreau's "Civil Disobedience" be approved? Would such classics as Richard Wright's *Native Son* or Shakespeare's *Macbeth* be acceptable?

7. The word *security* is a powerful political tool. Why is our national insurance plan for retirement and old age benefits named *Social Security*? What does *national security* mean? Does it differ in meaning from *national defense*?

Writing Assignments

1. From different newspapers or magazines select two articles on the same political event—local, national, or international. Contrast both the content and style of the articles. In looking at content, note not only the facts and opinions in each article but also the arrangement of the information. In analyzing the style, look at the word choice and sentence structure that set the tone. Your thesis should focus on what you see as significant differences in the two articles and why these differences are present.
2. Write a letter to the editor of your campus or community newspaper that challenges the careless or ambiguous use of political language in an editorial or a by-line article. Explain why the language is confusing and offer your own definition of the terms being discussed and a revision that clarifies the meaning of the original.
3. Abstract words such as *loyalty* and *democracy* have a different meaning for each of us, depending on our experiences with the word. By limiting the possible meanings of an abstraction, you shape the thinking of others by getting them to see the word as you see it. Choose one of the following pairs of words and write a paper that compares the meanings of the two words in order to prove the important difference between them despite their apparent similarities. Develop your paper by using the logical or dictionary definitions, comparisons (direct and metaphoric), contrasts, functions, descriptions, and examples. You might also consult the *Oxford English Dictionary* in your library for the history of your words.
   a. politician and statesman
   b. patriot and chauvinist
   c. war and conflict
   d. liberty and license
   e. peace and truce

4. Update Orwell's thesis—that the abuse of language leads to political and/or economic decline and vice versa—by writing a paper that is supported with examples from Watergate, "Billy-gate," ABSCAM, the wars in Lebanon and Central America, and/or other recent political events noted for their use of language to defend the indefensible, thus leading to doubletalk.
5. Censorship and the banning or even the burning of books is evidence that many people believe that books can create a decline in morals and/or civil disorder. Write a paper that defends or refutes the idea that a society should censor or ban books that are politically or morally radical. Cite incidents from history to support your position.

CHAPTER 8

© Sepp Seitz 1980/Woodfin Camp & Assoc.

The Media: Pressing the Limits of Power, Responsibility, and Freedom

GETTING STARTED: Ethics and Issues of the Media—Some Questions to Consider

For the past decade, prompted in part no doubt by the Watergate affair, criticism and praise of the press have reached new heights. The media have been both lavishly praised and caustically chastised for their reporting. Charges of bias—liberal, social, racial, sexual—of invasion of privacy, of generating the news they report, of taking an adversary position to the government are heard from one side while admiration of their investigative reporting, their on-the-spot coverage with portable videotape equipment, their skill in presenting so many events in so little time and space is heard from the other side. For those who see the press as exerting its power unethically, regulation is the answer; for those who see a free press as essential to our democratic ideals, any restriction on First Amendment rights is too much. Such complex issues as where freedom overshadows responsibility and colorful reporting becomes biased news require careful thought, open debate, and, perhaps, a willingness to judge particular situations rather than demand abstract rules.

As you read each of the selections in this chapter, keep in mind the following questions. They will help you focus on basic issues of media power and responsibility.

1. What does the First Amendment guarantee?
2. What is the responsibility of the media to their audience? To their sources?
3. Who should define this responsibility?
4. What power does the media have? Where does it come from?
5. What is the purpose of journalism?
6. What is ethical and unethical reporting?
7. When does reporting of the news become editorializing? Should all news articles containing analysis and opinion be clearly labeled as opinion?
8. What can we reasonably expect to be "true" in a news report? In what ways does the medium itself (TV, radio, print journalism) shape our perceptions of the events reported?

Why People Distrust the Press

Fred Bruning

With degrees in journalism and fine arts, Fred Bruning has worked at six newspapers and *Newsweek* magazine. He is currently a journalist at *Newsday,* a Long Island newspaper. The following article appeared in *Maclean's,* a Canadian newsmagazine, on January 16, 1984.

Alarmed by the pleasure some expressed over the prohibiting of reporters from covering America's invasion of Grenada, Bruning seeks to explain current attitudes toward the press and to remind us of journalism's role in our society.

1 Among the most striking peculiarities of the American democracy is the impatience of our people with democratic values. It is not unusual for one party, frustrated with the point of view of another, to suggest that his antagonist depart for more compatible environs. Typically, that kind of advice is delivered in the form of harsh interrogative. "Oh, yeah, Mac," a person might say. "You don't like it, why don't you shove off for Russia?" Quibbling about the rights and responsibilities of a citizen in an open society—why have free speech if its exercise is considered treasonous?—earns little more than further disapprobation. "Blow it out your ear" is the way the matter often is settled.

2 Eager to purge all deficient individuals, many Americans apparently would send packing that most suspect of institutions as well—that is, the press. In those heady days following the assault on Grenada,[1] our people celebrated more than just a victory of several thousand American soldiers over an enemy composed largely of Cuban handymen and bewildered local conscripts. Also thwarted was the media establishment, a comeuppance long awaited.

3 Military strategists had forbidden reporters access to the battlefront during the assault, citing the difficulties and dangers attendant with such an enterprise, and, in fact, held incommunicado a small group of journalists who gained a beachhead by way of a chartered fishing boat. So, during the most critical hours of the campaign, the government was able to carry out a questionable operation unencumbered by outside observers. The rout of Port Salines was recorded only by military cameramen and army public relations specialists. In this way was history poured into moulds, and marketed like chocolate kisses.

[1] An island in the Caribbean invaded by the U.S. military in the fall of 1983.—ED.

4 Reporters snarled, and media executives organized long luncheons to discuss the crisis. The public, on the other hand, seemed delighted. "I just want you to know the press had no business in Grenada and I'm glad they kept you out," said a caller to a New York newspaper. *"We loved it!"* the fellow added, speaking, one was invited to believe, for the millions of dutiful citizens who do not carry notebooks in their back pockets or seek comments from next of kin. Surveys proved the caller correct. The media got shellacked in the Caribbean, and who could say which was more inspiring, the defeat of Castro[2] or of Dan Rather?[3] A letter to *The New York Times* made the point well. The writer noted that during the Second World War journalists routinely accompanied troops, but, in those days, he said, "All our reporters were on *our* side."

5 Since Vietnam—at least since Vietnam—the press has been regarded as a contrary force ruined by its own dyspeptic nature and instinct for orneriness. The war did not go as planned, and, worse, the whole mess kept showing up on television and in the newspapers and magazines. Free-fire zones. Pacification. Fragging. My Lai. Haiphong. Tet offensive. Vietnamization. Trouble, trouble, trouble. Who needed such trouble? Spiro Agnew, a former federal employee, derided the "nattering nabobs of negativism" who hounded public officials, and some in the Reagan administration have similar outlooks.

6 Larry Speakes,[4] the presidential spokesman, recently claimed that two reporters peeked at documents on the desks of White House aides and dashed away in the hope of developing stories. The communiqués were phony, Speakes announced later, adding the reporters had bitten "like snakes" and revealed what hopeless bozos inhabit the press room. Speakes did not complain that stories were published (none was), only that reporters made a few phone checks. What exactly was proven then is not quite clear other than that the president's spokesman might better be employed as a production assistant on *Candid Camera.*

7 Tweaking the press is great sport, though, and one would expect politicians and their advance men to avail themselves of every opportunity. Tension exists between the sides—between the press and the powerful—and the air should crackle, there should be a tingle on the scalps of all concerned. Leaders want to protect their prerogatives; reporters are supposed to protect the public. "The business of journalism is to comfort the afflicted and to afflict the comfortable," remains the trade's most durable aphorism.

---

[2]Prime minister of Cuba since 1959.—Ed.

[3]Anchorman of the "CBS Evening News."—Ed.

[4]For the Reagan administration.—Ed.

8 The screwy thing is that the public doesn't want to be protected, at least not by the press. A recent survey by the National Opinion Research Center in Chicago showed that only 13.7 per cent of those questioned had confidence in journalists. They found doctors more trustworthy, and scientists, educators, the U.S. Supreme Court justices—even bankers. Incredibly, they considered members of Congress and executives of the federal government less reliable than reporters. What a sad state. People have no confidence in the press and wouldn't turn their backs on the folks who run the country. Instead, they place their faith in the pirates who brought us adjustable mortgage rates.

9 Certainly, the media leave much to be desired. Journalism is a booming corporate enterprise, there are times when the newspaper or television station may seem too accommodating of the business community—too intent on telling us what a swell Christmas selling season we've had. Reporters and editors tend to be white and middle class, and those demographics might give you concern if you're black and living on the wrong side of town. Some practitioners are lazy, self-aggrandizing, badly behaved and ever on the prowl for free tickets to the playoffs. And there are reporters who take too much for granted, or who are easily misled, or who have trouble asking questions that may prompt interviewees to reach for the duelling pistols.

10 But these are not the failings that induced our leaders to keep reporters out of Grenada. Nor does it seem that the public is aggravated because the press at times may be too timid, or tied to the power structure, or unwilling to pursue vigorously issues that ought to be pursued. The worry was, and is, that reporters will operate to capacity and get the bad news into print. Government doesn't want that. Often, readers don't either.

11 Perhaps when children are taught civics in this country, they are given the idea that our destiny is assured and that no one need mention if something seems amiss. Along the line, we may have come to think it wise to leave well enough alone—to cancel our subscriptions, turn out the lights and pretend there is comfort even in affliction.

Word Study List

environs	1	communiqués	6
disapprobation	1	bozos	6
conscripts	2	prerogatives	7
comeuppance	2	aphorism	7
incommunicado	3	demographics	9
unencumbered	3	self-aggrandizing	9
dyspeptic	5		

Questions

1. Bruning begins by observing that many Americans seem eager to send packing anyone expressing "negative" views about America's government or way of life. How does this point introduce Bruning's subject?

2. Bruning has written specifically in response to the 1983 invasion of Grenada by the American military. What was unique about this event that connects it to Bruning's subject? How did many respond to the media's exclusion from Grenada?

3. How does Bruning account for the current negative attitudes toward the media?

4. What does Bruning think is the business of journalism? Do you agree with him? Why or why not?

5. What objections could be made about some members of the media? Why does Bruning list some failings in paragraph 9?

6. What objections seem to be more current among government leaders and some readers? What is Bruning's attitude toward the worry that "reporters . . . will get the bad news into print"?

Exercises

1. Bruning says that people today do not trust journalists. Which groups do you trust the most? Place the following groups in a list from most trustworthy to least: bankers, bureaucrats, doctors, educators, elected officials, law enforcers, lawyers. Compare your order with classmates and be prepared to discuss differences.

2. Take either the group you trust the most or the least (see exercise 1) and explain, in a paragraph, why you hold that view. Is your attitude based on direct experiences or the attitudes of others?

3. Bruning says that people do not like the media's attention to "bad news." In reaction to this complaint, a journalist once said that the only news is bad news. What point about news stories was the journalist trying to make? What are some reasons why many don't want to read or hear about bad news? What could happen in our society if reporters stopped giving attention to bad news? Think about these questions as preparation for a class discussion of the issues Bruning raises.

Journalism and the Larger Truth

Roger Rosenblatt

Formerly a professor at Harvard and then a columnist for the *Washington Post,* Roger Rosenblatt (b. 1940) has been a senior writer at *Time* magazine since 1980. Many of his essays and his book *Children of War* (1983) have won awards. The following, a *Time* essay, appeared July 2, 1984.

Reflecting on the function of journalism, Rosenblatt asserts that reporters can and must stick to the facts but cannot provide the truth.

1 When journalists hear journalists claim a "larger truth," they really ought to go for their pistols. *The New Yorker*'s Alastair Reid[1] said the holy words last week: "A reporter might take liberties with the factual circumstances to make the larger truth clear." O large, large truth. Apparently Mr. Reid believes that imposing a truth is the same as arriving at one. Illogically, he also seems to think that truths may be disclosed through lies. But his error is more fundamental still in assuming that large truth is the province of journalism in the first place. The business of journalism is to present facts accurately—Mr. Reid notwithstanding. Those seeking something larger are advised to look elsewhere.

2 For one thing, journalism rarely sees the larger truth of a story because reporters are usually chasing quite small elements of information. A story, like a fern, only reveals its final shocking shape in stages. Journalism also reduces most of the stories it deals with to political considerations. Matters are defined in terms of where power lies, who opposes whom or what, where the special interests are. As a result, the larger truth of a story is often missed or ignored. By its nature, political thought limits speculative thought. Political realities themselves cannot be grasped by an exclusively political way of looking at things.

3 Then, too, journalism necessarily deals with discontinuities. One has never heard of the Falkland Islands.[2] Suddenly the Falklands are the center of the universe; one knows all there is to know about "kelpers" and Port Stanley; sheep jokes abound. In the end, as at the beginning, no one really knows anything about the Falkland Islands other than the war that gave it momentary celebrity—nothing about the people in the aftermath of the war, their concerns, isolation, or their true relationship to Argentina and Britain. Discontinuities are valuable because they point up the

---

[1]*New Yorker* staff writer who defended his revelation at a seminar that his non-fiction articles about Spain contain fictional embellishments.—ED.

[2]Islands near Argentina fought over by Britain and Argentina in 1981. They remain a part of the United Kingdom.—ED.

world's variety as well as the special force of its isolated parts. But to rely on them for truth is to lose one's grip on what is continuous and whole.

4 Journalism looks to where the ball is, and not where it is not. A college basketball coach, trying to improve the performance of one of his backcourt men, asked the player what he did when he practiced on his own. "Dribble and shoot," came the reply. The coach then asked the player to add up the total time he dribbled and shot during a scrimmage game, how many minutes he had hold of the ball. "Three minutes in all," came the reply. "That means," said the coach, "that you practice what you do in three minutes out of 40 in a game," Which means in turn that for every player, roughly 37 out of a possible 40 minutes are played away from the ball.

5 Journalism tends to focus on the poor when the poor make news, usually dramatic news like a tenement fire or a march on Washington. But the poor are poor all the time. It is not journalism's ordinary business to deal with the unstartling normalities of life. Reporters need a *story,* something shapely and elegant. Poverty is disorderly, anticlimactic and endless. If one wants truth about the poor, one must look where the ball is not.

6 Similarly, journalism inevitably imposes forms of order on both the facts in a story and on the arrangement of stories itself. The structures of magazines and newspapers impose one kind of order; radio and television another, usually sequential. But every form journalism takes is designed to draw the public's attention to what the editors deem most important in a day's or week's events. This naturally violates the larger truth of a chaotic universe. Oddly, the public often contributes its own hierarchical arrangements by dismissing editors' discriminations and dwelling on the story about the puppy on page 45 instead of the bank collapse on Page One. The "truth" of a day's events is tugged at from all sides.

7 Finally, journalism often misses the truth by unconsciously eroding one's sympathy with life. A seasoned correspondent in Evelyn Waugh's maliciously funny novel *Scoop* lectures a green reporter. "You know," he says, "you've got a lot to learn about journalism. Look at it this way. News is what a chap who doesn't care much about anything wants to read." The matter is not a laughing one. A superabundance of news has the benumbing effect of mob rule on the senses. Every problem in the world begins to look unreachable, unimprovable. What could one lone person possibly accomplish against a constant and violent storm of events that on any day include a rebellion of Sikhs, a tornado in Wisconsin, parents pleading for a healthy heart for their child? Sensibilities, overwhelmed, eventually grow cold; and therein monsters lie. Nobody wants to be part of a civilization that reads the news and does not care about it. Certainly no journalist wants that.

8 If one asks, then, where the larger truth is to be sought, the answer is where it has always been: in history, poetry, art, nature, education, conversation; in the tunnels of one's own mind. People may have come to

expect too much of journalism. Not of journalism at its worst; when one is confronted with lies, cruelty and tastelessness, it is hardly too much to expect better. But that is not a serious problem because lies, cruelty and tastelessness are the freaks of the trade, not the pillars. The trouble is that people have also come to expect too much of journalism at its best, because they have invested too much power in it, and in so doing have neglected or forfeited other sources of power in their lives. Journalists appear to give answers, but essentially they ask a question: What shall we make of this? A culture that would rely on the news for truth could not answer that question because it already would have lost the qualities of mind that make the news worth knowing.

9 If people cannot rely on the news for facts, however, then journalism has no reason for being. Alastair Reid may have forgotten that the principal reason journalists exist in society is that people have a need to be informed of and comprehend the details of experience. "The right to know and the right to be are one," wrote Wallace Stevens in a poem about Ulysses. The need is basic, biological. In that sense, everyone is a journalist, seeking the knowledge of the times in order to grasp the character of the world, to survive in the world, perhaps to move it. Archimedes[3] said he could move the world as long as he had a long enough lever. He pointed out, too, that he needed a ground to stand on.

Word Study List

discontinuities	3	eroding	7
hierarchical	6	superabundance	7

Questions

1. Reid's taking liberties with some facts is the occasion for Rosenblatt's essay. What three objections does Rosenblatt have to journalists' taking liberties with the facts?

2. One of Rosenblatt's three objections is also his thesis. What is that thesis?

3. Rosenblatt presents six reasons in support of his thesis. Summarize them in your own words, spotting each new point by finding the writer's transition words.

4. Rosenblatt explains one point by drawing a comparison from basketball. Explain the analogy.

[3]Greek mathematician (287?–212 B.C.) known for mechanical inventions.—ED.

5. If journalism cannot provide us with the truth, then what important contribution does it make to our getting at the truth? Where, according to Rosenblatt, should we look for the truth?

6. Rosenblatt says that journalists write about facts, not the truth. What, then, does he mean by the truth? Is this distinction between facts and truth new to you? In what ways is the distinction a useful one?

7. Bruning (see "Why People Distrust the Press," pp. 375–377) argues that people don't trust the press, whereas Rosenblatt asserts that we have come to expect too much of journalism. Are these views conflicting? Can they both be right?

Exercises

1. Rosenblatt offers several interesting generalizations. Select one from the list below and, in a paragraph, either develop or challenge Rosenblatt's idea.
   a. "Poverty is disorderly, anticlimactic and endless."
   b. "Political thought limits speculative thought."
   c. "This naturally violates the larger truth of a chaotic universe."
   d. "Nobody wants to be part of a civilization that reads the news and does not care about it."
2. We have noted Rosenblatt's distinction between the terms *facts* and *truth;* he also distinguishes between *political thought* and *speculative thought.* What is the difference between political and speculative thought? Why do we need to use both to understand politics? In a paragraph, develop an answer to either one of these questions.

Our All-Too-Timid Press

Tom Wicker

Tom Wicker (b. 1926) has been an associate editor and columnist of the *New York Times* since 1968. He has contributed articles to national magazines and has written both fiction and nonfiction books. Recent publications include *A Time to Die* (1975), a firsthand account of the Attica prison riots, *On Press* (1978), and *Unto This Hour* (1984), a novel about the Civil War. This article, the conclusion (with slight changes) to *On Press,* appeared in *Saturday Review,* March 4, 1978.

Wicker takes the position that our press is not too aggressive but rather too timid. He wants a press that risks being called irresponsible in order to publish what it sees as the truth. Wicker's discussion of press freedom and responsibility includes a rebuttal of arguments favoring controls designed to insure responsible reporting.

1 The First Amendment does not say anything about "responsibility." This observation, which I have offered to hundreds of disbelieving and usually disapproving audiences, invariably brings some challenger to his or her feet with something like the following inquiry (usually varied more in its degree of choler than in wording): "Do you mean to say that the press has a right to be irresponsible?"

2 I mean to say nothing of the sort, although it's true—just to be argumentative—that irresponsibility does not appear to the layman's eye to be a constitutional violation. But it's just as well for journalists in particular to recall the skeptical judgment in *The Federalist* of Alexander Hamilton—who opposed as unnecessary a Bill of Rights for the Constitution:

> What is the liberty of the press? Who can give it any definition which would not leave the utmost latitude for evasion? I hold it to be impracticable; and from this I infer that its security, whatever fine declarations may be inserted in any constitition respecting it, must altogether depend on public opinion, and on the general spirit of the people and of the government.

3 Just so. And with that in mind, no journalist should advocate to the public the idea that the press has "a right to be irresponsible"; no one could agree to that. Nor should any journalist wish the press or broadcast news to *be* irresponsible. Aside from their pride in their craft and its institutions, their desire to do their personal work well, and their concern that the public should be informed, all journalists know that popular contempt for and fear of press irresponsibility are as grave threats—and more justified ones—to a free press as are government attempts to silence it. And, as Hamilton foresaw, that part of the First Amendement might not long survive a hostile, determined public opinion.

4 Granting all that, a certain case for tolerance of irresponsibility still has to be made. That is to say, if the American press is to remain free—even in the somewhat limited sense that necessarily results from the conflict of this freedom with the other equally guaranteed freedoms in the Constitution and the Bill of Rights—it cannot have responsibility imposed on it by legislation, judicial interpretation, or any other process.

5 Freedom contains within itself the possibility of irresponsibility. No man is truly free who is not permitted occasionally to be irresponsible; nor is any institution. Responsibility, it goes without saying, is profoundly important; and the highest freedom of all may well be the freedom to conduct one's life and affairs responsibly—but by one's own standards of responsibility. It's a mean freedom in which a mere failure of responsibility brings a jail term or a fine or some other societally imposed penalty—and no freedom at all if standards of responsibility are uniform,

designed to prevent rather than to punish failures, and set by higher authority.

6 Yet some of the most sweeping restrictions on the freedom of the press have been proposed in the name of preventing press irresponsibility. What is lost sight of is that if responsibility can be imposed, freedom must be lost; and of those who advocate various means of ensuring the responsibility of a supposedly free press, two questions should be asked.

7 *Who defines responsibility?* In numerous instances, the difficulty editors and reporters have in determining a responsible course in disputed circumstances has, I believe, been demonstrated—notably in the case of the *New York Times*'s treatment of the Bay of Pigs[1] story. In literally thousands of other instances—most of them less important but many on the same level of seriousness—editors have no hard-and-fast rules to follow, save those of experience, ethics, and common sense—all of which vary from person to person. Editors may, and often do, differ on what is responsible—even as *Times* editors differed among themselves on handling the Bay of Pigs story. There simply is no certainty, in most instances, as to what constitutes a responsible course in an enormous number of cases that editors and reporters have to face.

8 Most journalists believe that the multiplicity of editorial decisions likely to result in any given case is a major safeguard against irresponsibility and misinformation. All editors won't make the same decision based on the same set of facts—a story played on page one by the *Times* may be printed inside *The Washington Post*; a quotation in the one story may not appear in the other; different lines of interpretation may well be taken by the two papers and by any number of others, with the result that the same story appears in many versions and with a greater or lesser degree of prominence. This rich diversity not only works against the possibility that any story can be covered up or manufactured but it also offers a reasonable guarantee that differing viewpoints on the same events will reach the public.

9 Not only, therefore, would the imposition of standards of responsibility on the press move it away from diversity and toward uniformity of presentation but it would require an instrument big enough and comprehensive enough to define responsibility in an immense number of instances, for a huge number of publications and broadcasters. No such instrument exists, save the government.

10 *Who enforces responsibility?* This is a simpler problem. Once responsibility is defined, obviously nothing of sufficient power and scope exists

---

[1] A secret Marine invasion of Cuba in an unsuccessful attempt to depose Fidel Castro. The mission, severely straining relations with Russia, was directed by the President and the CIA without consulting Congress.—Ed.

to force the defined responsibility on the entire press—again save the government.

11 Thus, if we are to be *sure* of a responsible press, the only way is through a government that both defines and enforces responsibility. Not just Richard Nixon would have leaped at *that* opportunity. It need scarcely even be pointed out that in such circumstances, the condition of the American press would be a far cry from freedom.

12 Would that matter?

13 Obviously, a totally government-controlled press would make much difference to liberty in America; but that is not what most of those who demand greater press responsibility have in mind. They more often set forth a supposedly middle course—yielding a little freedom in a beneficial trade-off to gain some responsibility.

14 The middle-course argument is respectable. It cannot be maintained by the most ardent First Amendment advocate that democracy is not reasonably healthy in Britain, where the press is under much greater restraint than it is in the United States. Libel laws that sharply restrict publication and broadcasting; a heavy bias toward privacy rather than publication in laws governing press reports on criminal justice proceedings and other actions of the courts; the Official Secrets Act that governments of both parties frequently invoke, apparently not always in matters of indisputable national security; and the quasi-governmental Press Council to monitor and criticize press activities—have these stifled the larger British democracy? From my side of the Atlantic, I cannot say that they have.

15 For whatever reasons, the history of British politics is by no means as marked by venality and corruption as is that of the United States, and governing ethics and traditions there appear so settled that serious violations of them—for example, a power grab such as that represented by the Watergate complex of offenses—are far less likely. Secrecy by the British government has been widely accepted for centuries. Profound policy miscalculations—the Suez War, for example—bring quick political retribution, Official Secrets Act or no, while more egregious American blunders in Vietnam and Cambodia for years produced in the United States mostly a "rally-round-the-President" effect, until the press—primarily television—finally turned the public against the war (by printing and broadcasting *news,* not editorials).

16 Therefore, press restraints perhaps amenable to British democracy—although not many British journalists really consider them so—would not necessarily be fitting in the United States. Should a Watergate occur in the United Kingdom, colleagues in the British press say, the governing party plausibly accused of conniving in the burglary of opposition party headquarters and then of obstructing justice to conceal the crime would soon be turned out of office, despite restrictions on reporting such a story. But it was a challenging American press that kept Watergate in

the public eye and ultimately forced the various actions that led to Richard Nixon's resignation—at that, two years after the offense.

17 But the existence of restrictions on the British press, together with the evident survival of the essential British democracy, leads many serious and reasonable persons to suggest not government control of the American press but similar instruments of responsibility in this country's journalistic practice.

18 When the Senate in 1977 established an oversight committee for the so-called intelligence community, for example, one of the committee's first studies was of the need, if any, for a limited form of Official Secrets Act in the United States—an effort to protect the CIA from the public rather than the public from the CIA that stood the committee's supposed responsibility on its head.

19 The discussed act's reach would ostensibly have been limited to barring disclosures of "sources and methods" of gathering intelligence—"ostensibly" because although "sources and methods" describes an arcane art and is a term therefore supposedly capable of being strictly defined and narrowly applied, both the FBI and the CIA have in the past shown themselves capable of slipping large abuses through tiny loopholes. It was, for example, supposedly to protect sources and methods that some of the CIA's mail-opening and surveillance operations were illegally pursued.

20 Whatever the situation in Britain, in this country—as I hope I have demonstrated—secrecy has too often been used to shield blunders, crimes, and ineptitude. Alert citizens should not accept without sharp questioning a secrecy law designed to give a secret agency even greater powers of covering up its operations than it already has. And unless Congress were to show an uncharacteristic willingness to include a "shield" provision for reporters—which it has never done in other legislation of less importance and which would be of dubious constitutionality—a likely consequence would be about as follows:

21 The leak of a secret protected by the act would appear as a news story in a newspaper or on a broadcast. An inquiry would be launched; but as usual, the identity of the leaker (who could be prosecuted under the new law) would not be learned. The reporter-recipient of the leak would be subpoenaed to appear before a grand jury and would be asked the identity of his source, with a view to prosecuting the leaker. It would be made clear that no other means existed of obtaining this information vital to enforcement of the Official Secrets Act and the orderly administration of government.

22 The reporter would abide by his professional code of ethics and would refuse to answer. He would then be held in contempt and ordered to jail—although there might be no evidence of any damage to national security as a consequence of his or her story. A lot of reporters would

have a lot of second thoughts—chilling indeed—about accepting leaks of so-called security secrets under such a threat.

23 Would that serve the cause of responsibility? Once again, the answer depends upon who defines responsibility in any given case; but those who place a high value upon a "robust and uninhibited press" and who have learned to be skeptical of the government's assertions of "national security" are not likely to think so.

24 But even if no such drastic step as instituting an Official Secrets Act was taken, why not more restrictive libel and privacy laws? Would they limit press freedom so severely as to threaten the public's right and need to know? And what about a non-governmental press council, at least to criticize—constructively, as well as punitively—press performance, even if the council had no real power to punish or penalize?

25 The question of more severe libel and privacy laws requires, essentially, a value judgment. There isn't much doubt that greater protection from press charges than is now provided for public officials would limit the ability of the press to act as a check on the power of government; but some reasonable persons believe the press has too much latitude to criticize government, expose its workings, penetrate needed confidentiality, and hinder its effectiveness. Similarly, no one should be in doubt that stricter protection of individual privacy from searching press inquiry would frequently prevent needed public exposure and discussion of personalities, institutions, and processes; but few in the press would deny that the power of the press has too often been the instrument by which have come unwarranted personal humiliations, embarrassments, misfortunes, and losses of reputation and livelihood.

26 As for a U.S. press council, the National News Council has been financed and supported by the Twentieth Century Fund, which is neither conservative nor antipress. Neither have been the first workings of the council, which is supported by many in the press and broadcasting and which has no connection with the government. Its purpose is to conduct quiet private investigations of controversial press or broadcasting decisions and to report publicly on whether or not those decisions were taken responsibly and on reasonable grounds. The council has no power, other than the force of its disapproval, to penalize news organizations.

27 Concerned journalists have argued that the press and broadcasting ought to cooperate wholeheartedly with the News Council. Most news organizations, they say, would have nothing to fear; and it would be better for those who might be culpable to be censured by a private group with press interests at heart than by unsympathetic courts or legislatures. Besides, say the advocates, by certifying in most disputed cases that editorial decisions had been responsibly and reasonably taken, the council would more often reassure the public than threaten the press.

28 In short, these journalists view the News Council as a good public

relations instrument for the press. Not only would news organizations appear to be trying to police their own work and that of colleagues but most would periodically be given a good bill of health by a respected panel of citizens, while irresponsible publications and broadcasts would be sternly reprimanded by a council backed by the press itself.

29 But there is another underlying reason why there has been considerable press support for the News Council. Seldom stated outside newsrooms, journalism classes, or press club bars, it is that the News Council idea offers a safe way to "clean up the press before the government comes in and does it for us." This suggests that even many who are themselves deeply involved in American journalism believe that there are so many excesses and malpractices that need to be cleaned up that the press really does face possible governmental control. And that points straight to the fundamental reason why I personally am opposed to the News Council, to more restrictive privacy and libel laws, and to all other schemes for enforcing the responsibility of a supposedly free press—reasonable as some of these schemes undoubtedly appear in their proposals for only limited sacrifices of freedom.

30 The overwhelming conclusion I have drawn from my life in journalism—nearly 30 years so far, from the *Sandhill Citizen* to *The New York Times*—is that the American press, powerful as it unquestionably is and protected though it may be by the Constitution and the laws, is not often "robust and uninhibited" but is usually timid and anxious—for respectability at least as much as for profitability. Those whose idea of the press is bounded by the exploits of Woodward and Bernstein on the one hand and by the Pentagon Papers[2] on the other do not usually understand that such remarkable efforts as these—whether or not they are viewed as necessary or excessive—are limited exceptions to long-established practice.

31 Undoubtedly, in the more than a decade since Dwight Eisenhower roused the Goldwaterites with his attack on "sensation-seeking columnists," the press has become more activist and challenging, particularly in covering politics and government—though *not* business and financial institutions. On the evidence of press performance in that decade—the disclosure of duplicity and ineptitude in Vietnam; the exposure of political corruption in the Nixon administration; the demonstration of grave threats to American liberty by the "Imperial Presidency," the FBI, the CIA, and other security agencies—I assert the necessity to encourage the developing tendency of the press to shake off the encumbrance of a falsely objective journalism and to take an adversary position toward the most powerful institutions of American life.

---

[2]Secret Pentagon documents concerning the Vietnam War that were stolen and then given to a *New York Times* reporter. The *New York Times* published the Papers, excluding names of CIA agents.—ED.

32 By "adversary position," I don't mean a necessarily hostile position; I use the word in the lawyer's sense of cross-examining, testing, challenging, the merits of a case in the course of a trial. Such an adversary is opposed only in the sense that he or she demands that a case be made: the law stated, the facts proven, the assumptions and conclusions justified, the procedure squared with common sense and good practice. An adversary press would hold truth—unattainable and frequently plural as it is—as its highest value and knowledge as its first responsibility.

33 Such a press should be encouraged in its independence, not investigated—even by its friends—when it asserts that independence. A relatively toothless News Council that nevertheless could summon editors and reporters, notes and documents, film and outtakes, in order to determine publicly whether editorial decisions had been properly made *by the News Council's standards* would be bound to have an ultimately inhibiting effect on editors, publishers, and broadcasters—not all of whom would therefore be dismayed. Most, it's safe to say, would rather be praised for someone else's idea of responsibility than risk being questioned or criticized for their own independence.

34 Somewhat similarly, tighter libel and privacy laws would surely narrow the area open to editorial judgment—and some editors and publishers might welcome such laws just for that reason. Some might even yearn privately for an Official Secrets Act because its proscriptions would relieve them of having to decide such difficult questions as whether or not to publish so-called national security stories and of the loud accusations of irresponsibility that inevitably follow such decisions, no matter how they are made.

35 My belief is that the gravest threat to freedom of the press is not necessarily from public animosity or mistrust, legislative action or court decision. Certainly, even though absolute press freedom may sometimes have to accommodate itself to other high constitutional values, the repeal or modification of the First Amendment seems unlikely. At least as great a threat, I believe, comes from the press itself—in its longing for a respectable place in the established political and economic order, in its fear of the reaction that boldness and independence will always evoke. Self-censorship silences as effectively as a government decree, and we have seen it far more often.

36 In the harsh sunlight of a robust freedom, after all, nothing stands more starkly exposed than the necessity to decide and to accept the responsibility for decision. If the true freedom of the press is to decide for itself what to publish and when to publish it, the true responsibiilty of the press must be to assert that freedom.

37 But my life in journalism has persuaded me that the press too often tries to guard its freedom by shirking its responsibility and that this leads to default on both. What the press in America needs is less inhibition, not more restraint.

Word Study List

choler	1	arcane	19
multiplicity	8	subpoenaed	21
imposition	9	punitively	24
quasi-governmental	14	culpable	27
venality	15	duplicity	31
egregious	15	encumbrance	31
amenable	16	proscriptions	34
ostensibly	19		

Questions

1. What is Wicker's thesis? Where in his essay can you find the best one-sentence statement of his thesis? Is it where you have been taught to look for a thesis? What is the effect of withholding one's main point until the case has been made for it?

2. Why must we tolerate some irresponsibility from the press, even though we do not wish it to be irresponsible? In Wicker's view, what is the connection between freedom and irresponsibility? Does Wicker's definition of freedom make sense to you?

3. Wicker says that if we insist on press responsibility at the cost of some freedom, two questions must be asked: "Who defines responsibility?" and "Who enforces responsibility?" How does Wicker answer both questions? What reason does he give for his answer?

4. While rejecting government control of the press, Wicker asserts that the "middle-course" argument has some merit and should be examined. What do "middle-course" advocates propose? Where do they get their ideas? Why does Wicker think that their suggestions will not work as well in the United States as in Britain?

5. Wicker offers a rather strong judgment when he says that American politics are more venal and corrupt than British politics. Why doesn't he offer any evidence to support this judgment? Are readers supposed to know that this is correct? Does Wicker simply hope that we will agree with him? Do you agree? Do you have evidence to support your judgment?

6. Why does Wicker think that many journalists and editors approve of a News Council? How does Wicker think the press behaves, generally? Why would they find comfort in a News Council? Why do so many people find comfort in clearly stated rules and regulations governing their behavior?

7. What kind of a press does Wicker want?

8. How is Wicker, in arguing for press freedom and responsibility, also arguing for a way of life for individuals and institutions? Do people and groups seem less willing, today, to want freedom and to accept responsibility?

Exercises

1. Find out what restrictions, if any, are placed on what your college newspaper can print. If there are restrictions, who imposes them?

2. What are the reasons for and against a college newspaper's having absolute freedom to print whatever it chooses? To what degree should the college administration serve as a parental substitute and moral arbiter? Is there a difference between restrictions on the freedom of the press imposed by a college administration and restrictions imposed by the government?

An Ethical Dilemma: Responsibility for 'Self-Generating' News

J. K. Hvistendahl

J. K. Hvistendahl (b. 1918) is an associate professor of journalism at Iowa State University. He has coauthored a book and written articles for professional journals. This article was first printed in *Grassroots Editor,* September/October 1973.

The author of "An Ethical Dilemma" poses the problems that arise from reporting news as correctly and impersonally as possible and advocates that reporters show some consideration, before publication, of the possible effects of certain news on the public.

1 During the McCarthy era[1] when an unusual amount of official and unofficial bigotry was in the air, the news director of a large Iowa radio station faced a problem in news ethics which is still unresolved. Are the news media responsible for the *effects* of what they publish, or just for getting the information from the source or the event to readers or listeners fairly and accurately?

[1]The early 1950s, when Senator Joseph McCarthy headed the Senate Un-American Activities Committee, whose goal was to identify presumed pro-Communists in this country.—Ed.

2 In this instance, a swastika was painted on a Jewish synagogue. The fact was routinely reported by the station. A second swastika was painted on another synagogue in another city. The event was again reported. Four more similar desecrations occurred, after which the news director told his staff:

> It is apparent that our reporting of these events is actually encouraging them to happen. Therefore, our policy as of now is to report no more stories about swastikas being painted on synagogues unless some entirely new angle develops.

3 The reporting of the swastika-paintings stopped and so did the painting of the swastikas.

4 The other option of the news director was to continue reporting the paintings until they lost news value or, more likely in Iowa, the swastika-painters had run out of synagogues. But he did what he thought was the "right" thing (read "ethical") despite the fact that the events still had news value.

5 Because he himself was not sure he had made the correct ethical decision, he reported the situation to a meeting of radio newsmen in the state.

6 "The effect on two-thirds of them," he says now, "was somewhat like arguing legalized abortion before the College of Cardinals. The other third seemed to agree that what I had done was right, but they may have just been trying to be polite."

7 This example is of only passing importance in the grander scale of press ethics but it serves to illuminate a basic philosophic difference among newsmen as to the responsibility of the press. The difference is seldom articulated as a philosophical problem, but newsmen almost always recognize the issue when it confronts them, and vehemently line up on one side or the other.

8 In the fall of 1972, the *New Yorker Magazine* in the "Talk of the Town" agonized over the "self-generating effect" of news which was apparent in the killing of the Kennedys and Martin Luther King, the shooting of George Wallace, and the possibility of the effect again manifesting itself in the letter-bomb assassinations of Israeli diplomats. Said the *New Yorker:*

> "NEW TYPE OF BOMB USED IN MAILING," says the paper in front of us, which then quotes "London sources" on the general procedure for making such a device and on the considerable destructive power of the explosive. This is freedom of the press, we think, which has its own ethics and its own logic, but it is also a means of providing information, and the information is provided in full knowledge of a now nearly universal propensity for madness, for wild, murderous faddism, which in recent years has all too amply shown the world—the world of newspaper editors as well as readers—its own deathly logic . . . Is it enough to say that everybody has been

doing his job—the reporter, the editor, the publisher? At this moment, we doubt it. A better way must be found, we think, of dealing with "news" of this sort, which is both "news" and something else.

9 Those who condemned the Iowa news director for refusing to report more swastika paintings probably would also condemn the *New Yorker* for suggesting that there is a serious ethical problem involved in "self generating" news. Many reporters and editors would reject the *New Yorker*'s conclusion that what is needed is:

> . . . some kind of coherent, responsible, nontrivial agreement among news organizations that they will play this kind of news down rather than up, and that whenever someone discovers, say, a new device for killing people, they will report the discovery with nondramatic coolness, and certainly not furnish us with how-to-do-it details of its construction. We (by which we mean those of us who are in the press and who care about the press) have to stop saying we are just doing our jobs, are fulfilling our functions, are being professional. No amount of professionalism can recover lives lost in a contagion of violence.

10 Those newsmen who disagree with both the *New Yorker* and the radio news director believe their function is to provide their readers with an uninterrupted flow of news based on the values of interest, significance, and importance. Any interruption of the flow of news, except for the exigencies of time and space, is unethical.

11 They believe their ethical compact is to quote the source correctly and describe the event accurately without the intrusion of their personal feelings of judgments. Beyond that, they disavow responsibility for the effect of what they write on readers and listeners, either temporary or cumulative. Their ethical responsibility is oriented more toward the source than the reader.

12 Those who subscribe to this philosophy of the press might be said to be practicing *"micro-ethics."*

13 The aphorisms of the profession attest that this philosophical position is real and broadly accepted. "We don't make the news, we just print it." "Give the people the facts, and they'll make the right decision." "What God in His wisdom has permitted to happen, I'm not too proud to print."

14 The philosophy of *micro-ethics* has worked well in reducing the influence of self-seeking pressure groups, advertisers, and politicians on the press. The key belief of *micro-ethics* is that in the long run humanity will benefit because the truth will be told without fear or favor; the guilty will be punished, exposed or at least identified, and the innocent will benefit. Full disclosure of the news is ethical because it is in the best interest of readers and listeners to know what is going on.

15 *But what is the ethical situation when the* unwanted *effects of a news article*

far overbalance the beneficial effects of the "right to know?" What if that which the reader learns benefits him little or not at all while the "self generating" effect triggers violent and destructive acts which make the reader or listener's world predictably worse rather than better?

16 It is at this point that those who practice *macro-ethics* depart from those who practice *micro-ethics.* The *macro-ethicists* follow the basic principles of the teleological philosophers, who claim that an act must be judged ethical or unethical by its consequences. If the effects of an act are more negative than positive for humanity as a whole, the act is considered unethical.

17 The *micro-ethicist* believes that the consequences of what he writes are outside of his responsibility. He believes that in supplying readers and listeners with all the information that could possibly interest, amuse, or inform them he is being both ethical and professional.

18 Those who take the *macro-ethics* view believe that the mass distribution of news to millions of people, rather than to thousands, demands a new journalistic ethic. The newsman, if he is to make a claim to being professional, must begin to take more of the responsibility for the unwanted effects of his stories.

19 Whether he is guided by *macro-* or *micro-ethics,* no newsman can hold himself responsible for miscellaneous and irrational effects which may result from even a routine news story. He cannot, for example, be expected to suffer pangs of conscience when, after he has written a story about the Dow-Jones averages dropping 36 points, one of his readers goes out of the window.

20 But the *macro-ethicist,* when he sees that publishing a certain article will be of only minor importance to many readers, but the consequences of publishing may have predictably bad results, believes it is his ethical duty to "cool," delay, or withhold parts of the story.

21 *The* micro-ethicist *will argue, with considerable justification that he indeed is being professional and serving a democratic society by* not specifying what *is in the interest of society. In a true democracy, no person or group, including reporters and editors, has the right to dictate what is in the best interests of others. The newsman who is the most professional is he who delivers the news "straight," holding nothing back, and presenting no point of view.*

22 He will argue that "consequences" are sufficiently ambiguous and unwieldy so as to make them a totally inadequate test of rightness or wrongness—only the reader or listener can determine that. Further the newsman is required not only to determine in advance what consequences are likely to accrue from what he writes, but he is forced to make the moral judgment as to whether the consequences are likely to be good or bad.

23 The *micro-ethicist* claims that his job is to hold a mirror up to society and reflect what is there. The *macro-ethicist* agrees, but points out that the mirror is raised *selectively.* Only a small fraction of the world's events reach

print or the airwaves. The minute the mirror comes up, the possibility exists that the nature of the event will be changed, especially for the millions who get the reflection from a distance and second hand. The mirror has become part of the event as it is perceived by the readers.

24 In most instances, the effect of the mirror is unimportant and leads to no serious consequences. But in other instances—like the swastika paintings—the mirror touches off a series of events that would not otherwise occur.

25 *The* macro-ethicist *claims that when it can be predicted with reasonable accuracy that the very process of raising the mirror will change the nature of the event, by intensifying it, glamorizing it, or causing it to be repeated, caution is in order. How, for example, does it serve the public interest to give the details of the construction of a letter bomb?*

26 Ethics are always easier to apply in the abstract than in the concete. In the swastika episode, the ethical decision based on ethics seems clear: The public had already become generally aware that swastikas were being painted. The news director was acting ethically in refusing to broadcast further stories once he was convinced the events were self generating, and perhaps media induced.

27 The letter bombings could hardly have been ignored under almost any ethical framework, but it seems unnecessary and contrary to the best interests of readers and listeners to show society's eccentrics how the bombs are made. Further, except in the New York and Washington, D.C. areas, where knowledge of the letter bombs might serve as a warning for diplomats and others, why was it necessary to run the story under a banner headline on page 1 as far away from the event as the West Coast?

28 How would the philosophy of *macro-ethics* square with the decision of the *New York Times* to publish the Pentagon Papers?[2] The case is a classical moral dilemma—the people's rights and need to know on one hand against the government executive's privilege to withhold and classify information—which he also considers in the public interest.

29 The *Times* deliberated—indeed agonized—and came to the conclusion that greater good would result for the American people through publishing the papers than in respecting the government's right to classify and withhold. The *Times* did its best to minimize the danger to the government by itself withholding some of the information and by going so far as to retain a cryptographic expert on the question of the possiblity of compromising government codes. But the *Times* published.

30 *Macro-ethicists* would agree that it is good to uphold the law. But when the law clashes with other considerations, the final ethical decision must be made on the same basis: what are the probable consequences,

---

[2]Secret Pentagon documents concerning the Vietnam War that were stolen and then given to a *New York Times* reporter. The *New York Times* published the Papers, excluding names of CIA agents.—ED.

which choice is ultimately better for the people? If Socrates had been publisher of the *New York Times* rather than Arthur Ochs Sulzberger, the Pentagon Papers probably wouldn't have been published. Socrates believed that law was of a higher order than individual moral considerations. If the state says you take the hemlock, it's "bottoms up." Greater harm to society results from eroding the law than in eliminating an aged philosopher, no matter how unjustly. (But Socrates was an old man; he might have made a different decision, as he himself admitted, if he had been a youth.)

31 The *Times* editors also made a *"macro"* decision when they decided not to tell the public all of what they knew about the impending Bay of Pigs[3] invasion during the Kennedy administration. In this case, they thought it in the best interest of the public to withhold the information, rather than publish it.

32 *In retrospect, the* Times *appears to have been wrong on this one. But when a newspaper accepts the responsibility of evaluating the news on the basis of probable effects, the probabilities are that once in awhile they are going to be wrong. The* micro *approach is much simpler: if it's legal and accurate, let the fallout drift where it may.*

33 No newspaper is likely to follow consistently either the *micro* or the *macro* pattern. *The Wall Street Journal,* which usually takes a *macro* approach to the news, went down the *micro* route in October of 1972 when a reporter was sent into North Carolina to interview low income and welfare recipients who were participating in a University of Wisconsin study on the effects of guaranteed annual wage. The published interviews, plus the additional publicity, could have destroyed the scientific validity of the research.

34 No question of legality was involved, but a dedicated *macro-ethicist* might ask what the public had to gain from the premature disclosure of research compared to the damage done to a research project which might answer some of the most vexing questions of public welfare.

35 The *macro* approach not only demands that a newspaper, magazine, radio or television station be responsible for the short term effects of its output, but that it also be responsible for the cumulative, long term effect. Richard Tobin, writing in the November 9, 1968 *Saturday Review,* quotes Psychologist Herbert Otto as saying, "The widely prevalent concept of what constitutes news is a narrow, destructive concept—a sick concept, destructive to society as a whole." When news is defined almost entirely in terms of catastrophe, disaster, crime, and cupidity, and when it is gathered from the four corners of the earth, the cumulative effect on the reader and listener is at best one-sided, and at worst psychologically disturbing.

---

[3]A secret Marine invasion of Cuba in an unsuccessful attempt to depose Fidel Castro. The mission, severely straining relations with Russia, was directed by the President and the CIA without consulting Congress.—ED.

36 *The* micro-ethicist *may insist that a controversial story be reasonably balanced, with both sides being given a square shake, but he is likely to deny that it is his responsibility to give a reasonably balanced picture of the world.*

37 *The approach of* macro-ethics *is that the communication media are a functioning part of the social system. The function of the media is not merely to mirror the rest of the social system but to participate actively in it, generating news as well as reporting it. The* macro *approach is centered more on the perceived needs of people, rather than in events in which people wittingly or unwittingly become involved.*

38 The full acceptance of *macro-ethics* would signal a new press in America: less strident, more willingness to accept responsibility for effects, a better balance of the "right" things in life with the wrong, less reporting of what officials say and more reporting of the effects of political institutions on people, more emphasis on news originating with people, less hysteria over the hysterical acts of others, less emphasis on recency and more emphasis on importance.

39 But the great attraction of the *macro* approach—accountability for predictable effects—could also be its greatest weakness. To what extent and to whom is the press to be accountable? If the press is accountable to government, we have an Agnew-Nixon press theory in which the press, out of patriotism, supports the president even when it appears to some newsmen that he may be lying or that he is totally wrong. If the press is accountable to business, labor unions, religious leaders, the rich, university professors, or others with vested viewpoints, it has sold its soul; the press is no longer accountable to the individual readers and listeners to whom it owes its strongest allegiance. Accountability in either approach, if it is to be consistent with the idea of an open, pluralistic society, must be to the individual, not to interest groups or government.

40 There may be less reason to fear the effects of self-generating news than a philosophy of news that says there are some things that the people ought not to be told. Yet, a more sophisticated press, with more insight into its effects and with more concern for readers and listeners, might be able to take the "cooler" *macro* approach without selling its soul to the devil. We may have reached a point in time where it is at least worth a try.

Word Study List

swastika	1	teleological	16
desecrations	2	accrue	22
articulated	7	eccentrics	27
vehemently	7	cyptographic	27
exigencies	10	eroding	30
disavow	11	cupidity	35
aphorisms	13	pluralistic	39

Questions

1. Hvistendahl defines two ethical positions journalists can take and labels them *micro-ethics* and *macro-ethics.* Explain, in your own words, each philosophical position. Which kind of ethics was the Iowa news director practicing?

2. Although Hvistendahl agrees that journalists cannot always accurately predict the consequences of their reports, he still believes that macro-ethics is possible and good. What guidelines does he offer for judging the effects of news reporting?

3. Micro-ethicists argue that the consequences of their actions are not their responsibility. Hvistendahl observes that the micro-ethics position is the simpler one. Why? How would Wicker, believing that freedom and responsibility go together, respond to the micro-ethicist?

4. Perhaps one of the best supports of the macro-ethics position lies in the recognition that journalists choose to report some events but not others. What events do newspapers choose to cover most often? What seems left out?

5. Another support for macro-ethics lies in perceiving that the press does not just report what happens; it shapes what happens by its reporting. Is this concept of "self-generating news" a new one for you? Can you think of examples of self-generating news events other than those given by Hvistendahl? Consider, for example, the scheduling of "media events" by politicians.

6. Finally, journalists not only create events by covering them, they also shape the reader's perception of reality. Herein lies the great power of the media according to most media analysts. How do journalists "see" the world they write about? Have you noticed any consistent patterns in news stories, patterns that sometimes seem imposed on the events?

7. How would the acceptance of macro-ethics change the press in America? Would these changes be in line with the kind of press that Wicker wants?

Exercises

1. Analyze the first section of a daily newspaper for a week, keeping a record of the events and people in the news. Look at your record and see what conclusions you can draw about the types of events (e.g., presidential decisions, disasters) and types of people (public officials, jet-setters) in the news.

2. To see if most news reporters use a pattern in writing up an event, select a front-page article, a feature story from the style or society section, and a sports story to analyze. What do they have in common? Pay particular attention to each story's organization.

Privacy and the Press

Arthur Schlesinger, Jr.

Arthur Schlesinger, Jr. (b. 1917), is Albert Schweitzer Professor of the Humanities at the City University of New York, winner of Pulitzer Prizes in history and biography, and a member of the *Wall Street Journal's* Board of Contributors. He has written many books on American politics and political figures from Andrew Jackson to Richard Nixon. This article appeared in the *Wall Street Journal,* October 24, 1978.

Schlesinger views the role of the press as invaluable in uncovering corruption and deceit that affects the political and economic activity of our country but argues that the press should draw the line at exposing secrets of people's private lives that in no way affect their public lives.

1 "The press," wrote Alexis de Tocqueville in *Democracy in America,* "is the chief democratic instrument of freedom." That sentiment, so banal today, was more daring in Tocqueville's time. When he visited the United States in the 1830s, newspapers were rowdy and irresponsible. Only a quarter century before Tocqueville arrived, President Thomas Jefferson had actually urged the governor of Pennsylvania to invoke the old English doctrine of seditious libel in order to prosecute disrespectful editors. "Nothing can now be believed," Jefferson observed soon thereafter, "which is seen in a newspaper." Nevertheless the French visitor declared a free press indispensable if liberty were to survive in the age of equality.

2 In the years since, the Tocqueville proposition has won general acceptance, and the press itself has become a good deal more careful, objective and sedate. Reflecting on "The Decay of Lying" toward the end of the 19th Century, Oscar Wilde remarked that even newspapers had degenerated; "they may now be absolutely relied upon." This process has continued in our own time. In recent years most newspapers have even come to the point of confessing error. Many run daily correction boxes. Some hire ombudsmen and print self-criticism in their own pages.

3 Yet, for all this, the press—and I use the word hereafter to include the news divisions of television networks and stations—seems to be in trouble; or at least supposes it is. Of course publishers and editors are not without a rather considerable talent for self-pity. In fact the communications industry has not done too badly in those occasional polls asking

Americans to rate their institutions on the scale of public trust. In any event it would be a poor country where no one is mad at the newspapers. Still journalists do seem honestly to feel these days that they are particularly set upon.

INVESTIGATIVE REPORTING'S ROLE

4 Much of this trouble springs from the current vogue of investigative reporting. Of course all reporting is in a sense investigative reporting; but in the strict sense investigative reporting aims at the uncovering of secrets that people, for good or bad reason, want to keep to themselves. The contemporary journalism of inquiry and exposure, Tom Wicker of *The New York Times* has suggested, may be creating a backlash that will in time turn the press back into a tame pussycat again.

5 One must hope that Mr. Wicker is wrong. The special capacity of the press for inquiry and exposure is one reason why men like Tocqueville have considered it the chief democratic instrument of freedom. American journalism has no more honored tradition than that of the muckrakers, who so brilliantly exposed abuse and corruption in political and economic life after the turn of the century. Nor can one doubt that *The Washington Post*'s crucial role in the Watergate affair has made aspiring journalists across the land today model themselves on those now legendary figures Woodward and Bernstein.

6 But investigative journalism appears to have generated a tendency on the part of the press to make undue, and perhaps unnecessary, claims for itself at the expense of other social interests. Does a reporter's right to conceal his sources really take precedence over the right of a man on trial for his life to have access to evidence that might prove his innocence? One can readily conceive an overriding social value in the protection of sources in certain definable circumstances, but is such protection really an absolute to which everything else must be sacrificed? I doubt whether that is true for journalism, and I am certain it cannot be true across the board. In the historian's trade it is precisely the writer that refuses to disclose his sources who is suspect.

7 Some of our current investigative journalists, moreover, misconstrue the Woodward-Bernstein model. For the Watergate exposé, like the work of the muckrakers, had an essential characteristic: it was aimed at public, not personal, conduct. But in the post-Watergate mood some newspaper and television reporters seem to have decided that the way to fame and influence is to uncover secrets and scandals in people's private lives. The traditional view was that a person's private life was relevant only if it significantly affected his public behavior. Modern investigative journalism too often regards digging into a person's private life as a legitimate and laudable end in itself.

8 Fifteen years ago J. Edgar Hoover made an assiduous effort to leak to the press tape recordings that were supposed to raise questions about Martin Luther King's personal habits. No newspaper or magazine would touch them. Senator Richard Russell of Georgia asked the Department of Justice what the FBI was going on about. When Nicholas Katzenbach briefed him, he "just wasn't interested," as Katzenbach later recalled; "wondered why I was wasting his time. He's a pretty good fellow on hitting below the belt. He said to me, 'You and I are a mile apart on civil rights, but I'll tell you, I'm a hundred miles away from George Wallace.'"

9 This was in 1964; Senator Russell was a gentleman of the old school; and newspapers still had standards. One doubts that Hoover would encounter the same difficulty in planting his scandal in 1978. And the rest of us are only too eager to believe the worst. In recent years we have been given to understand that Jefferson, FDR, Eisenhower, John Kennedy all had extramarital adventures. These are proper questions for a biographer to go into after a suitable passage of time. But what is morbid about the current atmosphere is the way it transforms biographical speculations into historical realities. There is simply no hard evidence, for example, that Jefferson ever dallied with Sally Hemings. But I have seen a dozen allusions in recent months to the supposed affair as if it were a proven and demonstrable fact.

JUSTICE BRANDEIS'S OPINION

10 If the press is in trouble today, it may be in part because it is forgetting the line that has traditionally divided proper from improper curiosity. If a politician takes a bribe, it is the public's business; if he has an affair, it ought to be his own. No one believed more fervently in the healthy effect of publicity than Louis D. Brandeis. Sunlight, he used to say, was the great disinfectant. But he rigorously confined the policy of exposure to secrets bearing on public concerns. When the press overstepped "the obvious bounds of propriety and decency" and intruded on personal matters, he was unsparing in his condemnation.

11 "Gossip," Brandeis wrote on one occasion, "is no longer the resource of the idle and the vicious, but has become a trade, which is pursued with industry as well as effrontery. To satisfy a prurient taste the details of sexual relations are spread broadcast in the columns of the daily papers." The result, he believed, was both to invade individual privacy and to lower moral and social standards. "Triviality destroys at once robustness of thought and delicacy of feeling. No enthusiasm can flourish, no generous impulse can survive under its blighting influence."

12 The addiction of our contemporary press and television to personal scandal represents a violation of what Brandeis called "the right to be let alone—the most comprehensive of rights and the right most valued by

civilized men." It would be a shame if resentment over the prurience of some journalists should create a backlash that would handicap others in their necessary and beneficial exposure of malfeasance in our society. Perhaps it is time to recall Theodore Roosevelt's celebrated warning: "Men with the muckrake are often indispensable to the well-being of society, but only if they know when to stop raking the muck."

Word Study List

seditious	1	assiduous	8
libel	1	effrontery	11
ombudsmen	2	prurient	11
muckrakers	5	blighting	11
laudable	7	malfeasance	12

Questions

1. Schlesinger is interested, like Hvistendahl, in establishing guidelines for deciding what to print. What, specifically, is Schlesinger's concern? What should and what should not be reported?

2. Schlesinger sees the problem of what to print as growing out of the "current vogue of investigative reporting." Who are the contemporary models for this kind of journalism? How have some reporters distorted this model?

3. Schlesinger reminds us that Woodward and Bernstein are in the good journalistic company of the muckrakers. Who were some of the famous muckrakers? What kinds of stories did they write? (A good encyclopedia or the subject catalog in your library will help you answer these questions.)

4. Do you agree with the distinction between gossip and private matters that are of legitimate public concern? How much right to privacy must a person relinquish in choosing a public life?

5. Think of all the words that have been written about the various Kennedys. Journalists must think that readers want gossip. Why are we so interested in the private lives of political leaders, movie stars, sports figures? What is the basis for our interest? A desire to emulate success? A desire to find flaws in the lives of apparently successful people?

6. Even if gossip sells, should journalists exercise restraint in revealing private matters? If we accept the power of the media, should we demand that journalists be more ethical than the general public?

Exercise

Examine an article about a famous person in *People* magazine, *Sports Illustrated, National Enquirer,* or a movie magazine. Has the article gone beyond the boundaries of propriety? What facts are reported? How much is opinion? Are details included that are irrelevant to the person's public life? Use Merrill's bias categories (see "How *Time* Stereotyped Three Presidents," Chapter 3) to measure the bias or slant of the article.

Must Reality Be Off the Record?

Meg Greenfield

A Smith College graduate and Cambridge University Fulbright Scholar, Meg Greenfield (b. 1930) has been Editorial Page editor of the *Washington Post* since 1979 and is also a biweekly columnist for *Newsweek*. She won a Pulitzer Prize for editorial writing in 1978. The following article appeared in *Newsweek* on April 16, 1984.

Deploring the "sitcom politics" of our time, Greenfield wonders if the media can't do a better job presenting political realities to us.

1 I have been in journalism for a few decades now, so I know all about the ground rules—all that on-the-record/off-the-record stuff. Like most reporters, I abide by the conditions set, think they sometimes have their reasonable uses and spend a certain amount of time arguing about what the ground rules actually were in various of my encounters. That said, I must observe that there is something wonderfully, if unintentionally, revealing in the argument that has been going on as to whether Jesse Jackson's use of the derogatory terms "Hymie" and "Hymietown" when he was talking to reporter Milton Coleman was on or off the record.[1] In this artless fashion do we in the political-journalistic complex reveal the basic misleading nature of our game. There we are, right out there in public, angrily disputing whether the *simulated* (read phony) "record" was supposed to include this bit of authenticity or not and whether its inclusion represents a breach of our ethics. The real fact—that Jackson talks that way—has become a secondary consideration.

2 In this and similar disputes we have given the game away—yet again—although no one seems particularly disturbed by its central fact, which is this: what we call the record often tends to be the precise oppo-

[1]In an interview during the Democratic primary campaign in the spring of 1984—Ed.

site of a record. It is, rather, the artifice, the cooked-up part, the image that the politician, with our connivance, hopes to convey and generally does. The off-the-record part is where the reality and authenticity are to be found and where they are generally supposed to remain forever obscure.

3 *Imprecations:* Maybe I overstate. But we in Washington do spend a great deal of time fabricating this incomplete reality that we call a record, and to some extent we live in it. I read in my morning paper today, for example, that Tip O'Neill and Ronald Reagan are having another titanic struggle, a hurling back and forth of imprecations. Does anyone in this country believe that these are real battles anymore? Surely your classic recurrent quarrel between Reagan and O'Neill has long since taken on the character of hoked-up wrestling: grunts and grimaces and sadistic leers and arms pinned behind backs while their owners howl—all this going on even though everybody knows none of it hurts. Secretary Shultz at a press lunch the other day expressed bemusement that one journalist had recently been very suspicious and resentful upon learning that an interview he was scheduled to get was going to be on the record. I thought: this probably tells you less about the particular journalist involved than it does about the meaning of the word record these days.

4 All this seems to me more than a little relevant to our politics this year [1984] and to people's ambivalence toward it. Consider the unease that is widely expressed about Gary Hart's apparent rearrangement of his persona from time to time. Hart is seen by many as an impersonator, sometimes of John F. Kennedy, sometimes merely of someone else who he is in the process of becoming. I don't like it any more than you do, but it hardly strikes me as being unique. Increasingly our politics has become the politics of impersonation. Cliché that it is by now, it is surely no accident that an accomplished actor sits in the White House or that every four years we seem to find ourselves faced with people who have been around somewhere for at least 40 years, but whose autobiography and very identity are oddly still open to question and revision.

5 When I speak of the American people's ambivalence about this condition of our political life, I have in mind several more and less attractive attributes. In some sense the very act of becoming an American has meant for all of our families and all of us a kind of personal reinvention of self. This is the reality behind all that inspirational Statue of Liberty prose and its less inspiring social-science version, the chatter about upward mobility and the rest. America is the chance to be whoever and whatever you choose. But of course there is a downside to it, too. This is all the primping, all the trimming, all the marketing of sheer illusions.

6 The trouble with the exasperation Americans periodically express with the artificial, cinematic quality of their politics is that half the time they seem to invite the situation, to relish and participate in it. For we are, remarkably, eager armchair connoisseurs of the little tricks and big deceptions being practiced on us. We have all become judges of the perfor-

mance of politicians, a nation of political movie critics talking endlessly about how this one did well or that one managed to look some way or other so that he must have wowed some particular group. Interestingly, it is almost always the way our leaders come across to other people, not to ourselves, that we talk about. The electorate spends a year writing reviews—raves and pans—and speculating as to how well the politicians will do with some other audience for an electorate that presumably exists elsewhere and is fairly gullible.

7 *Remarks:* In the end, alas, there comes every four years the bleak rediscovery that we ourselves are the audience, the ones who have to decide. I believe that this double preoccupation—one with the fun and phoniness of it all and the other a dead earnest search for authenticity in a candidate—is what makes our politics so hard to read and our politicians so frantically concerned with remaking themselves crazily overnight. In this the public can seem and be brutal. One day we are entertained by whether ugly remarks such as Jackson's were supposed to have been on or off the record. The next day we have reconstituted ourselves as detached analysts, contemplating how the candidate "handled" the embarrassment, how he "performed" under fire concerning it on a TV show. But finally we want to think about the reality, the fact, the real record as distinct from the made-up one.

8 We in the media (as the press are called when they've done something especially distasteful) contribute greatly to this first preoccupation of the public, to the sitcom politics everyone so enjoys. But I don't think we contribute nearly enough to making the real record available, the one people need to see if they are to make a genuine choice. Forgive me if I can't get sufficiently exercised about the ground rules under which Jesse Jackson uttered his remarks. Those remarks were part of the actual record. I think they also belonged on the one we put out for public consumption.

Word Study List

connivance	2	persona	4
imprecations	3	cinematic	6
fabricating	3	connoisseurs	6
hoked-up	3	gullible	6
sadistic	3	reconstituted	7

Questions

1. Like Bruning and Rosenblatt, Greenfield writes in response to a specific event—in this case, the reporting of Jackson's use of ethnic slurs. One issue is whether or not the words were spoken "off the record." The other issue is the fact that Jackson used the words. Which issue was debated in the press? Which issue was of secondary consideration?

2. What is Greenfield's attitude toward the two issues of the Jackson story?

3. Greenfield's column is not primarily about Jackson; what is her subject? What point about contemporary politics does she make?

4. Greenfield mentions Gary Hart's name change and Reagan's acting career. How do these facts connect to her subject? (See also Justin Kaplan's "Tune That Name," pp. 306–308.)

5. Greenfield asserts that we are ambivalent about our ongoing "sitcom politics." What attracts us? What distresses us?

6. Do you agree with Greenfield's analysis of us as viewers of the political show? Are we often more interested in analyzing performances than in understanding who the candidates really are? How can journalists help to keep us focused on the realities?

Exercises

1. Find two or three articles in newspapers and/or newsmagazines that have as their subject the "handling" of a problem by a current political figure. Analyze the articles to answer the question: Do the articles give more attention to the politician's performance or the moral and/or political consequences of the problem? Report your findings in a paragraph.

2. Read, if you have not yet done so, Bruning's "Why People Distrust the Press" (pp. 375–377) and Rosenblatt's "Journalism and the Larger Truth" (pp. 379–381). Then analyze the Bruning, Rosenblatt, and Greenfield articles as political essays. What characteristics do they share? How do they differ from one another? How do they differ from news stories? What elements of style do they share? (Look at word choice, sentence patterns, use of metaphors, tone.) Organize your analysis into a short essay.

Television News: Seeing Isn't Believing

Peter Funt

A contributor to numerous magazines and newspapers, including *TV Guide, Washington Journalism Review,* and the *New York Times,* Peter Funt (b. 1947) is editor and publisher of *On Cable* magazine. He has also worked as a radio news editor and in 1970 won an award for his radio news reporting.

This article on television news was printed in the November 1980 issue of *Saturday Review.*

Funt reminds us of the subjective nature of television news coverage, especially on network news shows that heavily edit their film.

1 History, other writers have noted, is what observers and historians choose to record. In centuries past, if no one wrote about an event—or passed on an oral tradition (of questionable reliability)—the event might just as well never have happened.

2 But in the age of video, it seems impossible that significant world events will ever escape objective preservation, since TV pictures never lie. Or do they? The taking of pictures, of course, is as subjective a process as selecting words: Which shots should you take, and which should you skip? The photographer, the moment he aims his camera, is performing an editorial function.

3 During the early stages of the hostage crisis in Iran, there were daily demonstrations outside the U.S. embassy building in Teheran. And night after night, American television viewers saw footage of the anti-American protests. The pictures themselves were not distorted, but some reporters who covered the story now believe the image was. Less than two blocks from the embassy, they note, there was business as usual in Teheran. Yet American viewers might have easily imagined that the entire city was in turmoil.

4 When rioting occurred in Miami early this summer [1980], exactly the opposite seems to have been the case. Several critics have observed that all three networks made a determined effort to avoid televising the full extent of the trouble, perhaps out of fear that such coverage would spark more rioting, or perhaps due to sensitivity about television's mishandling of riots back in the Sixties. In both cases, Teheran and Miami, television's coverage was not so much a window on the world as it was a peephole.

5 But whatever the extent to which television pictures can by themselves betray a news story, there is far greater danger of distortion when the film and tape images are subjected to the editing process. Editing of TV news material ranges from virtually nil—on live programs such as *Meet the Press,* or *Face the Nation*—to moderate—on the three networks' evening newscasts—to heavy—on "magazine" programs such as *20/20* and *60 Minutes. Sixty Minutes* relies more on the editing process than any other program on television, both in ratio of film shot to film actually used, and in the restructuring of questions and answers so that bits of one comment are strung together with pieces of another. As a consequence, it is probably harder to distinguish objective reality from editing on *60 Minutes* than on any other program.

6 To illustrate what can happen in the editing room, let us go back to one *60 Minutes* segment, first broadcast on November 12, 1978—a close-

up on the Franklin Mint titled "Limited Edition." In the report, co-anchor Morley Safer carried on at length about two fairly simple points. The first was that Franklin Mint collectibles—coins, plates, books, and the like—are not very good financial investments, particularly over a short term. The second point was that Franklin Mint customers are often misled about the first point.

7 As is often the case with *60 Minutes* segments, there was nothing revelatory here—both of Safer's major contentions had already been explored at length by print reporters. Still, none of the print pieces had so devastating an impact as the segment "Limited Edition." As it happens, Franklin Mint's chairman, Charles L. Andes, thought to have his own staff videotape the entire interveiw with Safer, thus providing a complete transcript against which the final *60 Minutes* segment can be measured.

8 One interesting fact that is immediately clear is that the entire interview, when typed single-spaced, runs 20 pages, while the final *60 Minutes* version takes up less than two. When Safer introduced the interview on the air, he said: " . . . we went to Franklin Mint, to their chairman of the board, Charles Andes, to hear their side of the story." That introduction alone might lead viewers to believe that what followed on film actually occurred shortly after Safer walked into Andes's office. In fact, what is shown first in Safer's finished piece actually appears on page 17 of the 20-page transcript.

9 Here is the final portion of the interview between Safer and Andes, exactly as presented on *60 Minutes:*

SAFER: —The fact is that something like, what, more than 75 percent, to be conservative, of all Franklin Mint issues have decreased massively in price, in value.

ANDES: Yes. Well, now, Morley, you're—you're absolutely right that there is a difference, and I was just going to point out, that there is a—there is a difference between the selling prices which are listed in here [a book] and the prices sold by the dealers—

SAFER: But that—that—that's what we're talking—

ANDES: —and one must realize that if you are going to sell to a dealer in the after-market—Franklin Mint medals or any kind of products in the—to a dealer—that the dealer will, of course, buy it wholesale and sell it retail. But what a collector must do then, if he's not willing to—to—to sell through a dealer, is to sell directly to another collector through ads placed in classified sections of newspapers, or in the numismatic sections of major papers, or in *Coin World* and *Numismatic News.*

SAFER: Well, let me tell you something. We went to *Coin World,* and we have a number of people who went to *Coin World,* and they found that when they advertised their collections in *Coin World,* they were offered roughly—either they were offered nothing or they were offered the spot bullion price for their collections.

ANDES: But that is not necessarily the case in every case. We have many instances where collectors have sold to other collectors, and know of many instances in our—from our monitoring of the market—

SAFER: At above the— at above the issue price?

ANDES: —where—where they sell it—no, not necessarily. In many—in some cases they are sold above issue price. There are a number of products that are sold above issue price.

10 End of interview. Safer then cut directly to an interview with a Franklin Mint customer and informed the astonished buyer that the Franklin Mint product is often sold back to dealers who in turn "sell it for scrap," and the scrap is "in many cases, or some cases, sold back to Franklin Mint."

11 Now let us return to the raw interview between Safer and Andes and edit it differently. By using portions never aired, but without changing any of the quotes by either man, we can create an interview that might just as well have been aired on *60 Minutes:*

SAFER: So far, what would you reckon that Franklin Mint has sold, roughly a billon dollars' worth of collectibles?

ANDES: Yes, that is about the figure, yes.

SAFER: And mainly in precious metals?

ANDES: Not mainly now but I suppose the sum total since the beginning of the company—the majority would be in silver.

SAFER: And even though the price of silver has gone up since you started selling, the price of Franklin mint material has not gone up with it.

ANDES: No, no. For the most part it is not so. That 62 percent of what the dealers report they sell, they sell above the original issue price.

SAFER: Would you say that investing in Franklin Mint collectibles would be a bad investment?

ANDES: We do not recommend investing in Franklin Mint products as a financial investment and we don't recommend—we don't believe—that people should invest in any kind of collectible or luxury product as a financial investment.

12 Thus might the interview have ended—perhaps no more fairly than in the actual CBS version, but certainly leaving the viewer with a vastly different impression of Franklin Mint.

13 The *60 Minutes* library is littered with such examples of the power of television editing. And those who have fallen victim to the *60 Minutes* techniques, regardless of their culpability in whatever is being "disclosed," invariably express surprise at how a recorded TV segment is put together. First, they are unnerved by the film-to-air ratio of about 10-to-one, claiming, in some cases, to have been worn down by the process and lulled into a false sense of security. Then, they are often startled when the interview ends and the camera is turned around to shoot so-called "reverse questions." With the camera aimed at him, the reporter rerecords all of his questions so that they may later be spliced together with the answers. Although all the networks insist that reverse questions match the original questions as closely as possible, there is no denying that the reporter is allowed to polish his performance, while the interview subject's answers must stand as first delivered.

14 Reverse questions, along with other random shots of the reporter nodding his head or writing in his notebook, are also used to camouflage edits in the final film or tape. Known in the trade as "cutaways," these devices make a segment look smooth and neat while at the same time doing the viewer a serious disservice. When an interview subject begins a sentence, then in the middle of that sentence a cutaway is inserted of the reporter's reaction, followed by what seems to be the remainder of the subject's sentence, chances are it was never one complete sentence in the first place. The sentence was probably patched together from two parts of the interview, with the cutaway covering the break.

15 A producer who has worked on *60 Minutes*—who requested anonymity—says that on more than one occasion he watched Mike Wallace record an interview during which Wallace smiled and encouraged the subject to continue talking, only to insert cutways in which Wallace has a stern, doubting expression, in effect changing the mood of the piece.

16 Such ploys can even trip up such broadcast veterans as Daniel Schorr, the former CBS correspondent who now works for the Cable News Network. Back in September 1976, Schorr decided to leak a secret house committee report on the CIA to the *Village Voice* newspaper. While under suspension from his job at CBS, Schorr agreed to tape an interview with Wallace for use on *60 Minutes.*

17 The full interview runs over 40 pages in double-spaced transcript form, but only a fraction of it actually went on the air. Among the portions *not* aired was Wallace's on-camera opening, "Dan, you have my profound admiration and that of your colleagues here and elsewhere I know, for the eloquent and persuasive case that you made for the protection of a reporter's sources." But the edited version belittled and humiliated the "admired" Schorr.

18 "What bothered me most about the interview," says Schorr upon reflection, "was not only the editing, but the way they set me up. Because they taped so much more than could have ever been broadcast, they recorded an entire story about reporters' rights before even touching on what they intended to use.

19 "At one point when I was discussing with [my lawyer] whether I would go on—and he was warning me about what might happen—I said 'I can take care of myself if we do this thing live.' [The executive producer of *60 Minutes* Don] Hewitt talked me out of that. He said, 'No, we never go live because too many things could go wrong. But don't worry.' Well, my answer is that the man with the scissors is the man with ultimate control."

20 Politicians and other famous figures are increasingly demanding live interviews or none at all. Last spring, for instance, Richard Nixon decided he was ready to talk about his new book. Don Hewitt of *60 Minutes* was quoted as saying he turned down a Nixon interview because Nixon insisted it be done live. According to Hewitt, the editing pencil—or scissors—is one of a journalist's most valuable tools, and should never be surrendered. Barbara Walters of ABC felt differently, however, and agreed to interview Nixon live on *20/20.*

21 "If you do a recorded interview," she says, "one of the advantages for the reporter is that he always comes out on top; he's always right. You've never seen a *60 Minutes* interview, or any taped interview, in which the reporter gets the worst of it. Doing live interviews has credibility."

22 Still, it is clear that filmed, taped, or live, the televised image is never more accurate or precise than the cameraman, editor, or reporter allows it to be. The same is true, of course, for the written word. But television's illusion of verifiable reality is so powerful that it is continually necessary to remind oneself that, even with television "news," seeing is not always believing.

Word Study List

revelatory	7	culpability	13
numismatic	9		

Questions

1. In what ways is television news edited without any cutting and splicing techniques being used? What two examples does Funt provide of "edited" coverage of news events?

2. Did you realize that there was, to use Funt's words, "moderate" editing on the network evening newcasts?

3. How much editing takes place on the magazine programs such as "60 Minutes"? What two examples of "60 Minutes'" editing does Funt provide?

4. What editing techniques are revealed by Funt in discussing and quoting from his two examples?

5. Do you think the reverse-questions technique is fair? Should "60 Minutes" be required to announce, at the start of each show, that extensive editing of the material has occurred?

6. What are famous people demanding now, before agreeing to interviews? How does this demand protect them?

7. Even though we know that television news must be shaped by someone's perspective on events, just as print news is shaped by reporter and editor, why do we need to remind ourselves continually of this fact?

Exercises

1. Is it true that most people know television news is edited—that is, really understand the extent to which our perceptions of events can be shaped by TV writers, camerapeople, and producers? Take a poll of at least ten people who are willing to answer the following question: Does editing of stories occur in:

	none	some	considerable
Newspaper articles TV network newscasts Interview shows such as "Meet the Press" Magazine shows such as "60 Minutes"			

   Tabulate your results to share with classmates.

2. Based on information gained from your poll and on what you have learned from Funt's article and others in this text, consider the issue of responsibility as it relates to TV news. Should extensive editing procedures be allowed? What constitutes "extensive"? Should edited pieces be identified? Should acknowledgment of editing be required or just encouraged? Prepare to debate this issue in class.

Research Topics

Using the articles in this chapter, appropriate works from the bibliography that follows, and additional materials, as needed, from your library, prepare a documented argument for a clear position on one of the following topics (or on a topic approved by your instructor):

1. Social, racial, or sex bias in newspapers, weekly newsmagazines, or television news coverage
2. A liberal or conservative bias in television news coverage
3. The negative effects of advertising on objective reporting
4. The ethics of printing personal details of people's lives that might be embarrassing or harmful to them, their friends, or their relatives when these details have no bearing on the political or economic responsibilities of these people
5. Government or self-imposed controls that define responsible news reporting
6. The power of the press to influence political events
7. The effect of the medium (TV, radio, print) on our perceptions of events
8. The function of journalism: to present facts, to explain to the world, or to tell us what to think

Remember that a topic and a position (or thesis) are not the same. After you select a topic and do some reading, you will need to narrow and focus your attention and take a stand that you can develop and support convincingly.

BIBLIOGRAPHY

Altheide, David L. *Creating Reality: How TV News Distorts Events.* Beverly Hills: Sage, 1976.

Bagdikian, Ben H. "The Best News Money Can Buy." *Human Behavior,* October 1978: 63–66.

———. *The Effete Conspiracy.* New York: Harper & Row, 1972.

Bailey, George A. "Interpretive Reporting of the Vietnam War by Anchormen." *Journalism Quarterly,* 53 (Summer 1976): 319–324.

———. "The War According to Walter: Network Anchormen and Vietnam." Milwaukee: Department of Mass Communications, University of Wisconsin, 1975.

Bethell, Tom. "The Myth of an Adversary Press." *Harper's,* January 1977: 33–40.

Childs, M. "Criticism and Control of the Press." *Intellect,* 104 (March 1976): 415.

Chomsky, Noam. "Reporting Indochina: The News Media and the Legitimation of Lies." *Social Policy,* 4 (September/October 1973): 4–19.

Cirino, Robert. *Power to Persuade: Mass Media and the News.* New York: Bantam, 1974.

Cockburn, A. "Wanted: An Irresponsible Press." *Harper's,* April 1981: 103–105.

Commission on Freedom of the Press. *A Free and Responsible Press.* Chicago: Chicago UP, 1947.

Darnton, Robert. "Writing News and Telling Stories." *Daedalus,* Spring 1975: 175–194.

Davis, Junetta. "Sexist Bias in Eight Newspapers." *Journalism Quarterly,* 59 (Autumn 1982): 456–460.

Diamond, Edwin. "The Fourth Estate: The Ostrich Effect." *Harper's,* April 1976: 105–106.

———. "The Miami Riots: Did TV Get the Real Story?" *TV Guide,* 30 August 1980: 18–22.

Downs, Hugh. "Rating the Media." *Center Magazine,* March 1978: 17–22.

Epstein, Edward J. *News from Nowhere: Television and the News.* New York: Random House, 1973.
Friedrich, Otto. "There are 00 Trees in Russia: The Function of Facts in Newsmagazines." *Harper's,* October 1964: 59–65.
Gans, Herbert J. *Deciding What's News: A Study of CBS Evening News, NBC Nightly News, Newsweek, and Time.* New York: Random House (Vintage Books), 1980.
Gerbner, George. "Television: The New State Religion?" *Et cetera,* June 1977: 145–150.
Glynn, Carroll J., and Albert R. Tims. "Sensationalism in Science Issues: A Case Study." *Journalism Quarterly,* 59 (Spring 1982): 126–131.
Griffith, Thomas. "Don't Tell Us What to Think." *Time,* 24 May 1982: 71.
———. "Putting Emotion Back In: Newspaper Readers' Opinions on Factual Journalism." *Time,* 7 May 1979: 98.
Harwood, Edwin. "The Pluralist Press." *Society,* 15 (November/December 1977): 10, 17–20.
Hearon, S. "Using Fiction Techniques for Nonfiction." *Writer,* 93 (January 1980): 22–23.
Henry, William H. "When News Is Almost a Crime." *Time,* 21 March 1983: 84.
Hentoff, Nat. "Privacy and the Press: Is Nothing Sacred?" *Saturday Review,* 21 July 1979: 22–23.
Hofstetter, C. Richard. *Bias in the News.* Columbus: Ohio State UP, 1976.
Hofstetter, C. Richard, and Terry F. Buss. "Bias in TV News Coverage of Political Events." *Journal of Broadcasting,* 22 (Fall 1978): 517–530.
Just, W. "Private Lives, Public Print." *Atlantic Monthly,* 244 (October 1979): 53–55.
Kraft, Joseph. "The Imperial Media." *Commentary,* May 1981: 36–47.
Lang, Kurt, and Gladys E. Lang. "The Unique Perspective of Television and Its Effect." *American Sociological Review,* 18 (February 1953): 3–12.
Lapham, Lewis. "Gilding the News." *Harper's,* July 1981: 31–39.
Levin, Eric. "How the Networks Decide What Is News." *TV Guide,* 2 July 1977: 4–10.
Lichty, Lawrence W., and George A. Bailey. "Violence in Television News: A Case Study of Audience Response." *Central States Speech Journal,* 23 (Winter 1972): 225–229.
Merrill, John C. *The Imperative of Freedom: A Philosophy of Journalistic Autonomy.* New York: Hastings House, Communication Arts Books, 1974.
Merrill, John C., and Ralph D. Barney, eds. *Ethics and the Press: Readings in Mass Media Morality.* New York: Hastings House, 1975.
Merrill, John C., and Everette E. Dennis. *Basic Issues in Mass Communication.* New York: Macmillan, 1984.
Miller, A. R. "Press and Privacy." *Current,* 204 (July 1978): 3–7.
Morrison, Donald. "Would This Magazine Print Innuendo?" *Psychology Today,* February 1982: 16–17.
Oster, P. R. "Free Press vs. Fair Trial: A Classic Collision." *U.S. News & World Report,* 23 February 1976: 44–45.
Patterson, Thomas E., and Robert D. McClure. *The Unseeing Eye: The Myth of Television Power in National Politics.* New York: G. P. Putnam's, 1976.
Phillips, Kevin. "Controlling Media Output." *Society,* 15 (November/December 1977): 10, 12–17.
Postman, Neil. "Television News Narcosis." *Nation,* 1 March 1980: 245–246.
Powers, T. "Schorr and a Free Press." *Commonweal,* 9 April 1976: 241–243.
"Press Freedom? Maybe a Little Too Much." *Nation's Business,* August 1979: 80.
Rivers, William L. *The Opinionmakers.* Boston: Beacon, 1965.
Roberts, Churchill. "The Presentation of Blacks in Television Network Newscasts." *Journalism Quarterly,* 52 (Spring 1975): 50–55.
Schmidt, Benno, Jr. *Freedom of the Press Versus Public Access.* New York: Praeger, 1975.
Sevareid, Eric. "Free Press for a Free People." *Society,* 15 (November/December 1977): 11, 23–25.
Small, William. *Political Power and the Press.* New York: W. W. Norton, 1972.
Smith, Adam. "And Now the Real News." *Esquire,* September 1982: 10, 12–13.
Sobran, J. "No-fault Media Bias." *National Review,* 25 January 1980: 103–107.
Tuchman, Gaye. *Making News: A Study in the Construction of Reality.* New York: Free Press, 1978.
———. "Objectivity as Strategic Ritual: An Examination of Newsmen's Notions of Objectivity." *American Journal of Sociology,* 77 (January 1972): 660–670.
Walfish, Andrew. "Sex Is In, Politics Is Out." *More,* September 1977: 25–31.
Weaver, Paul H. "Is Television News Biased?" *Public Interest,* 26 (Winter 1972): 57–74.

Welles, Chris. "The Numbers Magazines Live By." *Columbia Journalism Review,* 14 (September/October 1975): 22–27.
Wenglinsky, Martin. "Television News: A New Slant." *Columbia Forum,* Fall 1974: 2–9.
Whitney, Charles D., and Lee B. Becker. "Keeping the Gates for the Gatekeepers: The Effects of Wire News." *Journalism Quarterly,* 59 (Spring 1982): 60–65.
Wicker, Tom. *On Press.* New York: Viking, 1978.
Williams, Alden. "Unbiased Study of Television News Bias." *Journal of Communication,* 25 (Autumn 1975): 190–199.
Wise, David. *The Politics of Lying.* New York: Random House, 1973.

Glossary

ADJECTIVE Any word or word group that functions (in a sentence) as a modifier of nouns, e.g., *beautiful* cat, *white* cat, *purring* cat.

ANALYSIS The process of dividing an item (essay, poem) or concept (American foreign policy) into its component parts, usually for the purpose of understanding the nature or functioning of the item/concept being analyzed.

AUDIENCE Those likely to be reached by a speech or printed piece, or, as a writing concept, the particular knowledge and values characterizing the group being addressed.

CIRCUMLOCUTION Language characterized by wordiness and indirectness.

CLICHÉ A trite expression lacking punch through overuse, e.g., *sly as a fox.*

CONNOTATION The associations, emotional impact, and/or implications of a word, e.g., the word *mother* is usually associated with home, security, and love.

CONTEXT The words or sentences preceding and/or following a given word or statement and usually having an influence on the meaning of that word or statement.

DENOTATION The dictionary meanings of a word; in contrast to connotation, the more literal meanings of a word.

DIALECT The expressions, grammar, and pronunciation of a socially or geographically identifiable group of people.

DICTION A speaker or writer's word choice.

EUPHEMISM A vague, pleasant expression substituted for one considered too blunt or offensive, e.g., *powder room* for *toilet.*

EXPOSITORY WRITING Writing that explains a topic by means of logical organization of details.

FIGURE OF SPEECH An expression intended to convey a meaning beyond the literal meaning of the words, e.g., "It's raining cats and dogs" is not intended to produce a response from the animal shelter; rather, we are expected to understand that the rain is heavy.

GOBBLEDYGOOK Writing characterized by needlessly complex or fancy wording, jargon, and other techniques intended to obscure meaning and impress the reader.

GRAMMAR A description and codification of the sounds, words, and sentence structures of a language.

IDIOM An expression peculiar to a particular language either because of its grammatical construction or because the meaning of the phrase cannot be understood by knowing the meaning of each word; e.g., *we made friends with the neighbors.*

IMAGE The re-creation through language of an experience involving one or more of the five senses: smell, taste, sound, touch, and sight.

IMAGERY All of the images in a piece of writing, or the dominant kind of images that shape the nature and tone of a work, e.g., the *color imagery* in Hawthorne's *The Scarlet Letter.*

IRONY A figure of speech expressing the difference or incongruity between what is said and what is meant.

JARGON The vocabulary of a specialized group, e.g., *legal jargon.* The word *jargon* usually has a negative connotation, suggesting complex sentence structure and pretentious word choice.

LINGUISTICS The science of language; the study of sounds, words, and structures of language, including both the history of language and a description of language use.

MEDIA The various means of communication that reach large numbers of people, e.g., *radio, television, newspapers, magazines.*

METAPHOR A figure of speech that states or implies a comparison between two essentially dissimilar things, e.g., *the best mirror is an old friend.*

PARABLE A story, usually brief, that illustrates a truth or teaches a moral lesson, e.g., *the parable of the prodigal son.*

PARODY The exaggerated imitation of a composition, writer, or event for the purpose of ridicule or satire.

PREJUDICE Preconceived opinions or attitudes, usually hostile, held without knowledge or understanding, about any social, religious, racial, or national group.

PSYCHOBABBLE Words and phrases, borrowed from the popular psychology of encounter groups, transactional analysis, and meditation, that give the impression of a scientific understanding of human behavior and feelings.

PUN A play on words, e.g., from a car ad: "A beautiful way to stop *fueling* [*fooling*] around."

RHETORIC The art of influencing an audience through the effective use of language, including skill in organization, sentence structure, and figures of speech.

RHYME The repetition of the stressed vowel sound and final consonant sounds in two or more words, e.g., *know-though* or *ducking-bucking.*

SEMANTICS The study of the meanings of words, including changes in meanings, and the study of the relationship between language, thought, and behavior.

SIMILE A figure of speech that states a comparison between two unlike things using such connecting words as *like* or *seems.*

SLANG Highly informal, colorful, and imaginative words and expressions that are either absorbed into standard usage or become quickly dated, e.g., *to mooch.*

STEREOTYPE A set image or idea about a group that ignores differences among members of the group, e.g., *all athletes are dumb, all teenagers are lazy.*

STYLE A writer's or speaker's selection and arrangement of language.

SYMBOL An object that suggests meanings, associations, and emotions beyond those characteristic of its nature or function, e.g., the chauffeured limousine is associated with wealth, status, success, power.

SYNTAX The arrangement of words in a sentence.

THESIS The central idea or main point of a piece of writing; a thesis expresses the writer's message about and attitude toward his or her subject.

TONE A writer's or speaker's expression of attitude and the techniques of writing used to convey that attitude, e.g., a *serious tone,* an *angry tone.*

USAGE The customary way that a language is spoken or written.

VOICE The role or personality selected by a writer and conveyed to a reader through the writer's selection and arrangement of language.

About the Authors

Dorothy U. Seyler, Professor of English at Northern Virginia Community College, is a native of Washington, D.C. She received her education at the College of William and Mary (B.A.), Columbia University (M.A.), and the State University of New York at Albany (Ph.D.) and taught at Ohio State University, the University of Kentucky, and Nassau Community College before moving to Northern Virginia. Her teaching and research interests range from the drama and American literature to composition pedagogy. She is the author of articles on Chekhov and Marlowe and of three textbooks, *Thinking for Writing, Introduction to Literature: Reading, Analyzing, and Writing,* and *Read, Reason, Write.*

Carol J. Boltz has taught English composition, American literature, and business writing at Northern Virginia Community College. A native of North Carolina, she received her B.A. in English literature from the University of North Carolina at Chapel Hill and her M.Ed. from the University of Illinois at Urbana. Author of a composition text entitled *Language and Reality* (1979), she also served as Project Associate in the Northern Virginia Writing Project in 1978.